THE BHAGA

One of modern India's greatest sons, Professor S. Radhakrishnan (1888–1975) was a prominent philosopher, author and educationalist. He was equally at home in the European and Asiatic traditions of thought, and devoted an immense amount of energy to interpreting Indian religion, culture and philosophy for the rest of the world. He was a visiting professor at many foreign universities, and served as India's Ambassador Extraordinary to the USSR from 1949 to 1952. Despite his slight association with politics he was elected to the prestigious position of vice-president of India in 1957. He became the President of India in 1961 and held this rank until 1967, when he retired from public life.

He wrote a number of books for readers the world over. Some of his outstanding works are: *The Hindu View of Life, An Idealist View of Life* and *Indian Philosophy, Vols. I and II.*

He dedicated this translation to Mahatma Gandhi.

Other titles by S. Radhakrishnan

An Idealist View of Life
The Hindu View of Life
The Principal Upaniṣads
The Concept of Man
Recovery of Faith

THE BHAGAVADGĪTĀ

With an Introductory Essay,
Sanskrit Text,
English Translation and Notes

S. RADHAKRISHNAN

HarperCollins *Publishers* India

HarperCollins *Publishers* India Pvt Ltd
7/16 Ansari Road, Daryaganj, New Delhi 110 002

Published in 1993 by
HarperCollins *Publishers* India
Fourteenth impression 1998

First published in Great Britain 1948 by

ISBN 81-7223-087-7

Printed in India by
Gopsons Papers Ltd
A-14, Sector 60
Noida 201 301

PREFACE

WAR and post-war periods tend to bring into prominence the value of sciences, especially their practical applications. These are important for the conduct of wars and the comfort of citizens in peace. But if we have to give largeness and wisdom to men's outlook on life, we should lay stress on humanities also. The relation of sciences to humanities may be stated roughly to be one of means to ends. In our enthusiasm for the means we should not overlook the ends. The concepts of right and wrong do not belong to the sphere of science; yet it is, on the study of the ideas centring round these concepts, that human action and happiness ultimately depend. A balanced culture should bring the two great halves into harmony. The *Bhagavadgītā* is a valuable aid for the understanding of the supreme ends of life.

There are many editions of the *Bhagavadgītā* and several good English translations of it and there would be no justification for another, if all that was needed for English readers was a bare translation. Those who read the *Gītā* in English need notes at least as much as those who read it in Sanskrit, if they are not to miss their way in it. The classical commentaries indicate to us what the *Gītā* meant to the commentators and their contemporaries. Every scripture has two sides, one temporary and perishable, belonging to the ideas of the people of the period and the country in which it is produced, and the other eternal and imperishable, and applicable to all ages and countries. The intellectual expression and the psychological idiom are the products of time while the permanent truths are capable of being lived and seen by a higher than intellectual vision at all times. The vitality of a classic consists in its power to produce from time to time men who confirm and correct from their own experience truths enunciated in it. The commentators speak to us from experience and express in a new form, a form relevant to their age and responsive to its needs, the ancient wisdom of the scripture. All great doctrine, as it is repeated in the course of centuries, is coloured by the reflections of the age in which it appears and bears the imprint of the individual who restates it. Our times are different; our habits of thought, the mental background to which we relate our experience, are not quite the same as those of the classical commentators. The chief problem facing us today is the reconciliation of mankind. The *Gītā* is specially suited for the purpose, as it attempts to reconcile varied and apparently antithetical forms of the religious consciousness and emphasizes the root conceptions of religion which are neither ancient nor modern but eternal and belong to the very flesh of humanity, past, present and future. History poses our problems, and if we restate old principles in new ways, it is not because we will to do so but because we must. Such a restatement of the truths of eternity in the accents of our time is the only way in which a great scripture can be of living value to mankind. From this point of view, the general Introduction and the Notes may perhaps be found useful by the intelligent reader. There are many points in the detailed interpretations of the *Gītā* where there are differences among scholars. I have not done more than call attention to them in the Notes as the book is intended for the general reader who wishes to enlarge his spiritual environment rather than for the specialist.

A translation to serve its purpose must be as clear as its substance will permit. It must be readable without being shallow, modern without being unsympathetic. But no translation of the *Gītā* can bring out the dignity and grace of the original. Its melody and magic of phrase are difficult to recapture in another medium. The translator's anxiety is to render the thought, but he cannot convey fully the spirit. He cannot evoke in the reader the mood in which the thought was born and induce in him the ecstacy of the seer and the vision he beholds. Realizing that, for me at any rate, it is difficult to bring out, through the medium of English, the dignity of phrase and the intensity of utterance, I have given the text in Roman script also so that those who know Sanskrit can rise to a full comprehension of the meaning of the *Gītā* by pondering over the Sanskrit original. Those who do not know Sanskrit will get a fairly correct idea of the spirit of the poem from the beautiful English rendering by Sir Edwin Arnold. It is so full of ease and grace and has a flavour of its own which makes it acceptable to all but those who are scrupulous about scholarly accuracy.

I am much indebted to Professor M. Hiriyanna who read the typescript and Professor Franklin Edgerton who read the proofs for their valuable advice and help. S. R.

PREFACE TO THE SECOND EDITION

It is a pleasure to know that a second edition is called for and this has enabled me to correct many misprints and profit by the suggestions made by my friend Professor F. W. Thomas to whom I am greatly indebted.

S. R.

LIST OF ABBREVIATIONS

Bhagavadgītā	*Gītā* or B.G.
Indian Philosophy by Radhakrishnan	I.P.
Mahābhārata	M.B.
Śaṁkara	Ś.
Śaṁkara's Commentary on the *Brahma Sūtra*	S.B.
Śaṁkara's Commentary on the *Bhagavadgītā*	S.B.G.
Rāmānuja	R.
Upaniṣad	Up.

CONTENTS

THE BHAGAVADGĪTĀ

Taught by the blessed Nārāyaṇa Himself to Arjuna, compiled by Vyāsa, the ancient seer, in the middle of the Mahābhārata, I meditate on Thee, O Mother, O *Bhagavadgītā*, the blessed, of eighteen chapters, the bestower of the nectar of non-dualistic wisdom, the destroyer of rebirth.[1]

"This famous Gītāśāstra is an epitome of the essentials of the whole Vedic teaching. A knowledge of its teaching leads to the realization of all human aspirations."[2]

"I find a solace in the *Bhagavadgītā* that I miss even in the Sermon on the Mount. When disappointment stares me in the face and all alone I see not one ray of light, I go back to the *Bhagavadgītā*. I find a verse here and a verse there and I immediately begin to smile in the midst of overwhelming tragedies—and my life has been full of external tragedies—and if they have left no visible, no indelible scar on me, I owe it all to the teachings of the *Bhagavadgītā*." M. K. Gāndhi, *Young India* (1925), pp. 1078–1079.

[1] ***auṁ pārthāya pratibodhitāṁ bhagavatā nārāyaṇena svayam***
vyāsena grathitāṁ purāṇamuninā madhye mahābhāratām
advaitāmṛtavarṣiṇīṁ bhagavatīm aṣṭādaśādhyāyinīm
amba tvām anusandadhāmi bhagavadgīte bhavadveṣiṇīm.

[2] ***samastavedārthasārasaṁgrahabhūtam...samastapuruṣārthasiddhim.*** S.B.G. Introduction.

INTRODUCTORY ESSAY

I. *Importance of the Work*

The *Bhagavadgītā* is more a religious classic than a philosophical treatise. It is not an esoteric work designed for and understood by the specially initiated but a popular poem which helps even those "who wander in the region of the many and variable." It gives utterance to the aspirations of the pilgrims of all sects who seek to tread the inner way to the city of God. We touch reality most deeply, where men struggle, fail and triumph. Millions of Hindus,[1] for centuries, have found comfort in this great book which sets forth in precise and penetrating words the essential principles of a spiritual religion which are not contingent on ill-founded facts, unscientific dogmas or arbitrary fancies. With a long history

[1] The *Gītā* has exercised an influence that extended in early times to China and Japan and latterly to the lands of the West. The two chief works of Mahāyāna Buddhism, *Mahāyānaśraddhotpatti* (The Awakening of Faith in the Mahāyāna) and *Saddharmapuṇḍarīka* (The Lotus of the True Law) are deeply indebted to the teaching of the *Gītā*. It is interesting to observe that the official exponent of "the German Faith," J. W. Hauer, a Sanskrit scholar who served for some years as a missionary in India, gives to the *Gītā* a central place in the German faith. He calls it "a work of imperishable significance." He declares that the book "gives us not only profound insights that are valid for all times and for all religious life, but it contains as well the classical presentation of one of the most significant phases of Indo-Germanic religious history. . . . It shows us the way as regards the essential nature and basal characteristic of Indo-Germanic religion. Here Spirit is at work that belongs to our spirit." He states the central message of the *Gītā* in these words: "We are not called to solve the meaning of life but to find out the Deed demanded of us and to work and so, by action, to master the riddle of life." (Quoted in the *Hibbert Journal*, April 1940, p. 341.) The *Gītā*, however, bases its message of action on a philosophy of life. It requires us to know the meaning of life before we engage in action. It does not advocate a fanatical devotion to the practical to the disparagement of the dignity of thought. Its philosophy of the practical is a derivative from its philosophy of spirit, *brahmvidyāntargatakarmayogaśāstra*. Ethical action is derived from metaphysical realization. Ś. urges that the essential purpose of the *Gītā* is to teach us a way out of bondage and not merely enjoin action, *śokamohādisaṁsārakarmanivṛtyarthaṁ gītāśāstram, na pravartakam.*

of spiritual power, it serves even today as a light to all who will receive illumination from the profundity of its wisdom which insists on a world wider and deeper than wars and revolutions can touch. It is a powerful shaping factor in the renewal of spiritual life and has secured an assured place among the world's great scriptures.

The teaching of the *Gītā* is not presented as a metaphysical system thought out by an individual thinker or school of thinkers. It is set forth as a tradition which has emerged from the religious life of mankind. It is articulated by a profound seer who sees truth in its many-sidedness and believes in its saving power. It represents not any sect of Hinduism but Hinduism as a whole, not merely Hinduism but religion as such, in its universality, without limit of time or space,[1] embracing within its synthesis the whole gamut of the human spirit, from the crude fetishism of the savage to the creative affirmations of the saint. The suggestions set forth in the *Gītā* about the meaning and value of existence, the sense of eternal values and the way in which the ultimate mysteries are illumined by the light of reason and moral intuition provide the basis for agreement in mind and spirit so very essential for keeping together the world which has become materially one by the universal acceptance of the externals of civilization.

As the colophon indicates, the *Bhagavadgītā* is both metaphysics and ethics, *brahmavidyā* and *yogaśāstra*, the science of reality and the art of union with reality. The truths of spirit can be apprehended only by those who prepare themselves for their reception by rigorous discipline. We must cleanse the mind of all distraction and purge the heart from all corruption, to acquire spiritual wisdom.[2] Again, the

[1] Cp. Aldous Huxley: "The Gītā is one of the clearest and most comprehensive summaries of the Perennial Philosophy ever to have been made. Hence its enduring value, not only for Indians, but for all mankind. . . . The Bhagavadgītā is perhaps the most systematic spiritual statement of the Perennial Philosophy." Introduction to the *Bhagavadgītā* by Svāmi Prabhavānanda and Christopher Isherwood (1945).

[2] Cp. *jyotir ātmani nānyatra samaṁ tat sarvajantuṣu*
svayaṁ ca śakyate draṣṭuṁ susamāhitacetasā.

"God's light dwells in the self and nowhere else. It shines alike in every living being and one can see it with one's mind steadied."

perception of the truth results in the renewal of life. The realm of spirit is not cut off from the realm of life. To divide man into outer desire and inner quality is to violate the integrity of human life. The illumined soul acts as a member of the kingdom of God, affecting the world he touches and becoming a saviour to others.[1] The two orders of reality, the transcendent and the empirical, are closely related. The opening section of the *Gītā* raises the question of the problem of human action. How can we live in the Highest Self and yet continue to work in the world? The answer given is the traditional answer of the Hindu religion, though it is stated with a new emphasis.

By its official designation,[2] the *Gītā* is called an upaniṣad, since it derives its main inspiration from that remarkable group of scriptures, the Upaniṣads. Though the *Gītā* gives us a vision of truth, impressive and profound, though it opens up new paths for the mind of man, it accepts assumptions which are a part of the tradition of past generations and embedded in the language it employs. It crystallizes and concentrates the thoughts and feelings which were developing among the thinking people of its time. The fratricidal struggle is made the occasion for the development of a spiritual message based on the ancient wisdom, *prajñā purāṇī*, of the Upaniṣads.[3]

The different elements which, at the period of the composition of the *Gītā*, were competing with each other within the Hindu system, are brought together and integrated into a comprehensive synthesis, free and large, subtle and profound. The teacher refines and reconciles the different currents of thought, the Vedic cult of sacrifice, the Upaniṣad teaching of the transcendent Brahman, the Bhāgavata theism and tender piety, the Sāṁkhya dualism and the Yoga

[1] IV, 34.

[2] Cp. the colophon: *bhagavadgītāsu upaniṣatsu.*

[3] The popular verse from the *Vaiṣṇavīya Tantrasāra* makes out that the *Gītā* restates the central teachings of the Upaniṣads. The Upaniṣads are the cows and the cowherd's son, Kṛṣṇa, is the milker; Arjuna is the calf, the wise man is the drinker and the nectar-like gītā is the excellent milk.

sarvopaniṣado gāvo dogdhā gopālanandanaḥ
pārtho vatsaḥ sudhīr bhoktā dugdhaṁ gītāmṛtaṁ mahat.

meditation. He draws all these living elements of Hindu life and thought into an organic unity. He adopts the method, not of denial but of penetration and shows how these different lines of thought converge towards the same end.

2. *Date and Text*

The *Bhagavadgītā* is later than the great movement represented by the early Upaniṣads and earlier than the period of the development of the philosophic systems and their formulation in sūtras. From its archaic constructions and internal references, we may infer that it is definitely a work of the pre-Christian era. Its date may be assigned to the fifth century B.C., though the text may have received many alterations in subsequent times.[1]

We do not know the name of the author of the *Gītā*. Almost all the books belonging to the early literature of India are anonymous. The authorship of the *Gītā* is attributed to Vyāsa, the legendary compiler of the *Mahābhārata*. The eighteen chapters of the *Gītā* form Chapters XXIII to XL of the *Bhīṣmaparvan* of the *Mahābhārata*.

It is argued that the teacher, Kṛṣṇa, could not have recited the seven hundred verses to Arjuna on the battlefield. He must have said a few pointed things which were later elaborated by the narrator into an extensive work. According to Garbe, the *Bhagavadgītā* was originally a Sāṁkhya-yoga treatise with which the Kṛṣṇa-Vāsudeva cult got mixed up and in the third century B.C. it became adjusted to the Vedic tradition by the identification of Kṛṣṇa with Viṣṇu. The original work arose about 200 B.C. and it was worked into its present form by some follower of the Vedānta in the second century A.D. Garbe's theory is generally rejected. Hopkins regards the work as "at present a Kṛṣṇaite version of an older Viṣṇuite poem and this in turn was at first an unsectarian work, perhaps a late Upaniṣad."[2] Holtzmann

[1] I.P., Vol. I, pp. 522–5.

[2] *Religions of India* (1908), p. 389. Farquhar writes of it as "an old verse Upaniṣad, written rather later than the *Śvetāśvatara*, and worked up into the *Gītā* in the interests of Kṛṣṇaism by a poet after the Christian era." *Outline of the Religious Literature of India* (1920), Sec. 95.

looks upon the *Gītā* as a Viṣṇuite remodelling of a pantheistic poem. Keith believes that it was originally an Upaniṣad of the *Śvetāśvatara* type but was later adapted to the cult of Kṛṣṇa. Barnett thinks that different streams of tradition became confused in the mind of the author. Rudolf Otto affirms that the original *Gītā* was "a splendid epic fragment and did not include any doctrinal literature." It was Kṛṣṇa's intention "not to proclaim any transcendent dogma of salvation but to render him (Arjuna) willing to undertake the special service of the Almighty will of the God who decides the fate of battles."[1] Otto believes that the doctrinal treatises are interpolated. In this he is in agreement with Jacobi who also holds that the original nucleus was elaborated by the scholiasts into its present form.

These different opinions seem to arise from the fact that, in the *Gītā*, are united currents of philosophical and religious thought diffused along many and devious courses. Many apparently conflicting beliefs are worked into a simple unity to meet the needs of the time, in the true Hindu spirit, that over all of them broods the grace of God. The question whether the *Gītā* succeeds in reconciling the different tendencies of thought will have to be answered by each reader for himself after he completes the study of the book. The Indian tradition has always felt that the apparently incongruous elements were fused together in the mind of the author and that the brilliant synthesis he suggests and illuminates, though he does not argue and prove it in detail, fosters the true life of spirit.

For our purposes, we may adopt the text followed by Śaṁkara in his commentary as it is the oldest extant commentary on the poem.[2]

3. *Chief Commentators*

The *Gītā* has been recognized for centuries as an orthodox scripture of the Hindu religion possessing equal authority with the *Upaniṣads* and the *Brahma Sūtra* and the three

[1] *The Original Gītā:* E.T. (1939), pp. 12, 14.

[2] The few variations of the text which we find in the Kashmir Rescension do not affect the general teaching of the *Gītā*. See F. A. Schrader: *The Kashmir Rescension of the Bhagavadgītā* (1930).

together form the triple canon (*prasthāna-traya*). The teachers of the Vedānta are obliged to justify their special doctrines by an appeal to these three authorities and so wrote commentaries on them expounding how the texts teach their special points of view. The *Upaniṣads* contain many different suggestions about the nature of the Absolute and Its relation to the world. The *Brahma Sūtra* is so terse and obscure that it has been used to yield a variety of interpretations. The *Gītā* gives a more consistent view and the task of the commentators, who wish to interpret the texts to their own ends, becomes more difficult. After the decline of Buddhism in India, different sects arose, the chief being Advaita or non-dualism, Viśiṣṭādvaita or qualified non-dualism, Dvaita or dualism and Śuddhādvaita or pure non-dualism. The various commentaries on the *Gītā* were written by the teachers in support of their own traditions (*saṁpradāya*) and in refutation of those of others. These writers are able to find in the *Gītā* their own systems of religious thought and metaphysics, since the author of the *Gītā* suggests that the one eternal truth which we are seeking, from which all other truth derives, cannot be shut up in a single formula. Again, we receive from the study and reflection of the scripture as much living truth and spiritual influence as we are capable of receiving.

The commentary of Śaṁkara (A.D. 788–820) is the most ancient of the existing ones. There were other commentaries older than his, to which he refers in his Introduction, but they have not come down to us.[1] Śaṁkara affirms that Reality or Brahman is one without a second. The entire world of manifestation and multiplicity is not real in itself and seems to be real only for those who live in ignorance (avidyā). To be caught in it is the bondage in which we are all implicated. This lost condition cannot be removed by our efforts. Works are vain and bind us firmly to this unreal cosmic process (saṁsāra), the endless chain of cause and

[1] Ānandagiri in his comment on S.B.G., II, 10, says that the Vṛttikāra, who wrote a voluminous commentary on the *Brahma Sūtra* also wrote a Vṛtti or gloss on the *Gītā* urging that neither knowledge (jñāna) nor action (karma) by itself leads to spiritual freedom and a combined pursuit of them takes us to the goal.

effect. Only the wisdom that the universal reality and the individual self are identical can bring us redemption. When this wisdom arises, the ego is dissolved, the wandering ceases and we have perfect joy and blessedness.

Brahman is definable only in terms of being. As It is above all predicates, especially all distinctions of subject, object and the act of cognition, It cannot be regarded as personal and there can be no love or reverence for It.

Śaṁkara holds that while action is essential as a means for the purification of the mind, when wisdom is attained action falls away. Wisdom and action are mutually opposed as light and darkness.[1] He rejects the view of *jñānakarma-samuccaya.*[2] He believes that Vedic rites are meant for those who are lost in ignorance and desire.[3] The aspirants for salvation should renounce the performance of ritual works. The aim of the *Gītā*, according to Śaṁkara, is the complete suppression of the world of becoming[4] in which all action occurs, though his own life is an illustration of activity carried on, after the attainment of wisdom.

Śaṁkara's views are developed by Ānandagiri, who is probably as late as the thirteenth century, Śrīdhara (A.D. 1400) and Madhusūdana (sixteenth century), among others. The Marāṭha saints, Tukārām and Jñāneśvar, are great devotees though they accept the position of Śaṁkara in metaphysics.

Rāmānuja (eleventh century A.D.), in his commentary, refutes the doctrine of the unreality of the world and the path of renunciation of action. He follows the interpretation given by Yāmunācārya in his *Gītārthasaṁgraha*. Brahman, the highest reality, is Spirit, but not without attributes. He has self-consciousness with knowledge of Himself and a conscious will to create the world and bestow salvation on

[1] IV, 37; IV, 33.

[2] *tasmād gītāsu kevalād eva tattvajñānān mokṣaprāptih, na karma-samuccitāt.* S.B.G., II, 11. Even if karma may not be the immediate cause of liberation, still it is a necessary means for acquiring saving wisdom. Ś. admits it: "*karmaniṣṭhayā jñānaniṣṭhāprāptihetutvena puruṣārthahetutvaṁ na svātantryeṇa.*"

[3] *avidyākāmavata eva sarvāṇi śrautādīni darśitāni.*

[4] *gītāśāstrasya prayojanaṁ paraṁ niḥśreyasam, sahetukasya saṁsārasya atyantoparamalakṣaṇam.* S.B.G., Introduction.

His creatures. He is the sum of all ideal predicates, infinite and eternal, before and above all worlds, without any second. The Vedic gods are His servants created by Him and appointed in their places to perform their ordained duties. The world is no deception or illusion but is genuine and real. The world and God are one as body and soul are one. They are a whole but at the same time unchangeably different. Before creation, the world is in a potential form, undeveloped into the existing and diversified manifestations. In creation, it is developed into name and form (nāmarūpa). By representing the world as the body of God, it is suggested that the world is not made from something alien, a second principle but is produced by the Supreme out of His own nature. God is both the instrumental and the material cause of the world. The analogy of soul and body is used to indicate the absolute dependence of the world on God even as the body is absolutely dependent on the soul. The world is not only the body of God but His remainder, *īśvarasyaśeṣa*, and this phrase suggests the complete dependence and contingency of the world.

All consciousness presupposes a subject and an object which is different from consciousness which is regarded by Rāmānuja as a dependent substance (*dharmabhūtadravya*), capable of streaming out. The ego (jīva) is not unreal and is not extinguished in the state of liberation. The Upaniṣad passage, *tat tvam asi*, "that art thou," means that "God is my self" even as my soul is the self of my body. God is the supporting, controlling principle of the soul, even as the soul is the supporting principle of the body. God and soul are one, not because the two are identical but because God indwells and penetrates the soul. He is the inner guide, *antaryāmin*, who dwells deep within the soul and as such is the principle of its life. Immanence, however, is not identity. In time as well as in eternity, the creature remains distinct from the Creator.

Rāmānuja develops in his commentary on the *Gītā* a type of personal mysticism. In the secret places of the human soul, God dwells but He is unrecognized by it so long as the soul does not acquire the redeeming knowledge. We acquire this knowledge by serving God with our whole heart and soul. Perfect trust is possible only for those who are elected by divine grace. Rāmānuja admits that the paths of knowledge, devotion and action are all mentioned in the *Gītā*, but he holds that its main emphasis is on devotion. The wretchedness of sin, the deep longing for the Divine, the intense feeling of trust and faith in God's all-conquering love, the experience of being divinely elected are stressed by him.

The Supreme is Viṣṇu, for Rāmānuja. He is the only true god who will not share His divine honours with others. Liberation is service of and fellowship with God in Vaikuṇṭha or heaven.

Madhva (A.D. 1199 to 1276) wrote two works on the *Bhagavadgītā*, called the *Gītābhāṣya* and *Gītātātparya*. He attempts to derive from the *Gītā* tenets of dualistic (dvaita) philosophy. It is self-contradictory, he contends, to look upon the soul as identical with the Supreme in one sense and different from Him in another. The two must be regarded as eternally different from each other and any unity between them, partial or entire, is untenable. He interprets the passage "that art thou" as meaning that we must give up the distinction between mine and thine, and hold that everything is subject to the control of God.[1] Madhva contends that devotion is the method emphasized in the *Gītā*.

Nimbārka (A.D. 1162) adopts the theory of dvaitādvaita (dual-non-dual doctrine). He wrote on *Brahma Sūtra* and his disciple Keśavakāṣmīrin wrote a commentary on the *Gītā* called *Tattvaprakāśikā*. Nimbārka holds that the soul (jīva), the world (jagat) and God are different from each other; yet the existence and activity of the soul and the world depend on the will of God. Devotion to the Supreme is the principal theme of Nimbārka's writings.

Vallabha (A.D. 1479) develops what is called śuddhādvaita or pure non-dualism. The ego (jīva) when pure and unblinded by illusions and the Supreme Brahman are one. Souls are particles of God like sparks of fire and they cannot acquire the knowledge necessary for obtaining release except by the grace of the Supreme. Devotion to God is the most important

[1] *madīyaṁ tadīyam iti bhedam apahāya sarvam īśvarādhīnam iti sthitiḥ. Bhāgavatatātparya.*

means of obtaining release. Bhakti is truth associated with love.[1]

There have been several other commentators on the *Gītā* and in our own time, the chief are B. G. Tilak and Srī Aurobindo. Gandhi has his own views.

The differences of interpretation are generally held to be differences determined by the view-point adopted. The Hindu tradition believes that the different views are complementary. Even the systems of Indian philosophy are so many points of view or darśanas which are mutually complementary and not contradictory. The *Bhāgavata* says that the sages have described in various ways the essential truths.[2] A popular verse declares: "From the view-point of the body, I am Thy servant, from the view-point of the ego, I am a portion of Thee; from the view-point of the self I am Thyself. This is my conviction."[3] God is experienced as Thou or I according to the plane in which consciousness centres.

4. *Ultimate Reality*

The *Gītā* does not give any arguments in support of its metaphysical position. The reality of the Supreme is not a question to be solved by a dialectic which the vast majority of the human race will be unable to understand. Dialectic in itself and without reference to personal experience cannot give us conviction. Only spiritual experience can provide us with proofs of the existence of Spirit.

The Upaniṣads affirm the reality of a Supreme Brahman, one without a second, without attributes or determinations, who is identical with the deepest self of man. Spiritual experience centres round a sovereign unity which overcomes the duality between the known and the knowing. The inability to conceptualize the experience leads to such descriptions as identity, pure and simple. Brahman, the subsistent simplicity, is its own object in an intuition which is its very

[1] *premalakṣaṇā śraddhā. Amṛtataraṅgiṇī.*

[2] *"iti nānāprasaṁkhyānāṁ tattvānāṁ kavibhiḥ kṛtam."*

[3] *dehabuddhyā tu dāso'haṁ jīvabuddhyā tvad aṁśakaḥ:*
ātmabuddhyā tvam evāham iti me niścitā matiḥ.
See also Ānandagiri: *Śaṁkaradigvijaya.*

being. It is the pure subject whose existence cannot be ejected into the external or objective world.

Strictly speaking we cannot give any description of Brahman. The austerity of silence is the only way in which we can bring out the inadequacy of our halting descriptions and imperfect standards.[1] The *Bṛhadāraṇyaka Up.* says: "Where everything indeed has become the Self itself, whom and by what should one think? By what can we know the universal knower?"[2] The duality between knowing and knowable characteristic of discursive thought is transcended. The Eternal One is so infinitely real that we dare not even give It the name of One since oneness is an idea derived from worldly experience (*vyavahāra*). We can only speak of It as the non-dual, advaita,[3] that which is known when all dualities are resolved in the Supreme Identity. The Upaniṣads indulge in negative accounts, that the Real is not this, not this (na iti, na iti), "without sinews, without scar, untouched by evil,"[4] "without either shadow or darkness, without a

[1] Cp. Lao Tze: "The Tao which can be named is not the true Tao." "The reality of the formless, the unreality of that which has form—is known to all. Those who are on the road to attainment care not for these things, but the people at large discuss them. Attainment implies non-discussion; discussion implies non-attainment. Manifested Tao has no objective value; hence silence is better than argument. It cannot be translated into speech; better, then, say nothing at all. This is called the great attainment." Soothill: *The Three Religions of China*, second edition (1923), pp. 56–7. The Buddha maintained a calm silence when he was questioned about the nature of reality and nirvāṇa. Jesus maintained a similar silence when Pontius Pilate questioned him as to the nature of truth.

Cp. Plotinus: "If any one were to demand of nature why it produces, it would answer, if it were willing to listen and speak: You should not ask questions, but understand keeping silence as I keep silence, for I am not in the habit of speaking."

[2] II, 4, 12–14.

[3] Cp. *Kulārṇava Tantra.*

advaitaṁ kecid icchanti dvaitam icchanti cā'pare
mama tattvaṁ vijānanto dvaitādvaita vivarjitam.

Some editions read for *vijānantah, na jānanti.*

[4] *Īśa Up.*, 8. The Supreme, *tad ekam*, is without qualities and attributes, "neither existent nor non-existent." *Ṛg. Veda*, X, 129. The Mādhyamika Buddhists call the Ultimate Reality void or śūnya, lest by giving it any other name they may be betrayed into limiting it. For them it is that which shall be known when all oppositions are resolved in the Supreme Identity. Cp. St. John of Damascus:

within or a without."[1] The *Bhagavadgītā* supports this view of the Upaniṣads in many passages. The Supreme is said to be "unmanifest, unthinkable and unchanging,"[2] "neither existent nor nonexistent."[3] Contradictory predicates are attributed to the Supreme to indicate the inapplicability of empirical determinations. "It does not move and yet it moves. It is far away and yet it is near."[4] These predicates bring out the twofold nature of the Supreme as being and as becoming. He is parā or transcendent and aparā or immanent, both inside and outside the world.[5]

The impersonality of the Absolute is not its whole significance. The *Upaniṣads* support Divine activity and participation in nature and give us a God who exceeds the mere infinite and the mere finite. The interest which inspired Plato's instruction to the astronomers of the Academy "to save the appearances," made the seers of the *Upaniṣads* look upon the world as meaningful. In the words of the *Taittirīya Up.*, the Supreme is that "from which these beings are born, that by which they live and that into which, when departing, they enter." According to the *Veda*, "He is the God who is in fire, in water, who pervades the entire universe; He who is in plants, in trees, to Him we make our obeisance

"It is impossible to say what God is in Himself and it is more exact to speak of Him by excluding everything. Indeed He is nothing of that which is . . . above being itself."

[1] *Bṛhadāraṇyaka Up.*, III, 8, 8. In the M.B. the Lord who is the teacher tells Nārada that His real form is "invisible, unsmellable, untouchable, quality-less, devoid of parts, unborn, eternal, permanent and actionless." See *Śāntiparva*, 339, 21–38. It is the "cloud of unknowing" or what the Areopagite calls the "superluminous darkness," "the silent desert of the divinity . . . who is properly no being" in the words of Eckhart. Cp. Angelus Silesius: "God is mere nothing . . . to Him belongs neither now nor here." Cp. also Plotinus: "Generative of all, the Unity is none of all, neither thing nor quality, nor intellect nor soul, not in motion, not at rest, not in place, not in time; it is the self-defined, unique in form or, better, formless, existing before Form was or Movement or Rest, all of which are attachments of Being and make Being the manifold it is." (*Enneads*, E.T., by Mackenna, VI, 9.)

[2] II, 25. [3] XIII, 12; XIII, 15–17.

[4] *Īśa Up.*, 5: see also *Muṇḍaka Up.*, II, 1, 6–8; *Kaṭha Up.*, II, 14; *Bṛhadāraṇyaka Up.*, II, 37; *Śvetāśvatara Up.*, III, 17.

[5] *bahir antaś ca bhūtānām*, XIII, 15.

again and again."[1] "Who would have exerted, who would have lived, if this supreme bliss had not been in the heavens?"[2] The theistic emphasis becomes prominent in the *Śvetāśvatara Up.* "He, who is one and without any colour (visible form), by the manifold wielding of His power, ordains many colours (forms) with a concealed purpose and into whom, in the beginning and the end, the universe dissolves, He is the God. May He endow us with an understanding which leads to good actions."[3] Again "Thou art the woman, thou art the man; thou art the youth and also the maiden; thou as an old man totterest with a stick, being born. Thou art facing all directions."[4] Again, "His form is not capable of being seen; with the eye no one sees Him. They who know Him thus with the heart, with the mind, as abiding in the heart, become immortal."[5] He is a universal God who Himself is the universe which He includes within His own being. He is the light within us, *hṛdyantar jyotiḥ*. He is the Supreme whose shadow is life and death.[6]

In the *Upaniṣads*, we have the account of the Supreme as the Immutable and the Unthinkable as also the view that He is the Lord of the universe. Though He is the source of all that is, He is Himself unmoved for ever.[7] The Eternal Reality not only supports existence but is also the active power in the world. God is both transcendent, dwelling in light inaccessible and yet in Augustine's phrase "more intimate to the soul than the soul to itself." The *Upaniṣad* speaks of two birds perched on one tree, one of whom eats the fruits and the other eats not but watches, the silent witness withdrawn from enjoyment.[8] Impersonality and

[1] *yo devo'gnau yo'psu yo viśvam bhuvanam āviveśa*
yo oṣadhiṣu yo vanaspatiṣu tasmai devāya namonamaḥ.

[2] *ko hyevānyāt kaḥ prāṇyāt yad eṣa ākāśa ānando na syāt?*

[3] IV, 1. [4] IV, 3. [5] IV, 20.

[6] *Rg. Veda*, X, 121, 2: see also *Kaṭha Up.*, III, 1. Cp. *Deuteronomy:* "I kill and make alive," xxxii. 39.

[7] Cp. Rūmi: "Thy light is at once joined to all things and apart from all." *Shams-i-Tabriz* (E.T. By Nicholson), Ode IX.

[8] *Muṇḍaka Up.*, III, 1, 1–3. Cp. Boehme: "And the deep of the darkness is as great as the habitation of the light; and they stand not one distant from the other but together in one another and neither of them hath beginning nor end." *Three Principles*, XIV, 76.

personality are not arbitrary constructions or fictions of the mind. They are two ways of looking at the Eternal. The Supreme in its absolute self-existence is Brahman, the Absolute and as the Lord and Creator containing and controlling all, is Īśvara, the God. "Whether the Supreme is regarded as undetermined or determined, this Śiva should be known as eternal; undetermined He is, when viewed as different from the creation and determined, when He is everything."[1] If the world is a cosmos and not an amorphous uncertainty, it is due to the oversight of God. The *Bhāgavata* makes out that the one Reality which is of the nature of undivided consciousness is called Brahman, the Supreme Self or God.[2] He is the ultimate principle, the real self in us as well as the God of worship. The Supreme is at once the transcendental, the cosmic and the individual reality. In Its transcendental aspect, It is the pure self unaffected by any action or experience, detached, unconcerned. In Its dynamic cosmic aspect, It not only supports but governs the whole cosmic action and this very Self which is one in all and above all is present in the individual.[3]

Īśvara is not responsible for evil except in an indirect way. If the universe consists of active choosing individuals who can be influenced but not controlled, for God is not a dictator, conflict is inevitable. To hold that the world consists of free spirits means that evil is possible and probable. The alternative to a mechanical world is a world of risk and adventure. If all tendencies to error, ugliness and evil are to be excluded, there can be no seeking of the true, the beautiful and the good. If there is to be an active willing of these ideals of truth, beauty and goodness, then their opposites of error, ugliness and evil are not merely abstract possibilities but

[1] *nirguṇas saguṇas' ceti śivo jñeyaḥ sanātanaḥ*
nirguṇaḥ prakṛter anyaḥ, saguṇas sakala smṛtaḥ.

[2] *vadanti tat tattvavidaḥ tattvaṁ yaj jñānam advayam*
brahmeti paramātmeti bhagavān iti śabdyate.

Cp. also:

utpattiṁ ca vināśaṁ ca bhūtānām āgatiṁ gatim
vetti vidyām avidyāṁ ca sa vācyo bhagavān iti.

[3] Cp. Ś. on *Bṛhadāraṇyaka Up.*, III, 8, 12. Roughly we may say that the Self in its transcendental, cosmic and individual aspects answers to the Christian Trinity of Father, Son and Holy Ghost.

positive tendencies which we have to resist. For the *Gītā*, the world is the scene of an active struggle between good and evil in which God is deeply interested. He pours out His wealth of love in helping man to resist all that makes for error, ugliness and evil. As God is completely good and His love is boundless, He is concerned about the suffering of the world. God is omnipotent because there are no external limits to His power. The social nature of the world is not imposed on God, but is willed by Him. To the question, whether God's omniscience includes a foreknowledge of the way in which men will behave and use or abuse their freedom of choice, we can only say that what God does not know is not a fact. He knows that the tendencies are indeterminate and when they become actualized, He is aware of them. The law of karma does not limit God's omnipotence. The Hindu thinkers even during the period of the composition of the *Ṛg. Veda,* knew about the reasonableness and lawabidingness of nature. Ṛta or order embraces all things. The reign of law is the mind and will of God and cannot therefore be regarded as a limitation of His power. The personal Lord of the universe has a side in time, which is subject to change.

The emphasis of the *Gītā* is on the Supreme as the personal God who creates the perceptible world by His nature (prakṛti). He resides in the heart of every being;[1] He is the enjoyer and lord of all sacrifices.[2] He stirs our hearts to devotion and grants our prayers.[3] He is the source and sustainer of values. He enters into personal relations with us in worship and prayer.

The personal Īśvara is responsible for the creation, preservation and dissolution of the universe.[4] The Supreme has two natures, the higher (parā) and the lower (aparā).[5] The living souls represent the higher and the material medium the lower. God is responsible for both the ideal plan and the concrete medium through which the ideal becomes the

[1] XVIII, 61. [2] IX, 24. [3] VII, 22.

[4] Cp. Jacob Boehme: "Creation was the act of the Father; the incarnation that of the Son; while the end of the world will be brought about through the operation of the Holy Ghost."

[5] VII, 4–5.

actual, the conceptual becomes the cosmic. The concretization of the conceptual plan requires a fullness of existence, an objectification in the medium of potential matter. While God's ideas are seeking for existence, the world of existence is striving for perfection. The Divine pattern and the potential matter, both these are derived from God, who is the beginning, the middle and the end, Brahmā, Viṣṇu and Śiva. God with His creative ideas is Brahmā. God who pours out His love and works with a patience which is matched only by His love is Viṣṇu, who is perpetually at work saving the world. When the conceptual becomes the cosmic, when heaven is established on earth, we have the fulfilment represented by Śiva. God is at the same time wisdom, love and perfection. The three functions cannot be torn apart. Brahmā, Viṣṇu and Śiva are fundamentally one though conceived in a threefold manner. The *Gītā* is interested in the process of redeeming the world. So the aspect of Viṣṇu is emphasized. Kṛṣṇa represents the Viṣṇu aspect of the Supreme.

Viṣṇu is a familiar deity in the *Ṛg. Veda*. He is the great pervader, from *viṣ*, to pervade.[1] He is the internal controller who pervades the whole universe. He gathers to Himself in an ever increasing measure the position and dignity of the Eternal Supreme. *Taittirīya Āraṇyaka* says: "To Nārāyaṇa we bring worship; to Vāsudeva our meditations and in this may Viṣṇu assist us."[2]

Kṛṣṇa,[3] the teacher of the *Gītā*, becomes identified with Viṣṇu, the ancient Lord of the Sun, and Nārāyaṇa, an

[1] Amara states, *vyāpake parameśvare*. It is traced also from *viś*, to enter. *Taittirīya Up*. says: "Having created that world, he afterwards entered into it." See also *Padma Purāṇa*. Viṣṇu as the Lord entered into prakṛti. *sa eva bhagavān viṣṇuḥ prakṛtyām āviveśaḥ*.

[2] X, 1, 6. *nārāyaṇāya vidmahe vāsudevāya dhīmahi tan no viṣṇuḥ pracodayāt*. Nārāyaṇa says: "Being like the Sun, I cover the whole world with rays, and I am also the sustainer of all beings and am hence called Vāsudeva." M.B., XII, 341, 41.

[3] *karṣati sarvaṁ kṛṣṇaḥ*. He who attracts all or arouses devotion in all is kṛṣṇa. *Vedāntaratnamañjūṣā* (p. 52) says that Kṛṣṇa is so called because he removes the sins of his devotees, *pāpaṁ karṣayati, nirmūlayati*. Kṛṣṇa is derived from *kṛṣ*, to scrape, because he scrapes or draws away all sins and other sources of evil from his devotees. *kṛṣater vilekhanārthasya rūpaṁ bhaktajanapāpādidoṣakarṣaṇāt kṛṣṇaḥ*. S.B.G., VI, 34.

ancient God of cosmic character and the goal or resting place of gods and men.

The Real is the supracosmic, eternal, spaceless, timeless Brahman who supports this cosmic manifestation in space and time. He is the Universal Spirit, Paramātman, who ensouls the cosmic forms and movements. He is the Parameśvara who presides over the individual souls and movements of nature and controls the cosmic becoming. He is also the Puruṣottama, the Supreme Person, whose dual nature is manifested in the evolution of the cosmos. He fills our being, illumines our understanding and sets in motion its hidden springs.[1]

All things partake of the duality of being and non-being from Puruṣottama downwards. Even God has the element of negativity or māyā though He controls it. He puts forth His active nature (*svāṁ prakṛtīm*) and controls the souls who work out their destinies along lines determined by their own natures. While all this is done by the Supreme through His native power exercised in this changing world, He has another aspect untouched by it all. He is the impersonal Absolute as well as the immanent will; He is the uncaused cause, the unmoved mover. While dwelling in man and

[1] He brings to the ignorant the light of knowledge, to the feeble the power of strength, to the sinner the liberation of forgiveness, to the suffering the peace of mercy, to the comfortless comfort . . . *jñānam ajñānām, śaktir aśaktānām, kṣamā sāparādhānām, kṛpā duḥkhinām, vātsālyaṁ sadoṣānām, śīlaṁ mandānām, ārjavaṁ kuṭilānām, sauhārdyaṁ duṣṭahṛdayānām, mārdavaṁ viśleṣabhīrūṇām.*

Cp. also "Thou art joy and bliss, Thou the abode of peace: Thou dost destroy the sorrow of creatures and give them happiness."

"ānandāmṛtarūpas tvaṁ tvaṁ ca śāntiniketanam
harasi prāṇināṁ duhkhaṁ vidadhāsi sadā sukham."

"Thou art the refuge of the weak, the saviour of the sinful."
"dīnānāṁ śaraṇaṁ tvaṁ hi, pāpināṁ muktisādhanam."

See also: "Thou who art radiance, fill me with radiance, Thou who art valour, fill me with valour: Thou who art strength, give me strength: Thou who art vitality, endow me with vitality: Thou who art wrath (against wrong), instil that wrath into me: Thou who art fortitude, fill me with fortitude." *tejo'si tejo mayi dehi, vīryam asi vīryaṁ mayi dehi, balam asi balaṁ mayi dehi, ojo'si ojo mayi dehi, manyur asi manyuṁ mayi dehi, saho'si sahomayi dehi. Śukla Yajur Veda*, XIX, 9.

nature, the Supreme is greater than both. The boundless universe in an endless space and time rests in Him and not He in it.[1] The God of the *Gītā* cannot be identified with the cosmic process for He extends beyond it.[2] Even in it He is manifest more in some aspects than in others. The charge of pantheism in the lower sense of the term cannot be urged against the *Gītā* view.[3] While there is one reality that is ultimately perfect, everything that is concrete and actual is not equally perfect.

5. *Kṛṣṇa, the teacher*

So far as the teaching of the *Bhagavadgītā* is concerned, it is immaterial whether Kṛṣṇa, the teacher, is a historical individual or not. The material point is the eternal incarnation of the Divine, the everlasting bringing forth of the perfect and divine life in the universe and the soul of man.

There is, however, ample evidence in favour of the historicity of Kṛṣṇa. The *Chāndogya Up.* refers to Kṛṣṇa, devakīputra, the son of Devakī, and speaks of him as the pupil of Ghora Āṅgirasa[4] who is a priest of the sun, according to *Kauṣītaki Brāhmaṇa.*[5] After interpreting the meaning of sacrifice and making out that the true payment for the priests is in the practice of the virtues of austerity, charity, uprightness, non-violence and truthfulness,[6] the *Upaniṣad* continues "When Ghora Āṅgirasa explained this to Kṛṣṇa, the son of Devakī, he also said, that, in the final hour, one should take refuge in these three thoughts. "Thou art the indestructible (akṣita), thou art the immovable (acyuta), thou art the very essence of life (prāṇa)."[7] There is a great similarity between the teaching of Ghora Āṅgirasa in the *Upaniṣad* and that of Kṛṣṇa in the *Gītā.*

Kṛṣṇa plays an important part in the story of the M.B. where he is presented as the friend of Arjuna. Pāṇini refers to Vāsudeva and Arjuna as objects of worship.[8] Kṛṣṇa

[1] IX, 6, 10. [2] X, 41–2. [3] X, 21–37.
[4] III, 17, 6. [5] XXX, 6.
[6] *tapo dānam ārjavam ahiṁsā satyavacanam.* See B.G., XVI, 1–3.
[7] Cp. B.G., VIII, 11–13. He possibly composed hymn 74 of the 8th maṇḍala of *Ṛg. Veda* as he is called in *Kauṣītaki Brāhmaṇa,* Kṛṣṇa Āṅgīrasa. XXX, 9. [8] IV, 3, 98.

belonged to the ancient Vṛṣṇi or Sātvata branch of the family of Yadu, whose home was perhaps in the neighbourhood of Mathurā, a town with which Kṛṣṇa's name has been associated in history, tradition and legend. Kṛṣṇa was opposed to the sacerdotalism of the Vedic religion and preached the doctrines which he learnt from Ghora Āṅgirasa. His opposition to the Vedic cult comes out in passages where Indra when vanquished, humbled himself before Kṛṣṇa.[1] The *Gītā* has references to those who complain about Kṛṣṇa's teaching and express their lack of faith in him.[2] M.B. has indications that the supremacy of Kṛṣṇa was not accepted without challenge. In that epic Kṛṣṇa is represented both as an historical individual[3] and as an incarnation (avatāra). Kṛṣṇa taught the Sātvatas the worship of the Sun and the Sātvatas perhaps identified the teacher with the Sun he taught them to worship.[4] By the fourth century before Christ, the cult of Vāsudeva was well established. In the Buddhist work, *Niddesa* (fourth century B.C.) included in the Pāli Canon, the writer refers to the worshippers of Vāsudeva and Baladeva among others. Megasthenes (320 B.C.) states that Herakles was worshipped by the Saurasenoi (Śūrasenas) in whose land are two great cities, Methora (Mathura) and Kleisobora (Kṛṣṇapura). Heliodorus, the Greek Bhāgavata from Taxila, calls Vāsudeva, devadeva (god of gods) in the Besnagar inscription (180 B.C.). The Nānaghāt inscription, which belongs to the first century before the Christian era, mentions Vāsudeva among the deities invoked in the opening verse. Some of the principal personages like Rādhā, Yaśodā and Nanda figure in Buddhist legends. Patañjali, in his *Mahābhāṣya*, commenting on

[1] "I am Indra of the devas but thou hast gained Indra's power over the cows. As Govinda the people will ever praise thee." *Harivaṁśa*, 4004 ff.

[2] III, 32; IX, 11; XVIII, 67.

[3] The story of his early life with legends and fancies is found in the *Bhāgavata* and the *Harivaṁśa*.

[4] According to *Bhāgavata*, the Sātvatas worship the Supreme as Bhagavān and as Vāsudeva. IX. 9, 50. Yāmunācārya in his *Āgamaprāmāṇya* says that those who worship God in purity of spirit are called Bhāgavata and Sātvata: *sattvād bhagavān bhajyate yaiḥ paraḥ pumān te sātvatā bhāgavatā ity ucyante dvijottamaiḥ.*

Pāṇini, IV, 3, 98, calls Vāsudeva Bhagavat. The book is called *Bhagavadgītā* because Kṛṣṇa is known in the Bhāgavata religion as Śrī Bhagavān. The doctrine which he preaches is the Bhāgavata creed. In the *Gītā*, Kṛṣṇa says that he is not expressing any new view but is only repeating what has been preached by him to Vivasvān and by Vivasvān to Manu and by Manu to Ikṣvāku.[1] M.B. says that "the Bhāgavata religion has been traditionally handed down by Vivasvān to Manu and by Manu to Ikṣvāku."[2] The two traditions similarly propagated must have been the same. There are other evidences also. In the exposition of the Nārāyaṇīya or the Bhāgavata religion, it is said that this religion was described by the Lord previously in the *Bhagavadgītā*.[3] Again, it is declared that it "was taught by the Lord when, during the fight between the Kauravas and the Pāṇḍavas, both the armies had got ready for war and Arjuna had become depressed."[4] This is the religion of monotheism (ekāntika).

In the *Gītā* Kṛṣṇa is identified with the Supreme Lord, the unity that lies behind the manifold universe, the changeless truth behind all appearances, transcendent over all and immanent in all. He is the manifested Lord,[5] making it easy for mortals to know, for those who seek the Imperishable Brahman reach Him no doubt but after great toil. He is called Paramātman which implies transcendence; he is jīva-bhūta, the essential life of all.

How can we identify an historical individual with the Supreme God? The representation of an individual as identical with the Universal Self is familiar to Hindu thought. In the *Upaniṣads*, we are informed that the fully awakened soul, which apprehends the true relation to the Absolute sees that it is essentially one with the latter and declares itself to be so. In the *Ṛg. Veda*, IV, 26, Vāmadeva says: "I am Manu, I am Sūrya, I am the learned sage Kakṣivān. I have adorned the sage Kutsa, the son of Arjuni. I am the

[1] IV, 1, 3.
[2] *Śāntiparva*, 348, 51–2.
[3] *kathito harigītāsu. Śāntiparva*, 346, 10.
[4] *samupoḍheṣvanīkeṣu kurupāṇḍavayor mṛdhe*
arjune vimanaskeca gītā bhagavatā svayam. Śāntiparva, 348, 8.
[5] XII, 1 ff.

wise Uśaṇā; look at me. . . ." In the *Kauṣītaki Up.* (III), Indra says to Pratardana "I am the vital breath. I am the conscious self. Worship me as life, as breath. He who worships me as life, as immortality, obtains full life in this world. He obtains immortality and indestructibility in the heavenly regions."[1] In the *Gītā*, the author says: "Delivered from passion, fear and anger, absorbed in Me, taking refuge in Me, many purified by the austerity of wisdom have attained to My state of being."[2] The ego holds something other than itself, to which it should abandon itself. In this abandonment consists its transfiguration. A liberated soul uses his body as a vehicle for the manifestation of the Eternal. The divinity claimed by Kṛṣṇa is the common reward of all earnest spiritual seekers. He is not a hero who once trod the earth and has now left it, having spoken to His favourite friend and disciple, but is everywhere and in every one of us, as ready to speak to us now as He ever was to any one else. He is not a bygone personality but the indwelling spirit, an object for our spiritual consciousness.

God is never born in the ordinary sense. Processes of birth and incarnation which imply limitation do not apply to Him. When the Lord is said to manifest Himself at a particular

[1] Ś., commenting on this, observes: "That is, Indra, a deva, looking on his own self as the Supreme Brahman by the vision of the sages according to the Śāstras, says, 'Know me' just as the sage Vāmadeva seeing the same truth, felt, 'I am Manu, I am Sūrya.' In the Śruti (that is the *Bṛhadāraṇyaka Up.*) it is said, 'The worshipper becomes one with the god he truly sees.' "

[2] IV, 10. Jesus spent his life in solitary prayer, meditation and service, was tempted like any of us, had spiritual experiences like the great mystics and in a moment of spiritual anguish, when he lost the sense of the presence of God, cried out, "My God, my God, why hast thou forsaken me?" (*Mark* xv, 34). Throughout, he felt his dependence on God. "The father is greater than I": (*John* xiv, 28). "Why callest thou me good? None is good, save one, even God" (*Luke* xviii, 19). "But of that day and that hour knoweth no one, not even the angels in heaven, neither the Son but the Father" (*Mark* xiii, 32). "Father, into Thy hands I commend my spirit" (*Luke* xxiii, 46). Though conscious of his imperfections, Jesus recognized the grace and love of God and willingly submitted himself entirely to Him. Thus delivered from all imperfection and taking refuge in Him, he attained to a divine status. "I and the Father are one" (*John* x, 30).

time, on a particular occasion, it only means that it takes place with reference to a finite being. In Chapter XI the whole world is seen in God. The subjective and the objective processes of the world are only the expressions of the higher and lower natures of the Supreme; yet in whatever is glorious, beautiful and strong, God's presence becomes more manifest. When any finite individual develops spiritual qualities and shows large insight and charity, he sits in judgment on the world and starts a spiritual and social upheaval and we say that God is born for the protection of the good, the destruction of the evil and the establishment of the kingdom of righteousness. As an individual, Kṛṣṇa is one of millions of forms through which the Universal Spirit manifests Itself. The author of the *Gītā* mentions Kṛṣṇa of history as one of many forms along with his disciple Arjuna.[1] The avātara is the demonstration of man's spiritual resources and latent divinity. It is not so much the contraction of Divine majesty into the limits of the human frame as the exaltation of human nature to the level of Godhead by its union with the Divine.

Theism, however, makes out that Kṛṣṇa is an incarnation (avataraṇa) or descent of the Divine into the human frame. Though the Lord knows no birth or change, He has many times been born. Kṛṣṇa is the human embodiment of Viṣṇu. He is the Supreme who appears to the world as though born and embodied.[2] The assumption of human nature by the Divine Reality, like the creation of the world, does not take away from or add to the integrity of the Divine.

[1] X, 37.

[2] Ś. writes: *sa ca bhagavān jñānaiśvaryaśaktibalavīryatejobhiḥ, sadā sampannaḥ, triguṇātmikāṁ vaiṣṇavīṁ svāṁ māyāṁ mūlaprakṛtīṁ vaśīkṛtya, ajo avyayo bhūtānām īśvaro nityaśuddhabuddhamukta-svabhāvopi san svamāyayā dehavān iva jāta iva, lokānugrahaṁ kurvaniva lakṣyate. aṁśena sambabhūva* does not mean that Kṛṣṇa is born of a part or is a partial incarnation. Ānandagiri interprets *aṁśena* to mean "in a phenomenal form created by his own will" *svecchānirmitena māyāmayeṇa svarūpeṇa*. While the Apostle's Creed lays stress on the human nature of the Son of God, "who was conceived by the Holy Ghost, born of the Virgin Mary, suffered under Pontius Pilate, was crucified, dead and buried," the Nicene Creed adds that he "came down from heaven and was made flesh." This coming down or descent of God into flesh is the avataraṇa.

Creation and incarnation both belong to the world of manifestation and not to the Absolute Spirit.[1]

If the Infinite God is manifested in finite existence throughout time, then Its special manifestation at one given moment and through the assumption of one single human nature is but the free fulfilment of that same movement by which the Divine plenitude freely fulfils itself and inclines towards the finite. It does not raise any fresh problem apart from that of creation. If a human organism can be made in the image of God, if new patterns can be woven into the stuff of repetitive energy, if eternity can be incorporated in these ways into succession, then the Divine Reality can express His absolute mode of being in and through a completely human organism. The scholastic theologians tell us that God is present in the creatures, "by essence, presence, power." The relation between the Absolute, infinite, self-existent and immutable and the finite human individual who is enmeshed in the temporal order is unimaginably intimate though difficult to define and explain. In the great souls we call incarnations, God who is responsible for the being and dignity of man has more wonderfully renewed it. The penetration of successiveness by the Eternal which is present in every event of the cosmic is manifested in a deeper sense in the incarnations. When once God has granted us free will, He does not stand aside leaving us to make or unmake ourselves. Whenever by the abuse of freedom unrighteousness increases and the world gets stuck in a rut, He creates Himself to lift the world from out of its rut and set it on new tracks. Out of His love He is born again and again to renew the work of creation on a higher plane. According to a passage in the M.B., the Supreme who is ever ready to protect the worlds has four forms. One of them dwells on earth practising penance; the second keeps watch over the actions of erring humanity; the third is engaged in activity in the world of men, and the fourth is plunged in the slumber of a thousand

[1] Cp. Hooker: "This admirable union of God with man can enforce in that higher nature no alternation because with God there is nothing more natural than not to be subject to any change." *Ecclesiastical Polity* (1888 ed.), vol. ii, p. 234.

years.[1] Absolute impassivity is not the only side of Divine nature. The Hindu tradition makes out that the avatāras are not confined to the human level. The presence of pain and imperfection is traced not to man's rebellious will but to a disharmony between the creative purpose of God and the actual world. If suffering is traced to the "fall" of man, we cannot account for the imperfections of innocent nature, for the corruption that infects all life, for the economy of disease. The typical question, Why is there cancer in the fish? cannot be avoided. The *Gītā* points out that there is a Divine Creator who imposes His forms on the abysmal void. Prakṛti is the raw material, the chaos out of which order is to be evolved, a night which is to be illumined. In the struggle between the two, whenever a deadlock is created, there is Divine interference to release the deadlock. Besides, the idea of one unique revelation is hardly consistent with our present views of the universe. The tribal God gradually became the God of the earth and the God of the earth has now become the God of the universe, perhaps only one of many universes. It is inconceivable that the Supreme is concerned only with one part of one of the smallest of planets.

The theory of avatāra is an eloquent expression of the law of the spiritual world. If God is looked upon as the saviour of man, He must manifest Himself, whenever the forces of evil threaten to destroy human values. An avatāra is a descent of God into man and not an ascent of man into God, which is the case with the liberated soul. Though every conscious being is such a descent, it is only a veiled manifestation. There is a distinction between the self-conscious being of the Divine and the same shrouded in ignorance.

The fact of descent or avataraṇa indicates that the Divine is not opposed to a full vital and physical manifestation. We can live in the physical body and yet possess the full

[1] *caturmūrtir ahaṁ śavśal lokatrāṇārtham udvataḥ*
ātmānaṁ pravibhajveha lokānāṁ hitam ādadhe
ekāmūrtis tapascaryāṁ kurute me bhuvi sthitā
aparā paśyati jagat kurvāṇaṁ sādhvasādhunī
aparā kurute karma mānuṣaṁ lokam āsritā
s'ete caturthī tvaparā nıdrāṁ varṣasahasrikīṁ.
Droṇaparva, XXIX, 32-34.

truth of consciousness. Human nature is not a fetter but can become an instrument of divine life. Life and body with us, ordinary mortals, remain ignorant, imperfect and impotent means of expression but they need not always be so. The Divine Consciousness uses these for Its purpose while the unfree human consciousness has not this absolute control, over the physical, vital and mental forces.

Though the *Gītā* accepts the belief in avatāra as the Divine limiting Himself for some purpose on earth, possessing in His limited form the fullness of knowledge, it also lays stress on the eternal avatāṛa, the God in man, the Divine consciousness always present in the human being. The two views reflect the transcendent and the immanent aspects of the Divine and are not to be regarded as incompatible with each other. The teacher, who is interested in the spiritual illumination of the human race, speaks from the depths of the Divine in him. Kṛṣṇa's avatāra is an illustration of the revelation of the Spirit in us, the Divine hidden in gloom. According to the *Bhāgavata*,[1] "at midnight, in the thickest darkness, the Dweller in every heart revealed Himself in the divine Devakī for the Lord is the self hidden in the hearts of all beings."[2] The glorious radiance arises from the blackest of black nights. In mysteries and revelations the night is rich. The presence of night does not make the existence of light less real. Indeed but for night there could be no human consciousness of light. The meaning of the birth of Kṛṣṇa is the fact of redemption in the dark night. In the hour of

[1] *niśīthe tamodbhūte jāyamāne janārdane*
devakyāṁ devarūpiṇyāṁ viṣṇuḥ sarvaguhāśayaḥ. . . .
vasudevagṛhe sākṣāt bhagavān puruṣaḥ paraḥ janiṣyate. Bhagavata.

Cp. what is said about the Incarnation of Jesus Christ: "Whilst all things were in quiet silence and night was in the midst of her swift course; thine Almighty Word leapt down from heaven out of thy royal throne. Alleluia." The doctrine of the Incarnation agitated the Christian world a great deal. Arius maintained that the Son is not the equal of the Father but created by Him. The view that they are not distinct but only different aspects of one Being is the theory of Sabellius. The former emphasized the distinctness of the Father and the Son and the latter their oneness. The view that finally prevailed was that the Father and the Son were equal and of the same substance; they were, however, distinct persons.

[2] X, 20; XVIII, 61.

calamity and enslavement the Saviour of the world is born.

Kṛṣṇa is said to be born of Vasudeva and Devakī. When our sattva nature is purified,[1] when the mirror of understanding is cleansed of the dust of desire, the light of pure consciousness is reflected in it. When all seems lost, light from heaven breaks, enriching our human life more than words can tell. A sudden flash, an inward illumination we have and life is seen fresh and new. When the Divine birth takes place within us, the scales fall from our eyes, the bolts of the prison open. The Lord abides in the heart of every creature and when the veil of that secret sanctuary is withdrawn, we hear the Divine voice, receive the Divine light, act in the Divine power. The embodied human consciousness is uplifted into the unborn eternal.[2] The incarnation of Kṛṣṇa is not so much the conversion of Godhead into flesh as the taking up of manhood into God.

The teacher slowly guides his pupil to attain the status which he has, *mama sādharmyam*. The pupil, Arjuna, is the type of the struggling soul who has not yet received the saving truth. He is fighting with the forces of darkness, falsehood, limitation, and mortality which bar the way to the higher world. When his whole being is bewildered, when he does not know the valid law of action, he takes refuge in his

[1] *sattvaṁ viśuddhaṁ vasudeva śabditam. Bhāgavata.* Devakī is *daivī prakṛti*, divine nature.

[2] This, to my mind, is the meaning of the Christian doctrine of resurrection. The physical resurrection of Jesus is not the important thing but the resurrection of the Divine. The rebirth of man as an event that happens within his soul, resulting in a deeper understanding of reality and a greater love for God and man, is the true resurrection which lifts human life to an awareness of its own Divine content and purpose. God is perpetual creativity, ceaseless action. He is the Son of Man for in man is God reborn. When the veil between the eternal and the temporal is lifted, man walks with God and as He directs.

Cp. Angelus Silesius: Though Christ a thousand times
In Bethlehem be born,
If He's not born in thee
Thy soul is still forlorn.
The Cross on Golgotha
Will never save thy soul,
The Cross in thine own heart
Alone can make thee whole.

higher self, typified as Kṛṣṇa, the world teacher, *jagadguru*[1] and appeals for the grace of enlightenment. "I am thy disciple. Illumine my consciousness. Remove what is dark in me. Give me that which I have lost, a clear rule of action." The rider in the chariot of the body is Arjuna but the charioteer is Kṛṣṇa and He has to guide the journey. Every individual is a pupil, an aspirant for perfection, a seeker of God and if he seeks earnestly, with faith, God the goal becomes God the guide. It is of little moment, so far as the validity of the teaching is concerned, whether the author is a figure of history or the very god descended into man, for the realities of spirit are the same now as they were thousands of years ago and differences of race and nationality do not affect them. The essential thing is truth or significance; and the historical fact is nothing more than the image of it.[2]

6. *The Status of the World and the Concept of Māyā*

If the fundamental form of the Supreme is *nirguṇa*, quality-less and *acintya*, inconceivable, the world is an appearance which cannot be logically related to the Absolute. In the unalterable eternity of Brahman, all that moves and evolves is founded. By It they exist, they cannot be without It, though It causes nothing, does nothing, determines nothing.

[1] Cp. *ajñānatimirāndhasya jñānāñjanaśalākayā*
cakṣur unmīlitaṁ yena tasmai śri gurave namaḥ.
I bow to the divine teacher, who opens the eyes of one blinded by the disease of ignorance by means of the principle (collyrium) of knowledge.

[2] Cp. Spinoza: "It is not in the least needful for salvation to know Christ according to the flesh; but concerning that so-called eternal Son of God (de aeterno illo Dei filio), that is, God's eternal wisdom, which is manifested in all things, and chiefly in the mind of man, and most particularly in Christ Jesus, the case is far otherwise. For without this no man can arrive at a state of blessedness, inasmuch as nothing else can teach him what is true or false, what is good or evil." Thus Spinoza distinguishes between the historical Jesus and the ideal Christ. The divinity of Christ is a dogma that has grown in the Christian conscience. Christological doctrine is the theological explanation of the historic fact. Loisy observes: "The Resurrection of Jesus was not the last step of His terrestrial career, the last act of His ministry amongst men, but the first article of the faith of the Apostles and the spiritual foundation of Christianity." Maude Petre: *Loisy* (1944), pp. 65–66.

While the world is dependent on Brahman, the latter is not dependent on the world. This one-sided dependence and the logical inconceivability of the relation between the Ultimate Reality and the world are brought out by the word, "māyā." The world is not essential being like Brahman; nor is it mere non-being. It cannot be defined as either being or non-being.[1] The sudden discovery through religious experience of the ultimate reality of spirit inclines us sometimes to look upon the world as an illusion rather than as a misapprehension or a misconstruction. Māyā does not imply that the world is an illusion or is non-existent absolutely. It is a delimitation distinct from the unmeasured and the immeasurable. But why is there this delimitation? The question cannot be answered, so long as we are at the empirical level.

In every religion, the Supreme Reality is conceived as infinitely above our time order, with its beginning and end, its movements and fluctuations. God, in the Christian religion, is represented as without variableness or shadow of turning. He dwells in the eternal now seeing the end from the beginning. If this were all, there would be an absolute division between the Divine life and this pluralistic world, which would make all communion between the two impossible. If the Supreme Reality were unique, passive and immobile, there would be no room for time, for movement, for history. Time, with its processes of change and succession, would become a mere appearance. But God is a living principle, a consuming fire. It is not a question of either an Absolute with an apparent multiplicity or a living God working in this pluralistic universe. The Supreme is both this and that. Eternity does not mean the denial of time or of history. It is the transfiguration of time. Time derives from eternity and finds fulfilment in it. In the *Bhagavadgītā*, there is no antithesis between eternity and time. Through the figure of Kṛṣṇa, the unity between the eternal and the historical is indicated. The temporal movement is related to the inmost depths of eternity.

The Spirit which transcends all dualities, when looked at from the cosmic end becomes sundered into the transcendental subject facing the transcendental object. Subject and

[1] *sadasadbhyām anirvacanīyam.*

object are the two poles of the one Reality. They are not unrelated. The principle of objectivity, mūlaprakṛti, the unmanifested (avyakta) potentiality of all existence is of the very nature of the creative Logos, Īśvara. The eternal "I" confronts the pseudo-eternal "not I," Nārāyaṇa broods over the waters. As the "not-I," prakṛti, is a reflection of the Self, it is subordinate to the Self. When the element of negation is introduced into the Absolute, its inwardness is unfolded in the process of becoming. The original unity becomes pregnant with the whole course of the world.

Cosmic process is the interaction between the two principles of being and non-being. God is the upper limit with the least affection by and complete control of non-being and matter or prakṛti is the lower limit with the least affection by being. The whole cosmic process is the Supreme God working on prakṛti which is conceived as a positive entity because it has the power of resistance. As resisting form, it is evil. Only in God is it completely penetrated and overcome. In the rest of the created world, it is there in some degree or other, obscuring the light.

The *Gītā* does not uphold a metaphysical dualism; for the principle of non-being is dependent on being. Non-being is a necessary moment in reality for the unfolding of the Supreme. If the world is what it is, it is because of the tension. The world of time and change is ever striving to reach perfection. Non-being which is responsible for the imperfections is a necessary element in the world, for it is the material in which the ideas of God are actualized.[1] The Divine forms (puruṣa) and matter (prakṛti) belong to one spiritual whole. When the whole world is delivered from bondage, when it is lifted into incorruption, when it becomes completely illuminated, the purpose of the Supreme is realized and the world is restored to its origin in pure Being, above all distinctions.

Why is there non-being? Why is there the fall or the precipitation from absolute being to becoming? This is to ask why is there the world with its perpetual strife between being and non-being? Absolute being, the one Godhead, is behind

[1] Cp. Proclus who regards matter as a "child of God" which is bound to be transformed into spirit.

and beyond the world and in the world; He is also the Supreme Living God, loving the world and redeeming it by His grace. Why is the world what it is with its graduated hierarchy? We can only say, it is the nature of the Supreme to express Itself in this way. We cannot account for the fact of the world but can only construe its nature, which is a strife between being and non-being in the process of becoming. Pure being is above the world and pure non-being is below the lowest existent. If we go lower still we have nothing, it is absolute non-entity. In the world of true becoming, saṁsāra, we have the conflict between the two principles of being and non-being.

The first product of the interaction is the cosmic egg (brahmāṇḍa) which includes within itself the totality of manifested being. All later developments are contained within it in a germinal form. It contains the past, the present and the future in a supreme now. Arjuna sees the whole Viśvarūpa, world-form, in one vast shape. He sees the form of the Divine bursting the very bounds of existence, filling the whole sky and the universe, worlds coursing through it like cataracts.

Those who look upon the Supreme as impersonal and relationless regard the conception of Īśvara with his power of self-manifestation as the result of ignorance (avidyā).[1] The power of thought that produces forms which are transient and therefore unreal compared with the Eternal Reality, this power of producing appearances is called avidyā. But avidyā is not something peculiar to this or that individual. It is said to be the power of self-manifestation possessed by the Supreme. The Lord says that though He, in reality, is birthless, He comes to birth by His own power *ātmamāyayā*.[2] Māyā is derived from the root, *mā*, to form, to build, and

[1] Ś. says: "The names and forms imagined to exist in the Supreme Īśvara as a result of the ignorance of the nature of the Ātman, of which it is not possible to say whether they are different, or non-different from the Supreme are in Śruti and Smṛti texts called māyā, śakti, prakṛti of the all knowing Parameśvara." S.B., II, 1, 14.

[2] IV, 6. "The Supreme Lord chose to sport in the exercise of His power of Yoga."

bhagavān api rantuṁ manascakre yogamāyām upaśṛtaḥ. Bhāgavata, X, 29, 1. Divine activity is not undertaken for the fulfilment of any

originally meant the capacity to produce forms. The creative power by which God fashions the universe is called *yoga māyā.* There is no suggestion that the forms, the events and the objects produced by māyā or the form-building power of God, the māyin, are only illusory.

Māyā is sometimes said to be the source of delusion (moha). "Deluded by these threefold modes of nature (guṇa), this whole world does not recognize Me who am above them and imperishable."[1] Through the force of māyā we have a bewildering partial consciousness which loses sight of the reality and lives in the world of phenomena. God's real being is veiled by the play of prakṛti and its modes. The world is said to be deceptive because God hides Himself behind His creation. The world is not a deception but the occasion for it. We must shatter all forms, get behind the veil to find the reality. The world and its changes constitute the self-concealment of God (*tirodhāna*) or obscuring of the Creator by His creation. Man is inclined to turn towards the objects of the world instead of directing his mind to the Creator. God seems to be the great deceiver as He creates the world and its sense objects and turns our senses outward.[2] The proneness to self-deception lies in the desire for the things of sense which actually leads man away from God. The glamour of the world casts its spell on us and we become slaves to its prizes. The world or objectivized nature or saṁsāra is fallen, enslaved, alienated and it is full of suffering, as alienation from inward being is suffering. When it is said that "this divine māyā of mine is hard to over-

purpose of his own, because God is *nityatṛpta.* This feature of disinterestedness is brought out by the use of the word sport. *lokavat tu līlā kaivalyam. Brahma Sūtra,* II, 1, 33. *Rādhā Up.* says that the One God is eternally at play in the varied activities of the world. *eko devo nityalīlānuraktaḥ,* IV, 3.

[1] VII, 13. Cp. *Nārada Pañcarātra.* "One only is the Lord always, in all and in each. All beings come into existence by His action; but they are deceived by His māyā." II, 1, 22. In M.B. it is said: "O, Nārada, that which you see is the māyā which has been created by Me. Do not think that I possess the qualities, which are to be found in the created world."

māyā hy eṣa mayā sṛṣṭā yan māṁ paśyasi nārada
sarvabhūtaguṇair yuktaṁ naiva tvaṁ jñātum arhasi.

Śāntiparva, 339, 44.

[2] *Kaṭha Up.,* IV, 1.

come," it means that we cannot easily pierce behind the universe and its activities.[1]

We may here distinguish the different senses in which the word "māyā" is used and indicate its place in the *Gītā.* (1) If the Supreme Reality is unaffected by the events of the world, then the rise of these events becomes an inexplicable mystery. The author of the *Gītā* does not use the term, "māyā," in this sense, however much it may be implied in his views. The conception of a beginning-less, and at the same time unreal, avidyā causing the appearance of the world, does not enter the mind of the author. (2) The personal Īśvara is said to combine within Himself, sat and asat, the immutability of Brahman as well as the mutation of becoming.[2] Māyā is the power which enables Him to produce mutable nature. It is śakti or the energy of Īśvara, or *ātmavibhūti*, the power of self-becoming. Īśvara and māyā in this sense are mutually dependent and beginning-less.[3] This power of the Supreme is called māyā in the *Gītā*.[4] (3) Since the Lord is able to produce the universe by means of the two elements of His being, prakṛti and puruṣa, matter and consciousness, they are said to be māyā (higher and lower) of God.[5] (4) Gradually, māyā comes to mean the lower prakṛti, since puruṣa is said to be the seed which the Lord casts into the womb of prakṛti for the generation of the universe. (5) As the manifested world hides the real from the vision of mortals, it is said to be delusive in character.[6] The world is not an illusion, though by regarding it as a mere mechanical determination of nature unrelated to God, we fail to perceive its Divine essence. It then becomes a source of delusion. The Divine māyā becomes *avidyāmāyā.* It is so, however, only for us mortals, shut off from the truth; to God who knows all and controls it, it is *vidyāmāyā.* God seems to be enveloped in the immense cloak of māyā.[7] (6) Since the world is only

[1] VII, 14; see also *Īśa Up.*, 16. [2] IX, 19.
[3] See *Śāṇḍilya Sūtra*, II, 13 and 15; *Śvetāśvatara Up.*, IV, 10.
[4] XVIII, 61; IV, 6. [5] IV, 16. [6] VII, 25 and 14.
[7] māyā which does not produce avidyā is said to be *sāttvikī māyā.* When it is polluted, it breeds ignorance or avidyā. Brahman reflected in the former is Īśvara, while that reflected in the latter is jīva, or the individual self. This is later Vedānta; see *Pañcadaśī*, I, 15–17. *Gītā* is not aware of this view.

an effect of God, who is the cause and since everywhere the cause is more real than the effect, the world as effect is said to be less real than God the cause. This relative unreality of the world is confirmed by the self-contradictory nature of the process of becoming. There is a struggle of opposites in the world of experience, and the real is above all opposites.[1]

7. *The Individual Self*

Reality is, in its own nature, infinite, absolute, untramelled, inalienably possessed of its own unity and bliss. In the cosmic process, dualities and oppositions which obscure the infinite undivided reality arise. In the terms of the *Taittirīya Up.*, the cosmic process has assumed the five stages of matter[2] (anna), life (prāṇa), mind (manas), intelligence (vijñāna) and bliss (ānanda). There is an inner direction given to things by reason of their participation in the creative onrush of life. The human being is at the fourth stage of vijñāna or intelligence. He is not master of his acts. He is aware of the universal reality which is operating in the whole scheme. He seems to know matter, life and mind. He has mastered, to a large extent, the material world, the vital existence and even the obscure workings of mentality but has not yet become the completely illumined consciousness. Even as matter is succeeded by life, life by mind and mind by intelligence, even so the intelligent man will grow into a higher and divine life. Progressive self-enlargement has been the impulse of nature. God's purpose for the world or the cosmic destiny for man is the realization of the immortal aspiration through this mortal frame, the achievement of the Divine life in and through this physical frame and intellectual consciousness.

The Divine dwells in the inmost being of man and cannot be extinguished. It is the inner light, the concealed witness, that which endures and is imperishable from birth to birth, untouched by death, decay or corruption. It is the principle of the jīva, the psychic person which changes and grows from life to life and when the ego is completely harmonized by the Divine, it ascends into spiritual existence which is

[1] II, 45; VII, 28; IX, 33.

[2] Literally food.

its destiny and until this happens it travels between birth and death.

All forms of existence are found in each being for, under the well-fixed traits of the human form, are the contours of materiality, organization and animality. The matter, life and mind that fill the world are in us as well. We partake of the forces that work in the outer world. Our intellectual nature produces self-consciousness; it leads to the emergence of the human individual from its original solidarity with nature. The security which he derives from the instinctive adherence to the group is lost and has to be regained at a higher level without the elimination of his individuality. By the integration of his self, his unity with the world has to be achieved in a spontaneity of love and unselfish work. Arjuna, in the opening scene, faces the world of nature and society and feels utterly alone. He does not wish to buy inward security by submission to the social standard. So long as he looks upon himself as a kṣatriya required to fight, so long as he is chained to his station and its duties, he is unaware of the full possibilities of his individual action. Most of us, by finding our specific place in the social world, give a meaning to our life and gain a feeling of security, a sense of belonging. Normally, within limits, we find scope for the expression of our life and the social routine is not felt as a bondage. The individual has not yet emerged. He does not conceive of himself except through the social medium. Arjuna could have overcome his feeling of helplessness and anxiety by submitting completely to the social authority. But that would be to arrest his growth. Any sense of satisfaction and security derived by submission to external authority is bought at the price of the integrity of the self. Modern views like the totalitarian declare that the individual can be saved by his absorption into society. They forget that the group exists only to secure the complete unfolding of human personality. Arjuna disentangles himself from the social context, stands alone and faces the perilous and overpowering aspects of the world. Submission is not the human way of overcoming loneliness and anxiety. By developing our inner spiritual nature, we gain a new kind of relatedness to the world and grow into the freedom, where the integrity of the self is not compromised. We then become aware of ourselves as active creative individuals, living, not by the discipline of external authority but by the inward rule of free devotion to truth.

The individual self is a portion of the Lord,[1] a real, not an imaginary form of the Supreme, a limited manifestation of God. The soul which derives from the Supreme Īśvara is not so much an emanation as a member of the Supreme. It draws its ideal from this superior principle which is like a father who has given it existence. The soul's substantial existence springs from the Divine intellect and its expression in life is effected by virtue of its vision of the Divine who is its father and its ever-present companion. Its distinctiveness is determined by the divine pattern and the context of the senses and the mind which it draws to itself. The universal is embodied in a limited context of mental—vital-physical sheaṭh.[2] No individual is quite like his fellow; no life repeats another and yet a single pattern runs through them all. The essence of the ego, the distinguishing characteristic of human personality is a certain creative unity, an inner purposiveness, a plan which has gradually shaped itself into an organic unity. As our purpose is, so is our life. Any form which the individual assumes is bound to be superseded, for he always tries to transcend himself and this process will continue till becoming reaches its end in being. The jīvas are movements in the being of God, individualized. When the ego is lost in a false identification with the not-self and its forms, it is bound; but when through the development of proper understanding, it realizes the true nature of the self and the not-self and allows the apparatus produced by the not-self to be illumined completely by the self, then it is freed. This realization is possible through the proper functioning of buddhi or vijñāna.

The problem facing man is the integration of his personality, the development of a divine existence in which the spiritual principle has the mastery over all the powers of soul and body. This integral life is created by the spirit. The distinction between soul and body which links man with the life of nature is not an ultimate one. It does not exist in the

[1] XV, 7. Many names are given to this divine essence of the soul—apex, ground, abyss, spark, fire, inner light. [2] XIII, 21.

radical sense in which Descartes affirmed it. The life of the soul permeates the life of the body, even as the bodily life has its effect on the soul. There is a vital unity of soul and body in man. The real dualism is between spirit and nature, between freedom and necessity. In the integrated personality we have the victory of the spirit over nature, of freedom over necessity. The *Gītā* which looks upon both these as aspects of the Supreme, affirms that we can spiritualize nature and communicate another quality to it. We need not crush or destroy nature.

The problem of freedom *vs.* determinism has meaning only with reference to human individuals. It has no application to the Absolute which is above all opposites or to the sub-human species of plants and animals. If man is but the simple creature of instinct, if his desires and decisions are only the resultants of the forces of heredity and environment, then moral judgments are irrelevant. We do not condemn the lion for its ferocity or praise the lamb for its meekness. Man is the possessor of freedom.[1] After describing the whole philosophy of life, the teacher asks Arjuna to do as he chooses.[2] The whole teaching of the *Gītā* requires man to choose the good and realize it by conscious effort. There are however many impediments to this freedom of choice.

Man is a complex multi-dimensional being, including within him different elements of matter, life, consciousness, intelligence and the divine spark. He is free when he acts from the highest level and uses the other elements for the realization of his purpose. But when he is on the level of objective nature, when he does not recognize his distinction from not-self, he becomes a slave to the mechanism of nature. But, even when he falsely identifies himself with the objective universe, and feels that he is subjected to the necessities of nature, he is not without hope, for the One Spirit operates at all levels of being. Even matter is a manifestation of the Supreme. There is an element of spontaneity and creativity inexplicable in terms of mechanical forces even in the lowest forms of nature. Each plane of our being has its own consciousness, its surface thoughts, its habitual ways of feeling, thought and action. The ego should not persist in retaining

[1] *svatantraḥ kartā.* [2] XVIII, 63.

its obscure and limited consciousness, which is a distortion of its true nature. When we subdue the senses and keep them under control, the flame of spirit burns bright and clear "like a lamp in a windless place." The light of consciousness stands in its own nature and the empirical self with its shifting tides of experience is controlled by buddhi in which is reflected the light of consciousness. Then we rise above the play of prakṛti and see the real self from which creative forces arise; we cease to belong to that which is moved about and are no more helpless tools of nature. We are free participants of the world above into the world below. Nature is an order of determinism but not a closed order. Forces of spirit may break upon it and change its course. Every act of the self is a creative one, while all acts of the not-self are truly passive. It is in our inner life that we confront primary reality, the deeps of being. The law of karma holds in the realm of the not-self where heredity, biological and social, holds but in the subject is the possibility of freedom, of triumph over the determinism of nature, over the compulsion of the world. Man, the subject, should gain mastery over man, the object. Object indicates determinism from without; subject means freedom, indetermination. The ego, in its self-confinement, in its automatism, psychical and social, is a distortion of the true subject. The law of karma can be overcome by the affirmation of the freedom of spirit. In several passages[1] the *Gītā* affirms that there is no radical dualism between the supernatural and the natural. The cosmic forces to which man is exposed represent the lower *prakṛti*. But his spirit can burst the circle of nature and realize its kinship with the Divine. Our bondage consists in our dependence on something alien. When we rise above it, we can make our nature the medium for the incarnation of the spiritual. Through struggle and suffering, man can pass from his freedom to choose good or evil to the higher freedom that abides in the steadfastly chosen good. Liberation is a return to inward being, to subjectivity; bondage is enslavement to the object world, to necessity, to dependence.

Neither nature nor society can invade our inner being

[1] See VII, 5.

without permission. Even God acts with a peculiar delicacy in regard to human beings. He woos our consent but never compels. Human individuals have distinctive beings of their own which limit God's interference with their development. The world is not fulfilling a prearranged plan in a mechanical way. The aim of creation is the production of selves who freely carry out God's will. We are asked to control our impulses, shake off our wanderings and confusions, rise above the current of nature and regulate our conduct by reference to buddhi or understanding, as otherwise, we will become the victims of "lust which is the enemy of man on earth."[1] The *Gītā* lays stress on the individual's freedom of choice and the way in which he exercises it. Man's struggles, his sense of frustration and self-accusation are not to be dismissed as errors of the mortal mind or mere phases of a dialectic process. This would be to deny the moral urgency of life. When Arjuna expresses his sense of awe and dread in the presence of the Eternal, when he asks for forgiveness, he is not acting a part but passing through a crisis.

Nature does not absolutely determine. Karma is a condition, not a destiny. It is only one of the five factors involved in the accomplishment of any act, which are *adhiṣṭhāna* or the basis or centre from which we work, *kartṛ* or doer, *karaṇa* or the instrumentation of nature, *ceṣṭā* or effort and *daiva* or fate.[2] The last is the power or powers other than human, the cosmic principle which stands behind, modifying the work and disposing of its fruits in the shape of act and its reward. We must make a distinction between that part which is inevitable in the make-up of nature, where restraint does not avail and the part where it could be controlled and moulded to our purpose. There are certain factors in our lives which are determined for us by forces over which we have no control. We do not choose how or when or where or in what condition of life we are born. On the theory of rebirth, even these are chosen by us. It is our past karma that determines our ancestry, heredity and environment. But when we look from the standpoint of this life, we can say that we were not consulted about our nationality, race, parentage or social status. But subject to these limi-

[1] III, 37; VI, 5–6. [2] XVIII, 14.

tations, we have freedom of choice. Life is like a game of bridge. We did not invent the game or design the cards. We did not frame the rules and we cannot control the dealing. The cards are dealt out to us, whether they be good or bad. To that extent, determinism rules. But we can play the game well or play it badly. A skilful player may have a poor hand and yet win the game. A bad player may have a good hand and yet make a mess of it. Our life is a mixture of necessity and freedom, chance and choice. By exercising our choice properly, we can control steadily all the elements and eliminate altogether the determinism of nature. While the movements of matter, the growth of plants and the acts of animals are controlled more completely, man has understanding which enables him to co-operate consciously with the work of the world. He can approve or disapprove, give or withhold his consent to certain acts. If he does not exercise his intelligent will, he is acting in a way contrary to his humanity. If he acts blindly according to his impulses and passions, he acts more like an animal than a man. Being human, he justifies his actions.

Some of our acts are ours only seemingly. The sense of spontaneity is only apparent. We sometimes carry out suggestions given to us in the hypnotic condition. We may believe that we think, feel and will the acts but in so doing we may be giving expression to the suggestions conveyed to us during the hypnotic state. What is true of the hypnotic situation is true of many of our acts which may seem spontaneous but are really not so. We repeat the latest given opinions and believe that they are the result of our own thinking. Spontaneous acting is not compulsive activity to which the individual is driven by his own isolation and helplessness. It is the free acting of the total self. The individual should become transparent to himself and the different elements should reach a fundamental integration for spontaneous or creative activity to be possible. It is man's duty to control his rajas and tamas by means of his sattva nature which seeks for the truth of things and the right law of action. But even when we act under the influence of our sattva nature we are not entirely free. Sattva binds us quite as much as rajas and tamas. Only our desires for truth and virtue are nobler. The sense of ego is still operative. We must rise above our ego and grow into the Supreme Self of which the ego is an expression. When we make our individual being one with the Supreme, we rise above nature with its three modes, become triguṇātīta,[1] and freed from the bonds of the world.

8. *Yoga-śāstra*

Every system of Indian philosophic thought gives us a practical way of reaching the supreme ideal. Though we begin with thought, our aim is to go beyond thought to the decisive experience. Systems of philosophy give not only metaphysical theories, but also spiritual dynamics. It may be argued that, if man is a part of the Divine, what he needs is not redemption as an awareness of his true nature. If he feels himself a sinner estranged from God, he requires a technique by which he reminds himself that he is essentially a part of God and any feeling to the contrary is illusory. This awareness is not intellectual but integral; so man's whole nature requires overhauling. The *Bhagavadgītā* gives us not only a metaphysics (brahmavidyā) but also a discipline (yogaśāstra). Derived from the root, *yuj*, to bind together, yoga means binding one's psychic powers, balancing and enhancing them.[2] By yoking together and harnessing our energies by the most intense concentration of personality, we force the passage from the narrow ego to the transcendent personality. The spirit tears itself away from its prison house, stands out of it and reaches its own innermost being.

The *Gītā* gives a comprehensive yoga-śāstra, large, flexible and many-sided, which includes various phases of the soul's development and ascent into the Divine. The different yogas are special applications of the inner discipline which leads to the liberation of the soul and a new understanding of the unity and meaning of mankind. Everything that is related to this discipline is called a yoga such as jñāna-yoga or the way of knowledge, bhakti-yoga or the way of devotion, karma-yoga or the way of action.

[1] XIV, 21.

[2] It is used in different senses; *yujyate etad iti yogaḥ*; (ii) *yujyate anena iti yogaḥ;* (iii) *yujyate tasminn iti yogaḥ.*

Perfection at the human level is a task to be accomplished by conscious endeavour. The image of God operating in us produces a sense of insufficiency. Man has a haunting sense of the vanity, the transience and the precariousness of all human happiness. Those who live on the surface of life may not feel the distress, the laceration of spirit, and may not feel any urge to seek their true good. They are human animals (*puruṣapaśu*), and like animals they are born, they grow, they mate and leave offspring and pass away. But those who realize their dignity as men are acutely aware of the discord and seek a principle of harmony and peace.

Arjuna typifies the representative human soul seeking to reach perfection and peace but in the opening section we find that his mind is clouded, his convictions unsettled, his whole consciousness confused. Life's anxieties touch him with a gnawing distress. For every individual there comes an hour sometime or other, for nature is not in a hurry, when everything that he can do for himself fails, when he sinks into the gulf of utter blackness, an hour when he would give all that he has for one gleam of light, for one sign of the Divine. When he is assailed by doubt, denial, hatred of life and black despair, he can escape from them only if God lays His hand on him. If the divine truth which is free of access to all mankind, is attained only by a few, it shows that only a few are willing to pay the price for it. The sense of insufficiency, of barrenness and dust, is due to the working of the Perfection, the mystery that lurks at the heart of creation. The invisible impulse to seek God produces the agony that inspires heroic idealism and human fulfilment. The image of God in us expresses itself in the infinite capacity for self-transcendence.[1]

1 "There is a principle which is pure, placed in the human mind, which in different places and ages hath had different names; it is, however, pure and proceeds from God. It is deep, and inward, confined to no forms of religion, nor excluded from any, where the heart stands in perfect sincerity. In whomsoever this takes root and grows, of what nation soever, they become brethren in the best sense of the expression." John Woolman, the American Quaker saint.

9. *Jñāna or Saving Wisdom*

How is the goal of perfection to be attained? Saṁsāra is historical becoming. It is the temporal procession of changes from one state into the next. What keeps the world going is action or karma. If the world is nothing but ebb and flow, continual becoming, it is due to action. At the human level action is caused by desire or attachment, kāma. The root cause of desire is avidyā or ignorance of the nature of things. The roots of desire lie in the ignorant belief in the individual's self-sufficiency, in the attribution of reality and permanence to it. So long as ignorance persists, it is not possible to escape from the vicious circle of becoming. We cannot cure desires by fresh desires; we cannot cure action by more action. The eternal cannot be gained by that which is temporal.[1] Whether we are bound by good desires or bad desires, it is still a question of bondage. It makes little difference whether the chains which bind us are made of gold or of iron. To escape from bondage we must get rid of ignorance, which is the parent of ignorant desires and so of ignorant actions. Vidyā or wisdom is the means of liberation from the chain of *avidyā-kāma-karma.*

Wisdom is not to be confused with theoretical learning or correct beliefs, for ignorance is not intellectual error. It is spiritual blindness. To remove it, we must cleanse the soul of its defilement and kindle the spiritual vision. The fire of passion and the tumult of desire must be suppressed.[2] The mind, inconstant and unstable, must be steadied so as to reflect the wisdom from above. We must control the senses, possess the faith which no intellectual doubts disturb and train the understanding (buddhi).[3]

Wisdom is direct experience which occurs as soon as obstacles to its realization are removed. The effort of the seeker is directed to the elimination of the hindrances, to the removal of the obscuring tendencies of avidyā. According to Advaita Vedānta, this wisdom is always present. It is not a thing to be acquired; it has only to be revealed. Our casual apprehensions, backed by our wishes and prejudices, do not reveal reality. Utter silence of the mind and

[1] *Kaṭha Up.*, II, 10. [2] IV, 39. [3] II, 44.

the will, an emptying of the ego produces illumination, wisdom, the light by which we grow into our true being. This is life eternal, the complete fulfilment of our capacity of love and knowledge, "the completely simultaneous and perfect possession of unlimited life at a single moment," to use the words of Boethius.

Jñāna and ajñāna, wisdom and ignorance are opposed as light and darkness.[1] When wisdom dawns, ignorance dies and the evil is cut off at the root. The liberated soul overcomes the world. There is nothing to conquer or create. Action no more binds. When we grow into this wisdom, we live in the Supreme.[2] This consciousness is not an abstract one. It is "that by which thou shalt see all existences without exception in the Self, then in Me." The true human individual pursues this ideal of perfection with a devotion similar to that which he offers to an adored woman.[3]

10. *The Way of Knowledge: Jñāna-mārga*

We can reach the goal of perfection, attain the saving truth in three different ways, by a knowledge of Reality (jñāna) or adoration and love (bhakti) of the Supreme Person or by the subjection of the will to the Divine purpose (karma). These are distinguished on account of the distribution of emphasis on the theoretical, emotional and practical aspects. Men are of different types, reflective, emotional or active but they are not exclusively so. At the end, knowledge, love and action mingle together. God Himself is sat, cit and ānanda, reality, truth and bliss. To those seeking knowledge, He is Eternal Light, clear and radiant as the sun at noonday, in which is no darkness; to those struggling for virtue, He is Eternal Righteousness, steadfast and impartial; and to those emotionally inclined, He is Eternal Love and Beauty of Holiness. Even as God combines in Himself these features, man aims at the integral life of spirit. Cognition, will and feeling, though logically distinguishable, are

[1] *Svarūpajñāna* or the Real as consciousness always *is*. Its constant presence does not dispel, according to Advaita Vedānta, ajñāna or ignorance. It rather reveals it. Wisdom as *sākṣātkāra* is a vṛtti and so an effect like any other kind of jñāna.

[2] V, 20.

[3] *muktikāntā*.

not really separable in the concrete life and unity of mind. They are different aspects of the one movement of the soul.[1]

Jñāna as the intellectual pathway to perfection is different from jñāna as spiritual wisdom. The spiritual apprehension of the real is not an act of service or of devotion or for that matter, of cognition, however much these acts may lead up to it. As the same word "jñāna" is employed for both the goal of perfection and the way to it, for the recognition of reality as well as the scheme of spiritual knowledge, some are led to think that the intellectual path is superior to the other methods of approach.

Wisdom, pure and transcendent, is different from scientific knowledge, though it is not discontinuous from it. Every science expresses, after its own fashion, within a certain order of things, a reflection of the higher immutable truth of which everything of any reality necessarily partakes. Scientific or discriminative knowledge prepares us for the higher wisdom. The partial truths of science are different from the whole truth of spirit. Scientific knowledge is useful since it dispels the darkness oppressing the mind, shows up the incompleteness of its own world and prepares the mind for something beyond it. For knowing the truth, we require a conversion of the soul, the development of spiritual vision. Arjuna could not see the truth with his naked eyes and so was granted the divine sight.

[1] Cp. Plotinus: "There are different roads by which this end (of spiritual apprehension) may be reached; the love of beauty which exalts the poet; that devotion to the one and that ascent of science which make the ambition of the philosopher; that love and those prayers by which some devout and ardent soul tends in its moral purity towards perfection. These are the great highways conducting to that height above the actual and the particular, where we stand in the immediate presence of the Infinite, who shines out as from the deeps of the soul." *Letter to Flaccus.*

Madhusūdana holds that to attain the perfect Godhead who is of the nature of Being, Wisdom and Bliss, the Vedas are of three sections, dealing with action, worship and knowledge; similarly these three sections are embodied in the eighteen chapters of the *Gītā.*

saccidānandarūpaṁ tat pūrṇaṁ viṣṇoḥ paraṁ padam,
yat prāptaye samārabdhā vedāḥ kāṇḍatrayātmikāḥ,
karmopāstis tathā jñānam iti kāṇḍatrayaṁ kramāt,
tadrūpā'ṣṭādaśadhyāyair gītā kāṇḍatrayātmikā.

Ascent to higher levels of being, losing oneself to find the higher self can be achieved through jijñāsā or disinterested passion for knowledge. It lifts man out of his narrow limits and makes him forget his self in the contemplation of the universal principles of existence. Knowledge pursued for the sake of power or fame does not take us far. It must be sought for attaining truth.

The metaphysical creed accepted by the *Gītā* with certain fundamental modifications is that of the Sāṁkhya philosophy. Profound faith in God and belief in redemption require us to assume three entities, the soul which has to be redeemed, the fetter which binds it, from which it has to be redeemed, and God, the Being who releases us from this bondage. The Sāṁkhya philosophy elaborates the dualism between puruṣa (self) and prakṛti (not-self); only the *Gītā* makes them both subordinate to God. The selves are many and remain for ever separate. The self is the permanent entity behind all the changes of conscious life. It is not the soul in the usual sense but the pure, inactive, self-luminous principle, which is not derived from or dependent on or determined by the world. It is unique and integral. Man is not self but possesses self and can become self. Not-self or prakṛti is another ultimate principle which is conceived as being at first undifferentiated matter with all its constituents in equilibrium. As such, it is the unmanifested or the avyakta. All mental and material phenomena are explained as the outcome of the evolution of prakṛti. It has three modes or guṇas, literally strands of a rope. These, by appearing in different proportions, produce the variety of actual existence. With reference to matter, they act as lightness (*sattva*), movement (*rajas*) and heaviness (*tamas*). As forms of mental phenomena, they act as goodness, passion and dullness respectively. When the self realizes that it is free from all contact with prakṛti, it is released. The *Gītā* accepts this account with the fundamental modification that the dualities of Sāṁkhya, puruṣa and prakṛti, are the very nature of the Supreme Principle, God.

Evil is caused by the bondage to the guṇas. It arises because the seed of life or the spirit cast into matter becomes fettered by the guṇas. According to the preponderance of one or the other of the guṇas the soul rises or falls. When we recognize the self as distinct from prakṛti with its guṇas, we are released. Metaphysical knowledge[1] is transformed into realization[2] by means of yoga or the method of concentration. From the earliest times, yoga has been employed to describe practices and experiences of a special kind which have been later adapted to the teachings of the different methods, jñāna, bhakti and karma. Each of them uses the practices of *dhyānayoga* or the way of meditation. Yoga is the suppression of the activities of the mind, according to Patañjali.[3] *Muṇḍaka Up.* says, "As fire deprived of fuel is extinguished in its own hearth, so when mental activities are suppressed (*vṛttikṣayāt*), citta is extinguished in its own seat."[4] It is by a mighty exercise of will that we can achieve this suppression of the clamour of ideas and of the rabble of desires. By ceaseless action the yogī is called upon to achieve control.[5]

Man knows only a part of his being, his surface mentality. There is a good deal beneath the surface of which he has no knowledge though it has effects on his conduct. We are sometimes completely overcome by emotions, instinctive and involuntary reactions that upset the rule of conscious reason. While the lunatic is completely overcome by them, many of us are also subject to their influence, though such conditions are temporary with normal individuals. Under the stress of strong emotions of love or of hatred, we say or do things which we regret afterwards when we regain control. Our language, "He is beside himself," "He forgot himself," "He is not himself," suggests the truth of the primitive view that the man who is overcome by a strong emotion is possessed by a devil or a spirit.[6] When strong emotions are aroused, we become increasingly suggestible and all sorts of wild ideas take possession of us. Normally the subconscious collaborates with the conscious and we do not even suspect

[1] *parokṣajñāna.* [2] *aparokṣabrahmasākṣātkāra.*

[3] *yogaś cittavṛttinirodhaḥ.* [4] VI, 34. *cittaṁ svayonau upaśāmyate.*

[5] *nirvikāreṇa karmaṇā. Harivaṁśa.* XI, 736.

[6] "Fascination, bewitchment, loss of soul, possession and so on are clearly phenomena of dissociation, repression and suppression of consciousness by unconscious contents." Jung: *The Integration of the Personality.* E.T. (1940), p. 12.

its presence but if we get off the track of our original instinctive pattern, we realize the full force of the subconscious. Unless the individual has complete self-awareness, he cannot become master of his life. Besides, body, life and mind require to be integrated. As a selfconscious being, man is actually aware of the deeper discords in him. He generally resorts to working compromises and leads a precarious life. But until a perfect harmony, an organic balance, of his many-sided possibilities is achieved, he is not fully master of himself. The process of integration is never completed, so long as he is subject to temptations as Arjuna was. A growing personality requires unceasing care and fostering. By developing purity of intention, passions directed towards mundane objects die, producing tranquillity of mind which in turn gives rise to the inward silence in which the soul begins to establish contact with the Eternal from which it is sundered, and experience the presence of the Indwelling God. In stillness which is the rest of the soul from earthly encounter, insight is born and man becomes what he is.

Our consciousness when united with the body is turned outward in order to accomplish its work of controlling the outer world by means of the senses. In its outward functioning, it employs concepts to achieve an understanding of the sensible. By turning inward, it normally gets an inferential apprehension of the self, through the acts which are apprehended immediately, in the sense that the objects apprehended are known by no other intermediary than the apprehension itself. All this does not tell us what the self, in its essential nature, is. We know about the phenomena of the self but not of the self itself. To get at the existential experience of the self, we should get free from the diversity of objects, external and internal, which impedes and prevents the direct or intuitive vision of the essence of the self. Normally, the phenomenal content, external and internal, occupies the stage and the self is not perceived in its essentiality. The more we obscure ourselves psychologically, that is, through introspection or reflection, the more are we in contact with the phenomenal manifestations of the self. We should adopt a different discipline, if we are to confront the Supreme Self in us. We must fold up the phenomenal series, go against the grain of our nature, strip ourselves naked, escape from the apparent ego and get at the abyss of pure subjectivity, the Absolute Self.

The *Bhagavadgītā* describes to us how the aspirant avoids bodily excesses of indulgence or abstinence, goes to a place free from external distractions, chooses a comfortable seat, regulates his breathing, focuses his mind on one point and becomes harmonized (yukta) and detached from all desire for the fruit of action. When he attains this unity, he arrives at a perfect understanding with his fellow beings through sympathy and love and not because it is a matter of duty. We have the example of Gautama the Buddha, the greatest jñāni or seer whose love for humanity led to his ministry of mankind for forty years. To know the truth is to lift up our hearts to the Supreme and adore Him. The knower is also a devotee and the best of them.[1]

The systematic cultivation of yoga results incidentally in the development of supernatural powers but to practise yoga for the sake of obtaining these powers is vain and futile. Often it results in neurosis and failure. The aspirant for spiritual life is warned about the attraction of the supernatural powers. They may lead us to worldly advancement but are not directed to saintliness. They are spiritually meaningless and irrelevant. The occultist, who is able to see hyper-physical spheres, has developed certain potentialities which put him above the ordinary human beings even as those who are familiar with modern technology are better equipped than the primitive peasants. But the advance is in the external direction and not in the interiorization of the soul. Yoga is to be practised for the sake of attaining truth, of gaining contact with Reality. Kṛṣṇa is the lord of yoga (yogeśvara)[2] who helps us in our life to save ourselves. He is the supreme lord of spiritual experience who conveys those moments of celestial glory when man gets beyond the veil of the flesh and also indicates their true relation to the problems of daily existence.

II. *The Way of Devotion: Bhakti-mārga*

Bhakti or devotion is a relationship of trust and love to a personal God. Worship of the unmanifested (*avyaktopāsana*)

[1] VII, 17. [2] XVIII, 78.

is difficult for ordinary human beings, though there are instances of great advaitins (non-dualists) who have given to the Impersonal Reality a warm emotional content.[1] Worship of the Personal God is recommended as the easier way open to all, the weak and the lowly, the illiterate and the ignorant.[2] The sacrifice of love is not so difficult as the tuning of the will to the Divine purpose or ascetic discipline or the strenuous effort of thinking.

The origin of the way of devotion is hidden in the mists of long ago. The praises and prayers of the Ṛg. Veda, the upāsanas of the *Upaniṣads* and the ardent piety of the Bhāgavata religion influenced the author of the *Gītā*. He struggles to develop an order of ideas belonging to the religious side of the *Upaniṣads* to which they were not able to give free and unambiguous utterance. The Supreme is not a God who sleeps in serene abstraction while hearts heavy laden cry out for help, but a saving God of love believed and experienced as such by the devotee. He bestows salvation on those who believe in Him. He declares:

[1] The devotees dismiss the Advaita emphasis on knowledge as a damnable heresy or a soul-killing error, though Ś. recognizes the value of devotion as a preparation for gradual release.

[2] IX, 32; see also XI, 53–4; XII, 1–5. "What were the good practices of Vyādha? What was the age of Dhruva? What was the learning of Gajendra? What was the prowess of Ugrasena? What was the beauty of Kubjā? What was the wealth of Sudāma? The Lord, who is the lover of devotion, is pleased with devotion and does not bother about (other) qualities."

vyādhasyācaraṇaṁ, dhruvasya ca vayo, vidyā gajendrasya kā,
kā jātir vidurasya, yādavapater ugrasya kiṁ pauruṣam,
kubjāyāḥ kamanīyarūpamadhikaṁ kiṁ tat sudāmno dhanam
bhaktyā tuṣyati kevalaṁ na tu guṇaih bhakti priyo mādhavaḥ.

A verse attributed to Ś. reads: "Let the state of birth be that of a man or an angel or of a beast of the hill and the forest, of a mosquito, of the cattle, of an insect, of a bird or such others, if the heart longs to revel incessantly in this life in the contemplation of Thy lotus feet, that flood of supreme bliss, how does the embodiment matter?"

naratvaṁ devatvaṁ nagavanamṛgatvaṁ maśakatā paśutvaṁ kīṭatvam bhavatu vihagatvādi jananam
sadā tvat pādābjasmaraṇaparamānandalaharī vihārāsaktam ced hṛdayam iha kiṁ tena vapuṣā.

This is rather an exaggerated way of emphasizing the importance of bhakti.

"This is my word of promise, that He who loveth me shall not perish."[1]

Bhakti is derived from the root, *bhaj*, to serve, and means service of the Lord. It is loving attachment to God. Nārada defines it as intense love for God.[2] For Śaṇḍilya, it is supreme longing for God,[3] for its own sake.[4] It is surrender in trusting appropriation of the grace of the Lord. It is *īśvarapraṇidhāna* of *Yoga Sūtra*, which, according to Bhoja, is "the love in which, without seeking results, such as sense enjoyment, etc., all works are dedicated to the teacher of teachers."[5] It is a profound experience which negates all desire and fills the heart with love for God.[6] Advocates of the way of devotion are not interested so much in supramundane redemption as in absolute subjection to the abiding will of God. The human soul draws near to the Divine by contemplation of God's power, wisdom and goodness, by constant remembrance of Him with a devout heart, by conversing about His qualities with others, by singing His praises with fellow men and by doing all acts as His service.[7] The devotee directs his whole being to God. Adoration is the essence of religion. It involves a duality between the worshipper and the worshipped. If a philosophy of immanentism is so interpreted as to destroy man's sense of creatureliness or God's trans-

1 IX, 31.

2 *paramapremarūpā.*

3 *sā parānuraktir īśvare.* I, 1, 2.

4 *nirhetuka.* Cp. *Bhāgavata: ahetukavyavahitā yā bhaktiḥ puruṣottame:* see also B.G., XII, 5; IX, 17–18.

Cp. Caitanya: "I desire not, O Lord, wealth or retinue or a beautiful woman or poetic genius; I pray for spontaneous devotion to the Supreme in every birth of mine."

na dhanaṁ na janaṁ sundarīṁ kavitāṁ vā jagadīśa kāmaye
mama janmani janmanī'śvare bhavatād bhaktir ahaitukī tvayi.
Śikṣāṣṭaka, 4.

5 I, 23. It is *buddhānusmṛti* of *Mahāvastu.*

6 Cp. Nārada: *Bhakti Sūtra* 54; *guṇarahitaṁ, kāmanārahitaṁ, pratikṣaṇavardhamānam, avicchinnaṁ, sūkṣmataram, anubhavarūpam.*

7 *Nārada Sūtra*, 16–18. The *Bhāgavata* describes the nine stages of bhakti:

śravaṇaṁ kīrtanaṁ viṣṇoḥ, smaraṇaṁ pādasevanam
arcanaṁ, vandanaṁ, dāśyaṁ, sakhyam, ātmanivedanam."

Again: "I abide not in heaven nor in the hearts of yogis; I dwell where My devotees sing My glory."

nāhaṁ vasāmi vaikuṇṭhe, yogināṁ hṛdaye na ca
madbhaktā yatra gāyanti tatra tiṣṭhāmi nārada.

cendence, it has no place for devotion and worship. The distinction between creature and creator is the ontological basis of the religion of bhakti. The Eternal One is viewed in the *Bhagavadgītā* not so much as the God of philosophical speculation as the God of grace such as the heart and the soul need and seek, who inspires personal trust and love, reverence and loyal self-surrender. "Before the rise of knowledge, duality is misleading but when our understanding is enlightened, we perceive that duality is more beautiful than even non-duality and is conceived so that there might be worship."[1] Again, "The truth is non-duality; but duality is for the sake of worship; and thus, this worship is a hundred times greater than liberation."[2]

Bhakti, in the *Gītā*, is not an *amor intellectualis* which is more reflective and contemplative. It is sustained by knowledge but is not knowledge. It involves no reference to yoga technique or longing for speculative knowledge of the Divine. Śāṇḍilya argues that it gives us spiritual peace even without knowledge as in the case of milkmaids.[3] The devotee has a sense of utter humility. In the presence of the Ideal, he feels that he is nothing. God loves meekness,[4] the utter prostration of the self.

As a rule, the particular qualities associated with bhakti, love and devotion, mercy and tenderness are to be found more in women than in men. As bhakti emphasizes humility, obedience, readiness to serve, compassion and gentle love, as the devotee longs to surrender himself, renounce self-will and experience passivity, it is said to be more feminine in character. Women expect, suffer, hope and receive. They long for compassion, mercy, peace. Femininity is in all beings. In the *Bhāgavata*, it is said that the girls prayed to the Supreme Goddess, Kātyāyanī, to get for them Kṛṣṇa as their husband.[5] When they are most truly themselves, women give everything,

[1] *dvaitaṁ mohāya bodhāt prāk jāte bodhe manīṣayā*
bhaktyarthaṁ kalpitaṁ dvaitam advaitād api sundaram.

[2] *pāramārthikam advaitam dvaitam bhajanahetave*
tādriśī yadi bhaktiḥ syāt sā tu muktiśatādhikā.

[3] *ata eva tad abhāvād vallavīnām.*

[4] *dainyapriyatvam. Nārada Sūtra,* 27.

[5] *kātyāyani mahāmāye mahāyoginy adhīśvari*
nandagopasutaṁ devi patiṁ me kuru te namaḥ.
X, 22, 4.

claim nothing; they want to love and be loved. Rādhā typifies the loving soul. In relation to God, bhaktas are more like women. "The Supreme Lord is the only man; all others from Brahmā downwards are like women (who long to be united with Him)."[1]

When the soul surrenders itself to God, He takes up our knowledge and our error and casts away all forms of insufficiency and transforms all into His infinite light and the purity of the universal good. Bhakti is not merely the "flight of the alone to the Alone," the soul's detachment from the world and attachment to God, but is active love for the Divine who enters into the world for redeeming it.

The view that we cannot win the grace of the Lord by our own efforts results in an intense emotional pietism. While bhakti requires faith and love, in prapatti we simply surrender ourselves to God, place ourselves in His hands leaving it to Him to deal with us as He elects. It stresses the simple and austere purity of the relationship of surrender in a humble and direct attitude of trust. It perceives genuine piety in the completeness of the surrender rather than in the intensity of the bhakti discipline. When we are emptied of our self, God takes possession of us. The obstacles to this God-possession are our own virtues, pride, knowledge, our subtle demands and our unconscious assumptions and prejudices. We must empty ourselves of all desires and wait in trust on the Supreme Being. To fit God's pattern, all our claims are to be surrendered.[2] The difference between bhakti and prapatti is symbolized by the ape way (*markaṭakiśoranyāya*) and the cat way (*mārjārakiśoranyāya*). The young ape clings fast to the mother and is saved. A little effort on the part of the young is called for. The mother cat takes the young in her mouth. The young one does nothing to secure its safety. In bhakti the grace of God is earned to an extent; in prapatti it is freely bestowed. There is no reference in the latter to one's own worthiness or the service performed.[3] This view finds support in the earlier tradition, "When alone this Self

[1] *sa eva vāsudevo'sau sākṣāt puruṣa ucyate,*
strīprāyam itarat sarvaṁ jagad brahmapurassaram.'

[2] XVIII, 66.

[3] prapatti has the following accessories: good will to all (*ānukūlyasya saṁkalpaḥ*); (ii) absence of ill will (*prātikūlyasya varjanam;*

chooses, by him can He be reached, to him the Self shows His form."[1] Arjuna is told that the Divine Form was revealed to him by the grace of the Lord.[2] Again, it is said, "From Me are memory and knowledge as well as their loss."[3] Even Śaṁkara admits that the Supreme alone can grant us the saving wisdom.[4] The distinction of prapatti and bhakti relates to the issue in Christian thought which is as old as St. Augustine and Pelagius, whether man as a fallen creature is to be saved only by the grace of God or whether he can make something of himself and contribute by his own effort to his salvation.

Pelagius believed in free will, questioned the doctrine of original sin and asserted that men acted of their own moral effort. Augustine disputed the Pelagian theory and taught that Adam before the Fall had possessed free will, but after he and Eve ate the apple, corruption entered into them and descended to all their posterity. None of us can abstain from sin of our own power. Only God's grace can help us to be virtuous. Since we have all sinned in Adam, we are all condemned in him. Yet by God's free grace some of us are elected for heaven, not because we deserve it or we are good but because God's grace is bestowed on us. No reason except God's unmotived choice can be given as to why some are saved and others damned. Damnation proves God's justice because we are all wicked. St. Paul, in some passages of the

(iii) faith that the Lord will protect (*rakṣiṣyatīti viśvāsaḥ*); (iv) resort to Him as saviour (*goptṛitva varaṇam*); (v) a sense of utter helplessness (*kārpaṇyam*); (vi) complete self-surrender (*ātmanikṣepaḥ*). The last is traditionally regarded as equivalent to *prapatti*, which is the end and aim *aṅgin* while the remaining five are accessories *aṅgas*. Cp. the statement *ṣaḍvidhā śaranāgatiḥ* which is explained on the analogy of *aṣṭāṅga-yoga* where *samādhi* is really the end and the other seven are aids to it.

[1] *Kaṭha Up.*, II, 23. [2] XI, 47. [3] XV, 15.

[4] *tad anugrahahetukenaiva ca vijñānena mokṣasiddhir bhavitum arhati S.B.* The first verse of the *Avadhūta Gītā* reads:

īśvarānugrahād eva puṁsām advaitavāsanā
mahadbhayaparitrāṇāt viprāṇām upajāyate

"It is only with the grace of God that in men with knowledge is born the inclination for nondual experience which protects them from great danger." Another reading for the second line is mahābhaya-paritrānā dvitrānām upajāyate.

Epistle to the Romans, St. Augustine and Calvin adopt the view of universal guilt. That in spite of it some of us are saved shows God's mercy. Damnation and salvation both manifest the goodness of God, his justice or mercy. The *Gītā* is inclined to the Pelagian doctrine.

Man's effort is involved in the total surrender to the Supreme. It cannot be unintentional or effortless. The doctrine of grace is not to be interpreted as one of special election, as such a conception conflicts with the general trend of the *Gītā* that the Supreme is "the same to all beings."[1]

Faith (śraddhā) is the basis of bhakti. So the gods in whom people have faith are tolerated. Some love is better than none, for if we do not love we become shut up within ourselves. Besides, the lower gods are accepted as forms of the One Supreme.[2] There is insistence on the fact that, while other devotees reach other ends, only he who is devoted to the Supreme reaches infinite bliss.[3] So long as worship is done with devotion, it purifies the heart and prepares the mind for the higher consciousness. Every one shapes God in the likeness of his longing. For the dying, He is everlasting life, for those who grope in the dark, He is the light.[4] Even as the horizon remains at a level with our eyes, however high we may climb, the nature of God cannot be higher than the level of our consciousness. In the lower stages we pray for wealth and life and the Divine is regarded as the provider of material needs. Later it is meditation where we identify ourselves with the good cause which is God's cause. In the highest stages, God is the final satisfaction, the other which completes and fulfils the human spirit. Madhusūdana defines bhakti as a mental state in which the mind moved by an ecstasy of love assumes the shape of God.[5] When

[1] IX, 29; cp. *Yogavāśiṣṭha*. II, 6, 27.

[2] IX, 23.

[3] VII, 21. Madhva comments "*antobrahmādi bhaktānāṁ madbhaktānām anantatā*.

[4] Cp. *rujāsu nāthah paramaṁ hi bheṣajaṁ tamaḥ pradīpo viṣameṣu saṁkramaḥ*
bhayeṣu rakṣā vyasaneṣu bāndhavo bhavaty agādhe viṣayāmbhasi plavaḥ.

[5] *dravībhāvapūrvikā hi manaso bhagavadākāratā savikalpaka vṛttirūpā bhaktiḥ*.

the emotional attachment to God becomes highly ecstatic, the devout lover forgets himself in God.[1] Prahlāda in whom we find the spiritual condition of complete concentration in God expresses his unity with the Supreme Person. Such self-forgetful ecstatic experiences cannot be regarded as supporting advaita metaphysics. In *aparokṣānubhava* or the ultimate state in which the individual is absorbed in the Absolute, the separate individual as such does not survive.

Bhakti leads to jñāna or wisdom. For Rāmānuja, it is smṛtisantāna. Even prapatti is a form of jñāna. When the devotion glows, the Lord dwelling in the soul imparts to the devotee by His grace the light of wisdom. The devotee feels united intimately with the Supreme, who is experienced as the being in whom all antitheses vanish. He sees God in himself and himself in God. Prahlāda says that the supreme end for man is absolute devotion to God and a feeling of His presence everywhere.[2] "For her who loves, it is the same whether she, in the ardour of love, plays on the bosom of the lover or whether she caresses with tenderness his feet. Thus to him who knows, whether he remain in a superconscious ecstasy or serves God with worship, the two are the same."[3] For the devotee, the higher freedom is in surrender to God.[4] Participation in God's work for the world is the duty of all devotees.[5] "Those who give up their duties and simply proclaim the name of the Lord, Kṛṣṇa, Kṛṣṇa, are verily the enemies of the Lord and sinners for the very Lord has taken birth for protecting righteousness."[6] When the devotee truly surrenders himself to the Divine, God

[1] "The Vṛṣṇis . . . lost themselves in thought about Kṛṣṇa and completely forgot their own separate existence." *Bhaktiratnāvali*. 16.

[2] *ekāntabhaktir govinde yatsarvatra tad īkṣaṇam*. *Bhāgavata* VII, 7, 35.

[3] *priyatamahṛdaye vā khelatu premarītyā,*
padayugaparicaryāṁ preyasī vā vidhattām
viharatu viditārtho nirvikalpe samādhau
nanu bhajanavidhau vā tulyam etad dvayaṁ syāt.

[4] *līnatā haripādābje muktir ity adhidhīyate.*

[5] Cp. *Majjhima Nikāya: yo mām passati sa dhammaṁ passati.* He who sees me sees dharma.

[6] *svadharmakarmavimukhāh kṛṣṇakṛṣṇetivādinaḥ*
te harer dveṣiṇo mūḍhāh dharmārthaṁ janma yad hareḥ.

Viṣṇu Purāṇa. See also B.G., IX, 30; cp. I *John* ii, 9-11, iv, 18-20; cp. "Not everyone that calls 'Christ' Lord, but he that does the will of the Father, shall enter into the kingdom of Heaven."

becomes the ruling passion of his mind, and whatever the devotee does, he does for the glory of God. Bhakti, in the *Bhagavadgītā*, is an utter self-giving to the Transcendent. It is to believe in God, to love Him, to be devoted to Him, to enter into Him. It is its own reward. Such a devotee has in him the content of the highest knowledge as well as the energy of the perfect man.[1]

12. *The Way of Action: Karma-mārga*

In determining the purpose of any treatise, we must see the question with which it opens (upakrama) and the conclusion to which it leads (upasaṁhāra). The *Gītā* opens with a problem. Arjuna refuses to fight and raises difficulties. He puts up a plausible plea for abstention from activity and for retreat from the world, an ideal which dominated certain sects at the time of the composition of the *Gītā*. To convert him is the purpose of the *Gītā*. It raises the question whether action or renunciation of action is better and concludes that action is better. Arjuna declares that his perplexities are ended and he would carry out the command to fight. Right through, the teacher emphasizes the need for action.[2] He does not adopt the solution of dismissing the world as an illusion and action as a snare. He recommends the full active life of man in the world with the inner life anchored in the Eternal Spirit. The *Gītā* is therefore a mandate for action. It explains what a man ought to do not merely as a social being but as an individual with a spiritual destiny. It deals fairly with the spirit of renunciation as well as with the ceremonial piety of the people which are worked into its code of ethics.[3] The Sāṁkhya, which is another name

[1] *Bhāgavata* says that "devotion directed to Lord Vāsudeva produces soon dispassion and wisdom by which the vision of the Supreme is obtained."

vāsudeve bhagavati bhaktiyogaḥ prayojitaḥ
janayaty āśu vairāgyaṁ jñānaṁ yad brahmadarśanam.

Cp. *vimalamatir vimatsaraḥ praśāntaḥ sucarito'khilasattvamitrabhūtaḥ*
priyahitavacano' stamānamāyo vasati sadā hṛdi yasya vāsudevaḥ.
Viṣṇu Purāṇa, III, 7.

[2] II, 18, 37; III, 19; IV, 15; VIII, 7; XI, 33; XVI, 24; XVIII, 6; 72.

[3] Cp. M.B., *Śāntiparva*, 348, 53.

yatīnāṁ cāpi yo dharmaḥ sa te pūrvaṁ nṛpottama
kathito harigītāsu samāsa vidhi kalpitaḥ.

for jñāna in the *Gītā*, requires us to renounce action. There is the well-known view that created beings are bound by karma or action and are saved by knowledge.[1] Every deed, whether good or bad produces its natural effect and involves embodiment in the world and is an obstacle to liberation. Every deed confirms the sense of egoism and separateness of the doer, and sets in motion a new series of effects. Therefore, it is argued, one must renounce all action and become a saṁnyāsin. Śaṁkara, who upholds the method of jñāna as a means of salvation, argues that Arjuna was a *madhyamādhikāri* for whom renunciation was dangerous and so he was advised to take to action. But the *Gītā* adopts the view developed in the Bhāgavata religion which has the twofold purpose of helping us to obtain complete release and do work in the world.[2] In two places, Vyāsa tells Śuka that the most ancient method of the Brāhmin is to obtain release by knowledge and perform actions.[3] *Īśa Up.* adopts a similar view. It is incorrect to assume that Hindu thought strained excessively after the unattainable and was guilty of indifference to the problems of the world. We cannot lose ourselves in inner piety when the poor die at our doors, naked and hungry. The *Gītā* asks us to live in the world and save it.

The teacher of the *Gītā* points out the extreme subtlety of the problem of action, *gahanā karmaṇo gatiḥ*.[4] It is not possible for us to abstain from action. Nature is ever at work and we are deluded if we fancy that its process can be held up. Nor is cessation from action desirable. Inertia is not freedom. Again, the binding quality of an action does not lie in its mere performance but in the motive or desire that prompts it. Renunciation refers, not to the act itself but to the

[1] *karmaṇā badhyate jantur, vidyayā tu pramucyate.* M.B., *Śāntiparva*, 240, 7.

[2] *nārāyaṇaparo dharmaḥ punarāvṛttidurlabhaḥ*
pravṛttilakṣaṇaścaiva dharmo nārāyaṇātmakaḥ.
M.B., *Śāntiparva*, 347, 80–1.

Again *pravṛttilakṣaṇaṁ dharmaṁ ṛṣir nārāyano'bravīt.* ibid., 217, 2.

[3] *eṣā pūrvatarā vṛttir brāhmaṇasya vidhīyate*
jñanavān eva karmāṇi kurvan sarvatra siddhyati.
M.B., *Śāntiparva*, 237, 1; 234, 29.

See also *Īśa Up.*, 2, and *Viṣṇu Purāṇa*, VI, 6, 12.

[4] IV, 17.

frame of mind behind the act. Renunciation means absence of desire. So long as action is based on false premises, it binds the individual soul. If our life is based on ignorance, however altruistic our conduct may be, it will be binding. The *Gītā* advocates detachment from desires and not cessation from work.[1]

When Kṛṣṇa advises Arjuna to fight, it does not follow that he is supporting the validity of warfare. War happens to be the occasion which the teacher uses to indicate the spirit in which all work including warfare will have to be performed. Arjuna takes up a pacifist attitude and declines to participate in a fight for truth and justice. He takes a human view of the situation and represents the extreme of non-violence. He winds up:

> "Better I deem it, if my kinsmen strike,
> To face them weaponless, and bare my breast
> To shaft and spear, than answer blow with blow."[2]

Arjuna does not raise the question of the right or wrong of war. He has faced many battles and fought many enemies. He declares against war and its horrors because he has to destroy his own friends and relations (*svajanam*).[3] It is not a question of violence or non-violence but of using violence against one's friends now turned enemies. His reluctance to fight is not the outcome of spiritual development or the predominance of sattvaguṇa but is the product of ignorance and passion.[4] Arjuna admits that he is overcome by weakness and ignorance.[5] The ideal which the *Gītā* sets before us is ahiṁsā or non-violence and this is evident from the description of the perfect state of mind, speech and body in Chapter VII, and of the mind of the devotee in Chapter XII. Kṛṣṇa advises Arjuna to fight without passion or ill-will, without anger or attachment and if we develop such a frame of mind violence becomes impossible. We must fight against what is wrong but if we allow ourselves to hate, that ensures our spiritual defeat. It is not possible to kill people in a state of absolute serenity or absorption in

[1] Arjuna says:
asaktah saktavat gacchan nissaṅgo muktabandhanaḥ
samah śatrau ca mitre ca sa vai mukto mahīpate.
M.B., XII, 18, 31.

[2] I, 46. Edwin Arnold's E.T.

[3] I, 31; I, 27; I, 37; I. 45.

[4] XVIII, 7, 8.

[5] II, 7.

God. War is taken as an illustration. We may be obliged to do painful work but it should be done in a way that does not develop the sense of a separate ego. Kṛṣṇa tells Arjuna that one can attain perfection even while doing one's duties. Action done devotedly and wholeheartedly, without attachment to the results makes for perfection. Our action must be the result of our nature. While Arjuna is a householder belonging to the warrior caste, he speaks like a saṁnyāsin not because he has risen to the stage of utter dispassion and love for humanity but because he is overcome by false compassion. Everyone must grow upward from the point where he stands. The emphasis of the *Gītā* on lokasaṁgraha, world-solidarity, requires us to change the whole pattern of our life. We are kindly, decent men who would be shocked and indignant if a dog is hurt, we would fly to the protection of a crying child or a maltreated woman and yet we persist in doing wrong on a large scale to millions of women and children in the comforting belief that by doing so, we are doing our duty to our family or city or the state. The *Gītā* requires us to lay stress on human brotherhood. Where-ever the imperative to fight is employed, Śaṁkara points out that it is not mandatory (vidhi), but refers only to the prevailing usage.[1] The *Gītā* belongs to a period of upheaval through which humanity periodically passes in which intellectual, moral, social and political forms are at strife and when these are not properly adjusted, violent convulsions take place. In the conflict between the self-affirming law of good and the forms that impede it, force is sometimes necessary to give the law of good a chance of becoming a psychological fact and an historic process. We have to act in the world as it is, while doing our best to improve it. We should not be defiled by disgust even when we look at the worst that life can do to us, even when we are plunged in every kind of loss, bereavement and humiliation. If we act in the spirit of the *Gītā* with detachment and dedication, and have love even for our enemy, we will help to rid the world of wars.[2]

[1] *tasmād yuddhasvety anuvādamātram, na vidhiḥ; na hyatra yuddhakartavyatā vidhīyate.* S.B.G., II, 18.

[2] Cp. the Vedic prayer: "Whatever here is heinous, cruel and sinful, may all that be stilled, may everything be good and peaceful to us."

yad iha ghoram, yad iha krūram, yad iha pāpaṁ
tac chāntaṁ tac chivaṁ sarvam eva samastu naḥ.

If we cultivate the spirit of detachment from results and dedication to God, we may engage in action. One who acts in this spirit is a perpetual saṁnyāsin.[1] He accepts things as they come and leaves them without regret, when necessary.

If there is hostility to the method of works, it is not hostility to work as such but to the theory of salvation by works. If ignorance, avidyā, is the root evil, wisdom or jñāna is the sovereign remedy. Realization of wisdom is not what is accomplished in time. Wisdom is ever pure and perfect and is not the fruit of an act. An eternal attainment devoid of change cannot be the result of a temporary act. But karma prepares for wisdom. In his commentary on *Sanatsujātīya*, Śaṁkara says: "Liberation is accomplished by wisdom, but wisdom does not spring without the purification of the heart. Therefore, for the purification of the heart one should perform all acts of speech, mind and body, prescribed in the śrutis and the smṛtis, dedicating them to the Supreme Lord."[2] Work done in such a spirit becomes a yajña or sacrifice. Sacrifice is a making sacred to the Divine. It is not deprivation or self-immolation but a spontaneous self-giving, a surrender to a greater consciousness of which we are a limitation. By such a surrender, the mind becomes purified of its impurities and shares the power and knowledge of the Divine. Action performed in the spirit of a yajña or sacrifice ceases to be a source of bondage.

The *Bhagavadgītā* gives us a religion by which the rule of karma, the natural order of deed and consequence, can be transcended. There is no element of caprice or arbitrary interference of a transcendent purpose within the natural order. The teacher of the *Gītā* recognizes a realm of reality where karma does not operate and if we establish our relations with it, we are free in our deepest being. The chain of karma can be broken here and now, within the flux

[1] V, 3: cp. also *Yājñavalkya Smṛti* where, after an account of the state of the renouncer (saṁnyāsin) it is said, that even the householder who is a devotee of knowledge and speaks the truth attains release (without taking saṁnyāsa). III, 204–5.

[2] *jñānenaiva mokṣah siddhyati kiṁtu tad eva jñānaṁ sattvaśuddhiṁ vinā notpadyate . . . tasmāt sattvaśuddhyarthaṁ sarveśvaram uddiśya sarvāṇi vāṅmanaḥkāyalakṣaṇāni śrautasmārtāni karmāṇi samācaret.*

of the empirical world. We become masters of karma by developing detachment and faith in God.

For the wise sage who lives in the Absolute, it is contended that nothing remains to be done, *tasyakāryaṁ na vidyate*.[1] The seer of truth has no longer the ambition to do or to achieve. When all desires are destroyed, it is not possible to act. *Uttaragītā* states the objection thus: "For the yogi who has become accomplished as the result of having drunk the nectar of wisdom, no further duty remains; if any remains, he is not a real knower of truth."[2] All knowledge, all striving is a means to attain to this ultimate wisdom, this last simplicity. Every act or achievement would be less than this act of being. All action is defective.[3]

Śaṁkara admits that there is no objection to the performance of work until one reaches death, even after the attainment of wisdom.[4] Such a one is said to be above all duties only from the theoretical standpoint.[5] This means that in principle there is no contradiction between spiritual freedom and practical work. Though, strictly speaking, there is nothing that remains to be done by the wise sage as by God, yet both of them act in the world, for the sake of world-maintenance and progress, lokasaṁgraha. We may even say that God is the doer, as the individual has emptied himself of all desires.[6] He does nothing, *na kiñcit karoti*. As he has no ulterior purpose, he lays claim to nothing and surrenders him-

[1] III, 17.

[2] *jñānāmṛtena tṛptasya kṛtakṛtyasya yoginaḥ*
na cāsti kiñcit kartavyam asti cen na sa tattvavit.
I, 23.

[3] *Nyāya Sūtra*, I, 1, 18.

[4] S.B., III, 3, 32; S.B.G., II, 11; III, 8 and 20. There is a natural shirking from outward works by those who are afraid of being distracted from their contemplation of God.

[5] *alaṁkāro hi ayam asmākaṁ yad brahmātmāvagatau satyām sarvakartavyatāhāniḥ*. S.B., I, 1, 4.

[6] *Jaiminīya Up.*: Thou (God) art the doer thereof: *tvaṁ vai tasya kartāsi*. "We have the mind of Christ" (*Cor.* ii, 16); "I live, yet no longer I, but Christ liveth in me" (*Gal.* ii, 20). Tauler: "By their works they cannot go again. . . . If any man is to come to God, he must be empty of all works and let God work alone." *Following of Christ*, 16, 17, St. Thomas Aquinas: "The works of a man who is led by the Holy Ghost are the works of the Holy Ghost rather than his own." *Summa Theol.*, II, 1, 93, 6 and 1.

self to spontaneity. Then God acts through him and the question of right and wrong does not arise, though it is impossible for such a one to do any wrong.[1] Poised in the serenity of the Self, he becomes the doer of all works, *kṛtsnakarmakṛt*. He knows that he is only the instrument for the work of God, *nimittamātram*.[2] When the long agony of Arjuna had borne its fruit, he learned that in God's will is his peace.[3] Under the control of the Lord, nature (prakṛti) carries on its work. The individual intelligence, mind and senses function for the great universal purpose and in its light. Victory or defeat does not disturb, as it is willed by the Universal Spirit. Whatever happens, the individual accepts without attachment or aversion. He has passed beyond the dualities (dvandvātīta). He does the duty expected of him, *kartavyaṁ karma*, without travail and with freedom and spontaneity.

The man of the world is lost in the varied activities of the world. He throws himself into the mutable world (kṣara). The quietist withdraws into the silence of the Absolute (akṣara) but the ideal man of the *Gītā* goes beyond these two extremes and works like Puruṣottama who reconciles all possibilities in the world without getting involved in it. He is the doer of works who yet is not the doer, *kartāram akartāram*. The Lord is the pattern of an unwearied and active worker who does not, by His work forfeit His integrity of spirit. The liberated soul is eternally free like Kṛṣṇa and Janaka.[4] Janaka carried on his duties and was not per-

[1] Cp. St. John's words: "Whosoever is born of God doth not commit sin."

[2] XI, 33.

[3] XVIII, 73.

[4] *Iśa Up.* asks us to look upon the whole world as dwelling in the Supreme and to perform actions, as such actions do not bind us: *na karma lipyate nare*. Cp. *yaḥ kriyāvān sa paṇḍitaḥ*. M.B., *Vanaparva*, 312, 108. Ānandagiri in his comment on Ś. on *Kaṭha Up.*, II, 19, says:

vivekī sarvadā muktaḥ kurvato nāsti kartṛtā
alepavādam āśritya śrīkṛṣṇa janakau yathā.

In the *Adhyātma Ramāyaṇa*, Rāma tells Lakṣmaṇa: "He who has fallen in the stream of this world remains unsullied even though he may outwardly perform all kinds of actions."

pravāhapatitaḥ kāryaṁ kurvann api na lipyate
bāhye sarvatra kartṛtvam āvahann api rāghava.

turbed by the events of the world.[1] The freed souls work for the guidance of men who follow the standards set by the thoughtful. They live in the world but as strangers. They endure all hardships in the flesh[2] and yet they live not after the flesh. Their existence is on earth but their citizenship is in heaven. "As the unlearned act from attachment to their work, so should the learned also act but without any attachment, with the desire to maintain the world-order."[3]

While the Buddhist ideal exalts a life of contemplation, the *Gītā* attracts all those souls who have a relish for action and adventure. Action is for self-fulfilment. We must find out the truth of our own highest and innermost existence and live it and not follow any outer standard. Our svadharma, outward life, and svabhāva, inner being, must answer to each other. Only then will action be free, easy and spontaneous. We can live in God's world as God intends us to live only by keeping alive the precious unearthly flame of uniqueness. By placing ourselves in the hands of the Divine, by making ourselves perfect instruments for His use do we attain the highest spiritual wisdom.

Karmayoga is an alternative method of approach to the goal of life according to the *Gītā* and culminates in wisdom.[4] In this sense, Śaṁkara is correct in holding that karma and bhakti are means to spiritual freedom. But spiritual freedom is not inconsistent with activity. Duty *as such* drops away but not all activity. The activity of the liberated is free and

1 "Infinite indeed is my wealth of which nothing is mine. If Mithilā is burnt, nothing that is mine is burnt."

anantam bata me vittaṁ yasya me nāsti kiñcana
mithilāyāṁ pradīptāyāṁ na me kiñcit pradahyate.

M.B., *Śāntiparva*, VII, 1.

S. says that the saints, the great ones, live in peace. Like the spring season, they confer good on the world. Themselves having crossed the mighty ocean of saṁsāra, they enable others to cross the same, with no apparent motive in doing so.

śāntā mahānto nivasanti santāḥ vasantaval lokahitaṁ carantaḥ
tīrṇāḥ svayaṁ bhīmabhavārṇavaṁ janān ahetunānnyānapi tārayantaḥ.

2 Cp. *Bhāgavata*: The good people suffer for the sorrows of the world. *prāyaśo lokatāpena tapyante sādhavo janāḥ.* They consume themselves in order that they may light the world.

3 III, 25. 4 IV, 33.

spontaneous and not obligatory. They act for the sake of the welfare of the world even though they have attained wisdom.[1] Work is not practised as a *sādhana* but becomes a *lakṣaṇa*. Even when we accept the saṁnyāsa āśrama, the duties of the other āśramas are abandoned but not those of the saṁnyāsa. The common virtues (*sādhāraṇadharma*) obligatory on all, such as the practice of kindness, are adopted. So work and liberation are not inconsistent with each other.[2]

The *Gītā* takes up the various creeds and codes that were already competing with each other and transforms them into aspects of a more inward religion, free, subtle, and profound. If popular deities are worshipped, it must be understood that they are only varied manifestations of the One Supreme. If sacrifices are to be offered, they must be of the spirit and not of material objects. A life of self-control or disinterested action is a sacrifice. The Veda is of use but it is like a tank when compared to the widely spreading flood of the teaching of the *Gītā*. The *Gītā* teaches the doctrine of the Brahman-

[1] S.B.G., III. 20.

[2] Maṇḍana Miśra in his *Brahmasiddhi* mentions seven different theories about the relation of karma and jñāna. (1) The injunctions in the ritual part of the Veda tend to turn men away from their natural activities in the direction of meditative activity enjoined for the realization of the self. (2) These injunctions are intended to destroy desires through a process of enjoyment and thus prepare the way for meditation leading to knowledge of the self. (3) The performance of karma is necessary to discharge the three debts (ṛṇatraya) which is the essential prerequisite for self-knowledge. (4) The activities prescribed have a dual function (saṁyogapṛthaktva) of leading to the fulfilment of desires expected of them and of preparing for self-knowledge. (5) All karma is intended to purify men and prepare them for self-knowledge. (6) That self-knowledge is to be regarded as a purificatory aid to the agent, serving the requirements of the various activities prescribed in the karmakāṇḍa. (7) Karma and jñāna are opposed to each other.

Maṇḍana Miśra is inclined to accept the views indicated in 4 and 5. The performance of rites is a valuable accessory to the contemplation on the content of verbal knowledge (śabda jñāna) arising from the great texts (mahāvākyas) of the Upaniṣads in bringing about the final manifestation (abhivyakti) of the eternally self-luminous light of ātman. While the saṁnyāsins reach realization of self exclusively through contemplative discipline with the performance of scriptural rites, the householders (gṛhasthas) reach the goal through the performance of rites, etc.

Ātman which the followers of the Upaniṣads seek and proclaim. The yoga of concentration is useful but the Supreme is the Lord of yoga. The dualism of the Sāṁkhya is taken over into non-dualism, for puruṣa and prakṛti are the two natures of the Supreme Lord, Puruṣottama. He alone dispenses grace. He is the true object of devotion. For Him must all work be done. Saving wisdom is of Him. The traditional rules of dharma are to be followed because He established them and He upholds the moral order. The rules are not ends in themselves, for union with the Supreme is the final goal. The teacher of the *Gītā* reconciles the different systems in vogue and gives us a comprehensive eirenicon which is not local and temporary but is for all time and all men. He does not emphasize external forms or dogmatic notions but insists on first principles and great facts of human nature and being.

13. *The Goal*[1]

The *Gītā* insists on the unity of the life of spirit which cannot be resolved into philosophic wisdom, devoted love or strenuous action. Work, knowledge and devotion are complementary both when we seek the goal and after we attain it. We do not proceed on the same lines but that which we seek is the same. We may climb the mountain by different paths but the view from the summit is identical for all. Wisdom is personified as a being whose body is knowledge and whose heart is love. Yoga, which has for its phases, knowledge and meditation, love and service is the ancient road that leads from darkness to light, from death to immortality.

The goal of transcendence is represented as the ascent to the world of the Creator (*brahmaloka*), or the attainment of the status of the Impersonal Supreme (*brahmabhāva* or *brāhmīsthiti*). One side of it is isolation from the world (*kaivalya*). The *Gītā* mentions all these views. Many passages

[1] The end of perfection is called the highest (III, 19), emancipation (III, 31; IV, 15), the eternal state (XVIII, 56), the path from which there is no return (V, 17), perfection (XII, 10), the highest rest (IV, 39), the entering into God (IV, 9, 10 and 24), contact with God (VI, 28), rest in Brahman (II, 72), transformation into Divine existence (XIV, 26), transmutation into Godhead (V, 24).

suggest that, in the state of release, duality disappears and the released soul becomes one with the Eternal Self. It is a condition beyond all modes and qualities, impassive, free and at peace. If we have a body clinging to us, nature will go on acting till the body is shaken off as a discarded shell. The jīvanmukta or the freed soul possessing the body reacts to the events of the outer world without getting entangled in them. On this view, spirit and body are an unreconciled duality and we cannot think of any action of the released soul.

The main emphasis of the *Gītā* is not on such a view. For it, the state of spiritual freedom consists in the transformation of our whole nature into the immortal law and power of the Divine. Equivalence with God (*sādharmya*) and not identity (*sāyūjya*) is emphasized. The freed soul is inspired by Divine knowledge and moved by the Divine will. He acquires the mode of being (*bhāva*) of God. His purified nature is assimilated into the Divine substance. Any one who attains this transcendent condition is a *yogin*, a *siddhapuruṣa*, a realized soul, a *jitātman*, a *yuktacetas*, a disciplined and harmonized being for whom the Eternal is ever present. He is released from divided loyalties and actions. His body, mind and spirit, the conscious, the pre-conscious, and the unconscious, to use Freud's words, work flawlessly together and attain a rhythm expressed in the ecstasy of joy, the illumination of knowledge and the intensity of energy. Liberation is not the isolation of the immortal spirit from the mortal human life but is the transfiguration of the whole man. It is attained not by destroying but by transfiguring the tension of human life. His whole nature is subdued to the universal vision, is wrought to splendour and irradiated by the spiritual light. His body, life and mind are not dissolved but are rendered pure and become the means and mould of the Divine Light, and he becomes his own masterpiece. His personality is raised to its fullness, its maximum expression, pure and free, buoyant and unburdened. All his activities are for the holding together of the world, *cikīrṣur lokasaṁgraham.*[1] The liberated souls take upon themselves the burden of the redemption of the whole world. The end of the dynamic of

[1] III, 25.

the spirit and its ever new contradictions can only be the end of the world. The dialectic development cannot stop until the whole world is liberated from ignorance and evil. According to the Sāṁkhya system, even those persons who are qualified for the highest wisdom and liberation on account of their solicitousness for the good of others do not give up the world. Merging themselves in the body of prakṛti and using its gifts, these *prakṛtilīna* selves serve the interests of the world. The world is to move forward to its ideal and those who are lost in ignorance and bewilderment are to be redeemed by the effort and example, the illumination and strength of the freed.[1] These elect are the natural leaders of mankind. Anchored in the timeless foundation of our spiritual existence, the freed soul, the eternal individual works for the jīvaloka;[2] while possessing individuality of body, life and mind he yet retains the universality of spirit. Whatever action he does, his constant communion with the Supreme is undisturbed.[3] As to what happens if and when the cosmic process reaches its fulfilment, when universal redemption takes place, it is difficult for us to say. The Supreme, which is infinite possibility, may take another possibility for expression.

The *Gītā* admits that the Real is the absolute Brahman, but from the cosmic point of view, it is the Supreme Īśvara. The latter is the only way in which man's thought, limited as it is, can envisage the highest reality. Though the relation between the two is inconceivable by us from the logical standpoint, it is got over when we have the direct apprehension of Reality. In the same way, the two views of the ultimate state of freedom are the intuitional and the intellectual representations of the one condition. The freed spirits have no need for individuality but still assume it by self-limitation. Both views agree that so long as the freed spirits continue to live in the world, they are committed to some action or other. They work in a freedom of the spirit and with an inner joy and peace which does not depend on externals for its source or continuance.

The *Gītā* represents *brahmaloka* or the world of God, not as itself the Eternal, but as the farthest limit of manifes-

[1] IV, 34. [2] XV, 7. [3] VI, 31.

tation. Ānanda is the limit of our development and we grow into it from the level of vijñāna. It belongs to the cosmic manifestation. The Absolute is not the *ānandamaya ātmā*, not the divinized self.[1] The pure Self is different from the five sheaths.[2] When the purpose of the cosmos is reached, when the kingdom of God is established, when it is on earth as it is in heaven, when all individuals acquire the wisdom of spirit and are superior to the levels of being in which birth and death take place, then this cosmic process is taken over into that which is beyond all manifestations.

[1] Nor is this ānandamaya self the Supreme Spirit since it is subject to conditions and is a modification of prakṛti, an effect and the sum of all the results of good acts. *Vivekacūḍāmaṇi*, 212.

[2] *pañcakośavilakṣaṇaḥ*. *Vivekacūḍāmaṇi*, 214.

CHAPTER I

The Hesitation and Despondency of Arjuna

The Question

dhṛtarāṣṭra uvāca

1. *dharmakṣetre kurukṣetre*
samavetā yuyutsavaḥ
māmakāḥ pāṇḍavāś cai 'va
kim akurvata saṁjaya

Dhṛtarāṣṭra said:

(1) In the field of righteousness, the field of the Kurus, when my people and the sons of Pāṇḍu had gathered together, eager for battle, what did they do, O Saṁjaya?

dharmakṣetre: in the field of righteousness. The quality of deciding what is right or dharma is special to man. Hunger, sleep, fear and sex are common to men and animals. What distinguishes men from animals is the knowledge of right and wrong.[1]

The world is dharmakṣetra, the battleground for a moral struggle. The decisive issue lies in the hearts of men where the battles are fought daily and hourly. The ascent from earth to heaven, from suffering to spirit, is through the path of dharma. Even in our corporeal existence, through the practice of dharma, we can reach up to safety where every difficulty culminates in joy The world is dharmakṣetra, the nursery of saints where the sacred flame of spirit is never permitted to go out. It is said to be karmabhūmi where we work out our karma and fulfil the purpose of soul-making.

The aim of the *Gītā* is not so much to teach a theory as to enforce practice, dharma. We cannot separate in theory what is not separable in life. The duties of civic and social life provide religion with its tasks and opportunities. Dharma is what promotes

[1] *āhāranidrābhayamaithunaṁ ca sāmānyam etat paśubhir narāṇām*
dharmo hi teṣām adhiko viśeṣo dharmeṇa hīnāḥ paśubhiḥ samānāḥ.
Hitopadeśa.

worldly prosperity and spiritual freedom.[1] The *Gītā* does not teach a mysticism that concerns itself with man's inner being alone. Instead of rejecting the duties and relationships of life as an illusion, it accepts them as opportunities for the realization of spiritual freedom. Life is offered to us that we may transfigure it completely.

The battlefield is called dharmakṣetra or the field of righteousness for the Lord who is the protector of dharma is actively present in it.

kurukṣetre: in the field of the Kurus. Kurukṣetra is the land of the Kurus, a leading clan of the period.[2]

The words, "dharmakṣetre kurukṣetre," suggest the law of life by death. God, the terrible, is a side of the vision that Arjuna sees on the field of battle. Life is a battle, a warfare against the spirit of evil. Creative process is one of perpetual tension between two incompatibles, each standing against the other. By their mutual conflict, the development is advanced and the cosmic purpose furthered. In this world are elements of imperfection, evil and irrationality, and through action, dharma, we have to change the world and convert the elements, which are now opaque to reason, transparent to thought. War is a retributory

[1] *prāṇināṁ sākṣād abhyudayaniḥśreyasahetur yaḥ sa dharmaḥ.*

[2] It is a vast field near Hastināpura in the neighbourhood of modern Delhi. When Dhṛtarāṣṭra, the blind king of the Kurus, decided to give his throne to Yudhiṣṭhira, who is also known as Dharmarāja, the embodiment of virtue, in preference to his own eldest son, Duryodhana, the latter, by tricks and treachery, secured the throne for himself and attempted to destroy Yudhiṣṭhira and his four brothers. Kṛṣṇa, the head of the Yādava clan, sought to bring about a reconciliation between the cousins. When all attempts failed, a fratricidal war between the Kauravas and the Pāṇḍavas became inevitable. Kṛṣṇa proposed that he and his vassals would join the two sides and left the choice to the parties. The vassals were selected by Duryodhana and Kṛṣṇa himself joined the Pāṇḍavas as the charioteer of Arjuna. M.B., *Udyogaparva*: VI, 147. "Some put their trusts in chariots and some in horses but we will trust in the Lord, our God," as the Old Testament says. The Pāṇḍavas and the Kauravas represent the conflict between the two great movements, the upward and the downward, the divine and the demoniac, the dharma which helps us to grow in our spiritual stature and the adharma which drags us down deeper into entanglement with matter. The two are not irreconcilable as they spring from the same source. The Pāṇḍavas and the Kauravas are cousins and have a common ancestry.

judgment as well as an act of discipline. Kurukṣetra is also called tapaḥkṣetra, the field of penance, of discipline.[1] War is at once punishment and cleansing for mankind. God is judge as well as redeemer. He destroys and creates. He is Śiva and Viṣṇu.

māmakāh: my people.[2] This sense of mineness is the result of ahaṁkāra which is the source of evil. Mamakāra or selfishness on the part of the Kauravas which leads to the love of power and domination is brought out.

Saṁjaya.

Saṁjaya is the charioteer of the blind king, Dhṛtarāṣṭra, who reports to him the events of the war.

The Two Armies

saṁjaya uvāca

2. *dṛṣṭvā tu pāṇḍavānīkaṁ*
vyūḍhaṁ duryodhanas tadā
ācāryam upasaṁgamya
rājā vacanam abravīt

Saṁjaya said:

(2) Then, Duryodhana the prince, having seen the army of the Pāṇḍavas drawn up in battle order, approached his teacher and spoke this word:

ācārya: teacher, one who knows the meaning of the scriptures, teaches it to others and practises the teaching himself:

Droṇa, the ācārya, taught the art of war to the princes on both sides.

3. *paśyai 'tāṁ pāṇḍuputrāṇām*
ācārya mahatīṁ camūm
vyūḍhāṁ drupadaputreṇa
tava śiṣyeṇa dhīmatā

(3) Behold, O Teacher, this mighty army of the sons of Pāṇḍu organized by thy wise pupil, the son of Drupada.[3]

[1] See *Manu*, II, 19 and 20.

[2] *mameti kāyantīti māmakāh, avidyāpuruṣāh.*
Abhinavagupta.

[3] Dhṛṣṭadyumna is the son of Drupada, the king of Pāñcāla.

4. *atra śūrā maheṣvāsā*
bhīmārjunasamā yudhi
yuyudhāno virāṭaś ca
drupadaś ca mahārathaḥ

(4) Here are heroes, great bowmen equal in battle to Bhīma and Arjuna—Yuyudhāna, Virāṭa and Drupada, a mighty warrior.[1]

5. *dhṛṣṭaketuś cekitānaḥ*
kāśirājaś ca vīryavān
purujit kuntibhojaś ca
śaibyaś ca narapuṁgavaḥ

(5) Dhṛṣṭaketu, Cekitāna and the valiant King of Kāśi, also Purujit, Kuntibhoja and Śaibya the foremost of men.[2]

6. *yudhamanyuś ca vikrānta*
uttamaujāś ca vīryavān
saubhadro draupadeyāś ca
sarva eva mahārathāḥ

(6) Yudhāmanyu, the strong and Uttamauja, the brave; and also the son of Subhadrā and sons of Draupadī, all of them great warriors.

Saubhadraḥ is Abhimanyu, the son of Arjuna and Subhadrā.

7. *asmākaṁ tu viśiṣṭā ye*
tān nibodha dvijottama
nāyakā mama sainyasya
saṁjñārthaṁ tān bravīmi te

(7) Know also, O Best of the twiceborn, the leaders of my

[1] *Bhīma* is Yudhiṣṭhira's Commander-in-Chief, though nominally Dhṛṣṭadyumna holds that office.
Arjuna is the friend of Kṛṣṇa and the great hero of the Pāṇḍavas.
Yuyudhāna is Kṛṣṇa's charioteer, also called Sātyaki. *Virāṭa* is the prince in whose state the Pāṇḍavas lived for some time in disguise.

[2] *Dhṛṣṭaketu* is the king of the Cedis.
Cekitāna is a famous warrior in the army of the Pāṇḍavas.
Purujit and *Kuntibhoja* are two brothers. Sometimes Purujit Kuntibhoja is taken as one.
Śaibya is a king of the Śibi tribe.

army, those who are most distinguished among us. I will name them now for thy information.

dvijottama: O best of the twiceborn. A dvija is one who is invested with the sacred thread, literally, one who is twice-born. Initiation into the life of spirit is the aim of education. We are born into the world of nature; our second birth is into the world of spirit; *tad dvitīyaṁ janma, mātā sāvitrī, pitā tu ācāryah*: The individual born a child of nature grows up into his spiritual manhood and becomes a child of light.

8. *bhavān bhīṣmaś ca karṇaś ca*
kṛpaś ca samitiṁjayaḥ
aśvatthāmā vikarṇaś ca
saumadattis tathai 'va ca

(8) Thyself and Bhīṣma and Karṇa and Kṛpa, ever victorious in battle; Asvatthāman, Vikarṇa, and also the son of Somadatta.[1]

9. *anye ca bahavaḥ śūrā*
madarthe tyaktajīvitāh
nānāśastrapraharaṇāḥ
sarve yuddhaviśāradāḥ

(9) And many other heroes who have risked their lives for my sake. They are armed with many kinds of weapons and are all well skilled in war.

10. *aparyāptaṁ tad asmākaṁ*
balaṁ bhīṣmābhirakṣitam
paryāptaṁ tv idam eteṣāṁ
balaṁ bhīmābhirakṣitam

(10) Unlimited is this army of ours which is guarded by Bhīṣma, while that army of theirs which is guarded by Bhīma is limited.

aparyāptam: insufficient. Śrīdhara.

[1] *Bhīṣma* is the old sage-warrior who brought up Dhṛtarāṣṭra and Pāṇḍu.
Karṇa is half-brother to Arjuna.
Kṛpa is the brother-in-law of Droṇa.
Aśvatthāman is the son of Droṇa.
Vikarṇa is the third of the hundred sons of Dhṛtarāṣṭra.
Somadatti is the son of Somadatta, the King of the Bāhikas.

11. *ayaneṣu ca sarveṣu*
yathābhāgam avasthitāḥ
bhīṣmam evā 'bhirakṣantu
bhavantaḥ sarva eva hi

(11) Therefore do ye all support Bhīṣma, standing firm in all the fronts, in your respective ranks.

The Sounding of the Conchshells

12. *tasya saṁjanayan harṣaṁ*
kuruvṛddhaḥ pitāmahaḥ
siṁhanādaṁ vinadyo 'ccaiḥ
śaṅkhaṁ dadhmau pratāpavān

(12) In order to cheer him up, the aged kuru, his valiant grandsire, roared aloud like a lion and blew his conch.

With him and others, loyalty to duty counted far more than individual conviction. Social order generally depends on obedience to authority. Did not Socrates tell Crito that he would not break the Laws of Athens which brought him up, guarded and watched over him?

Roared aloud like a lion: Bhīṣma declared emphatically his confidence.

13. *tataḥ śaṅkhāś ca bheryaś ca*
paṇavānakagomukhāḥ
sahasai 'vā 'bhyahanyanta
sa śabdas tumulo 'bhavat

(13) Then conches and kettledrums, tabors and drums and horns suddenly were struck and the noise was tumultuous.

14. *tataḥ śvetair hayair yukte*
mahati syandane sthitau
mādhavaḥ pāṇḍavaś cai 'va
divyau śaṅkhau pradadhmatuḥ

(14) When stationed in their great chariot, yoked to white horses, Kṛṣṇa and Arjuna blew their celestial conches.

Throughout the Hindu and the Buddhist literatures, the chariot stands for the psychophysical vehicle. The steeds are the senses, the reins their controls, but the charioteer, the guide is the spirit or real self, ātman. Kṛṣṇa, the charioteer, is the Spirit in us.[1]

15. *pāñcajanyaṁ hṛṣīkeśo*
devadattaṁ dhanaṁjayaḥ
pauṇḍraṁ dadhmau mahāśaṅkhaṁ
bhīmakarmā vṛkodaraḥ

(15) Kṛṣṇa blew his Pāñcajanya and Arjuna his Devadatta and Bhīma of terrific deeds blew his mighty conch, Pauṇḍra.

These indicate readiness for battle.

16. *anantavijayaṁ rājā*
kuntīputro yudhiṣṭhiraḥ
nakulaḥ sahadevaś ca
sughoṣamaṇipuṣpakau

(16) Prince Yudhiṣṭhira,[2] the son of Kuntī, blew his Anantavijaya and Nakula and Sahadeva blew their Sughoṣa and Maṇipuṣpaka

17. *kāśyaś ca parameṣvāsaḥ*
śikhaṇḍī ca mahārathaḥ
dhṛṣṭadyumno virāṭaś ca
sātyakiś cā 'parājitaḥ

(17) And the king of Kāśi, the Chief of archers, Śikhaṇḍin, the great warrior, Dhṛṣṭadyumna and Virāṭa and the invincible Sātyaki.

18. *drupado draupadeyāś ca*
sarvaśaḥ pṛthivīpate
saubhadraś ca mahābāhuḥ
śaṅkhān dadhmuḥ pṛthak-pṛthak

[1] Cp. *Kaṭha Up.*, III, 3. See also Plato, *Laws*, 898 C; *Milindapañha*, 26–8.

[2] *Yudhiṣṭhira* is the eldest of the five sons of Pāṇḍu.
Nakula is the fourth of the Pāṇḍu princes. *Sahadeva* is the youngest of them.

(18) Drupada and the sons of Draupadī, O Lord of earth, and the strong-armed son of Subhadrā, on all sides blew their respective conches.

19. *sa ghoṣo dhārtarāṣṭrāṇāṁ*
hṛdayāni vyadārayat
nabhaś ca pṛthivīṁ cai 'va
tumulo vyanunādayan

(19) The tumultuous uproar resounding through earth and sky rent the hearts of Dhṛtarāṣṭra's sons.

Arjuna Surveys the Two Armies

20. *atha vyavasthitān dṛṣṭvā*
dhārtarāṣṭrān kapidhvajaḥ
pravṛtte śastrasaṁpāte
dhanur udyamya pāṇḍavaḥ

(20) Then Arjuna, whose banner bore the crest of Hanumān, looked at the sons of Dhṛtarāṣṭra drawn up in battle order; and as the flight of missiles (almost) started, he took up his bow.

pravṛtte śastrasaṁpāte: as the flight of missiles started. The crisis throws Arjuna into great anguish. The opposing hosts are drawn up in battle array, the conches are blown, the thrill of anticipated battle is on them all, when, suddenly in a moment of self-analysis, Arjuna realizes that the struggle means that the whole scheme of life, the great ideals of race and family, of law and order, of patriotism and reverence for the teacher, which he had loyally carried out till then, will have to be abandoned.

21. *hṛṣīkeśaṁ tadā vākyam*
idam āha mahīpate
senayor ubhayor madhye
rathaṁ sthāpaya me 'cyuta

(21) And, O Lord of earth, he spoke this word to Hṛṣīkeśa (Kṛṣṇa): Draw up my chariot, O Acyuta (Kṛṣṇa), between the two armies.

Acyuta: immovable is another name for Kṛṣṇa[1]

22. *yāvad etān nirīkṣe 'haṁ*
yoddhukāmān avasthitān
kair mayā saha yoddhavyam
asmin raṇasamudyame

(22) So that I may observe these men standing, eager for battle, with whom I have to contend in this strife of war.

23. *yotsyamānān avekṣe 'haṁ*
ya ete 'tra samāgatāḥ
dhārtarāṣṭrasya durbuddher
yuddhe priyacikīrṣavaḥ

(23) I wish to look at those who are assembled here, ready to fight and eager to achieve in battle what is dear to the evil-minded son of Dhṛtarāṣṭra.

All the preparations for war are ready. That very morning, Yudhiṣṭhira looks at the impenetrable formation organized by Bhīṣma. Trembling with fear, he tells Arjuna, "How can victory be ours in the face of such an army?"[2] Arjuna encourages his brother by quoting an ancient verse, "they, that are desirous of victory, conquer not so much by might and prowess as by truth, compassion, piety and virtue. Victory is certain to be where Kṛṣṇa is. . . . Victory is one of his attributes, so also is humility."[3] Kṛṣṇa advises Arjuna to purify himself and pray to Durgā for success. Arjuna descends from his chariot and chants a hymn in praise of the Goddess. Pleased with his devotion, She blesses

[1] Other names used for Kṛṣṇa are Madhusūdana (slayer of the demon Madhu), Arisūdana (slayer of enemies), Govinda (herdsman or giver of enlightenment), Vāsudeva (son of Vasudeva), Yādava (descendant of Yadu), Keśava (having fine hair), Mādhava (the husband of Lakṣmī), Hṛṣīkeśa (lord of the senses, hṛṣīka, īśa), Janārdana (the liberator of men).

Other names used for Arjuna are Bhārata (descended of Bharata), Dhanaṁjaya (winner of wealth), Guḍākeśa (having the hair in a ball), Pārtha (son of Pṛthā), Paraṁtapa (oppressor of the enemy).

[2] *dhanaṁjaya kathaṁ śakyam asmābhir yoddhum āhave.* M.B., *Bhīṣmaparva*, 21, 31.

[3] *yudhyadhvam anahaṁkāraḥ yato dharmaṣ tato jayaḥ . . . yataḥ kṛṣṇas tato jayaḥ.* ibid., 21, 11–12.

Arjuna: "O Son of Pāṇḍu, you will vanquish your enemy in no time. You have Nārāyaṇa Himself to help you." And yet, as a man of action, Arjuna did not think out the implications of his enterprise. The presence of his teacher, the consciousness of the Divine, helps him to realize that the enemies he has to fight are dear and sacred to him. He has to cut social ties for the protection of justice and the suppression of lawless violence.

The establishment of the kingdom of God on earth is a co-operative enterprise between God and man. Man is a co-sharer in the work of creation.

24. *evam ukto hṛṣīkeśo*
guḍākeśena bhārata
senayor ubhayor madhye
sthāpayitvā rathottamam

(24) Thus addressed by Guḍākeśa (Arjuna), Hṛṣīkeśa (Kṛṣṇa) drew up that best of chariots, O Bhārata (Dhṛtarāṣṭra), between the two armies.

25. *bhīṣmadroṇapramukhataḥ*
sarveṣāṁ ca mahīkṣitām
uvāca pārtha paśyai 'tān
samavetān kurūn iti

(25) In front of Bhīṣma, Droṇa and all the chiefs he said: "Behold, O Pārtha (Arjuna), these Kurus assembled (here)."

26. *tatrā 'paśyat sthitān pārthaḥ*
pitṝn atha pitāmahān
ācāryān mātulān bhrātṝn
putrān pautrān sakhīṁs tathā

(26) There saw Arjuna standing fathers and grandfathers, teachers, uncles, brothers, sons and grandsons as also companions.

27. *śvaśurān suhṛdaś cai 'va*
senayor ubhayor api
tān samīkṣya sa kaunteyaḥ
sarvān bandhūn avasthitān

(27) And also fathers-in-law and friends in both the armies. When the son of Kuntī (Arjuna) saw all these kinsmen thus standing arrayed.

svajanam: his own people, kinsmen. It is not so much slaughter but slaughter of one's own people that causes distress and anxiety to Arjuna. See also I, 31, 37, and 45. We are generally inclined to take a mechanical view of wars and get lost in statistics. But, with a little imagination, we can realize how our enemies are human beings, "fathers and grandfathers" with their own individual lives, with their longings and aspirations. Later on, Arjuna asks whether victory is worth much after we make the place a desert waste. See I, 36.

28. *kṛpayā parayā 'viṣṭo*
viṣīdann idam abravīt
dṛṣṭve 'maṁ svajanaṁ kṛṣṇa
yuyutsuṁ samupasthitam

(28) He was overcome with great compassion and uttered this in sadness;

The Distress of Arjuna

When I see my own people arrayed and eager for fight O Kṛṣṇa,

29. *sīdanti mama gātrāṇi*
mukhaṁ ca pariśuṣyati
vepathuś ca śarīre me
romaharṣaś ca jāyate

(29) My limbs quail, my mouth goes dry, my body shakes and my hair stands on end.

30. *gāṇḍīvaṁ sraṁsate hastāt*
tvak cai 'va paridahyate
na ca śaknomy avasthātuṁ
bhramatī 'va ca me manaḥ

(30) (The bow) Gāṇḍīva slips from my hand and my skin too is burning all over. I am not able to stand steady. My mind is reeling.

Arjuna's words make us think of the loneliness of man oppressed by doubt, dread of waste and emptiness, from whose being the riches of heaven and earth and the comfort of human affection are slipping away. This intolerable sadness is generally the experience of all those who aspire for the vision of Reality.

31. *nimittāni ca paśyāmi*
viparītāni keśava
na ca śreyo 'nupaśyāmi
hatvā svajanam āhave

(31) And I see evil omens, O Keśava (Kṛṣṇa), nor do I foresee any good by slaying my own people in the fight.

Arjuna's attention to omens indicates his mental weakness and instability.

32. *na kāṅkṣe vijayaṁ kṛṣṇa*
na ca rājyaṁ sukhāni ca
kiṁ no rājyena govinda
kiṁ bhogair jīvitena vā

(32) I do not long for victory, O Kṛṣṇa, nor kingdom nor pleasures. Of what use is kingdom to us, O Kṛṣṇa, or enjoyment or even life?

In moments of great sorrow we are tempted to adopt the method of renunciation.

This verse indicates Arjuna's inclination for renunciation of the world: *saṁnyāsasādhanasūcanam.* Madhusūdana.

33. *yeṣām arthe kāṅkṣitaṁ no*
rājyaṁ bhogāḥ sukhāni ca
ta ime 'vasthitā yuddhe
prāṇāṁs tyaktvā dhanāni ca

(33) Those for whose sake we desire kingdom, enjoyments and pleasures, they stand here in battle, renouncing their lives and riches.

34. *ācāryāḥ pitaraḥ putrās*
tathai 'va ca pitāmahāḥ
mātulāḥ śvaśurāḥ pautrāḥ
śyālāḥ saṁbandhinas tathā

(34) Teachers, fathers, sons and also grandfathers; uncles and fathers-in-law, grandsons and brothers-in-law and (other) kinsmen.

35. *etān na hantum icchāmi*
ghnato 'pi madhusūdana
api trailokyarājyasya
hetoḥ kiṁ nu mahīkṛte

(35) These I would not consent to kill, though they kill me, O Madhusūdana (Kṛṣṇa), even for the kingdom of the three worlds; how much less for the sake of the earth?

The three worlds refer to the Vedic idea of earth, heaven and atmosphere (antarikṣa).

36. *nihatya dhārtarāṣṭrān naḥ*
kā prītiḥ syāj janārdana
pāpam evā 'śrayed asmān
hatvai 'tān ātatāyinaḥ

(36) What pleasure can be ours, O Kṛṣṇa, after we have slain the sons of Dhṛtarāṣṭra? Only sin will accrue to us if we kill these malignants.

How shall we benefit by this bloody sacrifice? What is that goal we expect to reach over the dead bodies of all that we hold dear?

Arjuna is being guided by social conventions and customary morality and not by his individual perception of the truth. He has to slay the symbols of this external morality and develop inward strength. His former teachers who gave him guidance in life have to be slain before he can develop the wisdom of the soul. Arjuna is still talking in terms of enlightened selfishness.

Even though the enemies are the aggressors, we should not kill them, *na pāpe pratipāpaḥ syāt*. Do not commit a sin in retaliation for another sin. "Conquer the anger of others by non-anger; conquer evil doers by saintliness; conquer the miser by gifts; conquer falsehood by truth."[1]

[1] *akrodhena jayet krodham, asādhuṁ sādhunā jayet*
iayet kadaryaṁ dānena, jayet satyena cānṛtam.
M.B., *Udyogaparva*, 38, 73, 74.

See *Dhammapada*, 223.

37. *tasmān nā 'rhā vayaṁ hantuṁ*
dhārtarāṣṭrān svabāndhavān
svajanaṁ hi kathaṁ hatvā
sukhinaḥ syāma mādhava

(37) So it is not right that we slay our kinsmen, the sons of Dhṛtarāṣṭra. Indeed, how can we be happy, O Mādhava (Kṛṣṇa), if we kill our own people?

38. *yady apy ete na paśyanti*
lobhopahatacetasaḥ
kulakṣayakṛtaṁ doṣaṁ
mitradrohe ca pātakam

(38) Even if these whose minds are overpowered by greed, see no wrong in the destruction of the family and no crime in treachery to friends;

39. *kathaṁ na jñeyam asmābhiḥ*
pāpād asmān nivartitum
kulakṣayakṛtaṁ doṣaṁ
prapaśyadbhir janārdana

(39) Why should we not have the wisdom to turn away from this sin, O Janārdana (Kṛṣṇa), we who see the wrong in the destruction of the family?

They are stricken blind by greed and have no understanding, but we are able to see the wrong. Even if we assume that they are guilty of selfish passion and greed, it is a wrong to slay them and it is a greater wrong because they who are blinded by passion are unconscious of the guilt they are committing, but our eyes are open and we see that it is a sin to slay.

40. *kulakṣaye praṇaśyanti*
kuladharmāḥ sanātanāḥ
dharme naṣṭe kulaṁ kṛtsnam
adharmo 'bhibhavaty uta

(40) In the ruin of a family, its ancient laws are destroyed: and when the laws perish, the whole family yields to lawlessness

Wars tend to tear us away from our natural home surroundings and uproot us from social traditions which are the distillation of the mature will and experience of the people.

41. *adharmābhibhavāt kṛṣṇa*
praduṣyanti kulastriyaḥ
strīṣu duṣṭāsu vārṣṇeya
jāyate varṇasaṁkaraḥ

(41) And when lawlessness prevails, O Vārṣṇeya (Kṛṣṇa), the women of the family become corrupted and when women are corrupted, confusion of castes arises.

Varṇa is usually translated by caste, though the present system of caste in no way corresponds to the *Gītā* ideal.

42. *saṁkaro narakāyai 'va*
kulaghnānāṁ kulasya ca
patanti pitaro hy eṣāṁ
luptapiṇḍodakakriyāḥ

(42) And to hell does this confusion bring the family itself as well as those who have destroyed it. For the spirits of their ancestors fall, deprived of their offerings of rice and water.

It refers to the belief that the deceased ancestors require these offerings for their welfare.

43. *doṣair etaiḥ kulaghnānāṁ*
varṇasaṁkarakārakaiḥ
utsādyante jātidharmāḥ
kuladharmāś ca śāśvatāḥ

(43) By the misdeeds of those who destroy a family and create confusion of varṇas, the immemorial laws of the caste and the family are destroyed.

When we shatter the ideals enshrined in immemorial traditions, when we disturb the social equilibrium, we only bring chaos into the world.

44. *utsannakuladharmāṇāṁ*
manuṣyāṇāṁ janārdana
narake niyataṁ vāso
bhavatī 'ty anuśuśruma

(44) And we have heard it said, O Janārdana (Kṛṣṇa), that the men of the families whose laws are destroyed needs must live in hell.

45. *aho bata mahat pāpaṁ*
kartuṁ vyavasitā vayam
yad rājyasukhalobhena
hantuṁ svajanam udyatāḥ

(45) Alas, what a great sin have we resolved to commit in striving to slay our own people through our greed for the pleasures of the kingdom!

46. *yadi mām apratīkāram*
aśastraṁ śastrapāṇayaḥ
dhārtarāṣṭrā raṇe hanyus
tan me kṣemataraṁ bhavet

(46) Far better would it be for me if the sons of Dhṛtarāṣṭra, with weapons in hand, should slay me in the battle, while I remain unresisting and unarmed.

Another reading is *priyataram* for *kṣemataram.*

Arjuna's words are uttered in agony and love. He has his mind on the frontiers of two worlds. He is struggling to get something done as man has struggled from the beginning, and yet he is incapable of decision because of his inability to understand either himself or his fellows or the real nature of the universe in which he is placed. He is stressing the physical pain and the material discomfort which warfare involves. The main end of life is not the pursuit of material happiness. We are bound to miss it as we approach the end of life, with its incidents of old age, infirmity, death. For the sake of an ideal, for justice and love, we must stand up to tyranny and face pain and death. On the very edge of the battle, Arjuna loses heart and all worldly considerations persuade him to abstain from the battle. He has yet to realize that wives and children, teachers and kinsmen, are dear not for their own sake but for the sake of the Self. Arjuna has still to listen to the voice of the teacher who declares that he should lead a life in which his acts will not have their root in desire, that there is such a thing as niṣkāma karma—desireless action.

47. *evam uktvā 'rjunaḥ saṁkhye*
rathopastha upāviśat
visṛjya saśaraṁ cāpaṁ
śokasaṁvignamānasaḥ

(47) Having spoken thus on the (field of) battle, Arjuna sank down on the seat of his chariot, casting away his bow and arrow, his spirit overwhelmed by sorrow.

The distress of Arjuna is a dramatization of a perpetually recurring predicament. Man, on the threshold of higher life, feels disappointed with the glamour of the world and yet illusions cling to him and he cherishes them. He forgets his divine ancestry and becomes attached to his personality and is agitated by the conflicting forces of the world. Before he wakes up to the world of spirit and accepts the obligations imposed by it, he has to fight the enemies of selfishness and stupidity, and overcome the dark ignorance of his self-centred ego. Man cut off from spiritual nature has to be restored to it. It is the evolution of the human soul that is portrayed here. There are no limits of time and space to it. The fight takes place every moment in the soul of man.

ity śrīmad bhagavadgītāsūpaniṣatsu brahmavidyāyām yogaśāstre śrīkṛṣṇārjunasaṁvāde arjunaviṣādayogo nāma prathamo 'dhyāyaḥ

In the Upaniṣad of the *Bhagavadgītā*, the science of the Absolute, the scripture of Yoga and the dialogue between Śrīkṛṣna and Arjuna, this is the first chapter entitled The Depression of Arjuna.[1]

brahmavidyā: the science of the Absolute. What is reality? Is this perpetual procession of events all or is there anything else which is not superseded? What is it that is capable of this mani-

[1] This is the usual colophon which is not a part of the text. There are slight variations in the titles of the chapters in the different versions, but they are not worth recording.

fold manifestation? What compels or impels this exuberant play of infinite possibilities? Have they any aim, any meaning? To help us to understand the nature of reality is the purpose of brahmavidyā. Logical investigation is an aid to the attainment of spiritual wisdom. Ś., in his *Aparokṣānubhūti*, observes that, without inquiry, wisdom cannot be attained by any other means, even as things of the world cannot be seen without light.[1]

yoga-śāstra: the scripture of yoga. There are many who regard philosophy as irrelevant to life. It is said that philosophy deals with the changeless universe of reality and life with the transitory world of process. This view received plausibility from the fact that, in the West, philosophic speculation originated in the city states of ancient Greece, where there were two classes of a wealthy and leisured aristocracy indulging in the luxury of philosophic speculation and a large slave population devoid of the pursuit of the fine and practical arts. Marx's criticism, that philosophers interpret the world while the real task is to change it, does not apply to the author of the *Gītā*, who gives us not only a philosophical interpretation, brahmavidyā, but also a practical programme, yogaśāstra. Our world is not a spectacle to contemplate; it is a field of battle. Only for the *Gītā* improvement in the individual nature is the way to social betterment.

kṛṣṇārjunasaṁvāda: the dialogue between Kṛṣṇa and Arjuna. The author of the *Gītā* gives dramatic expression to the felt presence of God in man.

When Arjuna is tempted to abstain from his proper duty, the Logos in him, his own authentic inspiration, reveals the ordained path, when he is able to set aside the subtle whisperings of his lower self. The innermost core of his soul is also the divine centre of the whole universe. Arjuna's deepest self is Kṛṣṇa.[2] Man and God need a third party as intermediary no more than do two lovers. No one is so close to God as oneself and to get at Him we require only an ardent heart, a pure intention. Arjuna stands naked and alone without intermediaries opposite his God. There

[1] *notpadyate vinā jñānaṁ vicāreṇā'nyasādhanaiḥ*
yathā padārthabhānaṁ hi prakāśena vinā kvacit.

[2] Cp. Tauler: "The soul in this profundity has a likeness and ineffable nearness to God. . . . In this deepest, most inner and most secret depth of the soul, God essentially, really and substantially exists."

is perpetual communion between God and man and the dialogue proceeds until complete harmony of purpose is reached.

This Divine Principle is not at a distance but close to us. God is not a detached spectator or a distant judge of the issue but a friend, sakhā who is with us at all times, *vihāraśayyāsanabhojaneṣu* (XI, 42). *Ṛg. Veda* speaks of two birds, beautiful of wing, friends by nature who live together on one tree.[1]

viṣāda: depression. The Chapter ends in dejection and sorrow and this is also called *Yoga* as this darkness of the soul is an essential step in the progress to spiritual life. Most of us go through life without facing the ultimate questions. It is in rare crises, when our ambitions lie in ruins at our feet, when we realize in remorse and agony the sad mess we have made of our lives, we cry out "Why are we here?" "What does all this mean and whither do we go from here?" "My God, my God, why hast thou forsaken me?". Draupadī cries: "I have no husbands, no sons, no kinsmen, no brothers, no father, not even you, O Kṛṣṇa."[2] Arjuna passes through a great spiritual tension. When he detaches himself from his social obligations and asks why he should carry out the duty expected of him by society, he gets behind his socialized self and has full awareness of himself as an individual, alone and isolated. He faces the world as a stranger thrown into a threatening chaos. The new freedom creates a deep feeling of anxiety, aloneness, doubt and insecurity. If he is to function successfully, these feelings must be overcome.

[1] Cp. also: "Thou all-knowing God, Thou art always present near us; Thou dost see whatever sins there may be without and within."

sarvajñatvaṁ svayaṁ nityaṁ sannidhau vartase ca naḥ
antar bahiś ca yat kiñcit pāpaṁ tat paśyati svayam.

[2] *naiva me patayas santi, na putrā, na ca bāndhavāḥ*
na bhrātaro, na ca pitā, naiva tvaṁ madhusūdana.

CHAPTER II

Sāṁkhya Theory and Yoga Practice

Kṛṣṇa's rebuke and exhortation to be brave

saṁjaya uvāca

1. *taṁ tathā kṛpayā 'viṣṭam*
aśrupūrṇākulekṣaṇam
viṣīdantam idaṁ vākyam
uvāca madhusūdanaḥ

Saṁjaya said:

(1) To him (who was) thus overcome by pity, whose eyes were filled with tears and troubled and (who was) much depressed in mind, Madhusūdana (Kṛṣṇa) spoke this word.

The pity of Arjuna has nothing in common with Divine compassion. It is a form of self-indulgence, a shrinking of the nerves from an act which requires him to hurt his own people. Arjuna recoils from his task in a mood of sentimental self-pity and his teacher rebukes him. That the Kauravas were his kinsmen he had known before.

śrībhagavān uvāca

2. *kutas tvā kaśmalam idaṁ*
viṣame samupasthitam
anāryajuṣṭam asvargyam
akīrtikaram arjuna

The Blessed Lord said:

(2) Whence has come to thee this stain (this dejection) of spirit in this hour of crisis? It is unknown to men of noble mind (not cherished by the Aryans); it does not lead to heaven; (on earth) it causes disgrace, O Arjuna.

anāryajuṣṭam: un-Aryan. The Aryans, it is contended by some, are those who accept a particular type of inward culture and social practice, which insists on courage and courtesy, nobility and straight dealing.

In his attempt to release Arjuna from his doubts, Kṛṣṇa refers to the doctrine of the indestructibility of the self, appeals to his sense of honour and martial traditions, reveals to him God's purpose and points out how action is to be undertaken in the world.

3. *klaibyaṁ mā sma gamaḥ pārtha*
nai 'tat tvayy upapadyate
kṣudraṁ hṛdayadaurbalyaṁ
tyaktvo 'ttiṣṭha paraṁtapa

(3) Yield not to this unmanliness, O Pārtha (Arjuna), for it does not become thee. Cast off this petty faintheartedness and arise, O Oppressor of the foes (Arjuna).

Arjuna's Doubts are Unresolved

arjuna uvāca

4. *kathaṁ bhīṣmam ahaṁ saṁkhye*
droṇaṁ ca madhusūdana
iṣubhiḥ pratiyotsyāmi
pūjārhāv arisūdana

Arjuna said:

(4) How shall I strike Bhīṣma and Droṇa who are worthy of worship, O Madhusūdana (Kṛṣṇa), with arrows in battle, O Slayer of foes (Kṛṣṇa.)?

5. *gurūn ahatvā hi mahānubhāvān*
śreyo bhoktuṁ bhaikṣyam apī 'ha loke
hatvā 'rthakāmāṁs tu gurūn ihai 'va
bhuñjīya bhogān rudhirapradigdhān

(5) It is better to live in this world by begging than to slay these honoured teachers.[1] Though they are mindful of their gains, they are my teachers and by slaying them, only, I would enjoy in this world delights which are smeared with blood.

[1] *mahānubhāvān śrutādhyayana-tapa-ācārādi nibandhanaḥ prabhāvo yeṣām tān hi mahānubhāvān ity ekam vā padam. himaṁ jāḍyam apahantīti himahā ādityo' gnir vā tasyevānubhāvaḥ sāmarthyaṁ yeṣāṁ tān.* Madhusūdana. The latter is a fanciful explanation.

rudhirapradigdhān: smeared with blood. If we make real to ourselves the victims of every bloodstained page of history, if we hear the woes of women, the cries of children, the tales of calamity, of oppression and of injustice in its myriad forms, no one with any human feelings would delight in such bloodstained conquests.

6. *na cai 'tad vidmaḥ kataran no garīyo*
yad vā jayema yadi vā no jayeyuḥ
yān eva hatvā na jijīviṣāmas
te 'vasthitāḥ pramukhe dhārtarāṣṭrāḥ

(6) Nor do we know which for us is better, whether we conquer them or they conquer us. The sons of Dhṛtarāṣṭra, whom if we slew we should not care to live, are standing before us in battle array.

7. *kārpaṇyadoṣopahatasvabhāvaḥ*
pṛcchāmi tvāṁ dharmasaṁmūḍhacetāḥ
yac chreyaḥ syān niścitaṁ brūhi tan me
śiṣyas te 'haṁ śādhi māṁ tvāṁ prapannam

(7) My very being is stricken with the weakness of (sentimental) pity. With my mind bewildered about my duty, I ask Thee. Tell me, for certain, which is better. I am Thy pupil; teach me, who am seeking refuge in Thee.

niścitam: for certain; Arjuna is driven not only by despair, anxiety and doubt but also by an ardent wish for certainty.

To realize one's unreason is to step towards one's development to reason. The consciousness of imperfection indicates that the soul is alive. So long as it is alive, it can improve even as a living body can heal, if it is hurt or cut to a point. The human being is led to a higher condition through a crisis of contrition.

It is the general experience of seekers that they are assailed by doubts and difficulties, even when they are on the threshold of light. The light as it begins to shine in any soul provokes the darkness to resist it. Arjuna faces difficulties, outward and inward, such as the resistance of relations and friends, doubts and fears, passions and desires. They must all be laid on the altar and consumed in the fire of wisdom. The struggle with darkness will continue until the light fills one's whole being.

Weighed down by wretchedness, confused about what is right and wrong, Arjuna seeks light and guidance from his teacher, the Divine with him, within his self. Man cannot be left to his own devices. When one's world is in ruins, one can only turn within and seek illumination as the gift of God's infinite compassion.

Arjuna does not ask for a metaphysic as he is not a seeker of knowledge; as a man of action he asks for the law of action, for his dharma, for what he has to do in this difficulty. "Master, what wouldst thou have me to do?"

Like Arjuna, the aspirant must realize his weakness and ignorance and yet be anxious to do God's will and discover what it is.

8. *na hi prapaśyāmi mamā 'panudyād*
yac chokam ucchoṣaṇam indriyāṇām
avāpya bhūmāv asapatnam ṛddhaṁ
rājyaṁ surāṇām api cā 'dhipatyam

(8) I do not see what will drive away this sorrow which dries up my senses even if I should attain rich and unrivalled kingdom on earth or even the sovereignty of the gods.

The conflict in Arjuna must be healed. He must attain to a new, integral, comprehensive consciousness.

saṁjaya uvāca

9. *evam uktvā hṛṣīkeśaṁ*
guḍākeśaḥ paraṁtapaḥ
na yotsya iti govindam
uktvā tūṣṇīṁ babhūva ha

Saṁjaya said:

(9) Having thus addressed Hṛiṣīkeśa (Kṛṣṇa), the mighty Guḍākeśa (Arjuna) said to Govinda (Kṛṣṇa) "I will not fight" and became silent.

na yotsye: "I will not fight." Arjuna, without waiting for the advice of the teacher, seems to have made up his mind. While he asks the teacher to advise him, his mind is not open. The task of the teacher becomes more difficult.

govinda. The omniscience of the teacher is indicated by this word. Madhusūdana.[1]

tūṣṇīm babhūva: became silent. The voice of truth can be heard only in silence.

10. *tam uvāca hṛṣīkeśaḥ*
prahasann iva bhārata
senayor ubhayor madhye
viṣīdantam idaṁ vacaḥ

(10) To him thus depressed in the midst of the two armies, O Bhārata (Dhṛtarāṣṭra), Hriṣīkeśa (Kṛṣṇa), smiling as it were, spoke this word.

In that moment of depression, the sinking heart of Arjuna heard the Divine voice of Kṛṣṇa. The smile indicates that he saw through Arjuna's attempt at rationalization or what is now known as wishful thinking. The attitude of the saviour God who knows all the sins and sorrows of suffering humanity is one of tender pity and wistful understanding.

The Distinction between Self and Body: We should not grieve for what is Imperishable

śrībhagavān uvāca
11. *aśocyān anvaśocas tvaṁ*
prajñāvādāṁś ca bhāṣase
gatāsūn agatāsūṁś ca
nā 'nuśocanti paṇḍitāḥ

The Blessed Lord said:

(11) Thou grievest for those whom thou shouldst not grieve for, and yet thou speakest words about wisdom Wise men do not grieve for the dead or for the living.

The Kashmir version has "thou dost not speak as an intelligent man": "prājñavat na abhibhāṣase."[2]

[1] *gāṁ vedalakṣāṇāṁ vāṇiṁ vindatīti vyutpattyā sarvavedopādānatvena sarvajñam.*

[2] Cp. Plotinus: "Murders, death in all its shapes, the capture and sacking of towns, all must be considered as so much stage-show, so many shiftings of scenes, the horror and outcry of a play; for here too, in all the changing doom of life, it is not the true man, the inner soul that grieves and laments but merely the phantasm of the man, the outer man, playing his part on the boards of the world." *Enneads*, III, 2, 15.—E. T.

The teacher explains in brief in verses 11–38 the wisdom of the Sāṁkhya philosophy. The Sāṁkhya does not refer to Kapila's system but to the teaching of the Upaniṣads.

12. *na tv evā 'haṁ jātu nā 'saṁ*
na tvaṁ ne 'me janādhipāḥ
na cai 'va na bhaviṣyāmaḥ
sarve vayam ataḥ param

(12) Never was there a time when I was not, nor thou, nor these lords of men, nor will there ever be a time hereafter when we all shall cease to be.

Ś. looks upon this reference to plurality as conventional. He argues that the plural number is used with reference to the bodies that are different and not with regard to the one Universal Self.[1]

R. lays stress on the distinction between Kṛṣṇa, Arjuna, and the princes as ultimate and holds that each individual soul is imperishable and coeval with the whole universe.

The reference here is not to the eternity of the Absolute Spirit but to the pre-existence and post-existence of the empirical egos. The plurality of egos is a fact of the empirical universe. Each individual is an ascent from initial non-existence to full existence as a real, from asat to sat. While the Sāṁkhya system postulates a plurality of souls, the *Gītā* reconciles this with the unity, the one Ksetrajña in whom we live, move and have our being. Brahman is the basis of all things and is not itself a thing. Brahman does not exist in time but time is in it. In this sense also, the egos have neither beginning nor end. Souls are like Brahman, for the cause and the effect are essentially one as the sayings, "I am Brahman," "That art Thou" indicate. Cp. Suso: "All creatures have existed eternally in the Divine essence as in their exemplar. So far as they conform to the Divine idea, all beings were before their creation, one with the essence of God."

The personal Lord, the Divine Creator, is coeval with the empirical universe. In a sense He is the totality of empirical existences. "The Lord of the beings travels in the wombs. Though unborn he is born in many ways."[2]

[1] *dehabhedānuvṛttyā bahuvacanam nā'tmabhedābhiprāyeṇa.*

[2] *prajāpatiś carati garbhe antar ajāyamāno bahudhā vijāyate. Vājasaneyi saṁhitā* XXXI, 19; see also XXXII, 4.

Ś. says "Of a truth God is the only transmigrant."[1] Compare with this Pascal's statement that Christ will be in agony till the end of the world. He takes upon himself the wounds inflicted on humanity. He suffers the conditions of created existence. Liberated souls suffer in time and enter peace at the end of time, though they participate in Divine life even now. Only if the Personal Supreme is freely limited, we are helplessly limited. If He is master of the play of prakṛti, we are subject to its play. Ignorance affects the individual spirit but not the Universal Spirit. Till the cosmic process ends, the multiplicity of individuals with their distinctive qualitative contents persists. The multiplicity is not separable from the cosmos. While the liberated souls know the truth and live in it, the unliberated ones pass from birth to birth, tied by the bondage of works.

13. *dehino 'smin yathā dehe*
kaumāraṁ yauvanaṁ jarā
tathā dehāntaraprāptir
dhīras tatra na muhyati

(13) As the soul passes in this body through childhood, youth and age, even so is its taking on of another body. The sage is not perplexed by this.

Cp. *Viṣṇu Smṛti:* XX, 49.

The human being makes himself fit for immortality by passing through a series of births and deaths. The changes in the body do not mean changes in the soul. None of its embodiments is permanent.

14. *mātrāsparśās tu kaunteya*
śītoṣṇasukhaduḥkhadāḥ
āgamāpāyino 'nityās
tāṁs titikṣasva bhārata

(14) Contacts with their objects, O Son of Kuntī (Arjuna), give rise to cold and heat, pleasure and pain. They come and go and do not last for ever, these learn to endure, O Bhārata (Arjuna).

[1] *satyaṁ neśvarād anyad saṁsārin.* (S.B., I, 1, 5.)

These opposites depend on limited and occasional causes whereas the joy of Brahman is universal, self-existent and independent of particular causes and objects. This indivisible being supports the variations of pleasure and pain of the egoistic existence which gets into contact with the multiple universe. These attitudes of pleasure and pain are determined by the force of habit. There is no obligation to be pleased with success and pained with failure. We can meet them with a perfect equanimity. It is the ego-consciousness which enjoys and suffers and it will continue to do so, so long as it is bound up with the use of life and body and is dependent on them for its knowledge and action. But when the mind becomes free and disinterested and sinks into that secret serenity, when its consciousness becomes illumined, it gladly accepts whatever happens, knowing full well that these contacts come and go and are not itself, though they happen to it.[1]

15. *yaṁ hi na vyathayanty ete*
puruṣaṁ puruṣarṣabha
samaduḥkhasukhaṁ dhīraṁ
so 'mṛtatvāya kalpate

(15) The man who is not troubled by these, O Chief of men (Arjuna), who remains the same in pain and pleasure, who is wise makes himself fit for eternal life.

Eternal life is different from survival of death which is given to every embodied being. It is the transcendence of life and death. To be subject to grief and sorrow, to be disturbed by the material happenings, to be deflected by them from the path of duty that has to be traversed, ***niyataṁ karma***, shows that we are still victims of avidyā or ignorance.

16. *nā 'sato vidyate bhāvo*
nā 'bhāvo vidyate sataḥ
ubhayor api dṛṣṭo 'ntas tv
anayos tattvadarśibhiḥ

[1] Cp. *Imitation.* "The desires of the senses draw us hither and thither, but, when the hour is past, what do they bring us but remorse of conscience and dissipation of spirit?"

(16) Of the non-existent there is no coming to be; of the existent there is no ceasing to be. The conclusion about these two has been perceived by the seers of truth.

sadākhyam brahma. Ś. defines real (sat) as that in regard to which our consciousness never fails and unreal (asat) as that in regard to which our consciousness fails.[1] Our consciousness of objects varies but not that of existence. The unreal which is the passing show of the world veils the unchanging reality which is for ever manifest.

According to R., the unreal is the body and the real is the soul. Madhva interprets the first quarter of the verse as asserting duality, vidyate-abhāvah. There is no destruction of the unmanifest (avyakta) prakṛti. Sat, of course is indestructible.

17. *avināśi tu tad viddhi*
yena sarvam idaṁ tatam
vināśam avyayasyā 'sya
na kaścit kartum arhati

(17) Know thou that that by which all this is pervaded is indestructible. Of this immutable being, no one can bring about the destruction.

tatam: pervaded. See also VIII, 22, 46; IX, 4; XI, 38 and M.B., XII, 240, 20. Ś. uses "*vyāptam.*"

Not even Īśvara, the Supreme Lord, can bring about the destruction of the Self.[2] Its reality is self-established, *svatassiddha*. It is not unknown to anybody.[3] The scriptures serve to remove the *adhyāropaṇa* or superposition of attributes alien to the Self and not to reveal what is altogether unknown.

R. means by *ātmatattva* the qualitative unity and equality in the midst of numerical plurality.

18 *antavanta ime dehā*
nityasyo 'ktāḥ śarīriṇaḥ
anāśino 'prameyasya
tasmād yudhyasva bhārata

[1] *yad viṣayā buddhir na vyabhicarati tat sat, yad viṣayā vyabhicarati tad asat.*

[2] *na kaścid ātmānaṁ vināśayituṁ śaknoti'śvaropi*. Ś.

[3] *na hy ātmā nāma kasyacid aprasiddho bhavati*. S.B.G., II, 18.

(18) It is said that these bodies of the eternal embodied (soul) which is indestructible and incomprehensible come to an end. Therefore fight, O Bhārata (Arjuna).

śarīri here refers to the true self of the individual as in the phrase *śārīraka mīmāṁsā*,[1] which is an enquiry into the nature of the individual self. It is incomprehensible because it is not known by the ordinary means of knowledge.

19. *ya enaṁ vetti hantāraṁ*
yaś cai 'naṁ manyate hatam
ubhau tau na vijānīto
nā 'yaṁ hanti na hanyate

(19) He who thinks that this slays and he who thinks that this is slain; both of them fail to perceive the truth; this one neither slays nor is slain.

The author is discriminating between the self and the not-self, puruṣa and prakṛti of the Sāṁkhya.[2]

20. *na jāyate mriyate vā kadācin*
nā 'yaṁ bhūtvā bhavitā vā na bhūyaḥ
ajo nityaḥ śāśvato 'yaṁ purāṇo
na hanyate hanyamāne śarīre

(20) He is never born, nor does he die at any time, nor having (once) come to be will he again cease to be. He is unborn, eternal, permanent and primeval. He is not slain when the body is slain.

See *Kaṭha Up.*, II, 18. Cp. *na vadhenāsya hanyate. Chāndogya Up.*, VIII, 1, 5. The soul is here spoken of as "having come to be." It is everlasting as a Divine form and derives its existence from God.

Ś. splits up the phrase into *bhūtvā-abhavitā*.

[1] Cp. *Bṛhadāraṇyaka Up. yat śākṣād aparokṣād brahma ya ātmā sarvāntaraḥ*. III, 4, 1.

[2] Cp. Emerson's *Brahma*.

"If the red slayer thinks he slays,
Or if the slain think he is slain,
They know not well the subtle ways
I keep and pass and turn again."

21. *vedā 'vināśinaṁ nityaṁ*
ya enam ajam avyayam
kathaṁ sa puruṣaḥ pārtha
kaṁ ghātayati hanti kaṁ

(21) He who knows that it is indestructible and eternal, uncreate and unchanging, how can such a person slay any one, O Pārtha (Arjuna), or cause any one to slay?

When we know the self to be invulnerable, how can anyone slay it?

22. *vāsāṁsi jīrṇāni yathā vihāya*
navāni gṛhṇāti naro 'parāṇi
tathā śarīrāṇi vihāya jīrṇāny
anyāni saṁyāti navāni dehī

(22) Just as a person casts off worn-out garments and puts on others that are new, even so does the embodied soul cast off worn-out bodies and take on others that are new.

The eternal does not move from place to place but the embodied soul moves from one abode to another. It takes birth each time and gathers to itself a mind, life and body formed out of the materials of nature according to its past evolution and its need for the future. The psychic being is the vijñāna which supports the triple manifestation of body (anna), life (prāṇa) and mind (manas). When the gross physical body falls away, the vital and mental sheaths still remain as the vehicle of the soul. Rebirth is a law of nature. There is an objective connection between the various forms of life. Cp. *Kaṭha Up.*, I, 6. "Like corn a mortal ripens and like corn is he born again."

Embodiments seem to be essential for the soul. Is it then right to kill the body? The world of concrete existence has a meaning.

23. *nai 'naṁ chindanti śastrāṇi*
nai 'naṁ dahati pāvakaḥ
na cai 'naṁ kledayanty āpo
na śoṣayati mārutaḥ

(23) Weapons do not cleave this self, fire does not burn him; waters do not make him wet; nor does the wind make him dry.

See also *Mokṣadharma*, 174. 17.

24. *acchedyo 'yam adāhyo 'yam*
akledyo 'śoṣya eva ca
nityaḥ sarvagataḥ sthāṇur
acalo 'yaṁ sanātanaḥ

(24) He is uncleavable, He cannot be burnt. He can be neither wetted nor dried. He is eternal, all-pervading, unchanging and immovable. He is the same for ever.

25. *avyakto 'yam acintyo 'yam*
avikāryo 'yam ucyate
tasmād evaṁ viditvai 'naṁ
nā 'nuśocitum arhasi

(25) He is said to be unmanifest, unthinkable and unchanging. Therefore, knowing him as such, thou shouldst not grieve.

Right through it is the puruṣa of the Sāṁkhya that is described here, not the Brahman of the Upaniṣads. The puruṣa is beyond the range of form or thought and the changes that affect mind, life and body do not touch him. Even when it is applied to the Supreme Self, which is one in all, it is the unthinkable (acintya) and immutable (avikārya) Self that is meant. Arjuna's grief is misplaced as the self cannot be hurt or slain. Forms may change; things may come and go but that which remains behind them all is for ever.[1]

We should not Grieve over what is Perishable

26. *atha cai 'naṁ nityajātaṁ*
nityaṁ vā manyase mṛtam
tathā 'pi tvaṁ mahābāho
nai 'naṁ śocitum arhasi

(26) Even if thou thinkest that the self is perpetually born and perpetually dies, even then, O Mighty-armed (Arjuna), thou shouldst not grieve.

[1] When Crito asks, "In what way shall we bury you, Socrates?" Socrates answers, "In any way you like, but first, you must catch *me*, the real me. Be of good cheer, my dear Crito, and say that you are burying my body only, and do with *that* whatever is usual and what you think best."

27. *jātasya hi dhruvo mṛtyur*
dhruvaṁ janma mṛtasya ca
tasmād aparihārye 'rthe
na tvaṁ śocitum arhasi

(27) For to the one that is born death is certain and certain is birth for the one that has died. Therefore for what is unavoidable, thou shouldst not grieve.

Cp. "In this rotating world of becoming, what dead person does not come to life again."[1] The realization of this fact will induce in us poise and proportion.[2]

Our existence is brief and death is certain. Our human dignity requires us to accept pain and suffering for the sake of the right.

The inevitability of death, however, cannot justify murders, suicides or wars. We cannot desire deliberately the death of others, simply because all men are bound to die. It is so that all life ends in death, that all progress is perishable, that nothing is permanent in the temporal sense of the term. But in every perfect realization of life, the eternal becomes actualized and the development in time is only the means to this essential aim. What is subject entirely to the rule of change or time is not of intrinsic importance; the eternal plan is the central truth whether cosmic accidents permit its full realization on earth or not.

[1] *parivartini saṁsāre mṛtaḥ ko vā na jāyate. Hitopadeśa.*

[2] Gautama the Buddha consoled the mother who lost her only son while yet a child by asking her to go into the town and bring him "a little mustard seed from any house where no man hath yet died." She went and found that there was no family where death had not entered. She discovered that it is the law of all things that they will pass away.

The Buddhist nun Paṭācārā is represented as consoling many bereaved mothers in the following words:

Weep not, for such is here the life of man
Unasked he came, unbidden went he hence
Lo! ask thyself again whence came thy son
To bide on earth this little breathing space
By one way come and by another gone. . . .
So hither and so hence—why should ye weep?

Psalms of the Sisters.
E.T. by Mrs. Rhys Davids (1909), p. 78.

28. *avyaktādīni bhūtāni*
vyaktamadhyāni bhārata
avyaktanidhanāny eva
tatra kā paridevanā

(28) Beings are unmanifest in their beginnings, manifest in the middles and unmanifest again in their ends, O Bhārata (Arjuna), What is there in this for lamentation?

29. *āścaryavat paśyati kaścid enam*
āścaryavad vadati tathai 'va cā 'nyaḥ
āścaryavac cai 'nam anyaḥ śṛṇoti
śrutvā 'py enaṁ veda na cai 'va kaścit

(29) One looks upon Him as a marvel, another likewise speaks of Him as a marvel; another hears of Him as a marvel; and even after hearing, no one whatsoever has known Him.

Though the truth of the Self is free of access to all mankind, it is attained only by very few who are willing to pay the price in self-discipline, steadfastness and non-attachment. Though the truth is open to all, many do not feel any urge to seek. Of those who have the urge, many suffer from doubt and vacillation. Even if they do not have doubts, many are scared away by difficulties. Only a few rare souls succeed in braving the perils and reaching the goal.

Cp. *Kaṭha Up.*, II, 7. "Even when one has beheld, heard and proclaimed it, no one has understood it." Ś.

30. *dehī nityam avadhyo 'yaṁ*
dehe sarvasya bhārata
tasmāt sarvāṇi bhūtāni
na tvaṁ śocitum arhasi

(30) The dweller in the body of every one, O Bhārata (Arjuna), is eternal and can never be slain, Therefore thou shouldst not grieve for any creature.

Man is a compound of Self which is immortal and body which is mortal. Even if we accept this position that body is naturally mortal, still as it is the means of furthering the interests of the Self it has to be preserved. This is not by itself a satisfactory reason. So Kṛṣṇa refers to Arjuna's duty as a warrior.

Appeal to a Sense of Duty

31. *svadharmam api cā 'vekṣya*
na vikampitum arhasi
dharmyād dhi yuddhāc chreyo 'nyat
kṣatriyasya na vidyate

(31) Further, having regard for thine own duty, thou shouldst not falter, there exists no greater good for a Kṣatriya than a battle enjoined by duty.

His svadharma or law of action, requires him to engage in battle. Protection of right by the acceptance of battle, if necessary, is the social duty of the Kṣatriya, and not renunciation. His duty is to maintain order by force and not to become an ascetic by "shaving off the hair."[1] Kṛṣṇa tells Arjuna that for warriors there is no more ennobling duty than a fair fight. It is a privilege that leads to heaven.

32. *yadṛcchayā co 'papannaṁ*
svargadvāram apāvṛtam
sukhinaḥ kṣatriyāḥ pārtha
labhante yuddham īdṛśam

(32) Happy are the Kṣatriyas, O Pārtha (Arjuna), for whom such a war comes of its own accord as an open door to heaven.

A Kṣatriya's happiness consists not in domestic pleasures and comfort but in fighting for the right.[2]

33. *atha cet tvam imaṁ dharmyaṁ*
saṁgrāmaṁ na kariṣyasi
tataḥ svadharmaṁ kīrtiṁ ca
hitvā pāpam avāpsyasi

[1] Cp. M.B., *daṇḍa eva hi rājendra kṣatradharmo na muṇḍanam. Śāntiparva*, 23, 46. "He who saves from destruction is a Kṣatriya." *kṣatād yo vai trāyati 'ti sa tasmāt kṣatriyaḥ smṛtaḥ*. M.B., XII, 29, 138.

[2] Cp. "O thou best of men, there are only two types who can pierce the constellation of the Sun (and reach the sphere of Brahman); the one is the saṁnyāsin who is steeped in Yoga and the other is the warrior who falls in the battlefield while fighting."

dvāv imau puruṣavyāghra sūryamaṇḍala bhedinau
parivāṅg yogayuktaś ca raṇe cā'bhimukho hataḥ.

M.B., *Udyogaparva*, 32, 65.

(33) But if thou doest not this lawful battle, then thou wilt fail thy duty and glory and will incur sin.

When the struggle between right and wrong is on, he who abstains from it out of false sentimentality, weakness or cowardice would be committing a sin.

34. *akīrtiṁ cā 'pi bhūtāni*
kathayiṣyanti te 'vyayām
saṁbhāvitasya cā 'kīrtir
maraṇād atiricyate

(34) Besides, men will ever recount thy ill-fame and for one who has been honoured, ill-fame is worse than death.

35. *bhayād raṇād uparataṁ*
maṁsyante tvāṁ mahārathāḥ
yeṣāṁ ca tvaṁ bahumato
bhūtvā yāsyasi lāghavam

(35) The great warriors will think that thou hast abstained from battle through fear and they by whom thou wast highly esteemed will make light of thee.

36. *avācyavādāṁś ca bahūn*
vadiṣyanti tavā 'hitāḥ
nindantas tava sāmarthyaṁ
tato duḥkhataraṁ nu kim

(36) Many unseemly words will be uttered by thy enemies, slandering thy strength. Could anything be sadder than that?

Contrast this with the central teaching of the *Gītā* that one should be indifferent to praise and blame.

37. *hato vā prāpsyasi svargaṁ*
jitvā vā bhokṣyase mahīm
tasmād uttiṣṭha kaunteya
yuddhāya kṛtaniścayaḥ

(37) Either slain thou shalt go to heaven; or victorious thou shalt enjoy the earth; Therefore arise, O Son of Kuntī (Arjuna), resolved on battle.

Whether we look at the metaphysical truth or the social duty, our path is clear. It is possible to rise higher through the performance of one's duty in the right spirit, and in the next verse Kṛṣṇa proceeds to indicate the spirit.

38. *sukhaduḥkhe same kṛtvā*
lābhālābhau jayājayau
tato yuddhāya yujyasva
nai 'vaṁ pāpam avāpsyasi

(38) Treating alike pleasure and pain, gain and loss, victory and defeat, then get ready for battle. Thus thou shall not incur sin.

Yet in the previous verses, Kṛṣṇa lays stress on sensibility to shame, the gain of heaven and earthly sovereignty. After urging worldly considerations, he declares that the fight has to be undertaken in a spirit of equal-mindedness. Without yielding to the restless desire for change, without being at the mercy of emotional ups and downs, let us do the work assigned to us in the situation in which we are placed. When we acquire faith in the Eternal and experience Its reality, the sorrows of the world do not disturb us.[1] He who discovers his true end of life and yields to it utterly is great of soul. Though everything else is taken away from him, though he has to walk the streets, cold, hungry and alone, though he may know no human being into whose eyes he can look and find understanding, he shall yet be able to go his way with a smile on his lips for he has gained inward freedom.

The Insight of Yoga

39. *eṣā te 'bhihitā sāṁkhye*
buddhir yoge tv imāṁ śṛṇu
buddhyā yukto yayā pārtha
karmabandhaṁ prahāsyasi

(39) This is the wisdom of the Sāṁkhya given to thee, O Pārtha (Arjuna). Listen now to the wisdom of the Yoga. If your intelligence accepts it, thou shalt cast away the bondage of works.

[1] Cp. Luther: "And though they take our life, goods, honour, children, wife, yet is their profit small; these things shall vanish all, the city of God remaineth."

Sāṁkhya in the *Gītā* does not mean the system of philosophy known by that name; nor does Yoga mean Pātañjalayoga. The scholastic version of the Sāṁkhya is a frank dualism of puruṣa (self) and prakṛti (not-self) which is transcended in the *Gītā*, which affirms the reality of a Supreme Self who is the Lord of all. Sāṁkhya gives an intellectual account of the intuition of the unchanging One.[1] It is the yoga of knowledge. The yoga of action is karma yoga. See III, 3. The knowledge hitherto described is not to be talked about and discussed academically. It must become an inward experience. In the *Gītā*, Sāṁkhya lays stress on knowledge and renunciation of desire and Yoga on action. How is one who knows that the self and body are distinct, that the self is indestructible and unmoved by the events of the world, to act? The teacher develops buddhiyoga or concentration of buddhi or understanding. Buddhi is not merely the capacity to frame concepts. It has also the function of recognition and discrimination. The understanding or buddhi must be trained to attain insight, constancy, equal-mindedness (samatā). The mind (manas), instead of being united to the senses, should be guided by buddhi which is higher than mind. III, 42. It must become united to buddhi (buddhiyukta).

The influence of the scholastic Sāṁkhya which was in the making at the time of the *Gītā* is here evident. According to it, the puruṣa is inactive, and bondage and liberation do not belong to it in reality. They are essentially the work of buddhi, one of the twenty-four cosmic principles. Out of prakṛti evolve successively five elemental conditions of matter, ether, air, fire, water and earth, five subtle properties of matter, sound, touch, form, taste and smell, buddhi or mahat which is the discriminating principle of intelligence and will, ahaṁkāra or self-sense, and mind with its ten sense functions, five of knowledge and five of action. Liberation is achieved when buddhi discriminates between puruṣa and prakṛti. This view is adapted to the *Gītā* theism. Buddhi is the driver of the chariot of the body drawn by the horses of the senses which are controlled by the reins of mind (manas). The self is superior to buddhi but is a passive witness. In the *Kaṭha Up.*, buddhi is the charioteer which controls the senses through

[1] Madhva quotes Vyāsa to this effect.
śuddhātmatattvavijñānaṁ sāṁkhyam ity abhidhīyate. Cp. *Śvetāśvatara Up. sāṁkhyayogādhigamyam.* VI, 13.

the mind and enables it to know the self.[1] If the buddhi is lit up by the consciousness of the self and makes it the master-light of its life, its guidance will be in harmony with the cosmic purpose. If the light of the ātman is reflected in buddhi in a proper way, that is, if the buddhi is cleared of all obscuring tendencies, the light will not be distorted, and buddhi will be in union with the Spirit. The sense of egoism and separateness will be displaced by a vision of the harmony in which each is all and all is each.

Sāṁkhya and Yoga are not in the *Gītā* discordant systems. They have the same aim but differ in their methods.

40. *ne 'hā 'bhikramanāśo 'sti*
pratyavāyo na vidyate
svalpam apy asya dharmasya
trāyate mahato bhayāt

(40) In this path, no effort is ever lost and no obstacle prevails; even a little of this righteousness (dharma) saves from great fear.

No step is lost, every moment is a gain. Every effort in the struggle will be counted as a merit.

41. *vyavasāyātmikā buddhir*
eke 'ha kurunandana
bahuśākhā hy anantāś ca
buddhayo 'vyavasāyinām

(41) In this, O joy of the Kurus (Arjuna), the resolute (decided) understanding is single; but the thoughts of the irresolute (undecided) are many-branched and endless.

The discursiveness of the irresolute buddhi is contrasted with the concentration, the single-mindedness of the resolute. Human life finds its fulfilment through self-devotion to a commanding end and not in the unfettered pursuit of endless possibilities. One-pointedness has to be acquired by cultivation. Distraction is our natural condition from which we have to be freed but not by the mysticisms of nature or sex, race or nation but by a genuine experience of Reality. Single-mindedness backed by such an experience is a supreme virtue and cannot be twisted to fanaticism.

[1] III, 3.

No Wisdom for the Worldly-Minded

42. *yām imāṁ puṣpitāṁ vācaṁ*
pravadanty avipaścitaḥ
vedavādaratāḥ pārtha
nā 'nyad astī 'ti vādinaḥ

43. *kāmātmānaḥ svargaparā*
janmakarmaphalapradām
kriyāviśeṣabahulāṁ
bhogaiśvaryagatiṁ prati

(42–43) The undiscerning who rejoice in the letter of the Veda, who contend that there is nothing else, whose nature is desire and who are intent on heaven, proclaim these flowery words that result in rebirth as the fruit of actions and (lay down) various specialized rites for the attainment of enjoyment and power.

The teacher distinguishes true karma from ritualistic piety. Vedic sacrifices are directed to the acquisition of material rewards but the *Gītā* asks us to renounce all selfish desire and work, making all life a sacrifice, offered with true devotion.

Cp. *Muṇḍaka Up.*, I, 2, 10. "These fools, who believe that only the performance of sacrificial ritual (iṣṭāpūrtam) is meritorious and nothing else is meritorious, come back to this mortal world, after having enjoyed happiness in heaven." See also *Īśa Up.*, 9, 12; *Kaṭha*, II, 5. The Vedic Aryans were like glorious children in their eager acceptance of life. They represent the youth of humanity whose life was still fresh and sweet, undisturbed by disconcerting dreams. They had also the balanced wisdom of maturity. The author however limits his attention to the karmakāṇḍa of the Veda which is not its whole teaching. While the Veda teaches us to work with a desire for recompense whether in a temporary heaven or in a new embodied life, buddhiyoga leads us to release.

44. *bhogaiśvaryaprasaktānāṁ*
tayā 'pahṛtacetasām
vyavasāyātmikā buddhiḥ
samādhau na vidhīyate

(44) The intelligence which discriminates between right and wrong, of those who are devoted to enjoyment and power and whose minds are carried away by these words (of the Veda) is not well-established in the Self (or concentration).

They will not have the one-pointedness of mind in God.[1] The intelligence which is intended to be well trained is seduced from its normal functioning.

45. *traiguṇyaviṣayā vedā*
nistraiguṇyo bhavā 'rjuna
nirdvandvo nityasattvastho
niryogakṣema ātmavān

(45) The action of the three-fold modes is the subject matter of the Veda; but do thou become free, O Arjuna, from this threefold nature; be free from the dualities (the pairs of opposites), be firmly fixed in purity, not caring for acquisition and preservation, and be possessed of the Self.

nityasattva. Arjuna is asked to stand above the modes and be firmly rooted in the sattva. This is not the mode of sattva which Arjuna is asked to go beyond, but is eternal truth. Ś. and R., however, take it to mean the sattvaguṇa. Ritualistic practices necessary for the maintenance of worldly life are the results of the modes. To gain the higher reward of perfection, we must direct our attention to the Supreme Reality. The conduct of the liberated, however, will be outwardly the same as that of one who is in the sattva condition. His action will be calm and disinterested. He acts with no interest in the fruits of action; not so the followers of the karmakāṇḍa of the Veda.

Yogakṣema is acquisition of the new and preservation of the old.[2]

ātmavān: be possessed of the self, ever vigilant.[3] Āpastamba declares that there is nothing higher than the possession of the self.[4] To know the Spirit which has neither commencement nor

[1] Cp. Śrīdhara: *samādhis cittaikāgryam, parameśvarābhimukhatvam iti yāvat; tasmin niścayātmikā buddhis tu na vidhīyate.*

[2] *anupāttasya upādānaṁ yogaḥ, upāttasya rakṣaṇaṁ kṣemaḥ.*

[3] *apramattaś ca bhava.* Ś.

[4] *ātmalābhān na paraṁ vidyate. Dharma Sūtra,* I, 7, 2.

decay, the Spirit which is immortal, to know Him whom we do not know is the true end of man. If we suppress this side we are slayers of the self,[1] to use the phrase of the Upaniṣad.

46. *yāvān artha udapāne*
sarvataḥ saṁplutodake
tāvān sarveṣu vedeṣu
brāhmaṇasya vijānataḥ

(46) As is the use of a pond in a place flooded with water everywhere, so is that of all the Vedas for the Brāhmin who understands.

Cp. "Just as one who gets water from the river does not attach importance to a well, so the wise do not attach any importance to ritual action."[2] For those of illumined consciousness, ritual observances are of little value.

Work Without Concern for the Results

47. *karmaṇy evā 'dhikāras te*
mā phaleṣu kadācana
mā karmaphalahetur bhūr
mā te saṅgo 'stv akarmaṇi

(47) To action alone hast thou a right and never at all to its fruits; let not the fruits of action be thy motive; neither let there be in thee any attachment to inaction.

This famous verse contains the essential principle of disinterestedness. When we do our work, plough or paint, sing or think, we will be deflected from disinterestedness, if we think of fame or income or any such extraneous consideration. Nothing matters except the good will, the willing fulfilment of the purpose of God. Success or failure does not depend on the individual but on other factors as well. Giordano Bruno says: "I have fought, that is much, victory is in the hands of fate."

[1] *ātmahano janāḥ.*

[2] *na te (jñāninaḥ) karma praśaṁsanti kūpaṁ nadyām pibann iva.* M.B., *Śāntiparva*, 240, 10.

48. *yogasthaḥ kuru karmāṇi*
saṅgaṁ tyaktvā dhanaṁjaya
siddhyasiddhyoḥ samo bhūtvā
samatvaṁ yoga ucyate

(48) Fixed in yoga, do thy work, O Winner of wealth (Arjuna), abandoning attachment, with an even mind in success and failure, for evenness of mind is called yoga.

yogasthaḥ: steadfast in inner composure.

samatvam: inner poise. It is self-mastery. It is conquest of anger, sensitiveness, pride and ambition.

We must work with a perfect serenity indifferent to the results. He who acts by virtue of an inner law is on a higher level than one whose action is dictated by his whims.

Those who do works for the sake of their fruits go to the region of the fathers or pitṛs, those who pursue wisdom go to the region of the gods or devas.[1]

49. *dūreṇa hy avaraṁ karma*
buddhiyogād dhanaṁjaya
buddhau śaraṇam anviccha
kṛpaṇāḥ phalahetavaḥ

(49) Far inferior indeed is mere action to the discipline of intelligence (buddhiyoga), O Winner of wealth (Arjuna), seek refuge in intelligence. Pitiful are those who seek for the fruits (of their action).

buddhiyoga. See also XVIII, 57.

50. *buddhiyukto jahātī 'ha*
ubhe sukṛtaduṣkṛte
tasmād yogāya yujyasva
yogaḥ karmasu kauśalam

(50) One who has yoked his intelligence (with the Divine) (or is established in his intelligence) casts away even here

[1] Cp. Ś. *dviprakāraṁ ca vittaṁ mānusaṁ daivaṁ ca, tatra mānusaṁ vittaṁ karmarūpam pitṛlokaprāptisādhanam, vidyāṁ ca daivaṁ vittam devalokaprāptisādhanam.* II, 11.

both good and evil. Therefore strive for yoga, yoga is skill in action.

He rises to a status higher than the ethical with its distinction of good and evil. He is rid of selfishness and therefore is incapable of evil. According to Ś., Yoga is evenness of mind in success or failure, possessed by one who is engaged in the performance of his proper duties, while his mind rests in God.[1]

51. *karmajaṁ buddhiyuktā hi*
phalaṁ tyaktvā manīṣiṇaḥ
janmabandhavinirmuktāḥ
padaṁ gacchanty anāmayam

(51) The wise who have united their intelligence (with the Divine) renouncing the fruits which their action yields and freed from the bonds of birth reach the sorrowless state.

Even when alive, they are released from the bond of birth and go to the highest state of Viṣṇu called mokṣa or liberation, which is free from all evil.[2]

52. *yadā te mohakalilaṁ*
buddhir vyatitariṣyati
tadā gantāsi nirvedaṁ
śrotavyasya śrutasya ca

(52) When thy intelligence shall cross the turbidity of delusion, then shalt thou become indifferent to what has been heard and what is yet to be heard.

Scriptures are unnecessary for the man who has attained the insight. See II, 46; VI, 44. He who attains the wisdom of the Supreme passes beyond the range of the Vedas and the Upaniṣads, *śabdabrahmātivartate*.

[1] *svadharmākhyeṣu karmasu vartamānasya yā siddhyasiddhyoḥ samatvabuddhir īśvarārpitacetas tayā.*

Cp. Śrīdhara. *karmajaṁ phalaṁ tyaktvā kevalam īśvarārādhanārtham eva karma kurvāṇā manīṣiṇo jñānino bhūtvā janmarūpeṇa bandhena vinirmuktāḥ.*

[2] *jīvanta eva janmabandhavinirmuktāḥ santaḥ padaṁ paramaṁ viṣṇor mokṣākhyaṁ gacchanty anāmayam sarvopadravarahitam.* Ś.

53. *śrutivipratipannā te*
yadā sthāsyati niścalā
samādhāv acalā buddhis
tadā yogam avāpsyasi

(53) When thy intelligence, which is bewildered by the Vedic texts, shall stand unshaken and stable in spirit (samādhi), then shalt thou attain to insight (yoga).

śrutivipratipannā: bewildered by the Vedic texts. As different schools of thought and practice profess to derive support from the Vedas, they bewilder.

samādhi is not loss of consciousness but the highest kind of consciousness.[1] The object with which the mind is in communion is the Divine Self. Buddhiyoga is the method by which we get beyond Vedic ritualism and do our duty without any attachment for the results of our action. We must act but with equanimity which is more important than any action. The question is not what shall we do, but how shall we do? In what spirit shall we act?

The Characteristics of the Perfect Sage

arjuna uvāca

54 *sthitaprajñasya kā bhāṣā*
samādhisthasya keśava
sthitadhīḥ kiṁ prabhāṣeta
kim āsīta vrajeta kim

Arjuna said:

(54) What is the description of the man who has this firmly founded wisdom, whose being is steadfast in spirit, O Keśava (Kṛṣṇa)? How should the man of settled intelligence speak, how should he sit, how should he walk?

In the Hindu scheme of life, there is the last stage of saṁnyāsa where the ritual is abandoned and social obligations surrendered. The first stage is that of student discipleship, the second that of the householder, the third that of retreat and the fourth and

[1] It is what Plato means when he exhorts the soul to "collect and concentrate itself in its self." *Phaedo,* 83A.

the last is that of total renunciation. Those who abandon the household life and adopt the homeless one are the renouncers. This state may be entered upon at any time, though normally it comes after the passage through the other three stages. The saṁnyāsins literally die to the world and even funeral rites are performed when they leave their homes and become parivrājakas or homeless wanderers. These developed souls, by their very example, affect the society to which they no longer belong. They form the conscience of society. Their utterance is free and their vision untrammelled. Though they have their roots in the Hindu religious organization, they grow above it and by their freedom of mind and universality of outlook are a challenge to the corrupting power and cynical compromise of the authoritarians. Their supersocial life is a witness to the validity of ultimate values from which other social values derive. They are the sages, and Arjuna asks for some discernible signs, some distinguishing marks of such developed souls.

śrībhagavān uvāca

55. *prajahāti yadā kāmān*
sarvān pārtha manogatān
ātmany evā 'tmanā tuṣṭaḥ
sthitaprajñas tado 'cyate

The Blessed Lord said:

(55) When a man puts away all the desires of his mind, O Pārtha (Arjuna), and when his spirit is content in itself, then is he called stable in intelligence.

Negatively, the state is one of freedom from selfish desires and positively, it is one of concentration on the Supreme.

56. *duḥkheṣv anudvignamanāḥ*
sukheṣu vigataspṛhaḥ
vītarāgabhayakrodhaḥ
sthitadhīr munir ucyate

(56) He whose mind is untroubled in the midst of sorrows and is free from eager desire amid pleasures, he from whom passion, fear, and rage have passed away, he is called a sage of settled intelligence.

It is self-mastery, conquest of desire and passion that is insisted on.[1]

57. *yaḥ sarvatrā 'nabhisnehas*
tat-tat prāpya śubhāśubham
nā 'bhinandati na dveṣṭi
tasya prajñā pratiṣṭhitā

(57) He who is without affection on any side, who does not rejoice or loathe as he obtains good or evil, his intelligence is firmly set (in wisdom).

Flowers bloom and they fade. There is no need to praise the former and condemn the latter. We must receive whatever comes without excitement, pain or revolt.

58. *yadā saṁharate cā 'yaṁ*
kūrmo 'ṅgānī 'va sarvaśaḥ
indriyāṇī 'ndriyārthebhyas
tasya prajñā pratiṣṭhitā

(58) He who draws away the senses from the objects of sense on every side as a tortoise draws in his limbs (into the shell), his intelligence is firmly set (in wisdom).

59. *viṣayā vinivartante*
nirāhārasya dehinaḥ
rasavarjaṁ raso 'py asya
paraṁ dṛṣṭvā nivartate

(59) The objects of sense turn away from the embodied soul who abstains from feeding on them but the taste for them remains. Even the taste turns away when the Supreme is seen.

The author is explaining the difference between outer abstention and inner renunciation. We may reject the objects but desire

[1] Cp. Lucretius: "Religion does not consist in turning unceasingly toward the veiled stone, nor in approaching all the altars, nor in throwing oneself prostrate on the ground, nor in raising the hands before the habitations of gods, nor in deluging the temples with the blood of beasts, nor in heaping vows upon vows; but in beholding all with a peaceful soul." *De rerum Natura.*

for them may remain. Even the desire is lost when the Supreme is seen.[1] The control should be both on the body and the mind. Liberation from the tyranny of the body is not enough; we must be liberated from the tyranny of desires also.

60. *yatato hy api kaunteya*
puruṣasya vipaścitaḥ
indriyāṇi pramāthīni
haranti prasabhaṁ manaḥ

(60) Even though a man may ever strive (for perfection) and be ever so discerning, O Son of Kuntī (Arjuna), his impetuous senses will carry off his mind by force.

61. *tāni sarvāṇi saṁyamya*
yukta āsīta matparaḥ
vaśe hi yasye 'ndriyāṇi
tasya prajñā pratiṣṭhitā

(61) Having brought all (the senses) under control, he should remain firm in yoga intent on Me; for he, whose senses are under control, his intelligence is firmly set.

matparaḥ: another reading is *tatparaḥ.*

Self-discipline is not a matter of intelligence. It is a matter of will and emotions. Self-discipline is easy when there is vision of the Highest. See XII, 5. The original Yoga was theistic. Cp. also *Yoga Sūtra,* I, 24. *kleśakarmavipākakṣayair aparāmṛṣṭaḥ puruṣaviśeṣa iśvaraḥ.*

62. *dhyāyato viṣayān puṁsaḥ*
saṅgas teṣū 'pajāyate
saṅgāt saṁjāyate kāmaḥ
kāmāt krodho 'bhijāyate

(62) When a man dwells in his mind on the objects of sense, attachment to them is produced. From attachment springs desire and from desire comes anger.

[1] Cp. Kālidāsa: "They whose minds are not disturbed when the sources of disturbance are present, are the truly brave."

vikārahetau sati vikriyante
yesāṁ na cetāṁsi ta eva dhīrāh.

Kumārasaṁbhava, I, 59.

kāma: desire. Desires may prove to be as resistless as the most powerful external forces. They may lift us into glory or hurl us into disgrace.

63. *krodhād bhavati saṁmohaḥ*
saṁmohāt smṛtivibhramaḥ
smṛtibhraṁśād buddhināśo
buddhināśāt praṇaśyati

(63) From anger arises bewilderment, from bewilderment loss of memory; and from loss of memory, the destruction of intelligence and from the destruction of intelligence he perishes.

buddhināśa: destruction of intelligence. It is failure to discriminate between right and wrong.

When the soul is overcome by passion, its memory is lost, its intelligence is obscured and the man is ruined. What is called for is not a forced isolation from the world or destruction of sense life but an inward withdrawal. To hate the senses is as wrong as to love them. The horses of senses are not to be unyoked from the chariot but controlled by the reins of the mind.

64. *rāgadveṣaviyuktais tu*
viṣayān indriyaiś caran
ātmavaśyair vidheyātmā
prasādam adhigacchati

(64) But a man of disciplined mind, who moves among the objects of sense, with the senses under control and free from attachment and aversion, he attains purity of spirit.

See V, 8. The sthitaprajña has no selfish aims or personal hopes. He is not disturbed by the touches of outward things. He accepts what happens without attachment or repulsion. He covets nothing, is jealous of none. He has no desires and makes no demands.[1]

[1] Cp. with this the following description of disciplined seers or ṛṣis.

ūrdhvaretās tapasyugro niyatāśī ca saṁyamī
śāpānugrahayoś śaktah satyasandho bhaved ṛṣiḥ
taponirdhūtapāpmānaḥ tathyā tathyābhidhāyinaḥ
vedavedāngatattvajnā ṛṣayah parikīrtitāḥ

65. *prasāde sarvaduḥkhānāṁ*
hānir asyo 'pajāyate
prasannacetaso hy āśu
buddhiḥ paryavatiṣṭhate

(65) And in that purity of spirit, there is produced for him an end of all sorrow; the intelligence of such a man of pure spirit is soon established (in the peace of the self).

66. *nā 'sti buddhir ayuktasya*
na cā 'yuktasya bhāvanā
na cā 'bhāvayataḥ śāntir
aśāntasya kutaḥ sukham

(66) For the uncontrolled, there is no intelligence; nor for the uncontrolled is there the power of concentration and for him without concentration, there is no peace and for the unpeáceful, how can there be happiness?

67. *indriyāṇāṁ hi caratāṁ*
yan mano 'nuvidhīyate
tad asya harati prajñāṁ
vāyur nāvam ivā 'mbhasi

(67) When the mind runs after the roving senses, it carries away the understanding, even as a wind carries away a ship on the waters.

68. *tasmād yasya mahābāho*
nigṛhītāni sarvaśaḥ
indriyāṇī 'ndriyārthebhyas
tasya prajñā pratiṣṭhitā

(68) Therefore, O Mighty-armed (Arjuna), he whose senses are all withdrawn from their objects his intelligence is firmly set.

69. *yā niśā sarvabhūtānāṁ*
tasyāṁ jāgarti saṁyamī
yasyāṁ jāgrati bhūtāni
sā niśā paśyato muneḥ

(69) What is night for all beings is the time of waking for

the disciplined soul; and what is the time of waking for all beings is night for the sage who sees (or the sage of vision).

When all beings are attracted by the glitter of sense-objects, the sage is intent on understanding reality. He is wakeful to the nature of reality to which the unwise is asleep or indifferent. The life of opposites which is the day or condition of activity for the unenlightened is night, a darkness of the soul to the wise. Cp. Goethe: "Error stands in the same relation to truth as sleeping to waking."

70. *āpūryamāṇam acalapratiṣṭhaṁ*
samudram āpaḥ praviśanti yadvat
tadvat kāmā yaṁ praviśanti sarve
sa śāntim āpnoti na kāmakāmī

(70) He unto whom all desires enter as waters into the sea, which, though ever being filled is ever motionless, attains to peace and not he who hugs his desires.

71. *vihāya kāmān yaḥ sarvān*
pumāṁś carati niḥspṛhaḥ
nirmamo nirahaṁkāraḥ
sa śāntim adhigacchati

(71) He who abandons all desires and acts free from longing, without any sense of mineness or egotism, he attains to peace.

Cp. the well-known saying of the *Upaniṣad.* "The human mind is of two kinds, pure and impure. That which is intent on securing its desires is impure; that which is free from attachment to desires is pure."[1]

carati: acts. He freely and readily spends himself without measure for something intuitively apprehended as great and noble.

śāntim: peace; the suppression of all the troubles of earthly existence.[2]

[1] *mano hi dvividhaṁ proktaṁ śuddhaṁ cāśuddham eva ca*
aśuddhaṁ kāmasaṁkalpaṁ śuddhaṁ kāmavivarjitam.

[2] *sarvasaṁsāraduḥkhoparamatvalakṣaṇāṁ, nirvāṇākhyām.* Ś.

72. *eṣā brāhmī sthitiḥ pārtha*
nai 'nāṁ prāpya vimuhyati
sthitvā 'syām antakāle 'pi
brahmanirvāṇam ṛcchati

(72) This is the divine state (brāhmīsthiti) O Pārtha (Arjuna), having attained thereto, one is (not again) bewildered; fixed in that state at the end (at the hour of death) one can attain to the bliss of God (brahmanirvāṇa).

brāhmīsthiti: life eternal.
nirvāṇam, mokṣam. Ś.
nirgataṁ vānaṁ gamanaṁ yasmin prāpye brahmaṇi tan nirvāṇam. Nīlakaṇṭha.

Nirvāṇa has been used to indicate the state of perfection in Buddhism. *Dhammapada* says: Health is the greatest gain, contentment is the greatest wealth, faith is the best friend and nirvāṇa is the highest happiness.[1]

These saints have points in common with the superman of Nietzsche, with the deity-bearers of Alexander. Joy, serenity, the consciousness of inward strength and of liberation, courage and energy of purpose and a constant life in God are their characteristics. They represent the growing point of human evolution. They proclaim, by their very existence, character and consciousness, that humanity can rise above its assumed limitations, that the tide of evolution is pushing forward to a new high level. They give us the sanction of example and expect us to rise above our present selfishness and corruption.

Wisdom is the supreme means of liberation, but this wisdom

[1] 204. See also M.B., 14, 543.
vihāya sarvasaṁkalpān buddhyā śārīramānasān
sa vai nirvāṇam āpnoti nirindhana ivānalaḥ.

Cp. Plato: "If the soul takes its departure in a state of purity, not carrying with it any clinging impurities which during life, it never willingly shared in, but always avoided; gathering itself into itself and making this separation from the body its aim and study . . . well then, so prepared the soul departs to that invisible region of the Divine, the Immortal, and the wise." *Phaedo*, Sec. 68.

The descriptions of the ideal man, the jñānin, the sthitaprajña, the yogārūḍha, the guṇātīta or the bhakta agree in all essentials. See VI, 4–32; X, 9–10; XII, 13–20; XIII, 7–11; XIV, 21–35; XVI, 1–3; XVIII, 50–60.

is not exclusive of devotion to God and desireless work. Even while alive, the sage rests in Brahman, and is released from the unrest of the world. The sage of steady wisdom lives a life of disinterested service.

iti . . . sāṁkhyayogo nāma dvitīyo 'dhyāyah

This is the second chapter entitled The Yoga of Knowledge.

CHAPTER III

Karma Yoga or the Method of Work

Why then work at all?

arjuna uvāca

1. *jyāyasī cet karmaṇas te*
matā buddhir janārdana
tat kiṁ karmaṇi ghore māṁ
niyojayasi keśava

Arjuna said:

(1) If thou deemest that (the path of) understanding is more excellent than (the path of) action, O Janārdana (Kṛṣṇa), why then dost thou urge me to do this savage deed, O Keśava (Kṛṣṇa)?

Arjuna misunderstands the teaching that work for reward is less excellent than work without attachment and desire and believes that Kṛṣṇa is of the view that knowledge without action is better than work and asks, if you think that knowledge is superior to action, why do you ask me to engage in this frightful work? If the Sāṁkhya method of gaining wisdom is superior, then action is an irrelevance.

2. *vyāmiśreṇe 'va vākyena*
buddhiṁ mohayasī 'va me
tad ekaṁ vada niścitya
yena śreyo 'ham āpnuyām

(2) With an apparently confused utterance thou seemest to bewilder my intelligence. Tell (me) then decisively the one thing by which I can attain to the highest good.

iva: confusion is only seeming. It is not the intention of the teacher to confuse Arjuna but yet Arjuna is confused.[1]

[1] *paramakāruṇikasya tava mohakatvaṁ nasty eva, tathāpi bhrāntyā mamaivam bhātītī'vaśabdenoktam.* Śrīdhara.

Life is Work; Unconcern for Results is Needful

śrībhagavān uvāca

3. *loke 'smin dvividhā niṣṭhā*
purā proktā mayā 'nagha
jñānayogena sāṁkhyānāṁ
karmayogena yoginām

The Blessed Lord said:

(3) O, blameless One, in this world a two-fold way of life has been taught of yore by Me, the path of knowledge for men of contemplation and that of works for men of action.

The teacher distinguishes, as modern psychologists do, two main types of seekers, introverts whose natural tendency is to explore the inner life of spirit and extroverts whose natural bias is towards work in the outer world. Answering to these, we have the yoga of knowledge, for those whose inner being is bent towards flights of deep spiritual contemplation, and the yoga of action for energetic personalities with love of action. But this distinction is not ultimate, for all men are in different degrees both introverts and extroverts.

For the *Gītā*, the path of works is a means of liberation quite as efficient as that of knowledge, and these are intended for two classes of people. They are not exclusive but complementary. The path is one whole including different phases. Cp. "Such are the two modes of life, both of which are supported by the Vedas—the one is the activistic path; the other that of renunciation."[1] The two modes of life are of equal value. The teacher points out that jñāna or wisdom is not incompatible with karma or action. Ś. admits that work is compatible with enlightenment. Work is adopted not as a means to the gaining of wisdom but as an example to the ordinary people. In the work of the enlightened as in that of the teacher of the *Gītā*, the self-sense and expectation of reward are absent.[2]

[1] *dvāv imav atha panthānau yasmin vedāḥ pratiṣṭhitāḥ*
pravṛttilakṣaṇo dharmaḥ nivṛttis ca vibhāṣitaḥ.
M.B., *Śāntiparva*, 240, 6.

[2] Abhinavagupta quotes this verse.
na kriyārahitaṁ jñānāṁ na jñānarahitā kriyā
jñānakriyāviniṣpannā ācāryaḥ paśupāśahā.
S.B.G., II, 11.

4. *na karmaṇām anārambhān*
naiṣkarmyaṁ puruṣo 'śnute
na ca saṁnyasanād eva
siddhiṁ samadhigacchati

(4) Not by abstention from work does a man attain freedom from action; nor by mere renunciation does he attain to his perfection.

Naiṣkarmya is the state where one is unaffected by work. The natural law is that we are bound by the results of our actions. Every action has its natural reaction and so is a source of bondage committing the soul to the world of becoming and preventing its union with the Supreme through the transcendence of the world. What is demanded is not renunciation of works, but renunciation of selfish desire.

5. *na hi kaścit kṣaṇam api*
jātu tiṣṭhaty akarmakṛt
kāryate hy avaśaḥ karma
sarvaḥ prakṛtijair guṇaiḥ

(5) For no one can remain even for a moment without doing work; every one is made to act helplessly by the impulses born of nature.

So long as we lead embodied lives, we cannot escape from action. Without work life cannot be sustained.[1] Ānandagiri points out that he who knows the self is not moved by the guṇas, but he who has not controlled the body and the senses is driven to action by the guṇas.

By implication the view that the released soul ceases to work, as all work is a derogation from the supreme state, a return to ignorance, is rejected. While life remains, action is unavoidable. Thinking is an act; living is an act—and these acts cause many effects. To be free from desire, from the illusion of personal interest, is the true non-action and not the physical abstention from

[1] Cp. "The eye cannot choose but see,
We cannot bid the ear be still,
Our bodies feel where'er they be
Against or with our will."
Wordsworth.

activity. When it is said that works cease for a man who is liberated, all that is meant is that he has no further personal necessity for works. It does not mean that he flees from action and takes refuge in blissful inaction. He works as God works, without any binding necessity or compelling ignorance, and even in performing work, he is not involved. When his egoism is removed, action springs from the depths and is governed by the Supreme secretly seated in his heart. Free from desire and attachment, one with all beings, he acts out of the profoundest depths of his inner being, governed by his immortal, divine, highest self.

6. *karmendriyāṇi saṁyamya*
ya āste manasā smaran
indriyārthān vimūḍhātmā
mithyācāraḥ sa ucyate

(6) He who restrains his organs of action but continues in his mind to brood over the objects of sense, whose nature is deluded is said to be a hypocrite (a man of false conduct).

We may control outwardly our activities but if we do not restrain the desires which impel them, we have failed to grasp the true meaning of restraint.

7. *yas tv indriyāṇi manasā*
niyamyā 'rabhate 'rjuna
karmendriyaiḥ karmayogam
asaktaḥ sa viśiṣyate

(7) But he who controls the senses by the mind, O Arjuna, and without attachment engages the organs of action in the path of work, he is superior.

The human will can triumph over the rigidity of law. We should not look upon the things of the world as means to our satisfaction. If we are to recover our lost equanimity, our lost integrity, our lost innocence we must see all things as manifestations of the Real and not as objects to be grasped and possessed. To develop this attitude of non-attachment to things, contemplation is essential.

In verse 6 the Lord condemns mere outer renunciation and in this verse commends the true spirit of inward detachment.

The Importance of Sacrifice

8. *niyatam kuru karma tvam*
karma jyāyo hy akarmaṇaḥ
śarīrayātrā 'pi ca te
na prasidhyed akarmaṇaḥ

(8) Do thou thy allotted work, for action is better than inaction; even the maintenance of thy physical life cannot be effected without action.

9. *yajñārthāt karmaṇo 'nyatra*
loko 'yam karmabandhanaḥ
tadartham karma kaunteya
muktasaṅgaḥ samācara

(9) Save work done as and for a sacrifice this world is in bondage to work. Therefore, O son of Kuntī (Arjuna), do thy work as a sacrifice, becoming free from all attachment.

Ś. equates yajña with Viṣṇu.

R. interprets it literally as sacrifice.

All work is to be done in a spirit of sacrifice, for the sake of the Divine. Admitting the Mīmāmsā demand that we should perform action for the purpose of sacrifices, the *Gītā* asks us to do such action without entertaining any hope of reward. In such cases the inevitable action has no binding power. Sacrifice itself is interpreted in a larger sense. We have to sacrifice the lower mind to the higher. The religious duty towards the Vedic gods here becomes service of creation in the name of the Supreme.

10. *sahayajñāḥ prajāḥ sṛṣṭvā*
puro 'vāca prajāpatiḥ
anena prasaviṣyadhvam
eṣa vo 'stv iṣṭakāmadhuk

(10) In ancient days the Lord of creatures created men along with sacrifice and said, "By this shall ye bring forth and this shall be unto you that which will yield the milk of your desires."

Kāmadhuk is the mythical cow of Indra from which one can get all one desires. By doing one's allotted duty one can be saved.

11. *devān bhāvayatā 'nena*
te devā bhāvayantu vaḥ
parasparaṁ bhāvayantaḥ
śreyaḥ param avāpsyatha

(11) By this foster ye the gods and let the gods foster you; thus fostering each other you shall attain to the supreme good.

See M.B., *Śāntiparva*, 340, 59–62, where the mutual dependence of gods and men is described in similar terms.

12. *iṣṭān bhogān hi vo devā*
dāsyante yajñabhāvitāḥ
tair dattān apradāyai 'bhyo
yo bhuṅkte stena eva saḥ

(12) Fostered by sacrifice the gods will give you the enjoyments you desire. He who enjoys these gifts without giving to them in return is verily a thief.

13. *yajñaśiṣṭāśinaḥ santo*
mucyante sarvakilbiṣaiḥ
bhuñjate te tv aghaṁ pāpā
ye pacanty ātmakāraṇāt

(13) The good people who eat what is left from the sacrifice are released from all sins but those wicked people who prepare food for their own sake—verily they eat sin.

Cp. *Manu*, III, 76, 118.[1]

14. *annād bhavanti bhūtāni*
parjanyād annasaṁbhavaḥ
yajñād bhavati parjanyo
yajñaḥ karmasamudbhavaḥ

(14) From food creatures come into being; from rain is the birth of food; from sacrifice rain comes into being and sacrifice is born of work.

Cp. *Manu*, III, 76.

[1] Cp. *Ṛg. Veda: kevalāgho bhavati kevalādi.* X, 117, 6.

15. *karma brahmodbhavaṁ viddhi*
brahmā 'kṣarasamudbhavam
tasmāt sarvagataṁ brahma
nityaṁ yajñe pratiṣṭhitam

(15) Know the origin of karma (of the nature of sacrifices) to be in Brahma (the Veda) and the Brahma springs from the Imperishable. Therefore the Brahma, which comprehends all, ever centres round the sacrifice.

Action is rooted in the Imperishable. But for the action of the Supreme, the world will fall into ruin. The world is a great sacrifice. We read in the *Ṛg Veda* (X, 90) that the One Puruṣa was offered as a sacrifice and his limbs were scattered to all the quarters of space. By this great sacrifice, the world's pattern is kept up. Action is a moral as well as a physical necessity for embodied beings.[1]

Brahma is also taken to be prakṛti as in XIV, 3–4. Nature springs from the Divine and the entire activity of the world is traceable to it.

16. *evaṁ pravartitaṁ cakraṁ*
nā 'nuvartayatī 'ha yaḥ
aghāyur indriyārāmo
moghaṁ pārtha sa jīvati

(16) He who does not, in this world, help to turn the wheel thus set in motion, is evil in his nature, sensual in his delight, and he, O Pārtha (Arjuna), lives in vain.

In these verses the Vedic conception of sacrifice as an interchange between gods and men is set in the larger context of the interdependence of beings in the cosmos. The deeds done in the sacrificial spirit are pleasing to God. God is the enjoyer of all sacrifices.[2] *yajño vai viṣṇuḥ*.[3] Sacrifice is the Supreme. It is also the law of life. The individual and the cosmos depend on each other. There is a constant interchange between human life and world life. He who works for himself lives in vain. The world is

[1] Śrīdhara says: *yajamānādi vyāpārarūpaṁ karma brahma vedaḥ; karma tasmāt pravṛttam.*

[2] See V, 29.

[3] *Taittirīya Saṁhitā*, I, 7, 4.

in progress because of this co-operation between the human and the divine. Only the sacrifice is not to the deities but to the Supreme of whom the deities are varied forms. In IV, 24, it is said that the act and the materials of the sacrifice, the giver and the receiver, the goal and the object of the sacrifice are all Brahman.

Be Satisfied in the Self

17. *yas tv ātmaratir eva syād*
ātmatṛptaś ca mānavaḥ
ātmany eva ca saṁtuṣṭas
tasya kāryaṁ na vidyate

(17) But the man whose delight is in the Self alone, who is content with the Self, who is satisfied with the Self, for him there exists no work that needs to be done.

He is freed from a sense of duty. He works not out of a sense of duty or for the progressive transformation of his being but because his perfected nature issues spontaneously in action.

18. *nai 'va tasya kṛtenā 'rtho*
nā 'kṛtene 'ha kaścana
na cā 'sya sarvabhūteṣu
kaścid arthavyapāśrayaḥ.

(18) Similarly, in this world he has no interest whatever to gain by the actions that he has done and none to be gained by the actions that he has not done. He does not depend on all these beings for any interest of his.

The next verse indicates that, though the liberated man has nothing to gain by action or non-action and is perfectly happy in the possession and enjoyment of Self, there is such a thing as desireless action which he undertakes for the welfare of the world.

19. *tasmād asaktaḥ satataṁ*
kāryaṁ karma samācara
asakto hy ācaran karma
param āpnoti pūruṣaḥ

(19) Therefore, without attachment, perform always the work that has to be done, for man attains to the highest by doing work without attachment.

Here work done without attachment is marked as superior to work done in a spirit of sacrifice which is itself higher than work done with selfish aims. Even the emancipated souls do work as the occasion arises.[1]

While this verse says that the man reaches the Supreme, param, performing actions, without attachment, Ś. holds that karma helps us to attain purity of mind which leads to salvation. It takes us to perfection indirectly through the attainment of purity of mind.[2]

Set an Example to Others

20. *karmaṇai 'va hi saṁsiddhim*
āsthitā janakādayaḥ
lokasaṁgraham evā 'pi
saṁpaśyan kartum arhasi

(20) It was even by works that Janaka and others attained to perfection. Thou shouldst do works also with a view to the maintenance of the world.

Janaka was the king of Mithilā and father of Sītā, the wife of Rāma. Janaka ruled, giving up his personal sense of being the worker. Even Ś. says that Janaka and others worked lest people at large might go astray, convinced that their senses were engaged in activity, *guṇā guṇeṣu vartante.* Even those who have not known the truth might adopt works for self-purification. II, 10.

lokasaṁgraha: world-maintenance. Lokasaṁgraha stands for the unity of the world, the interconnectedness of society. If the world is not to sink into a condition of physical misery and moral degradation, if the common life is to be decent and dignified, religious ethics must control social action. The aim of religion is to spiritualize society, to establish a brotherhood on earth.

[1] Cp. *Yogavāśiṣṭha.* "The knower has nothing to gain either by performing or by abstaining from action. Therefore he performs action as it arises." Again, "To me it is just the same whether something is done or not. Why should I insist on not performing action? I perform whatever comes to me."

jñasya nārthaḥ karmatyāgaiḥ nārthaḥ karmasamāśrayaiḥ
tena sthitaṁ yathā yad yat tat tathaiva karoty asau. VI, 199.
mama nāsti kṛtenārtho nākṛteneha kaścana
yathā prāptena tiṣṭhāmi hy akarmaṇi ka āgrahaḥ. Ibid., 216.

[2] *sattvaśuddhidvāreṇa.* See also S.B.G., III, 4.

We must be inspired by the hope of embodying ideals in earthly institutions. When the Indian world lost its youth, it tended to become other-worldly. In a tired age we adopt the gospel of renunciation and endurance. In an age of hope and energy we emphasize active service in the world and the saving of civilization. Boethius affirms that "he will never go to heaven who is content to go alone."

21. *yad-yad ācarati śreṣṭhas*
tad-tad eve 'taro janaḥ
sa yat pramāṇaṁ kurute
lokas tad anuvartate

(21) Whatsoever a great man does, the same is done by others as well. Whatever standard he sets, the world follows.

Common people imitate the standards set by the elect. Democracy has become confused with disbelief in great men. The *Gītā* points out that the great men are the pathmakers who blaze the trail that other men follow. The light generally comes through individuals who are in advance of society. They see the light shining on the mountain heights while their fellows sleep in the valley below. They are, in the words of Jesus, the "salt," the "leaven," the "light" of human communities. When they proclaim the splendour of that light, a few recognize it and slowly the many are persuaded to follow them.

22. *na me pārthā 'sti kartavyaṁ*
triṣu lokeṣu kiṁcana
nā 'navāptam avāptavyaṁ
varta eva ca karmaṇi

(22) There is not for me, O Pārtha (Arjuna), any work in the three worlds which has to be done nor anything to be obtained which has not been obtained; yet I am engaged in work.

Life of God and life of the world are not opposed to each other.[1]

[1] Cp. M.B. In the name of my lordship, I slave for the whole world, *dāsyam aiśvaryavādena jñātināṁ tu karomy aham.*

Cp. M.B., III, 313, 17.

tarko'pratiṣṭhaḥ śrutayo vibhinnā naiko munir yasyavacaḥ pramāṇam
dharmasya tattvaṁ nihitaṁ guhāyāṁ mahājano yena gataḥ sa panthāḥ.

23. *yadi hy ahaṁ na varteyaṁ*
jātu karmaṇy atandritaḥ
mama vartmā 'nuvartante
manuṣyāḥ pārtha sarvaśaḥ

(23) For, if ever I did not engage in work unwearied, O Pārtha (Arjuna), men in every way follow my path.

24. *utsīdeyur ime lokā*
na kuryāṁ karma ced aham
saṁkarasya ca kartā syām
upahanyām imāḥ prajāḥ

(24) If I should cease to work, these worlds would fall in ruin and I should be the creator of disordered life and destroy these people.

God, by His incessant activity, preserves the world and prevents it from falling back into non-existence.[1]

25. *saktāḥ karmaṇy avidvāṁso*
yathā kurvanti bhārata
kuryād vidvāṁs tathā 'saktaś
cikīrṣur lokasaṁgraham

(25) As the unlearned act from attachment to their work, so should the learned also act, O Bhārata (Arjuna), but without any attachment, with the desire to maintain the world-order.

Though the soul which is centred in the light has nothing further to accomplish for itself, it unites itself with the cosmic action, even as the Divine does. Its activity will be inspired by the light and joy of the Supreme.

26. *na buddhibhedaṁ janayed*
ajñānāṁ karmasaṅginām
joṣayet sarvakarmāṇi
vidvān yuktaḥ samācaran

[1] Cp. St. Thomas: "As the production of a thing into existence depends on the will of God, so likewise it depends on His will that things should be preserved; hence if He took away His action from them, all things would be reduced to nothing." *Summa Theol.* I, IX, 2c.

(26) Let him (jñānin) not unsettle the minds of the ignorant who are attached to action. The enlightened man doing all works in a spirit of yoga, should set others to act (as well).

na buddhibhedaṁ janayet: let him not unsettle the minds. Do not weaken religious devotion of any kind. The elements of duty, sacrifice and love seem to be the foundation of every religion. In the lower forms, they may be barely discernible and may centre round certain symbols which are accessories to the principles which they uphold. These symbols are vital to those who believe in them. They become intolerable only if they are imposed on those who cannot accept them and when they are suggested to be absolute and final forms of human thought. The absolute character of theological doctrine is incompatible with the mysterious character of religious truth. Faith is wider than belief. Again, if we know the better and do not adopt it, then we commit a wrong.

When the illiterate bow down to forces of nature, we know that they are bowing to the wrong thing and they are blind to the larger unity of Godhead. And yet they bow to something which is not their little self. Even crude views possess something by which men and women who want to live rightly are helped to do so. Traditional forms charged with historical associations are the vehicles of unspoken convictions, though they may not be well understood. The quality of mind and not the object determines whether the source is religious or not. It is true that every one should reach the highest level but this can be attained generally by slow steps and not by sudden jumps. Besides, our views of religion are not chosen by us. They are determined by our ancestry, upbringing and general environment. We should not speak contemptuously of them. We must approach the followers of simple faiths with reverence and not heedlessly disturb them, for the simple faiths have practical value and spiritual appeal. Modern anthropologists advise us that we should not, in our anxiety to "uplift" the aborigines, deprive them of their innocent joys, their songs and dances, their feasts and festivals. Whatever we should like to do for them, we should do with love and reverence. We must use their restricted apprehensions as steps to the larger vision.

Adopting the view that we should not throw out dirty water until we get in fresh, the Hindu pantheon has accommodated divinities worshipped by the different groups, those of the sky and the sea, the stream and the grove, the legendary figures of the distant past and the tutelary gods and goddesses of villages. In its anxiety to lose nothing in the march of ages, to harmonize every sincere conviction without renouncing any, it has become an immense synthesis combining within itself varied elements and motives. It is not surprising that the religion is full of superstitions, dark and primitive.

The Self is no Doer

27. *prakṛteḥ kriyamāṇāni*
guṇaiḥ karmāṇi sarvaśaḥ
ahaṁkāravimūḍhātmā
kartā 'ham iti manyate

(27) While all kinds of work are done by the modes of nature, he whose soul is bewildered by the self-sense thinks "I am the doer."

prakṛteh: pradhāna of the Sāṁkhya.[1] It is the power of māyā,[2] or the power of the Supreme God.[3]

The deluded soul attributes the acts of prakṛti to itself.[4]

There are different planes of our conscious existence and the self which becomes the ego attributes to itself the agency for actions forgetting the determinism of nature. According to the *Gītā*, when the ego soul is entirely subject to nature, it does not act freely. Body, life and mind belong to the side of the environment.

28. *tattvavit tu mahābāho*
guṇakarmavibhāgayoḥ
guṇā guṇeṣu vartanta
iti matvā na sajjate

[1] *prakṛtiḥ pradhānaṁ sattvarajastamasāṁ guṇānāṁ sāmyāvasthā.* Ś.

[2] *pradhānāśabdena māyāśaktir ucyate.* Ānandagiri.

[3] *prakṛteḥ parameśvaryāḥ sattvarajastamoguṇātmikāyāḥ, devātmaśaktiṁ svaguṇair nigūḍhām iti śrutiprasiddhāyāḥ śakter guṇaiḥ, kāryakāraṇa saṁghātātmakaiḥ.* Nīlakaṇṭha.

prakṛtir māyā sattvarajastamoguṇamayī mithyājñānātmikā pārameśvarī śaktiḥ. Madhusūdana.

[4] *anātmany ātmābhimānī.* Madhusūdana.

(28) But he who knows the true character of the two distinctions (of the soul) from the modes of nature and their works, O Mighty-armed (Arjuna), understanding that it is the modes which are acting on the modes, does not get attached.

Prakṛti and its modes represent the limits of human freedom such as the force of heredity and the pressure of environment. The empirical self is the product of works even as the whole cosmic process is the result of the operation of causes.

29. *prakṛter guṇasaṁmūḍhāḥ*
sajjante guṇakarmasu
tān akṛtsnavido mandān
kṛtsnavin na vicālayet

(29) Those who are misled by the modes of nature get attached to the works produced by them. But let no one who knows the whole unsettle the minds of the ignorant who know only a part.

We should not disturb those who act under the impulsion of nature. They should be slowly delivered from the false identification of the self with the ego subject to nature. The true self is the divine, eternally free and self-aware. The false self is the ego which is a part of nature, which reflects the workings of prakṛti. Here the true self, on the Sāṁkhya analysis, is described as inactive, while prakṛti is active and when puruṣa identifies itself with the activity of prakṛti, the sense of active personality is produced. The *Gītā* does not support the Sāṁkhya view of the withdrawal of puruṣa from prakṛti by complete inaction. Discernment does not imply inaction but it involves action done in a way that does not hinder the attainment of release. If we realize that the ātman or the true self is the detached witness, serene and impartial, no action binds us, though we engage in the great battle against imperfection and sorrow and work for world solidarity.

30. *mayi sarvāṇi karmāṇi*
saṁnyasyā 'dhyātmacetasā
nirāśīr nirmamo bhūtvā
yudhyasva vigatajvaraḥ

(30) Resigning all thy works to Me, with thy consciousness fixed in the Self, being free from desire and egoism, fight, delivered from thy fever.

By self-surrender to the Lord who presides over cosmic existence, and activity, we must engage in work. "Thy will be done" is to be our attitude in all work. We must do the work with the sense that we are the servants of the Lord.[1] See XVIII, 59–60 and 66.

31. *ye me matam idaṁ nityam*
anutiṣṭhanti mānavāḥ
śraddhāvanto 'nasūyanto
mucyante te 'pi karmabhiḥ

(31) Those men, too, who, full of faith and free from cavil, constantly follow this teaching of Mine are released from (the bondage of) works.

32. *ye tv etad abhyasūyanto*
nā 'nutiṣṭhanti me matam
sarvajñānavimūḍhāṁs tān
viddhi naṣṭān acetasaḥ

(32) But those who slight My teaching and do not follow it, know them to be blind to all wisdom, lost and senseless.

Nature and Duty

33. *sadṛśaṁ ceṣṭate svasyāḥ*
prakṛter jñānavān api
prakṛtiṁ yānti bhūtāni
nigrahaḥ kiṁ kariṣyati

(33) Even the man of knowledge acts in accordance with his own nature. Beings follow their nature. What can repression accomplish?

[1] *ahaṁ karteśvarāya bhṛtyavat karomīty anayā buddhyā.* Ś.
īśvarapreritohaṁ karomīty anayā buddhyā. Nīlakaṇṭha.
mayi sarvāṇi karmāṇi nāhaṁ karteti saṁnyasya svatantraḥ parameśvara eva sarvakartā nāhaṁ kaścid iti niścitya. Abhinavagupta.

Prakṛti is the mental equipment with which one is born, as the result of the past acts.[1] This must run its course. Ś. thinks that even God cannot prevent its operation. Even He ordains that the past deeds produce their natural effects.[2]

Restraint cannot avail since actions flow inevitably from the workings of prakṛti and the self is only an impartial witness.

This verse seems to suggest the omnipotence of nature over the soul and requires us to act according to our nature, the law of our being. It does not follow that we should indulge in every impulse. It is a call to find out our true being and give expression to it. We cannot, even if we will, suppress it. Violated nature will take its revenge.

34. *indriyasye 'ndriyasyā 'rthe*
rāgadveṣau vyavasthitau
tayor na vaśam āgacchet
tau hy asya paripanthinau

(34) For (every) sense attachment and aversion are fixed (in regard) to the objects of (that) sense. Let no one come under their sway for they are his (two) waylayers.

Men should act according to buddhi or understanding. If we are victims of our impulses, our life is as aimless and devoid of intelligence as that of the animals. If we do not interfere, attachments and aversions will determine our acts. So long as we act in certain ways because we like them and abstain from others because we dislike them, we will be bound by our actions. But if we overcome these impulses and act from a sense of duty, we are not victims of the play of prakṛti. The exercise of human freedom is conditioned and not cancelled by the necessities of nature.

35. *śreyān svadharmo viguṇaḥ*
paradharmāt svanuṣṭhitāt
svadharme nidhanaṁ śreyaḥ
paradharmo bhayāvahaḥ

(35) Better is one's own law though imperfectly carried out

[1] *prakṛtir nāma pūrvakṛta dharmādharmādi saṁskāro vartamāna-janmādāv abhivyaktaḥ.* Ś.

[2] *aham api pūrvakarmāpekṣayaiva tān pravartayāmīti bhāvaḥ.* Nīlakaṇṭhā.

than the law of another carried out perfectly. Better is death in (the fulfilment of) one's own law for to follow another's law is perilous.

There is more happiness in doing one's own work even without excellence than in doing another's duty well. Each one must try to understand his psychophysical make-up and function in accordance with it. It may not be given to all of us to lay the foundations of systems of metaphysics or clothe lofty thoughts in enduring words. We have not all the same gifts, but what is vital is not whether we are endowed with five talents or only one but how faithfully we have employed the trust committed to us. We must play our part, manfully, be it great or small. Goodness denotes perfection of quality. However distasteful one's duty may be, one must be faithful to it even unto death.

The Enemy is Desire and Anger

arjuna uvāca

36. *atha kena prayukto 'yaṁ*
pāpaṁ carati pūruṣaḥ
anicchann api vārṣṇeya
balād iva niyojitaḥ

Arjuna said:

(36) But by what is a man impelled to commit sin, as if by force, even against his will, O Vārṣṇeya (Kṛṣṇa)?

anicchannapi: even against his will. This is what Arjuna feels, that a man is forced to do things even against his will. But it is not really so. Man tacitly gives his consent as the use of the word kāṃa or craving by the teacher in the next verse indicates. Ś. says: what we speak of as the prakṛti or the nature of a person draws him to its course only through attachment and aversion.[1]

śrībhagavān uvāca

37. *kāma eṣa krodha eṣa*
rajoguṇasamudbhavaḥ
mahāśano mahāpāpmā
viddhy enam iha vairiṇam

[1] *yā hi puruṣasya prakṛtiḥ sā rāgadveṣapurassaraiva svakārye puruṣam pravartayati.* S.B.G., III, 34.

The Blessed Lord said:

(37) This is craving, this is wrath, born of the mode of passion, all devouring and most sinful. Know this to be the enemy here.

38. *dhūmenā 'vriyate vahnir*
yathā 'darśo malena ca
yatho 'lbenā 'vṛto garbhas
tathā tene 'dam āvṛtam

(38) As fire is covered by smoke, as a mirror by dust, as an embryo is enveloped by the womb, so is this covered by that (passion).

idam, this: this wisdom. Ś.
Everything is enveloped by passion.

39. *āvṛtaṁ jñānam etena*
jñānino nityavairiṇā
kāmarūpeṇa kaunteya
duṣpūreṇā 'nalena ca

(39) Enveloped is wisdom, O Son of Kuntī (Arjuna), by this insatiable fire of desire, which is the constant foe of the wise.

Cp. "Desire is never satisfied by the enjoyment of the objects of desire; it grows more and more as does the fire to which fuel is added."[1]

[1] *na jātu kāmaḥ kāmānām upabhogena śāmyati*
haviṣā kṛṣṇavartmeva bhūyaevābhivardhate.
Manu, II, 94.

Cp. Spinoza: "For the things which men, to judge by their actions, deem the highest good are Riches, Fame or Sensual pleasure. Of these the last is followed by satiety and repentance, the other two are never satiated; the more we have, the more we want; while the love of fame compels us to order our lives by the opinions of others. But if a thing is not loved, no quarrels will arise concerning it, no sadness will be felt if it perishes, no envy if another has it, in short no disturbances of the mind. All these spring from the love of that which passes away. But the love of a thing eternal and infinite fills the mind wholly with joy, and is unmingled with sadness. Therefore it is greatly to be desired, and to be sought with all our strength." *De Intellectus Emendations*. The fundamental social crime is appropriation in any form whatever, class privilege, race discrimination or national egotism, for it involves pain to others. There is no answer to Wordsworth,

"Never to blend our pleasure or our pride
With sorrow of the meanest thing that feels."
Hart-Leap Well.

40. *indriyāṇi mano buddhir*
asyā 'dhiṣṭhānam ucyate
etair vimohayaty eṣa
jñānam āvṛtya dehinam

(40) The senses, the mind and the intelligence are said to be its seat. Veiling wisdom by these, it deludes the embodied (soul).

41. *tasmāt tvam indriyāṇy ādau*
niyamya bharatarṣabha
pāpmānaṁ prajahi hy enaṁ
jñānavijñānanāśanam

(41) Therefore, O Best of Bharatas (Arjuna), control thy senses from the beginning and slay this sinful destroyer of wisdom and discrimination.

The wisdom of the Vedānta and the detailed knowledge of the Sāṁkhya may be meant by jñāna and vijñāna. Ś. explains jñāna as "knowledge of the self and other things acquired from the scriptures and the teachers," and vijñāna as "the personal experience, anubhava, of the things so taught."

For R., jñāna relates to ātmasvarūpa or the nature of the self and vijñāna to ātmaviveka or discriminatory knowledge of the self. In the translation here given jñāna is taken as spiritual wisdom and vijñāna as logical knowledge.

Śrīdhara supports both the interpretations.[1]

42. *indriyāṇi parāṇy āhur*
indriyebhyaḥ paraṁ manaḥ
manasas tu parā buddhir
yo buddheḥ paratas tu saḥ

(42) The senses, they say, are great, greater than the senses is the mind, greater than the mind is the intelligence but greater than the intelligence is he.

Kaṭha Up., III, 10; see also VI, 7. Consciousness must be raised step by step. The higher we rise the more free we are. If

[1] *jñānam ātmaviṣayaṁ, vijñānaṁ śāstrīyam . . . yadvā jñānaṁ śāstrācāryopadeśajaṁ, vijñānaṁ nididhyāsanajam.* Cp. *Amarakośa: mokṣe dhīḥ jñānam anyatra vijñānaṁ śilpaśāstrayoḥ.*

we act under the sway of the senses, we are least free. We are freer when we adopt the dictates of manas; still more free when our manas is united with buddhi; we attain the highest freedom when our acts are determined by buddhi suffused by the light from beyond, the self.

This verse gives us a hierarchy of levels of consciousness.

43. *evaṁ buddheḥ paraṁ buddhvā*
saṁstabhyā 'tmānam ātmanā
jahi śatruṁ mahābāho
kāmarūpaṁ durāsadam

(43) Thus knowing him who is beyond the intelligence, steadying the (lower) self by the Self, smite, O Mighty-armed (Arjuna), the enemy in the form of desire, so hard to get at.

kāma: desire.[1] Control the restless ego by the light of the Eternal Spiritual Self. He who knows becomes truly independent and asks guidance from no other power except his inner light.

This chapter expounds the necessity for the performance of work without any selfish attachment to results, with a view to securing the welfare of the world, with the realization that agency belongs to the modes of prakṛti or to God himself. Such is the view of Yāmunācārya.[2]

iti . . . karmayogo nāma tṛtīyo 'dhyāyah

This is the third chapter entitled The Yoga of Works.

[1] Cp. *kāmamaya evāyam puruṣaḥ.*

[2] *asaktyā lokarakṣāyai guṇeṣvāropya kartṛtām.*
sarveśvare vā nyasyoktā tṛtīye karmakāryatā.

CHAPTER IV

The Way of Knowledge

The Tradition of Jñāna Yoga

śrībhagavān uvāca

1. *imaṁ vivasvate yogaṁ*
proktavān aham avyayam
vivasvān manave prāha
manur ikṣvākave 'bravīt

The Blessed Lord said:

(1) I proclaimed this imperishable yoga to Vivasvān; Vivasvān told it to Manu and Manu spoke it to Ikṣvāku.[1]

2. *evaṁ paramparāprāptam*
imaṁ rājarṣayo viduḥ
sa kālene 'ha mahatā
yogo naṣṭaḥ paraṁtapa

(2) Thus handed down from one to another the royal sages knew it till that yoga was lost to the world through long lapse of time, O Oppressor of the foe (Arjuna).

rājarṣayah: royal sages. Rāma, Kṛṣṇa and Buddha were all princes who taught the highest wisdom.

kālena mahatā: by the great efflux of time. This teaching has become obscured by the lapse of ages. To renovate the faith for the welfare of humanity, great teachers arise. Kṛṣṇa now gives it to his pupil to reawaken faith in him and illumine his ignorance.

A tradition is authentic when it evokes an adequate response to the reality represented by it. It is valid, when our minds thrill and vibrate to it. When it fails to achieve this end, new teachers arise to rekindle it.

3. *sa evā 'yaṁ mayā te 'dya*
yogaḥ proktaḥ purātanaḥ
bhakto 'si me sakhā ce 'ti
rahasyaṁ hy etad uttamam

[1] Cp. M. B. *Śāntiparva:* 348 51–52
tretāyugādau ca tato vivasvān manave dadau
manuś ca lokabhṛtyarthaṁ sutāyekṣvākave dadau
ikṣvākuṇā ca kathito vyāpya lokān avasthitah

(3) This same ancient yoga has been today declared to thee by Me; for thou art My devotee and My friend; and this is the supreme secret.

yogah purātanah: ancient yoga. The teacher declares that he is not stating any new doctrine but is only restoring the old tradition, the eternal verity, handed down from master to pupil. The teaching is a renewal, a rediscovery, a restoration of knowledge long forgotten. All great teachers like Gautama the Buddha and Mahāvīra, Ś. and R. are content to affirm that they are only restating the teachings of their former masters. *Milindapañha* explains that it is an ancient way that had been lost that the Buddha opens up again.[1] When the Buddha returns to his father's capital in an ascetic's garb with a begging bowl in hand, his father asks him: "Why is this?" and the answer comes: "My father, it is the custom of my race." The king in surprise asks: "What race?" and the Buddha answers:

> "The Buddhas who have been and who shall be;
> Of these am I and what they did, I do,
> And this, which now befalls, so fell before
> That at his gate a king in warrior mail
> Should meet his son, a prince in hermit weeds."

The great teachers do not lay claim to originality but affirm that they are expounding the ancient truth which is the final norm by which all teachings are judged, the eternal source of all religions and philosophies, the *philosophia perennis*, the *sanātana dharma*, what Augustine calls the "wisdom that was not made; but is at this present, as it hath ever been and so shall ever be."[2]

bhaktosi me sakhā ceti: Thou art My devotee and My friend. Revelation is never closed. So long as the human heart has qualities of devotion and friendship, God will disclose His secrets to them. Divine self-communication is possible wherever we have sincerity and a sense of need. Religious revelation is not a past event; it is that which continues to be. It is possible for all beings and not the privilege of a few. "Every one that is of the Truth heareth my voice," said Jesus to Pilate.

[1] 217 ff.
[2] *Confessions*, IX, 10.

arjuna uvāca

4. *aparaṁ bhavato janma*
paraṁ janma vivasvataḥ
katham etad vijānīyāṁ
tvam ādau proktavān iti

Arjuna said:

(4) Later was Thy birth and earlier was the birth of Vivasvat. How then am I to understand that thou didst declare it to him in the beginning?

The Buddha claimed to have been the teacher of countless Bodhisattvas in bygone ages. *Saddharmapuṇḍarīka*, XV, 1. Jesus said: "Before Abraham was, I am." *John* viii, 58.

The Theory of Avatārs

śrībhagavān uvāca

5. *bahūni me vyatītāni*
janmāni tava cā 'rjuna
tāny ahaṁ veda sarvāṇi
na tvaṁ vettha paraṁtapa

The Blessed Lord said:

(5) Many are My lives that are past, and thine also, O Arjuna; all of them I know but thou knowest not, O Scourge of the foe (Arjuna).

6. *ajo 'pi sann avyayātmā*
bhūtānām īśvaro 'pi san
prakṛtiṁ svām adhiṣṭhāya
saṁbhavāmy ātmamāyayā

(6) Though (I am) unborn, and My self (is) imperishable, though (I am) the lord of all creatures, yet establishing Myself in My own nature, I come into (empiric) being through My power (māyā).

The embodiments of human beings are not voluntary. Driven by prakṛti through ignorance, they are born again and again.

The Lord controls prakṛti and assumes embodiment through His own free will. The ordinary birth of creatures is determined by the force of prakṛti, *avaśaṁ prakṛter vaśāt,*[1] while the Lord takes birth through his own power, *ātmamāyayā.*

prakṛtim adhiṣṭhāya: establishing in My own nature. He uses His nature in a way which is free from subjection to karma.[2] There is no suggestion here that the becoming of the one is a mere appearance. It is intended realistically. It is an actual becoming by māyā, "the capacity to render the impossible actual."

Ś.'s view that "I appear to be born and embodied, through My own power but not in reality unlike others"[3] is not satisfactory. Yogamāyā refers to the free will of God, His *svecchā,* His incomprehensible power. The assumption of imperfection by perfection, of lowliness by majesty, of weakness by power is the mystery of the universe. It is māyā from the logical standpoint.

7. *yadā-yadā hi dharmasya*
glānir bhavati bhārata
abhyutthānam adharmasya
tadā 'tmānaṁ sṛjāmy aham

(7) Whenever there is a decline of righteousness and rise of unrighteousness, O Bhārata (Arjuna), then I send forth (create incarnate) Myself.

"Whenever righteousness wanes, and unrighteousness increases the Almighty Lord, Hari, creates himself."[4] Wherever there is a serious tension in life, when a sort of all-pervasive materialism invades the hearts of human souls, to preserve the equilibrium, an answering manifestation of wisdom and righteousness is essential. The Supreme, though unborn and undying, becomes manifest in human embodiment to overthrow the forces of ignorance and selfishness.[5]

[1] IX, 8. [2] *karmapāratantryarahita.* Śrīdhara.

[3] *sambhavāmi dehavān iva, jāta iva, ātmamāyayā ātmano māyayā na paramārthato lokavat.*

[4] *yadāyadeha dharmasya kṣayo vṛddhiś ca pāpmanaḥ*
tadā tu bhagavān īśa ātmānaṁ sṛjate hariḥ.
Bhāgavata, IX, 24, 56.

[5] Cp. *Viṣṇu Purāṇa.*
yatrāvatīrṇaṁ kṛṣṇākhyaṁ paraṁ brahma narākṛti.

Avatāra means descent, one who has descended. The Divine comes down to the earthly plane to raise it to a higher status. God descends when man rises. The purpose of the avatār is to inaugurate a new world, a new dharma. By his teaching and example, he shows how a human being can raise himself to a higher grade of life. The issue between right and wrong is a decisive one. God works on the side of the right. Love and mercy are ultimately more powerful than hatred and cruelty. Dharma will conquer adharma, truth will conquer falsehood; the power behind death, disease and sin will be overthrown by the reality which is Being, Intelligence and Bliss.

Dharma literally means mode of being. It is the essential nature of a being that determines its mode of behaviour. So long as our conduct is in conformity with our essential nature, we are acting in the right way. Adharma is nonconformity to our nature. If the harmony of the world is derived from the conformity of all beings to their respective natures, the disharmony of the world is due to their nonconformity. God does not stand aside, when we abuse our freedom and cause disequilibrium. He does not simply wind up the world, set it on the right track and then let it jog along by itself. His loving hand is steering it all the time.

The conception of dharma is a development of the idea of ṛta which connotes cosmic as well as moral order in the *Ṛg. Veda*. The ṛta which gives logical significance and ethical elevation to the world is under the protection of Varuṇa. The god of the *Gītā*, is the upholder of righteousness *śāśvatadharmagoptā* (XI, 18), not a God beyond good and evil, remote and unconcerned with man's struggle with unrighteousness.

8. *paritrāṇāya sādhūnāṁ*
vināśāya ca duṣkṛtām
dharmasaṁsthāpanārthāya
saṁbhavāmi yuge-yuge

(8) For the protection of the good, for the destruction of the wicked and for the establishment of righteousness, I come into being from age to age.

It is the function of God as Viṣṇu, the protector of the world, to keep the world going on lines of righteousness. He assumes birth to re-establish right when wrong prevails.

9. *janma karma ca me divyam*
evaṁ yo vetti tattvataḥ
tyaktvā dehaṁ punarjanma
nai 'ti mām eti so 'rjuna

(9) He who knows thus in its true nature My divine birth and works, is not born again, when he leaves his body but comes to Me, O Arjuna.

Kṛṣṇa as an avatār or descent of the Divine into the human world discloses the condition of being to which the human souls should rise. The birth of the birthless means the revelation of the mystery in the soul of man.

The avatāra fulfils a number of functions in the cosmic process. The conception makes out that there is no opposition between spiritual life and life in the world. If the world is imperfect and ruled by the flesh and the devil, it is our duty to redeem it for the spirit. The avatāra points out the way by which men can rise from their animal to a spiritual mode of existence by providing us with an example of spiritual life. The Divine nature is not seen in the incarnation in its naked splendour but is mediated by the instrumentality of manhood. The Divine greatness is conveyed to us in and through these great individuals. Their lives dramatize for us the essential constituents of human life ascending to the fulfilment of its destiny. The *Bhāgavata* says, "The omnipresent Lord appears in the world, not only for destroying the demoniac forces but also for teaching mortals. How else could the Lord who is blissful in Himself experience anxieties about Sītā, etc."[1] . . . He knows hunger and thirst, sorrow and suffering, solitude and forsakenness. He overcomes them all and asks us to take courage from His example. He not only teaches us the true doctrine by which we can die to our separate temporal selfness and come to union with Timeless Spirit but He offers Himself to be a channel of grace. By inviting souls to trust and love Him, He promises to lead them to the knowledge of the Absolute. The historical fact is the illustration of a process

[1] *martyāvatārāstv iha martyaśikṣaṇaṁ*
rakṣovadhāyaiva na kevalaṁ vibhoḥ
kuto 'nyathā syād ramataḥ svātmanaḥ
sītākṛtāni vyasanānī'śvarasya.
V, 19, 5.

ever unfolding in the heart of man. The avatāra helps us to become what we potentially are. In Hindu and Buddhist systems of thought, there is no servitude to one historic fact. We can all rise to the divine status and the avatāras help us to achieve this inner realization. Cp. Gautama the Buddha: "Then the Blessed One spoke and said, 'Know Vasettha, that from time to time a Tathāgata is born into the world, a fully enlightened one, blessed and worthy, abounding in wisdom and goodness, happy with the knowledge of the worlds, unsurpassed as a guide to erring mortals, a teacher of gods and men, a Blessed Buddha. He proclaims the truth both in its letter and in its spirit, lovely in its origin, lovely in its progress, lovely in its consummation. A higher life doth he make known in all its purity and in all its perfectness.' "[1] According to Mahāyāna Buddhism there have been many previous Buddhas and Gautama would have a successor in Mettreya (Maitreya). Gautama himself passed through many births and acquired the qualities which enabled him to discover the Truth. It is possible for others to do the same. We hear of disciples taking the vow to attain the enlightenment of a Buddha. These systems do not believe in any exclusive revelation at one unique instant of time.

10. *vītarāgabhayakrodhā*
manmayā mām upāśritāḥ
bahavo jñānatapasā
pūtā madbhāvam āgatāḥ

(10) Delivered from passion, fear and anger, absorbed in Me, taking refuge in Me, many purified by the austerity of wisdom, have attained to My state of being.

madbhāvam: the supernatural being that I possess.

The purpose of incarnation is not simply to uphold the world order but also to help human beings to become perfected in their nature. The freed soul becomes on earth a living image of the Infinite. The ascent of man into Godhead is also the purpose of

[1] *Tevijja Sutta.* Cp. *Romans*: "For if we have grown into him by a death like his, we shall grow into him by a resurrection like his, knowing as we do that our old self has been crucified with him in order to crush the sinful body."
VI. 6. Moffatt's E.T.

the descent of God into humanity. The aim of the dharma is this perfection of man and the avatār generally declares that He is the truth, the way and the life.

11. *ye yathā mām prapadyante*
tāms tathai 'va bhajāmy aham
mama vartmā 'nuvartante
manuṣyāḥ pārtha sarvaśaḥ

(11) As men approach me so do I accept them: men on all sides follow my path, O Pārtha (Arjuna).

mama vartmā: My path; the way of worshipping Me.[1]

sarvaśah: on all sides; *sarvaprakāraiḥ*, in all ways, is another rendering.

This verse brings out the wide catholicity of the *Gītā* religion. God meets every aspirant with favour and grants to each his heart's desire. He does not extinguish the hope of any but helps all hopes to grow according to their nature. Even those who worship the Vedic deities with sacrifices and with expectation of reward find what they seek by the grace of the Supreme. Those who are vouchsafed the vision of truth convey it through symbols to ordinary people who cannot look upon its naked intensity. Name and form are used to reach the Formless. Meditation on any favourite form[2] may be adopted. The Hindu thinkers are conscious of the amazing variety of ways in which we may approach the Supreme, of the contingency of all forms. They know that it is impossible for any effort of logical reason to give us a true picture of ultimate reality. From the point of view of metaphysics (paramārtha), no manifestation is to be taken as absolutely true, while from the standpoint of experience (vyavahāra), every one of them has some validity. The forms we worship are aids to help us to become conscious of our deepest selves. So long as the object of worship holds fast the attention of the soul, it enters our mind and heart and fashions them. The importance of the form is to be judged by the degree in which it expresses ultimate significance.

The *Gītā* does not speak of this or that form of religion but

[1] *mamabhajanamārgam*. Śrīdhara.
[2] *yathābhimatadhyāna*.

speaks of the impulse which is expressed in all forms, the desire to find God and understand our relation to Him.[1]

The same God is worshipped by all. The differences of conception and approach are determined by local colouring and social adaptations. All manifestations belong to the same Supreme. "Viṣṇu is Śiva and Śiva is Viṣṇu and whoever thinks they are different goes to hell.[2] "He who is known as Viṣṇu is verily Rudra and he who is Rudra is Brahmā. One entity functions as three gods that is Rudra, Viṣṇu and Brahmā."[3] Udayanācārya writes: "Whom the Śaivas worship as Śiva, the Vedāntins as Brahman, the Buddhists as Buddha, the Naiyyāyikas who specialize in canons of knowledge as the chief agent, the followers of the Jaina code as the ever free, the ritualists as the principle of law, may that Hari, the lord of the three worlds, grant our prayers."[4] If he had been writing in this age, he would have added "whom the Christians devoted to work as Christ and the Mohammedans as Allah."[5] God is the rewarder of all who diligently seek Him,

[1] Cp. "All worship was to him sacred, since he believed that in its most degraded forms, among the most ignorant and foolish of worshippers, there has yet been some true seeking after the Divine, and that between these and the most glorious ritual or the highest philosophic certainty there lies so small a space that we may believe the Saints in paradise regard it with a smile." Elizabeth Waterhouse, *Thoughts of a Tertiary*; quoted in Evelyn Underhill, *Worship* (1937), p. 1.

[2] *harirūpī mahādevo lingarūpī janārdanaḥ*
īśad api antaraṁ nāsti bhedakṛn narakaṁ vrajet. Bṛhannāradīya.
Cp. also *Maitrāyaṇī Up. sa vā eṣa ekas tridhābhūtaḥ*. See also *Atharva veda*: The one light manifests itself in various forms *'ekaṁ jyoti bahudhā vibhāti*. XIII, 3, 17.

[3] *yo vai viṣṇuḥ sa vai rudro yo rudraḥ sa pitāmahaḥ*
ekamūrtis trayo devā rudraviṣṇupitāmahaḥ.

[4] *yaṁ śaivāḥ samupāsate śiva iti brahmeti vedāntinaḥ*
bauddhāḥ buddha iti pramāṇa paṭavaḥ karteti naiyyāyikāḥ
arhan nityātha jainaśāsanaratāḥ karmeti mīmāṁsakāḥ
so yaṁ vo vidadhātu vāñchitaphalaṁ trailokyanātho hariḥ.

[5] *kraistvāḥ krīstur iti kriyāpararatāḥ alleti māhammadāḥ.*
Abul Fazl describes the spirit of Akbar's Universal Faith in these words: "O God, in every temple I see people that seek Thee, and in every language I hear spoken, people praise Thee. Polytheism and Islam feel after Thee; each religion says 'Thou art One, without equal.' If it be a mosque, people murmur the holy prayer and if it be a Christian Church, people ring the bell from Love to Thee. Sometimes I frequent the Christian cloister, sometimes the mosque.

whatever views of God they may hold. The spiritually immature are unwilling to recognize other gods than their own. Their attachment to their creed makes them blind to the larger unity of the Godhead. This is the result of egotism in the domain of religious ideas. The *Gītā*, on the other hand, affirms that though beliefs and practices may be many and varied, spiritual realization to which these are the means is one.

A strong consciousness of one's own possession of the truth, the whole truth and nothing but the truth added to a condescending anxiety for the condition of those who are in outer darkness produces a state of mind which is not remote from that of an inquisitor.

12. *kāṅkṣantaḥ karmaṇāṁ siddhiṁ*
yajanta iha devatāḥ
kṣipraṁ hi mānuṣe loke
siddhir bhavati karmajā

(12) Those who desire the fruition of their works on earth offer sacrifices to the gods (the various forms of the one Godhead) for the fruition of works in this world of men is very quick.

The Desireless Nature of God's Work

13. *cāturvarṇyaṁ mayā sṛṣṭaṁ*
guṇakarmavibhāgaśaḥ
tasya kartāram api māṁ
viddhy akartāram avyayam

(13) The fourfold order was created by Me according to the divisions of quality and work. Though I am its creator, know Me to be incapable of action or change.

cāturvarṇyam: the fourfold order. The emphasis is on guṇa (aptitude) and karma (function) and not jāti (birth). The varṇa or the order to which we belong is independent of sex, birth or

But it is Thou whom I search from temple to temple. Thy elect have no dealings with either heresy or orthodoxy for neither of them stands behind the screen of Thy truth. Heresy to the heretic; and religion to the orthodox. But the dust of the rose petal belongs to the heart of the perfume seller." Blochmann, *Aini Akbari*, p. xxx.

breeding. A class determined by temperament and vocation is not a caste determined by birth and heredity. According to the M.B., the whole world was originally of one class but later it became divided into four divisions on account of the specific duties.[1] Even the distinction between caste and outcaste is artificial and unspiritual. An ancient verse points out that the Brāhmin and the outcaste are blood brothers.[2] In the M.B., Yudhiṣṭhira says that it is difficult to find out the caste of persons on account of the mixture of castes. Men beget offspring in all sorts of women. So conduct is the only determining feature of caste according to sages.[3]

The fourfold order is designed for human evolution. There is nothing absolute about the caste system which has changed its character in the process of history. Today it cannot be regarded as anything more than an insistence on a variety of ways in which the social purpose can be carried out. Functional groupings will never be out of date and as for marriages they will happen among those who belong to more or less the same stage of cultural development. The present morbid condition of India broken into castes and subcastes is opposed to the unity taught by the *Gītā*, which stands for an organic as against an atomistic conception of society.

akartāram: non-doer. As the Supreme is unattached, He is said to be a non-doer. Works do not affect His changeless being, though He is the unseen background of all works.

Action without Attachment does not lead to Bondage

14. *na māṁ karmāṇi limpanti*
na me karmaphale spṛhā
iti māṁ yo 'bhijānāti
karmabhir na sa badhyate

(14) Works do not defile Me; nor do I have yearning for their fruit. He who knows Me thus is not bound by works.

[1] *ekavarṇam idaṁ pūrṇaṁ viśvam āsid yudhiṣṭhira*
karmakriyāviśeṣeṇa cāturvarṇyam pratiṣṭhitam.

[2] *antyajo viprajātiś ca eka eva sahodaraḥ*
ekayoniprasūtaś ca ekaśākhena jāyate.

[3] *saṁkarāt sarvavarṇānām duṣparīkṣyeti me matiḥ*
sarve sdrvāsvapatyāni janayanti sadā narāḥ
tasmat śilaṁ pradḥāneṣṭaṁ viaur ye tattvadarśinaḥ.

15. *evaṁ jñātvā kṛtaṁ karma*
pūrvair api mumukṣubhiḥ
kuru karmai 'va tasmāt tvaṁ
pūrvaiḥ purvataraṁ kṛtam

(15) So knowing was work done also by the men of old who sought liberation. Therefore do thou also work as the ancients did in former times.

The ignorant perform action for self-purification (*ātma śuddhyartham*) and the wise perform action for the maintenance of the world (*lokasaṁgrahārtham*).

As the ancients carried out the work ordained by tradition, Arjuna is called upon to do his duty as a warrior. Cp. "Lord of the Universe, Supreme Spirit, Beneficent God, at Thy command only, I shall carry on this pilgrimage of life, for the good of the creatures and for Thy glory."[1]

Action and Inaction

16. *kiṁ karma kim akarme 'ti*
kavayo 'py atra mohitāḥ
tat te karma pravakṣyāmi
yaj jñātvā mokṣyase 'śubhāt

(16) What is action? What is inaction?—as to this even the wise are bewildered. I will declare to thee what action is, knowing which thou shalt be delivered from evil.

17. *karmaṇo hy api boddhavyaṁ*
boddhavyaṁ ca vikarmaṇaḥ
akarmaṇaś ca boddhavyaṁ
gahanā karmaṇo gatiḥ

(17) One has to understand what action is, and likewise one has to understand what is wrong action and one has to understand about inaction. Hard to understand is the way of work.

What is the right course is not generally obvious. The ideas of our time, the prescriptions of tradition, the voice of conscience

[1] *lokeśa caitanyamayādhideva māṅgalyaviṣṇo bhavad ājñayaiva hitāya lokasya tava priyārthaṁ saṁsārayātrām anuvartayiṣye.*

get mixed up and confuse us. In the midst of all this, the wise man seeks a way out by a reference to immutable truths, with the insight of the highest reason.

18. *karmaṇy akarma yaḥ paśyed*
akarmaṇi ca karma yaḥ
sa buddhimān manuṣyeṣu
sa yuktaḥ kṛtsnakarmakṛt

(18) He who in action sees inaction and action in inaction, he is wise among men, he is a yogin and he has accomplished all his work.

So long as we work in a detached spirit our mental balance is not disturbed. We refrain from actions which are born of desire and do our duties, with a soul linked with the Divine. So true non-activity is to preserve inner composure and to be free from attachment. Akarma means the absence of bondage resulting from work because it is done without attachment. He who works without attachment is not bound. We are acting even when we sit quiet without any outward action. Cp. *Aṣṭāvakragītā*. The turning away from action by fools due to perversity and ignorance amounts to action. The action of the wise (that is their desireless action) has the same fruit as that of renunciation.[1]

Ś. explains that in ātman there is no action; in the body however there is no rest, even when there seems to be rest.

R. holds that akarma is ātmajñāna. The wise man is he who sees jñāna in the true performance of karma. For him jñāna and karma go together.

According to Madhva, akarma is the inactivity of the self and the activity of Viṣṇu. Therefore the wise man is he who sees the activity of the Lord whether the individual is active or not.

19. *yasya sarve samārambhāḥ*
kāmasaṁkalpavarjitāḥ
jñānāgnidagdhakarmāṇaṁ
tam āhuḥ paṇḍitaṁ budhāḥ

(19) He whose undertakings are all free from the will of

[1] *nivṛttir api mūḍhasya pravṛttir upajāyate*
pravṛttir api dhīrasya nivṛttiphalabhāginī.
XVIII, 61.

desire, whose works are burned up in the fire of wisdom, him the wise call a man of learning.

Such a worker has the universality of outlook born of wisdom (jñāna) and freedom from selfish desire. Though he works, he really does nothing.

20 *tyaktvā karmaphalāsaṅgaṁ*
nityatṛpto nirāśrayaḥ
karmaṇy abhipravṛtto 'pi
nai 'va kiṁcit karoti saḥ

(20) Having abandoned attachment to the fruit of works, ever content, without any kind of dependence, he does nothing though he is ever engaged in work.

Cp. *Aṣṭāvakragītā.* "He who is devoid of existence and non-existence, who is wise, satisfied, free from desire, does nothing even if he may be acting in the eyes of the world."[1]

"He who, without attachment to them, surrenders to God all religious practices ordained by the scriptures, obtains the perfection of non-action; the promised fruit is only to attract us to action."[2]

21 *nirāśīr yatacittātmā*
tyaktasarvaparigrahaḥ
śārīraṁ kevalaṁ karma
kurvan nā 'pnoti kilbiṣam

(21) Having no desires, with his heart and self under control, giving up all possessions, performing action by the body alone, he commits no wrong.

śārīraṁ karma is work required for the maintenance of the body according to Ś. and Madhusūdana. It is work done by the body alone according to Vedānta Deśika.

Virtue or vice does not belong to the outer deed. When a man is rid of his passions and self-will, he becomes a mirror reflecting the will of the Divine. The human soul becomes the pure channel of Divine power.

[1] XVIII, 19. See also 20–6.

[2] *vedoktam eva kurvāṇo nissaṅgo'rpitam īśvare*
naiṣkarmyasiddhiṁ labhate rocanārtho phalaśrutiḥ.

22. *yadṛcchālābhasaṁtuṣṭo*
dvandvātīto vimatsaraḥ
samaḥ siddhāv asiddhau ca
kṛtvā 'pi na nibadhyate

(22) He who is satisfied with whatever comes by chance, who has passed beyond the dualities (of pleasure and pain), who is free from jealousy, who remains the same in success and failure, even when he acts, he is not bound.

Action by itself does not bind. If it does, then we are committed to a gross dualism between God and the world and the world becomes a cosmic blunder. The cosmos is a manifestation of the Supreme and what binds is not the act but the selfish attitude to action, born of ignorance which makes us imagine that we are so many separate individuals with our special preferences and aversions.

The teacher now proceeds to point out how the actor, the act and the action are all different manifestations of the one Supreme and action offered as a sacrifice to the Supreme does not bind.

Sacrifice and Its Symbolic Value

23. *gatasaṅgasya muktasya*
jñānāvasthitacetasaḥ
yajñāyā 'carataḥ karma
samagraṁ pravilīyate

(23) The work of a man whose attachments are sundered, who is liberated, whose mind is firmly founded in wisdom, who does work as a sacrifice, is dissolved entirely.

24 *brahmā 'rpaṇaṁ brahma havir*
brahmāgnau brahmaṇā hutam
brahmai 'va tena gantavyaṁ
brahmakarmasamādhinā

(24) For him the act of offering is God, the oblation is God. By God is it offered into the fire of God. God is that which is to be attained by him who realizes God in his works.

The Vedic yajña is here interpreted in a larger, spiritual way.

Though the performer of yajña does work, he is not bound by it,[1] for his earth life is brooded over by the sense of eternity.[2]

25. *daivam evā 'pare yajñaṁ*
yoginaḥ paryupāsate
brahmāgnāv apare yajñaṁ
yajñenai 'vo 'pajuhvati

(25) Some yogins offer sacrifices to the gods while others offer sacrifice by the sacrifice itself into the fire of the Supreme.

Ś. interprets yajña in the second half of the verse as ātman. "Others offer the self as self into the fire of Brahman."[3]

Those who conceive the Divine in various forms seek favours from them by performing the consecrated rites of action, while others offer all works to the Divine itself.

26. *śrotrādīnī 'ndriyāṇy anye*
saṁyamāgniṣu juhvati
śabdādīn viṣayān anya
indriyāgniṣu juhvati

(26) Some offer hearing and the other senses into the fires of restraint; others offer sound and the other objects of sense in the fires of sense.

By means of sacrifice interpreted here as means to mental control and discipline, we strive to make knowledge penetrate

[1] Cp. Śrīdhara: *tad evaṁ parameśvarārādhanalakṣaṇaṁ karma jñānahetutvena bandhakatvābhāvād akarmaiva.*

[2] Cp. *Mantiqu't-Tair. E. T.* by Fitzgerald.
"All you have been, and seen, and done and thought,
Not *you* but *I*, have seen and been and wrought. . . .
Pilgrim, pilgrimage and Road,
Was but Myself toward Myself; and your
Arrival but Myself at my own door . . .
Come, you lost Atoms, to your centre draw . . .
Rays that have wandered into Darkness wide,
Return, and back into your Sun subside."

Quoted from Ananda K. Coomaraswamy, *Hinduism and Buddhism* (1943), p. 42.

[3] Nīlakaṇṭha says: '*sopādhikaṁ jīvaṃ nirupādhikātmarūpeṇa juhvati.*

our whole being.[1] Our whole being is surrendered and changed. A right enjoyment of sense objects is compared to a sacrifice in which the objects are the offering and senses the sacrificial fires. Every form of self-control, where we surrender the egoistic enjoyment for the higher delight, where we give up lower impulses, is said to be a sacrifice.

27. *sarvāṇī 'ndriyakarmāṇi*
prāṇakarmāṇi cā 'pare
ātmasaṁyamayogāgnau
juhvati jñānadīpite

(27) Some again offer all the works of their senses and the works of the vital force into the fire of the yoga of self-control, kindled by knowledge.

28. *dravyayajñās tapoyajñā*
yogayajñās tathā 'pare
svādhyāyajñānayajñāś ca
yatayaḥ saṁśitavratāḥ

(28) Some likewise offer as sacrifice their material possessions, or their austerities or their spiritual exercises while others of subdued minds and severe vows offer their learning and knowledge.

29. *apāne juhvati prāṇaṁ*
prāṇe 'pānaṁ tathā 'pare
prāṇāpānagatī ruddhvā
prāṇāyāmaparāyaṇāḥ

(29) Others again who are devoted to breath control, having restrained the paths of prāṇa (the outgoing breath) and apāna (the incoming breath) pour as sacrifice prāṇa into apāna and apāna into prāṇa.

[1] Cp. Madhusūdana: *dhāraṇā dhyānam samādhir iti saṁyamaśabdenocyate: tathācāha bhagavān patañjaliḥ, trayam ekatra saṁyamaḥ iti. tatra hṛtpuṇḍarīkādau manasaścirakālasthāpanaṁ dhāraṇā; evam ekasya dhṛtasya cittasya bhagavadākāravṛttipravāho'ntarā'nyākārapratyayavyavahito dhyānam. sarvathā vijātīyapratyayāntaritaḥ sajātīyapratyayapravāhaḥ samādhiḥ.*

30. *apare niyatāhārāḥ*
prāṇān prāṇeṣu juhvati
sarve 'py ete yajñavido
yajñakṣapitakalmaṣāḥ

(30) While others, restricting their food, pour as sacrifice their life breaths into life breaths. All these are knowers of sacrifice (know what sacrifice is) and by sacrifice have their sins destroyed.

Restraint is the essence of all sacrifice and so all sacrifices may be regarded as means to spiritual growth.

31. *yajñaśiṣṭāmṛtabhujo*
yānti brahma sanātanam
nā 'yaṁ loko 'sty ayajñasya
kuto 'nyaḥ kurusattama

(31) Those who eat the sacred food that remains after a sacrifice attain to the eternal Absolute; this world is not for him who offers no sacrifice, how then any other world, O Best of the Kurus (Arjuna)?

The law of the world is sacrifice and he who violates it cannot obtain mastery either here or beyond.

32. *evaṁ bahuvidhā yajñā*
vitatā brahmaṇo mukhe
karmajān viddhi tān sarvān
evaṁ jñātvā vimokṣyase

(32) Thus many forms of sacrifice are spread out in the face of Brahman (i.e. set forth as the means of reaching the Absolute). Know thou that all these are born of work, and so knowing thou shalt be freed.

Wisdom and Work

33. *śreyān dravyamayād yajñāj*
jñānayajñaḥ paraṁtapa
sarvaṁ karmā 'khilaṁ pārtha
jñāne parisamāpyate

(33) Knowledge as a sacrifice is greater than any material sacrifice, O scourge of the foe (Arjuna), for all works without any exception culminate in wisdom.

The goal is the lifegiving wisdom, which gives us freedom of action and liberation from the bondage of work.

34. *tad viddhi praṇipātena*
paripraśnena sevayā
upadekṣyanti te jñānaṁ
jñāninas tattvadarśinaḥ

(34) Learn that by humble reverence, by inquiry and by service. The men of wisdom who have seen the truth will instruct thee in knowledge.

Wise men will teach us the truth if we approach them in a spirit of service and reverent inquiry. Until we realize the God within, we must act according to the advice of those who have had the experience of God. If we accept what is said in the śāstras or taught by the teacher in unthinking trust, that will not do. Reason must be satisfied. "He who has no personal knowledge but has only heard of many things cannot understand the meaning of scriptures even as a spoon has no idea of the taste of the soup."[1] We must combine devotion to the teacher with the most unrestricted right of free examination and inquiry. Blind obedience to an external authority is repudiated. Today there are several teachers who require of their followers unthinking obedience to their dictates. They seem to believe that the death of intellect is the condition of the life of spirit. Many credulous and simple-minded people are drawn to them not so much by their spiritual powers as by the publicity of their agents and the human weakness for novelty, curiosity and excitement. This is against the Hindu tradition which insists on jijñāsā or inquiry, manana or reflection or paripraśna in the words of the *Gītā*.

But mere intellectual apprehension will not do. Intellect can only give fragmentary views, glimpses of the Beyond, but it does not give the consciousness of the Beyond. We must open the

[1] *yasya nāsti nijā prajñā kevalaṁ tu bahuśrutaḥ*
na sa jānāti śāstrārthaṁ darvī sūtarasān iva.
M.B., II, 55. 1.

whole of our inner being to establish personal contact. The disciple has to tread the interior path. The ultimate authority is the inner light which is not to be confused with the promptings of desire. By the quality of service and self-effacement, we knock down the obstructing prejudices and let the wisdom in us shine. Truth achieved is different from truth imparted. Ultimately, what is revealed in the scriptures (praṇipātā-śravaṇa), what is thought out by the mind (paripraśna-manana) and what is realized by the spirit through service and meditation (śeva-nididhyāsana) must agree.[1] We must consort with the great minds of the past, reason about them and intuitively apprehend what is of enduring value in them.

This verse makes out that in spiritual life, faith comes first, then knowledge, and then experience.

Those who have experienced the truth are expected to guide us. The seers owe a duty to their less fortunate brethren and guide them to the attainment of illumination which they have reached.

In Praise of Wisdom

35. *yaj jñātvā na punar moham*
evaṁ yāsyasi pāṇḍava
yena bhūtāny aśeṣeṇa
drakṣyasy ātmany atho mayi

(35) When thou hast known it, thou shalt not fall again into this confusion, O Pāṇḍava (Arjuna), for by this thou shalt see all existences without exception in the Self, then in Me.

When the sense of difference is destroyed actions do not bind, since ignorance is the source of bondage and the self, having attained wisdom, is free from it.

[1] Cp. Plato: "A man should persevere till he has achieved one of two things: either he should discover the truth about them for himself or learn it from some one else; or if this is impossible he should take the best and most irrefragable of human theories and make it the raft on which he sails through life." *Phaedo*, 85. Cp. Plotinus: "Out of discussion we call to vision, to those desiring to see we point the path, our teaching is a guiding in the way, the seeing must be the very act of him who has made the choice." *Enneads*, VI, 9, 4.

36. *api ced asi pāpebhyaḥ*
sarvebhyaḥ pāpakṛttamaḥ
sarvaṁ jñānaplavenai 'va
vṛjinaṁ saṁtariṣyasi

(36) Even if thou shouldst be the most sinful of all sinners, thou shalt cross over all evil by the boat of wisdom alone.

37. *yathai 'dhāṁsi samiddho 'gnir*
bhasmasāt kurute 'rjuna
jñānāgniḥ sarvakarmāṇi
bhasmasāt kurute tathā

(37) As the fire which is kindled turns its fuel to ashes, O Arjuna, even so does the fire of wisdom turn to ashes all work.

38. *na hi jñānena sadṛśaṁ*
pavitram iha vidyate
tat svayaṁ yogasaṁsiddhaḥ
kālenā 'tmani vindati

(38) There is nothing on earth equal in purity to wisdom. He who becomes perfected by yoga finds this of himself, in his self in course of time.

Self-control discovers it to man at last.

Faith is Necessary for Wisdom

39. *śraddhāvāṁl labhate jñānaṁ*
tatparaḥ saṁyatendriyaḥ
jñānaṁ labdhvā parāṁ śāntim
acireṇā 'dhigacchati

(39) He who has faith, who is absorbed in it (i.e. wisdom) and who has subdued his senses gains wisdom and having gained wisdom he attains quickly the supreme peace.

śraddhā; faith. Faith is necessary for gaining wisdom. Faith is not blind belief. It is the aspiration of the soul to gain wisdom. It is the reflection in the empirical self of the wisdom that dwells in the deepest levels of our being. If faith is constant, it takes us to the realization of wisdom. Jñāna as wisdom is free from doubts while intellectual knowledge where we depend on sense data and logical inference, doubt and scepticism have their place. Wisdom is not acquired by these means. We have to live it inwardly and grow into its reality. The way to it is through faith and self-control.

parāṁ śāntim: the supreme peace. Nīlakaṇtha suggests that he attains the supreme state of bliss, after the karma which has commenced to operate completes its course.[1]

40. *ajñaś cā 'śraddadhānaś ca*
saṁśayātmā vinaśyati
nā 'yaṁ loko 'sti na paro
na sukhaṁ saṁśayātmanaḥ

(40) But the man who is ignorant, who has no faith, who is of a doubting nature, perishes. For the doubting soul, there is neither this world nor the world beyond nor any happiness.

We must have a positive basis for life, an unwavering faith which stands the test of life.

41. *yogasaṁnyastakarmāṇaṁ*
jñānasaṁchinnasaṁśayam
ātmavantaṁ na karmāṇi
nibadhnanti dhanaṁjaya

(41) Works do not bind him who has renounced all works by yoga, who has destroyed all doubt by wisdom and who ever possesses his soul, O winner of wealth (Arjuna).

The mutual relationship of true work, wisdom and self-discipline is here brought out.

yogasaṁnyastakarmāṇam: who has renounced all works by yoga. This may refer to those who develop even-mindedness with worship of God as its characteristic, and so dedicate all works to God or to those who have insight into the highest reality and so are detached from works.[2] Madhusūdana.

[1] *videhakaivalyam . . . prārabdhakarmasamāptausatyām.*

[2] *yogena bhagavadārādhanalakṣaṇasamatvabuddhirūpeṇa saṁnyastāni bhagavati samarpitāni karmāṇi yena yadvā paramārtha darśanalakṣaṇena yogena saṁnyastāni tyaktāni karmāṇi yena tam yogasaṁnyastakarmāṇam.*

ātmavantam: who possesses his self. While he does work for others, he remains his own self. In the eager pursuit of the good of others, he does not lose his hold on the self.

42. *tasmād ajñānasaṁbhūtaṁ*
hṛtsthaṁ jñānāsinā 'tmanaḥ
chittvai 'naṁ saṁśayaṁ yogam
ātiṣṭho 'ttiṣṭha bhārata

(42) Therefore having cut asunder with the sword of wisdom this doubt in thy heart that is born of ignorance, resort to yoga and stand up, O Bhārata (Arjuna).

Arjuna is here called upon to perform action with the help of knowledge and concentration. The doubt in his heart whether it is better to fight or abstain is the product of ignorance. It will be destroyed by wisdom. Then he will know what is right for him to do.

iti . . . jñānayogo nāma caturtho 'dhyāyaḥ

This is the fourth chapter entitled The Yoga of Divine Knowledge

Sometimes the chapter is entitled Jñāna Karmasaṁnyāsayoga, the yoga of knowledge and (true) renunciation of action.

CHAPTER V

True Renunciation

Sāṁkhya and Yoga lead to the same goal

arjuna uvāca

1 *saṁnyāsaṁ karmaṇāṁ kṛṣṇa*
punar yogaṁ ca śaṁsasi
yac chreya etayor ekaṁ
tan me brūhi suniścitam

Arjuna said:

(1) Thou praisest, O Kṛṣṇa, the renunciation of works and again their unselfish performance. Tell me for certain which one is the better of these two.

Ś. argues that the question is with reference to the unenlightened, for the man who has realized the Self has no longer any object to gain since he has achieved all. In III, 17, it is said that he has no more duties to perform. In such passages as III, 4 and IV, 6, the method of work is enjoined as an accessory to the acquisition of the knowledge of the Self, while in VI, 3, it is said that the man who has obtained right knowledge has no longer anything to do with work. Further, in IV, 21, all action is denied to him except that which is required for bodily maintenance. The man who knows the true nature of the Self is directed in V, 8, always to meditate with a concentrated mind on the idea that it is not "I" that do it. It is not possible to imagine even in a dream that the man who knows the Self can have anything to do with work so opposed to right knowledge and entirely based on illusory knowledge.[1] So Ś. contends that Arjuna's question relates only to those who have not known the Self. For the ignorant, work is better than renunciation.

The intention of the *Gītā* right through seems to be that the work to be abandoned is selfish work which binds us to the chain

[1] *ātmatattvavidaḥ, saṁyagdarśanaviruddho mithyājñānahetukah karmayogaḥ svapnepi na sambhāvayituṁ śakyate.*

of karma and not all activity. We cannot be saved by works alone, but works are not opposed to saving wisdom.

śrībhagavān uvāca

2. *saṁnyāsaḥ karmayogaś ca*
niḥśreyasakarāv ubhau
tayos tu karmasaṁnyāsāt
karmayogo viśiṣyate

The Blessed Lord said:

(2) The renunciation of works and their unselfish performance both lead to the soul's salvation. But of the two, the unselfish performance of works is better than their renunciation.[1]

The Sāṁkhya method involves the renunciation of works and the Yoga insists on their performance in the right spirit. They are at bottom the same but the Yoga way comes more naturally to us. The two ways are not inconsistent. In Sāṁkhya, jñāna or insight is emphasized. In Yoga, volitional effort is stressed. In one, we know the Self by thinking away the alien elements; in the other, we will them away.

3. *jñeyaḥ sa nityasaṁnyāsī*
yo na dveṣṭi na kāṅkṣati
nirdvandvo hi mahābāho
sukhaṁ bandhāt pramucyate

(3) He who neither loathes nor desires should be known as one who has ever the spirit of renunciation; for free from dualities he is released easily, O Mighty-armed (Arjuna), from bondage.

nityasaṁnyāsi: one who has ever the spirit of renunciation. The true worker (karmayogin) is also the true renouncer (nitya saṁnyāsin), for he does his work in a detached spirit.[2]

4. *sāṁkhyayogau pṛthag bālāḥ*
pravadanti na paṇḍitāḥ
ekam apy āsthitaḥ samyag
ubhayor vindate phalaṁ

[1] See III, 8.
[2] *sa karmāṇi pravṛttopi nityaṁ saṁnyāsīti jñeyaḥ.* Madhusūdana.

(4) The ignorant speak of renunciation (Sāṁkhya) and practice of works (Yoga) as different, not the wise. He who applies himself well to one, gets the fruit of both.

In this chapter, Yoga means karmayoga and Sāṁkhya means the intellectual way with renunciation of works.

5. *yat sāṁkhyaiḥ prāpyate sthānaṁ*
tad yogair api gamyate
ekaṁ sāṁkhyaṁ ca yogaṁ ca
yaḥ paśyati sa paśyati

(5) The status which is obtained by men of renunciation is reached by men of action also. He who sees that the ways of renunciation and of action are one, he sees (truly).

5(*b*) appears elsewhere in the M.B., *Śāntiparva*, 305, 19; 316, 4.[1] The true renouncer is not he who remains completely inactive but he whose work is done in a spirit of detachment. Renunciation is a mental attitude, the casting-off of desire in work; true work is work with all desire renounced. There is not any opposition between the two. Cp. "When actions are performed by the wise man or the fool, the body (that is the external act) is the same but the inward understanding is different.[2] M.B. says that the Bhāgavata religion is equal in merit to the Sāṁkhya religion."[3]

6. *saṁnyāsas tu mahābāho*
duḥkham āptum ayogataḥ
yogayukto munir brahma
nacireṇā 'dhigacchati

(6) But renunciation, O Mighty-armed (Arjuna), is difficult to attain without yoga; the sage who is earnest in yoga (the way of works) attains soon to the Absolute.

[1] Cp. *yad eva yogāḥ paśyanti tat sāṁkhyair api dṛśyate*
ekaṁ sāṁkhyaṁ ca yogaṁ ca yaḥ paśyati sa tattvavit.

[2] *prājñasya mūrkhasya ca kāryayoge*
samatvam abhyeti tanur na buddhiḥ.—*Avimāra*, V, 5.

[3] *sāṁkhyayogena tulyo hi dharma ekāntasevitaḥ*. *Śāntiparva*, 348, 71.

7. *yogayukto viśuddhātmā*
vijitātmā jitendriyaḥ
sarvabhūtātmabhūtātmā
kurvann api na lipyate

(7) He who is trained in the way of works, and is pure in soul, who is master of his self and who has conquered the senses, whose soul becomes the self of all beings, he is not tainted by works, though he works.

He renounces all actions inwardly, not outwardly. Even Ś. admits that such action is quite consistent with the knowledge of Self. Even if he acts for the sake of world-solidarity, he is not bound by actions.[1]

8. *nai 'va kiṁcit karomī 'ti*
yukto manyeta tattvavit
paśyañ śṛṇvan spṛśañ jighrann
aśnan gacchan svapañ śvasan

(8) The man who is united with the Divine and knows the truth thinks "I do nothing at all" for in seeing, hearing, touching, smelling, tasting, walking, sleeping, breathing;

9. *pralapan visṛjan gṛhṇann*
unmiṣan nimiṣann api
indriyāṇī 'ndriyārtheṣu
vartanta iti dhārayan

(9) In speaking, emitting, grasping, opening and closing the eyes he holds that only the senses are occupied with the objects of the senses.

We are called upon to realize the self in us which is pure and free and distinct from the factors of prakṛti or objective universe. The constituents of the ego are impermanent, a flux which changes from moment to moment. There is no changeless centre or immortal nucleus in these pretenders to selfhood.

[1] *saḥ . . . lokasaṁgrahāya karma kurvann api na lipyate, na karmabhir badhyate.*

10. *brahmaṇy ādhāya karmāṇi*
saṅgaṁ tyaktvā karoti yaḥ
lipyate na sa pāpena
padmapattram ivā 'mbhasā

(10) He who works, having given up attachment, resigning his actions to God, is not touched by sin, even as a lotus leaf (is untouched) by water.

The *Gītā* requires us, not to renounce works but to do them, offering them to the Supreme in which alone is immortality. When we renounce our attachment to the finite ego and its likes and dislikes and place our actions in the Eternal, we acquire the true renunciation which is consistent with free activity in the world. Such a renouncer acts not for his fleeting finite self but for the Self which is in us all.[1]

brahmaṇy ādhāya karmāṇi. R. makes Brahman equivalent to prakṛti.

11. *kāyena manasā buddhyā*
kevalair indriyair api
yoginaḥ karma kurvanti
saṅgaṁ tyaktvā 'tmaśuddhaye

(11) The yogins (men of action) perform works merely with the body, mind, understanding or merely with the senses, abandoning attachment, for the purification of their souls.

12. *yuktaḥ karmaphalaṁ tyaktvā*
śāntim āpnoti naiṣṭhikīm
ayuktaḥ kāmakāreṇa
phale sakto nibadhyate

(12) The soul earnest (or devoted) attains to peace well-founded, by abandoning attachment to the fruits of works, but he whose soul is not in union with the Divine is impelled by desire, and is attached to the fruit (of action) and is (therefore) bound.

[1] Cp. Emerson:
"Teach me your mood, O patient stars;
Who climb each night the ancient sky,
Leaving on space no shade, no scars,
No trace of age, no fear to die."

yuktaḥ, or disciplined in action:

śāntim. When the peace of God descends on us, Divine knowledge floods our being with a light which illumines and transforms, making clear all that was before dark and obscure.

The Enlightened Self

13. *sarvakarmāṇi manasā*
saṁnyasyā 'ste sukhaṁ vaśī
navadvāre pure dehī
nai 'va kurvan na kārayan

(13) The embodied (soul), who has controlled his nature having renounced all actions by the mind (inwardly) dwells at ease in the city of nine gates, neither working nor causing work to be done.

Cp. *Kaṭha Up.*, V, 1.

The nine gates are the two eyes, the two ears, the two nostrils, and the mouth and the two organs of excretion and generation. See *Śvetāśvatara Up.*, III, 18.

14. *na kartṛtvaṁ na karmāṇi*
lokasya sṛjati prabhuḥ
na karmaphalasaṁyogaṁ
svabhāvas tu pravartate

(14) The Sovereign Self does not create for the people agency, nor does He act. Nor does He connect works with their fruits. It is nature that works out (these).

Prabhuḥ is the Sovereign Self of the knower, the Real Self which is one with all that is.

15. *nā 'datte kasyacit pāpaṁ*
na cai 'va sukṛtaṁ vibhuḥ
ajñānenā 'vṛtaṁ jñānaṁ
tena muhyanti jantavaḥ

(15) The All-pervading Spirit does not take on the sin or the merit of any. Wisdom is enveloped by ignorance; thereby creatures are bewildered.

vibhuḥ: all-pervading. Each soul is not a separate monad, eternal and changeless. Vibhuḥ refers either to the Self of the jñānin or the Supreme Self, which are identical in Advaita Vedānta.

ajñānena: by ignorance. It is the ignorance which makes us believe in the ultimateness of the multiplicity.

jñānam: wisdom. It is the wisdom which is the one basis of all distinctions.[1]

16. *jñānena tu tad ajñānaṁ*
yeṣāṁ nāśitam ātmanaḥ
teṣām ādityavaj jñānaṁ
prakāśayati tat param

(16) But for those in whom ignorance is destroyed by wisdom, for them wisdom lights up the Supreme Self like the sun.

tatparam: paramārtha tattvam: ultimate reality. Ś.

The Self above the ego is not touched by sin or merit, by joy or sorrow. It is the witness of all.

17. *tadbuddhayas tadātmānas*
tanniṣṭhās tatparāyaṇāḥ
gacchanty apunarāvṛttiṁ
jñānanirdhūtakalmaṣāḥ

(17) Thinking of That, directing one's whole conscious being to That, making That their whole aim, with That as the sole object of their devotion, they reach a state from which there is no return, their sins washed away by wisdom.

The false ego determined by works disappears and the jīva realizes its identity with the Supreme Self and works from that centre.

18. *vidyāvinayasaṁpanne*
brāhmaṇe gavi hastini
śuni cai 'va śvapāke ca
paṇḍitāḥ samadarśinaḥ

[1] *ajñānenāvaraṇavikṣepaśaktimatā māyākhyenā'nṛtena tamasā jñānaṁ jīveśvarajagadbhedabhramādhiṣṭhānabhūtaṁ nityaṁ svaprakāśaṁ saccidānāndarūpam advitīyaṁ paramārthasatyam.* Madhusūdana

(18) Sages see with an equal eye, a learned and humble Brahmin, a cow, an elephant or even a dog or an outcaste.

vidyāvinayasaṁpanne: great learning brings great humility. As our knowledge increases we become increasingly aware of the encircling darkness. It is when we light the candle that we see how dark it is. What we know is practically nothing compared to what we do not know.[1] A little knowledge leads to dogmatism, a little more to questioning and a little more takes us to prayer. Besides, humility comes from the knowledge that we are sustained in existence by the love of God. The greatest thinkers of all ages were deeply religious men.

vinaya: humility or rather modesty which is the result of cultivation or discipline. The first division of the Buddhist *Tipitaka* is called *vinaya* or discipline. *vinaya* is the opposite of pride or insolence. The recognition of dependence on non-human factors produces cosmic piety. The truly learned are humble.

samadarśinaḥ: see with an equal eye. The Eternal is the same in all, in animals, as in men, in learned Brahmins as in despised outcasts. The light of Brahman dwells in all bodies and is not affected by the differences in the bodies it illumines.

The characteristics of the Supreme, being, consciousness and bliss, are present in all existences and the differences relate to their names and forms, that is, their embodiments.[2] When we look at things from the standpoint of the Ultimate Reality present in all, we "see with an equal eye."[3] The fundamental dualism is that of spirit and nature and not of soul and body. It is the distinction between the subject and the object. Nature is the world of objectivization, of alienation, of determinability. There we have, the distinction of minerals, plants and animals and men, but they all have an inner non-objective existence. The

[1] The familiar sentence of the great Newton illustrates this: "I do not know what I may appear to the world; but to myself I seem to have been only like a boy playing on the seashore, and diverting myself in now and then finding a smoother pebble or a prettier shell than ordinary, while the great ocean of truth lay undiscovered before me." I might transcribe a sentence of Henry Adams. "After all, man knows mighty little, and may some day learn enough of his own ignorance to fall down and pray."

[2] *asti bhāti priyaṁ rūpaṁ nāmacet' aṁśapañcakam*
ādyaṁ trayaṁ brahmarūpaṁ jagadrūpaṁ tato dvayam.

[3] *carācaraṁ jagad brahmadṛṣṭyaiva paśyanti.* Nīlakaṇṭha.

subject, Reality, dwells in all of them. This affirmation of basic identity is not inconsistent with the empirical variety. Even Ś. admits that the one eternal reality is revealing itself in higher and higher forms through successive stages of manifestation.[1] The empirical variety should not hide from us the metaphysical reality which all beings have in common. This view makes us look upon our fellow beings with kindliness and compassion. The wise see the one God in all beings and develop the quality of equalmindedness which is characteristic of the Divine.

19. *ihai 'va tair jitaḥ sargo*
yeṣāṁ sāmye sthitaṁ manaḥ
nirdoṣaṁ hi samaṁ brahma
tasmād brahmaṇi te sthitāḥ

(19) Even here (on earth) the created (world) is overcome by those whose mind is established in equality. God is flawless and the same in all. Therefore are these (persons) established in God.

See *Chāndogya Up.*, II, 23. 1.
The state of liberation is one which we can attain here on earth.

20. *na prahṛṣyet priyaṁ prāpya*
no 'dvijet prāpya cā 'priyam
sthirabuddhir asaṁmūḍho
brahmavid brahmaṇi sthitaḥ

(20) One should not rejoice on obtaining what is pleasant nor sorrow on obtaining what is unpleasant. He who is (thus) firm of understanding and unbewildered, (such a) knower of God is established in God.

brahmaṇi sthitaḥ: established in God. He gets at It, reaches It, enters into It and is fairly established in It.

21. *bāhyasparśeṣv asaktātmā*
vindaty ātmani yat sukham
sa brahmayogayuktātmā
sukham akṣayam aśnute

[1] *ekasyāpi kūṭasthasya cittatāratamyāt, jñānaiśvaryāṇām abhivyaktiḥ pareṇa pareṇa bhūyasī bhavati.* S-B.I., 3, 30.

(21) When the soul is no longer attached to external contacts (objects) one finds the happiness that is in the Self. Such a one who is self-controlled in Yoga on God (Brahma) enjoys undying bliss.

He, who has freed himself from the phantoms of the senses and lives in the Eternal, enjoys the bliss divine.[1]

22. *ye hi saṁsparśajā bhogā*
duḥkhayonaya eva te
ādyantavantaḥ kaunteya
na teṣu ramate budhaḥ

(22) Whatever pleasures are born of contacts (with objects) are only sources of sorrow, they have a beginning and an end, O Son of Kuntī (Arjuna), no wise man delights in them.

See II, 14*n*.[2]

23. *śaknotī 'hai 'va yaḥ soḍhuṁ*
prāk śarīravimokṣaṇāt
kāmakrodhodbhavaṁ vegaṁ
sa yuktaḥ sa sukhī naraḥ

(23) He who is able to resist the rush of desire and anger, even here before he gives up his body, he is a yogin, he is the happy man.

The non-attachment from which inner peace, freedom and joy arise is capable of realization even here on earth, even when we lead embodied lives. In the midst of human life, peace within can be attained.

Peace from Within

24. *yo 'ntaḥsukho 'ntarārāmas*
tathā 'ntarjyotir eva yaḥ
sa yogī brahmanirvāṇaṁ
brahmabhūto 'dhigacchati

[1] Cp. Brother Lawrence: "I know, that, for the right practice of it, the heart must be empty of all else; because God wills to possess the heart alone; and as He cannot possess it alone unless it is empty of all else, so He cannot work in it what He would unless it be left vacant for Him." *The Practice of the Presence of God.*

[2] Cp. *Bhāgavata*
sukhasyānantaraṁ duḥkhaṁ duḥkhasyānantaraṁ sukham
cakravat parivarttete sukhaduḥkhe nirantaram.

(24) He who finds his happiness within, his joy within and likewise his light only within, that yogin becomes divine and attains to the beatitude of God (brahmanirvāṇa).

The yogin becomes unified in consciousness with the Eternal in him. The next verse indicates that this nirvāṇa is not mere annihilation. It is a positive state full of knowledge and self-possession.

25. *labhante brahmanirvāṇaṁ*
ṛṣayaḥ kṣīṇakalmaṣāḥ
chinnadvaidhā yatātmānaḥ
sarvabhūtahite ratāḥ

(25) The holy men whose sins are destroyed, whose doubts (dualities) are cut asunder, whose minds are disciplined and who rejoice in (doing) good to all creatures, attain to the beatitude of God.

sarvabhūtahite ratāh: the soul which has acquired wisdom and peace is also the soul of love and compassion. He who sees all existence in the Supreme, sees the Divine even in the fallen and the criminal, and goes out to them in deep love and sympathy.

To do good to others is not to give them physical comforts or raise their standard of living. It is to help others to find their true nature, to attain true happiness The contemplation of the Eternal Reality in whom we all dwell gives warmth and support to the sense of the service of fellow-creatures. All work is for the sake of the Supreme. *jagad hitāya kṛṣṇāya.* To overcome the world is not to become other-worldly. It is not to evade the social responsibilities.

The two sides of religion, the personal and the social, are emphasized by the *Gītā*. Personally, we should discover the Divine in us and let it penetrate the human; socially, society must be subdued to the image of the Divine. The individual should grow in his freedom and uniqueness and he should recognize the dignity of every man, even the most insignificant. Man has not only to ascend to the world of spirit but also to descend to the world of creatures.[1]

[1] Cp. *dṛṣṭiṁ jñānamayīṁ kṛtvā,*
paśyed brahmamayaṁ jagat.

26 *kāmakrodhaviyuktānāṁ*
yatīnāṁ yatacetasām
abhito brahmanirvāṇaṁ
vartate viditātmanām

(26) To those austere souls (yatis) who are delivered from desire and anger and who have subdued their minds and have knowledge of the Self, near to them lies the beatitude of God.

They live in the consciousness of Spirit. The possibility of blessed existence in this world is indicated here.

27 *sparśān kṛtvā bahir bāhyāṁś*
cakṣuś cai 'vā 'ntare bhruvoḥ
prāṇāpānau samau kṛtvā
nāsābhyantaracāriṇau

28. *yatendriyamanobuddhir*
munir mokṣaparāyaṇaḥ
vigatecchābhayakrodho
yaḥ sadā mukta eva saḥ

(27) and (28). Shutting out all external objects, fixing the vision between the eyebrows, making even the inward and the outward breaths moving within the nostrils, the sage who has controlled the senses, mind and understanding, who is intent on liberation, who has cast away desire, fear and anger, he is ever freed.

Cp. "When one fixes the thought on the midpoint between the two eyes the Light streams of its own accord."[1] It is symbolic of union with buddhi, that gives spiritual knowledge.

29. *bhoktāraṁ yajñatapasāṁ*
sarvalokamaheśvaram
suhṛdaṁ sarvabhūtānāṁ
jñātvā māṁ śāntim ṛcchati

(29) And having known Me as the Enjoyer of sacrifices and

[1] *The Secret of the Golden Flower.* E.T. by Wilhelm.

austerities, the Great Lord of all the worlds, the Friend of all beings, he (the sage) attains peace.

The transcendent God becomes the lord of all creation, the friend of all creatures, who does good to them without expecting any return.[1] God is not merely the distant world-ruler but an intimate friend and helper, ever ready to assist us in overcoming evil, if only we trust Him. The *Bhāgavata* says: "Of whom I am the beloved, the self, the son, the friend, the teacher, the relative and the desired deity."[2]

iti . . . karmasaṁnyāsayogo nāma pañcamo 'dhyāyaḥ

This is the fifth chapter entitled The Yoga of Renunciation of Action.

[1] *sarvaprāṇināṁ pratyupakāranirapekṣatayā upakāriṇam.* Ś. See also S.B.G., IX, 18.

[2] *yeṣām aham priya, ātmā, sutaś ca*
sakhā, guruḥ, suhṛdo, daivam iṣṭam.
III, 25, 38.

CHAPTER VI

The True Yoga

Renunciation and Action are One

śrībhagavān uvāca

1. *anāśritaḥ karmaphalaṁ*
kāryaṁ karma karoti yaḥ
sa saṁnyāsī ca yogī ca
na niragnir na cā 'kriyaḥ

The Blessed Lord said:

(1) He who does the work which he ought to do without seeking its fruit he is the saṁnyāsin, he is the yogin, not he who does not light the sacred fire, and performs no rites.

The teacher emphasizes that saṁnyāsa or renunciation has little to do with outward works. It is an inward attitude. To become a saṁnyāsin it is not necessary to give up the sacrificial fire and the daily ritual. To abstain from these without the spirit of renunciation is futile.

Ś., however, by the use of the word "kevalam," makes out that "he who does not light the sacred fire and performs no rites is not the only saṁnyāsin." This does not seem to be quite fair to the text.

2. *yaṁ saṁnyāsam iti prāhur*
yogaṁ taṁ viddhi pāṇḍava
na hy asaṁnyastasaṁkalpo
yogī bhavati kaścana

(2) What they call renunciation, that know to be disciplined activity, O Pāṇḍava (Arjuna), for no one becomes a yogin who has not renounced his (selfish) purpose.

saṁnyāsa: renunciation. It consists in the accomplishment of the necessary action without an inward striving for reward. This is true yoga, firm control over oneself, complete self-possession.

This verse says that disciplined activity (yoga) is just as good as renunciation (saṁnyāsa).

The Pathway and the Goal

3. *ārurukṣor muner yogaṁ*
karma kāraṇam ucyate
yogārūḍhasya tasyai 'va
śamaḥ kāraṇam ucyate

(3) Work is said to be the means of the sage who wishes to attain to yoga; when he has attained to yoga, serenity is said to be the means.

When we are aspirants for liberation (*sādhanāvasthā*), work done in the right spirit with inner renunciation helps us. When once we achieve self-possession (*siddhāvasthā*) we act, not for gaining any end but out of our anchorage in God-consciousness. Through work we struggle to obtain self-control; when self-control is attained, we obtain peace. It does not follow that we then abandon all action. For in VI, 1, it is stated that the true yogin is one who performs work and not one who renounces it. Śama does not mean the cessation of karma. It cannot be the cause (kāraṇa) of wisdom, for the perfected sage has already attained wisdom. V, 12 says that the yogin attains complete tranquillity by abandoning the fruit of action. He performs actions with a perfect equanimity. He overflows with a spontaneous vitality and works with a generosity which arises from his own inexhaustible strength.

4. *yadā hi ne 'ndriyārtheṣu*
na karmasv anuṣajjate
sarvasaṁkalpasaṁnyāsī
yogārūḍhas tado 'cyate

(4) When one does not get attached to the objects of sense or to works, and has renounced all purposes, then, he is said to have attained to yoga.

sarvasaṁkalpasaṁnyāsī: one who has renounced all purposes. We must give up our likes and dislikes, forget ourselves, leave ourselves out. By the abandonment of all purposes, by the mortification of the ego, by the total surrender to the will of the Supreme, the aspirant develops a condition of mind approximating to the Eternal. He partakes in some measure the undifferentiated timeless consciousness of that which he desires to apprehend.

The freed soul works without desire and attachment, without the egoistic will of which desires are born. Manu says that all desires are born of saṁkalpa.[1] M.B. says: "O desire, I know thy root. Thou art born of saṁkalpa or thought. I shall not think of thee and thou shalt cease to exist."[2]

5. *uddhared ātmanā 'tmānaṁ*
nā 'tmānam avasādayet
ātmai 'va hy ātmano bandhur
ātmai 'va ripur ātmanaḥ

(5) Let a man lift himself by himself; let him not degrade himself; for the Self alone is the friend of the self and the Self alone is the enemy of the self.

Cp. *Dhammapada*: "The Self is the lord of the self;"[3] "the Self is the goal of the self."[4]

The Supreme is within us. It is the consciousness underlying the ordinary individualized consciousness of every-day life but incommensurable with it. The two are different in kind, though the Supreme is realizable by one who is prepared to lose his life in order to save it. For the most part we are unaware of the Self in us because our attention is engaged by objects which we like or dislike. We must get away from them, to become aware of the Divine in us. If we do not realize the pointlessness, the irrelevance and the squalor of our ordinary life, the true Self becomes the enemy of our ordinary life. The Universal Self and the personal self are not antagonistic to each other. The Universal Self can be the friend or the foe of the personal self. If we subdue our petty cravings and desires, if we do not exert our selfish will, we become the channel of the Universal Self. If our impulses are under control, and if our personal self offers itself to the Universal

[1] *saṁkalpamūlaḥ kāmo vai yajñāḥ saṁkalpasaṁbhavāḥ*. II, 3.

[2] *kāma, jānāmi te mūlam, saṁkalpāt tvaṁ hi jāyase*
na tvāṁ saṁkalpayiṣyāmi tena me na bhaviṣyasi.
Śāntiparva, 77, 25.

[3] *attā hi attano nātho*. 160.

[4] *attā hi attano gati*. 380.

Self, then the latter becomes our guide and teacher.[1] Every one of us has the freedom to rise or fall and our future is in our own hands.

6. *bandhur ātmā 'tmanas tasya*
yenā 'tmai 'vā 'tmanā jitaḥ
anātmanas tu śatrutve
vartetā 'tmai 'va śatruvat

(6) For him who has conquered his (lower) self by the (higher) Self his Self is a friend but for him who has not possessed his (higher) Self, his very Self will act in enmity, like an enemy.

We are called upon to master the lower self by the higher. The determinism of nature is here qualified by the power to control nature. The lower self is not to be destroyed. It can be used as a helper, if it is held in check.

7. *jitātmanaḥ praśāntasya*
paramātmā samāhitaḥ
śītoṣṇasukhaduḥkheṣu
tathā mānāpamānayoḥ

(7) When one has conquered one's self (lower) and has attained to the calm of self-mastery, his Supreme Self abides ever concentrate, he is at peace in cold and heat, in pleasure and pain, in honour and dishonour.

[1] Boehme says: "Nothing truly but thine own willing, hearing and seeing do keep thee back from it, and do hinder thee from coming to this supersensual state. And it is because thou strivest so against that, out of which thou thyself art descended and derived, that thou thus breakest thyself off, with thine own willing, from God's willing, and with thy own seeing from God's seeing." St. John of the Cross says: "The more the soul cleaves to created things relying on its own strength, by habit and inclination, the less is it disposed for this union, because it does not completely resign itself into the hands of God, that He may transform it supernaturally."

Jāmi wrote in his *Lawā'iḥ*:

Make my heart pure, my soul from error free,
Make tears and sighs my daily lot to be,
And lead me on Thy road away from self,
That lost to self I may approach to Thee.

Whinfield's E. T.

This is the state of blessedness of the person who has established himself in unity with the Universal Self. He is a *jitātman* whose calm and serenity are not disturbed by the pains of the opposites.

paramātmā samāhitaḥ: Ś. says that the Supreme Self regards him as His very self.[1] The self in the body is generally absorbed by the world of dualities, cold and heat, pain and pleasure but when it controls the senses and masters the world, the self becomes free. The Supreme Self is not different from the self in the body. When the self is bound by the modes of prakṛti or nature, it is called kṣetrajña; when it is freed from them, the same self is called the Supreme Self.[2] This is certainly the position of Advaita (non-dual) Vedānta.

Those who are opposed to this view break up paramātmā into two words, param and ātmā, and look upon the word param as an adverb qualifying the verb samāhitaḥ.

R. takes param as an adverb and holds that the self is sublimely realized.

Śrīdhara says that such a person becomes concentrated in his self.[3] Ānandagiri holds that the self of such a person becomes completely concentrated.[4]

sama-āhita: firmly directed to equality. This is not, however, the usual explanation.

8. *jñānavijñānatṛptātmā*
kūṭastho vijitendriyaḥ
yukta ity ucyate yogī
samaloṣṭāśmakāñcanaḥ

(8) The ascetic (yogi) whose soul is satisfied with wisdom and knowledge, who is unchanging and master of his senses, to whom a clod, a stone and a piece of gold are the same, is said to be controlled (in yoga).

jñāna vijñāna: see III, 41 note.

kūṭastha: literally, set on a high place, immovable, changeless, firm, steady, tranquil.

[1] *sākṣāt ātmabhāvena vartate.*

[2] Cp. M.B. *ātmā kṣetrajña ity uktaḥ saṁyuktaḥ prākṛtair guṇaiḥ*
tair eva tu vinirmuktaḥ paramātmety udāhṛtaḥ.
Śantiparva, 187, 24.

[3] *samāhitaḥ ātmaniṣṭhaḥ bhavati.*

[4] *sam-ā-hita* cp. *samādhi: jitātmanaḥ nirvikāracittasya ātmā, cittaṁ param utkarṣeṇa samāhitaḥ samādhiṁ prāptaḥ bhavati.*

The yogin is said to be yukta or in yoga when he is concentrating on the Supreme above the changes of the world. Such a yogin is satisfied with the knowledge and experience of the Reality behind the appearances. He is unperturbed by things and happenings of the world and is therefore said to be equal-minded to the events of this changing world.

9. *suhṛnmitrāryudāsīna-*
madhyasthadveṣyabandhuṣu
sādhuṣv api ca pāpeṣu
samabuddhir viśiṣyate

(9) He who is equal-minded among friends, companions and foes, among those who are neutral and impartial, among those who are hateful and related, among saints and sinners, he excels.

Another reading for *viśiṣyate* is *vimucyate*. S.B.G.
How is one to attain to this yoga?

Eternal Vigilance over Body and Mind is Essential

10. *yogī yuñjīta satatam*
ātmānaṁ rahasi sthitaḥ
ekākī yatacittātmā
nirāśīr aparigrahaḥ

(10) Let the yogin try constantly to concentrate his mind (on the Supreme Self) remaining in solitude and alone, self-controlled, free from desires and (longing for) possessions.

Here the teacher develops the technique of mental discipline on the lines of Patañjali's *Yoga Sūtra*. Its main purpose is to raise our consciousness from its ordinary waking condition to higher levels until it attains union with the Supreme. The human mind is ordinarily turned outwards. Absorption in the mechanical and material sides of life leads to a disbalanced condition of consciousness. Yoga attempts to explore the inner world of consciousness and helps to integrate the conscious and the subconscious.

We must divest our minds of all sensual desires, abstract our attention from all external objects and absorb it in the object of meditation.[1] See B.G., XVIII, 72, where the teacher asks Arjuna whether he heard his teaching with his mind fixed to one point, *ekāgreṇa cetasā*. As the aim is the attainment of purity of vision, it exacts of the mind fineness and steadiness. Our present dimensions are not the ultimate limits of our being. By summoning all the energies of the mind and fixing them on one point, we raise the level of reference from the empirical to the real, from observation to vision and let the spirit take possession of our whole being. In the *Book of Proverbs*, it is said that "the spirit of man is the candle of the Lord." There is something in the inmost being of man which can be struck into flame by God.

satatam: constantly. The practice must be constant. It is no use taking to meditation by fits and starts. A continuous creative effort is necessary for developing the higher, the intenser form of consciousness.

rahasi: in solitude. The aspirant must select a quiet place with soothing natural surroundings such as the banks of rivers or tops of hills which lift our hearts and exalt our minds. In a world which is daily growing noisier, the duty of the civilized man is to have moments of thoughtful stillness. Cp. "Thou, when thou prayest, enter into thy closet—and shut the door."[2] We should retire into a quiet place and keep off external distractions. Cp. Origen's description of the first hermits: "They dwelt in the desert where the air was more pure and the heaven more open and God more familiar."

ekākī: alone. The teacher insists that the seeker should be alone to feel the gentle pressure, to hear the quiet voice.

yatacittātmā: self-controlled. He must not be excited, strained or anxious. To learn to be quiet before God means a life of control and discipline. ātmā is used in the sense of deha or body, according to Ś. and Śrīdhara. It is no use entering the closet with the daily paper and the business file. Even if we leave them outside and shut the doors and windows, we may have an unquiet time with all our worries and preoccupations. There should be no restlessness or turbulence. Through thoughts we appeal to the intellect; through silence we touch the deeper

[1] It is what Boehme calls the "stopping the wheel of the imagination and ceasing from self-thinking."

[2] *Matthew* vi, 6.

layers of being. The heart must become clean if it is to reflect God who is to be seen and known only by the pure in heart. We must centre down into that deep stillness and wait on the Light. "Commune with your Father which is in secret." The Living Presence of God is revealed in silence to each soul according to his capacity, and need.[1]

Plato's *Meno* begins with the question, "Can you tell me, Socrates, is virtue to be taught?" The answer of Socrates is, that virtue is not taught but "recollected." Recollection is a gathering of one's self together, a retreat into one's soul. The doctrine of "recollection" suggests that each individual should enquire within himself. He is his own centre and possesses the truth in himself. What is needed is that he should have the will and the perseverance to follow it up. The function of the teacher is not to teach but to help to put the learner in possession of himself. The questioner has the true answer in himself, if only he can be delivered of it. Every man is in possession of the truth and is dispossessed of it by his entanglement in the objective world. By identifying ourselves with the objective world, we are ejected or alienated from our true nature. Lost in the outer world, we desert the deeps. In transcending the object, physical and mental, we find ourselves in the realm of freedom.

nirāśi: free from desires. Worry about daily needs, about earning and spending money, disturbs meditation and takes us away from the life of the spirit. So we are asked to be free from desire and anxiety born of it, from greed and fear. The seeker should try to tear himself away from these psychic fetters and get detached from all distractions and prejudices. He must put away all clinging to mental preferences, vital aims, attachment to family and friends. He must expect nothing, insist on nothing.

aparigrahaḥ: free from longing for possessions. This freedom is a spiritual state, not a material condition. We must control the appetite for possessions, free ourselves from the tyranny of belongings. One cannot hear God's voice, if one is restless and self-centred, if one is dominated by feelings of pride, self-will or possessiveness. The *Gītā* points out that true happiness is inward.

[1] Cp. Wordsworth's statement, that "poetry takes its origin from emotion recollected in tranquillity." Rilke in his *Letters to a Young Poet* says: "I can give you no other advice than this, retire into yourself and probe the depths from which your life springs up."

It invites our attention to the manner of our life, the state of human consciousness, which does not depend on the outward machinery of life. The body may die and the world pass away but the life in spirit endures. Our treasures are not the things of the world that perish but the knowledge and love of God that endure. We must get out of the slavery to things to gain the glad freedom of spirit.[1]

11 *śucau deśe pratiṣṭhāpya*
sthiram āsanam ātmanaḥ
nā 'tyucchritaṁ nā 'tinīcaṁ
cailājinakuśottaram

(11) He should set in a clean place his firm seat, neither too high nor too low, covered with sacred grass, a deerskin and a cloth, one over the other.

12 *tatrai 'kāgraṁ manaḥ kṛtvā*
yatacittendriyakriyaḥ
upaviśyā 'sane yuñjyād
yogam ātmaviśuddhaye

(12) There taking his place on the seat, making his mind one-pointed and controlling his thought and sense, let him practise yoga for the purification of the soul.

yoga here means dhyāna yoga, meditation. To realize truth, man must be delivered from the clutches of practical interests which are bound up with our exterior and material life. The chief condition is a disciplined disinterestedness. We must develop the power to see things as a free undistorted intelligence would see them. For this we must get *ourselves* out of the way. When Pythagoras was questioned why he called himself a philo-

[1] To the rich man who said that he had kept all the commandments, Jesus answered, "Yet lackest thou one thing: sell all that thou hast, and distribute unto the poor, and thou shalt have treasure in heaven." When Jesus saw that the rich man was very sorrowful, he said: "How hardly shall they that have riches enter into the Kingdom of God! For it is easier for a camel to go through a needle's eye, than for a rich man to enter into the Kingdom of God." *St. Luke* xviii, 18–23.

sopher he gave the following story. He compared human life with the great festival at Olympia where all the world comes together in a motley crowd. Some are there to do business at the fair and enjoy themselves. Others wish to win the wreath in the contest and some others are merely spectators and these last are the philosophers. They keep themselves free from the urgencies of immediate problems and practical necessities. Ś. points out that the essential qualifications of a seeker of wisdom are a capacity to discriminate between the eternal and the non-eternal, detachment from the enjoyment of the fruits of action, terrestrial and celestial, self-control and an ardent desire for spiritual freedom.[1] For Plato, the aim of all knowledge is to raise us to the contemplation of the idea of good, the source alike of being and knowing, and the ideal philosopher is one whose goal, at the end of a life lived to the full, "is always a life of quiet, of indrawn stillness, of solitude and aloofness, in which the world forgetting, by the world forgot, he finds his heaven in lonely contemplation of the 'good.' That and that alone is really life." "Blessed are the pure in heart for they shall see God." This purification of the heart, cittaśuddhi, is a matter of discipline. Plotinus tells us that "wisdom is a condition in a being at rest."[2]

13. *samaṁ kāyaśirogrīvaṁ*
dhārayann acalaṁ sthiraḥ
saṁprekṣya nāsikāgraṁ svaṁ
diśaś cā 'navalokayan

(13) Holding the body, head and neck, erect and still, looking fixedly at the tip of his nose, without looking around (without allowing his eyes to wander).

Posture or āsana is here mentioned. Patañjali points out that the posture should be steady and pleasing so as to aid concentration. A right posture gives serenity of body. The body must be kept clean if the living image of God is to be installed in it.

saṁprekṣya nāsikāgram. The gaze is to be fixed on the tip of the nose. A wandering gaze is not a help to concentration.

[1] *nityānityavastuviveka, ihāmūtraphalabhogavirāgaḥ, śamādisādhana saṁpat, mumukṣutvam.*

[2] *Enneads*, IV, 4, 12.

14. *praśāntātmā vigatabhīr*
brahmacārivrate sthitaḥ
manaḥ saṁyamya maccitto
yukta āsīta matparaḥ

(14) Serene and fearless, firm in the vow of celibacy, subdued in mind, let him sit, harmonized, his mind turned to Me and intent on Me alone.

brahmacārivrate sthitaḥ: firm in the vow of celibacy. The aspirant for yoga must exercise control over sex impulses. Hindu tradition has insisted on brahmacarya from the beginning. In the *Praśna Up.*, Pippalāda asks the seekers to observe brahmacarya for a year more at the end of which he undertakes to initiate them into the highest wisdom. In *Chāndogya Up.*, Brahmā taught Indra the knowledge of Reality after making him undergo brahmacarya for 101 years. Brahmacarya is defined as abstinence from sex intercourse in thought, word and deed in all conditions and places and times.[1] The gods are said to have conquered death by brahmacarya and penance.[2] In *Jñānasaṁkalinī Tantra*, Śiva says that true tapas is brahmacarya and he who practises it uninterruptedly is divine, not human.[3] It is not ascetic celibacy that is meant by brahmacarya, but control. Hindu tradition affirms that a householder who controls his sex life is a brahmacāri

[1] Yājñavalkya writes:
karmaṇā manasā vācā sarvāvasthāsu sarvadā
sarvatra maithunatyāgo brahmacaryaṁ pracakṣate.

[2] *brahmacaryeṇa tapasā devā mṛtyum upāghnata. Atharva Veda.*

[3] *na tapas tapa ity āhuḥ brahmacaryaṁ tapottamam*
ūrdhvaretā bhaved yastu sa devo na tu mānuṣaḥ.

The difficulty of chastity is illustrated in the lives of many saints. St. Augustine used to pray: "Give me chastity and continence, only not yet." *Confessions*, Bk. VIII, Ch. VII. Rodin has the whole thing in a piece of sculpture called the Eternal Idol where a woman on her knees, but leaning backward, with body thrust forward and arms hanging loose receives between her breasts the bearded face of a man who kneels before her in servile longing for her embrace. There is hardly one man in a thousand who will not put aside his ideals, his highest vision, everything which for him represents God in order to get the woman he loves. In the opinion of many contemporaries chastity is a condition which is as selfish as it is dull. To them the Hindu emphasis on it may seem somewhat odd and exaggerated.

quite as truly as one who abstains from sex altogether.[1] To be a celibate is not to deaden the senses and deny the heart.

The qualities demanded for the practice of Yoga may be compared with the three Evangelical counsels of Poverty, Chastity and Obedience by which we overcome the world, the flesh and the devil.

The negative process of bringing all thoughts to a standstill has for its positive side, concentration on the Self. *Īśvara-praṇidhāna* is a recognized way in yoga discipline. The mind becomes still but not vacant, for it is fixed on the Supreme *maccittaḥ matparaḥ*.

Only the single-visioned see the Real. Spiritual life is not prayer or petition. It is profound devoutness, silent meditation, the opening of the consciousness to the innermost depths of the soul, which connect the individual self directly with the Divine Principle. Those who learn this art do not require any external assistance, any belief in dogma or participation in ritual. They acquire the creative vision since they combine absorption with detachment. They act in the world, but the passionless tranquillity of the spirit remains undisturbed. They are compared to the lotus on the lake which is unruffled by the tide.

15. *yuñjann evaṁ sadā 'tmānaṁ*
yogī niyatamānasaḥ
śāntiṁ nirvāṇaparamāṁ
matsaṁsthām adhigacchati

(15) The yogin of subdued mind, ever keeping himself thus harmonized, attains to peace, the supreme nirvāṇa, which abides in Me

16. *nā 'tyaśnatas tu yogo 'sti*
na cai 'kāntam anaśnataḥ
na cā 'tisvapnaśīlasya
jāgrato nai 'va cā 'rjuna

[1] *bhāryāṁ gacchan brahmacārī ṛtau bhavati vai dvijaḥ*. M.B. See also *Manu*.

Hindu tradition looks upon Ahalyā, Sītā, Maṇḍodarī, Draupadī and Tārā as models of chastity, *mahāpativratā*. They are also called *pañcamahākanyā*. Thomas Hardy asks us to look upon Tess as a pure woman Chastity is a condition of mind.

(16) Verily, yoga is not for him who eats too much or abstains too much from eating. It is not for him, O Arjuna, who sleeps too much or keeps awake too much.

We must be free from animal cravings. We must avoid excess in all things. Compare with this the middle path of the Buddhists, the golden mean of Aristotle.

17. *yuktāhāravihārasya*
yuktaceṣṭasya karmasu
yuktasvapnāvabodhasya
yogo bhavati duḥkhahā

(17) For the man who is temperate in food and recreation, who is restrained in his actions, whose sleep and waking are regulated, there ensues discipline (yoga) which destroys all sorrow.

It is not complete abstinence from action but restraint in action that is advised. When the ego is established in the Self, it lives in a transcendent and universal consciousness and acts from that centre.

The Perfect Yogi

18 *yadā viniyataṁ cittam*
ātmany evā 'vatiṣṭhate
niḥspṛhaḥ sarvakāmebhyo
yukta ity ucyate tadā

(18) When the disciplined mind is established in the Self alone, liberated from all desires, then is he said to be harmonized (in yoga).

Complete effacement of the ego is essential for the vision of truth. Every taint of individuality should disappear, if truth is to be known. There should be an elimination of all our prejudices and idiosyncrasies.

In these verses, the teacher gives the procedure by which the seeker can gain the experience of the Essential Self. In the ordinary experience of the outer or the inner world, the Self in union with the body is immersed in phenomenal multiplicity and remains veiled because of it. We should first of all empty the soul of every specific operation, rid it of every image, of every particular representation, of every distinct operation of mind. This is a negative process. It may be thought that by draining our consciousness of every image, we end in a pure and simple nothingness. The teacher makes out that the negative process is adopted to apprehend the Pure Self, to achieve the beatific vision. The silence is made perfect and the void is consummated through this apparently negative but intensely vital mystical contemplation, involving a tension of the forces of the soul. It is an experience which transcends all knowledge; for the Self is not an object expressible in a concept or presentable to mind as an object. It is inexpressible subjectivity.

19. *yathā dīpo nivātastho*
ne 'ṅgate so 'pamā smṛtā
yogino yatacittasya
yuñjato yogam ātmanaḥ

(19) As a lamp in a windless place flickereth not, to such is likened the yogi of subdued thought who practises union with the Self (or discipline of himself)

The yogi's thought is absorbed in the Ātman. Fleeting glimpses or passing visions should not be confused with the insight into Ātman which is the one safeguard against all delusions.

20. *yatro 'paramate cittaṁ*
niruddhaṁ yogasevayā
yatra cai 'vā 'tmanā 'tmānaṁ
paśyann ātmani tuṣyati

(20) That in which thought is at rest, restrained by the practice of concentration, that in which he beholds the Self through the self and rejoices in the Self;

21. *sukham ātyantikaṁ yat tad*
buddhigrāhyam atīndriyam
vetti yatra na cai 'vā 'yaṁ
sthitaś calati tattvataḥ

(21) That in which he finds this supreme delight, perceived by the intelligence and beyond the reach of the senses, wherein established, he no longer falls away from the truth;

See *Kaṭha Up.*, III, 12. While the Supreme is beyond perception by the senses, it is seizable by reason, not by the reason which deals with sense data and frames concepts on their basis but reason which works in its own right. When it does so, it becomes aware of things not indirectly, through the medium of the senses or the relations based on them, but by becoming one with them. All true knowledge is knowledge by identity.[1] Our knowledge through physical contact or mental symbols is indirect and approximate. Religion is contemplative realization of God.

22 *yaṁ labdhvā cā 'paraṁ lābhaṁ*
manyate nā 'dhikaṁ tataḥ
yasmin sthito na duḥkhena
guruṇā 'pi vicālyate

(22) That, on gaining which he thinks that there is no greater gain beyond it, wherein established he is not shaken even by the heaviest sorrow;

23. *taṁ vidyād duḥkhasaṁyoga-*
viyogaṁ yogasaṁjñitam
sa niścayena yoktavyo
yogo 'nirviṇṇacetasā

(23) Let that be known by the name of yoga, this disconnection from union with pain. This yoga should be practised with determination, with heart undismayed.

In verses 10–22 the intense fixation of the mind on its object with a view to liberation is taught. It is the repose of the liberated spirit in its own absoluteness and isolation. The self rejoices in the Self. It is the *kaivalya* of the Sāṁkhya puruṣa, though, in the *Gītā*, it becomes identified with blessedness in God.
anirviṇṇacetasā: nirvedarahitena cetasā. Ś. We must practise yoga without slackness of effort arising from the thought of prospective pain.

[1] Madhusūdana cites the verse.
samādhinirdhūtamalasya cetaso niveśitasy ātmani yat sukham bhavet na śakyate varṇayituṁ girā tadā svayaṁ tad antaḥkaraṇena gṛhyate.

24. *saṁkalpaprabhavān kāmāṁs*
tyaktvā sarvān aśeṣataḥ
manasai 've 'ndriyagrāmaṁ
viniyamya samantataḥ

(24) Abandoning without exception all desires born of (selfish) will, restraining with the mind all the senses on every side;

25. *śanaiḥ-śanair uparamed*
buddhyā dhṛtigṛhītayā
ātmasaṁsthaṁ manaḥ kṛtvā
na kiṁcid api cintayet

(25) Let him gain little by little tranquillity by means of reason controlled by steadiness and having fixed the mind on the Self, let him not think of anything (else).

26. *yato-yato niścarati*
manaś cañcalam asthiram
tatas-tato niyamyai 'tad
ātmany eva vaśaṁ nayet

(26) Whatsoever makes the wavering and unsteady mind wander away let him restrain and bring it back to the control of the Self alone.

27. *praśāntamanasaṁ hy enaṁ*
yoginaṁ sukham uttamam
upaiti śāntarajasaṁ
brahmabhūtam akalmaṣam

(27) For supreme happiness comes to the yogin whose mind is peaceful, whose passions are at rest, who is stainless and has become one with God.

brahmabhūtam: one with God. We become what we behold according to the rule of the wasp and the bee, *bhramarakīṭanyāya.* Even as the wasp which is threatened by the bee thinks of the bee so intently that it itself is transformed into the bee, so also the upāsaka (meditator) becomes one with the object of meditation (upāsya).

brahmatvaṃ prāptaṁ. Śrīdhara.[1]

Progress consists in the purification of body, life and mind. When the frame is perfected, the Light shines without any obstruction.

28. *yuñjann evaṁ sadā 'tmānaṁ*
yogī vigatakalmaṣaḥ
sukhena brahmasaṁsparśam
atyantaṁ sukham aśnute

(28) Thus making the self ever harmonized, the yogin, who has put away sin, experiences easily the infinite bliss of contact with the Eternal.

brahmasaṁsparśam: contact with the Eternal. God is no more a mere rumour, a vague aspiration, but a vivid reality with which we are in actual contact. Religion is not a matter of dialectic but a fact of experience. Reason may step in and offer a logical explanation of the fact but the reasoning becomes irrelevant, if it is not based on the solid foundation of fact.

Besides, these facts of religious experience are universal, in space and in time. They are found in different parts of the world and different periods of its history, attesting to the persistent unity and aspiration of the human spirit. The illuminations of the Hindu and the Buddhist seers, of Socrates and Plato, of Philo and Plotinus, of Christian and Muslim mystics, belong to the same family, though the theological attempts to account for them reflect the temperaments of the race and the epoch.

In the following verses the teacher describes the marks of the ideal yogin. His thought is subdued, his desire is cast off and he contemplates only the Self and is cut off from contact with pain and is at one with the Supreme Reality.

29. *sarvabhūtastham ātmānaṁ*
sarvabhūtāni cā 'tmani
īkṣate yogayuktātmā
sarvatra samadarśanaḥ

[1] Nilakaṇṭha believes that this state is one of samprajñāta samādhi and quotes *Yogabhāṣya*: *yastv ekāgre cetasi sadbhūtam artham pradyotayati karmabandhanāni śladhayati nirodham abhimukhī karoti kṣiṇotiśca kleśān sa samprajñāto yoga ity ākhyāyate.*

(29) He whose self is harmonized by yoga seeth the Self abiding in all beings and all beings in the Self; everywhere he sees the same.

Though, in the process of attaining the vision of Self, we had to retreat from outward things and separate the Self from the world, when the vision is attained the world is drawn into the Self. On the ethical plane, this means that there should grow a detachment from the world and when it is attained, a return to it, through love, suffering and sacrifice for it.

The sense of a separate finite self with its hopes and fears, its likes and dislikes is destroyed.

30. *yo māṁ paśyati sarvatra*
sarvaṁ ca mayi paśyati
tasyā 'haṁ na praṇaśyāmi
sa ca me na praṇaśyati

(30) He who sees Me every where and sees all in Me; I am not lost to him nor is he lost to Me.

It is personal mysticism as distinct from the impersonal one that is stressed in these tender and impressive words: "I am not lost to him nor is he lost to Me." The verse reveals the experience of the profound unity of all things in One who is the personal God. The more unique, the more universal. The deeper the self, the wider is its comprehension. When we are one with the Divine in us, we become one with the whole stream of life.

31 *sarvabhūtasthitaṁ yo māṁ*
bhajaty ekatvam āsthitaḥ
sarvathā vartamāno 'pi
sa yogī mayi vartate

(31) The yogin who established in oneness, worships Me abiding in all beings lives in Me, howsoever he may be active.

Whatever be his outer life, in his inward being he dwells in God. The true life of man is his inner life.

32. *ātmaupamyena sarvatra*
samaṁ paśyati yo 'rjuna
sukhaṁ vā yadi vā duḥkhaṁ
sa yogī paramo mataḥ

(32) He, O Arjuna, who sees with equality everything, in the image of his own self, whether in pleasure or in pain, he is considered a perfect yogi.

Ātma-aupamya means equality of others with oneself. Even as he desires good to himself, he desires good to all. He embraces all things in God, leads men to divine life and acts in the world with the power of Spirit and in that luminous consciousness. He harms no creature as, in the words of Ś., "he sees that whatever is pleasant to himself is pleasant to all creatures, and that whatever is painful to himself is painful to all beings."[1] He does not any more shrink from pleasure and pain. As he sees God in the world, he fears nothing but embraces all in the equality of the vision of the Self.

Control of Mind is Difficult but Possible

arjuna uvāca

33. *yo 'yaṁ yogas tvayā proktaḥ*
sāmyena madhusūdana
etasyā 'haṁ na paśyāmi
cañcalatvāt sthitiṁ sthirām

Arjuna said:

(33) This yoga declared by you to be of the nature of equality (evenness of mind), O Madhusūdana (Kṛṣṇa), I see no stable foundation for, on account of restlessness.

34. *cañcalaṁ hi manaḥ kṛṣṇa*
pramāthi balavad dṛḍham
tasyā 'haṁ nigrahaṁ manye
vāyor iva suduṣkaram

[1] *yathā mama sukham iṣṭaṁ tathā sarvaprāṇināṁ sukham anukūlaṁ yadi vā yacca duḥkhaṁ mama pratikūlam aniṣṭaṁ yathā tathā sarvaprāṇināṁ duḥkham aniṣṭam . . . na kasyacit pratikūlam ācarati ahiṁsaka ity arthaḥ.*

(34) For the mind is verily fickle, O Kṛṣṇa, it is impetuous, strong and obstinate. I think that it is as difficult to control as the wind.

śrībhagavān uvāca

35. *asaṁśayaṁ mahābāho*
mano durnigrahaṁ calam
abhyāsena tu kaunteya
vairāgyeṇa ca gṛhyate

The Blessed Lord said:

(35) Without doubt, O Mighty-armed (Arjuna), the mind is difficult to curb and restless but it can be controlled, O Son of Kuntī (Arjuna), by constant practice and non-attachment.

Cp. *Yoga Sūtra*, I, 12. *abhyāsavairāgyābhyāṁ tan nirodhaḥ.* The teacher points out that the restless mind, accustomed to act on impulse, can be controlled only by non-attachment[1] and practice.

Arjuna realizes that there is so much of obstinacy and violence, waywardness and self-will in human nature. We are inclined to shut our eyes to the defects of our nature and harden our hearts against the Light. Tapasya is what is needed.

36. *asaṁyatātmanā yogo*
duṣprāpa iti me matiḥ
vaśyātmanā tu yatatā
śakyo 'vāptum upāyataḥ

(36) Yoga is hard to attain, I agree, by one who is not self-controlled; but by the self-controlled it is attainable by striving through proper means.

[1] When there is earth to lie upon, why trouble about bed? When one's arm is readily available, why need pillows? When there is the palm of one's hand, why seek for plates and utensils? When there is the atmosphere, the bark of trees, etc., what need is there of silks?

satyāṁ kṣitau kiṁ kaśipoḥ prayāsaiḥ bāhau saṁsiddhe hy upa barhaṇaiḥ kim

ṣatyaṁjalau kiṁ purudhānnapātraiḥ digvalkalādau sati kiṁ dukūlaiḥ. Bhāgavata, II, 1.

Arjuna asks what happens to the soul who attempts and fails.

Defeat is temporary: He who starts well reaches the End.

arjuna uvāca

37. *ayatiḥ śraddhayo 'peto*
yogāc calitamānasaḥ
aprāpya yogasaṁsiddhiṁ
kāṁ gatiṁ kṛṣṇa gacchati

(37) He who cannot control himself though he has faith, with the mind wandering away from yoga, failing to attain perfection in yoga, what way does he go, O Kṛṣṇa?

Arjuna's question refers to the future of those, who, when they die are not at war with Eternal Goodness though they are not disciplined enough to contemplate the splendour of Eternal Purity. Are the alternatives eternal heaven and everlasting hell as some believe or is there a chance for such individuals to grow towards perfection after death?

38. *kaccin no 'bhayavibhraṣṭaś*
chinnābhram iva naśyati
apratiṣṭho mahābāho
vimūḍho brahmaṇaḥ pathi

(38) Does he not perish like a rent cloud, O Mighty-armed (Kṛṣṇa), fallen from both and without any hold and bewildered in the path that leads to the Eternal?

Fallen from both, *ito bhraṣṭaḥ tato bhraṣṭaḥ*, is he left in a no man's world? Does he miss both this life and the life eternal? What happens to those numerous persons who have not succeeded in pursuing the extremely difficult path of yoga to its end? Are their exertions useless altogether? Is it any good beginning a course which one may not be able to complete?

39. *etan me saṁśayaṁ kṛṣṇa*
chettum arhasy aśeṣataḥ
tvadanyaḥ saṁśayasyā 'sya
chettā na hy upapadyate

(39) Thou shouldst dispel completely this, my doubt, O Kṛṣṇa, for there is none else than Thyself who can destroy this doubt.

śrībhagavān uvāca

40\. *pārtha nai 've 'ha nā 'mutra*
vināśas tasya vidyate
na hi kalyāṇakṛt kaścid
durgatiṁ tāta gacchati

The Blessed Lord said:

(40) O, Pārtha (Arjuna), neither in this life nor hereafter is there destruction for him; for never does any one who does good, dear friend, tread the path of woe.

No man of honest life can come to grief. No good man can come to an evil end. God knows our weaknesses and the efforts we make to overcome them. We must not despair for even failure here is success and no sincere attempt will go without its reward. Eckhart says: "If thou do not fail in intention, but only in capacity, verily, thou hast done all in the sight of God." Cp. Goethe: "Whoever strives and labours, him may we bring redemption."

41\. *prāpya puṇyakṛtāṁ lokān*
uṣitvā śāśvatīḥ samāḥ
śucīnāṁ śrīmatāṁ gehe
yogabhraṣṭo 'bhijāyate

(41) Having attained to the world of the righteous and dwelt there for very many years, the man who has fallen away from yoga is again born in the house of such as are pure and prosperous.

śāśvatīh: very many; not everlasting.

śucīnām: righteous. In VI, 11, cleanliness refers to the outer side; here inward purity is indicated.[1]

[1] *śaucaṁ tu dvividhaṁ proktam bāhyam ābhyantaraṁ tathā mṛjjalābhyāṁ smṛtaṁ bāhyam, bhāvaśuddiś tathā'ntaram.*
Vyāghrapāda quoted in *Mādhavapārāśara.*

42. *athavā yoginām eva*
kule bhavati dhīmatām
etad dhi durlabhataraṁ
loke janma yad īdṛśam

(42) Or he may be born in the family of yogins who are endowed with wisdom. For such a birth as this is more difficult to obtain in the world.

43. *tatra taṁ buddhisaṁyogaṁ*
labhate paurvadehikam
yatate ca tato bhūyaḥ
saṁsiddhau kurunandana

(43) There he regains the (mental) impressions (of union with the Divine) which he had developed in his previous life and with this (as the starting point) he strives again for perfection, O Joy of the Kurus (Arjuna).

Progress on the path to perfection is slow and one may have to tread through many lives before reaching the end. But no effort is wasted. The relations we form and the powers we acquire do not perish at death. They will be the starting point of later developments.

44. *pūrvābhyāsena tenai 'va*
hriyate hy avaśo 'pi saḥ
jijñāsur api yogasya
śabdabrahmā 'tivartate

(44) By his former practice, he is carried on irresistibly. Even the seeker after the knowledge of yoga goes beyond the Vedic rule.

śabdabrahma: Vedic rule. It refers to the Veda and the injunctions set forth in it. By practising the Vedic rule, we are helped to get beyond it. Cp. "Brahman is of two kinds, the śabdabrahma and the other beyond it. When a person has become well versed in the śabdabrahma, he reaches the Brahman which is beyond it."[1] Then faith ends in experience, tongues shall cease and doctrine shall fade away. The stimulus to religion is generally

[1] *Maitrī Up.*, VI, 22. Cp. also *Viṣṇu Purāṇa : śabdabrahmaṇi niṣṇātaḥ paraṁ brahmādhigacchati*, VI, 5.

supplied by the study of holy writ or participation in a cult. This is helpful until spontaneity becomes so great and absolute as to require no indirect help. Ordinarily the study of the Veda is a quickening influence. But when once we have the awakening which is sufficient unto itself, we need no external aid and so pass beyond śabdabrahma or any institutional guidance. One who proposes to cross a river needs a boat, but "let him no longer use the Law as a means of arrival when he has arrived." *Majjhima Nikāya*, I, 135. R. takes śabdabrahma to mean prakṛti.

45. *prayatnād yatamānas tu*
yogī saṁśuddhakilbiṣaḥ
anekajanmasaṁsiddhas
tato yāti parāṁ gatim

(45) But the yogi who strives with assiduity, cleansed of all sins, perfecting himself through many lives, then attains to the highest goal.

Though he may fail through weakness to reach the goal of perfection in this life, the lessons of his effort will abide with him after death and help him in his progress in other lives until he attains the goal. God's purpose will not be accomplished until all human beings are redeemed by forgiveness, repentance and healing discipline and restored into communion with the Supreme. Every soul will be won back to God who created him in His own image. God's love wi l finally restore into harmony with itself even the most rebellious elements. The *Gītā* gives us a hopeful belief in the redemption of all.

The Perfect Yogi

46. *tapasvibhyo 'dhiko yogī*
jñānibhyo 'pi mato 'dhikaḥ
karmibhyaś cā 'dhiko yogī
tasmād yogī bhavā 'rjuna

(46) The yogin is greater than the ascetic; he is considered to be greater than the man of knowledge, greater than the man of ritual works, therefore do thou become a yogin, O Arjuna.

Here the teacher is making out that the yogin here described is superior to the tapasvin, who retires to the forest for performing severe fasts and arduous practices, to the jñānin who adopts the way of knowledge for obtaining release, with renunciation of action, to the karmin who performs the rites enjoined in the Vedas for obtaining rewards. The yoga which is said to be superior to the tapas, jñāna and karma, has the best of all the three and includes devotion also. Such a yogin pours himself forth in utter worship of the Divine seated within the hearts of all and his life is one of self-forgetful service under the guidance of the Divine light.

Yoga or union with God which is attained through bhakti is the highest goal. The next verse points out that even among yogins, the greatest is the devotee or the bhakta.

Jñāna here means *śāstrapāṇḍitya* or scriptural learning (Ś.) and not spiritual realization.

47 *yoginām api sarveṣāṁ*
madgatenā 'ntarātmanā
śraddhāvān bhajate yo māṁ
sa me yuktatamo mataḥ

(47) And of all yogins, he who full of faith worships Me, with his inner self abiding in Me, him, I hold to be the most attuned (to me in Yoga).

After giving a long account of the yoga discipline, the obstacles to be overcome, the teacher concludes that the great yogin is the great devotee (bhakta).

iti . . . dhyānayogo nāma ṣaṣṭho 'dhyāyaḥ

This is the sixth chapter entitled The Yoga of Meditation

CHAPTER VII

God and the World

God is Nature and Spirit

śrībhagavān uvāca

1. *mayy āsaktamanāḥ pārtha*
yogaṁ yuñjan madāśrayaḥ
asaṁśayaṁ samagraṁ māṁ
yathā jñāsyasi tac chṛṇu

The Blessed Lord said:

(1) Hear then, O Pārtha (Arjuna), how, practising yoga, with the mind clinging to Me, with Me as thy refuge, thou shalt know Me in full, without any doubt.

The author wishes to give a complete or integral knowledge of the Divine, not merely the Pure Self but Its manifestation in the world.

2. *jñānaṁ te 'haṁ savijñānam*
idaṁ vakṣyāmy aśeṣataḥ
yaj jñātvā ne 'ha bhūyo 'nyaj
jñātavyam avaśiṣyate

(2) I will declare to thee in full this wisdom together with knowledge by knowing which there shall remain nothing more here left to be known.

See III, 41 note. Jñāna is interpreted as wisdom, the direct spiritual illumination and vijñāna as the detailed rational knowledge of the principles of existence. We must have not merely knowledge of the relationless Absolute but also of Its varied manifestation. The Supreme is in man and nature though these do not limit Him.

3. *manuṣyāṇāṁ sahasreṣu*
kaścid yatati siddhaye
yatatām api siddhānāṁ
kaścin māṁ vetti tattvataḥ

(3) Among thousands of men scarcely one strives for perfection and of those who strive and succeed, scarcely one knows Me in truth.

Another reading: *yatatām ca sahasrāṇām*: "and of thousands of strivers." Most of us do not even feel the need for perfection. We grope along by the voice of tradition and authority. Of those who strive to see the truth and reach the goal, only a few succeed. Of those who gain the sight, not even one learns to walk and live by the sight.

The Two Natures of the Lord

4. *bhūmir āpo 'nalo vāyuḥ*
khaṁ mano buddhir eva ca
ahaṁkāra itī 'yaṁ me
bhinnā prakṛtir aṣṭadhā

(4) Earth, water, fire, air, ether, mind and understanding and self-sense—this is the eightfold division of My nature.

prakṛtiḥ. Nature, which is identified with śakti or māyā,[1] the basis of the objective world.[2]

These are the forms which unmanifested nature, prakṛti, takes when it becomes manifested. This is an early classification which later becomes elaborated into twenty-four principles. See XIII, 5. The senses, mind and understanding, indriyas, manas and buddhi, belong to the lower, the material nature. For, according to the Sāṁkhya psychology, which is accepted by the Vedānta, they effect contact with objects and consciousness results only when the spiritual subject, puruṣa, illuminates them. When the self illumines, the activities of the senses, of mind and of understanding become processes of knowledge and objects become objects of knowledge. Ahaṁkāra or the self-sense belongs to the "object" side. It is the principle by which the ego relates objects to itself. It attributes to itself the body and the senses connected with it. It effects the false identification of the body with the spiritual subject and the sense of "I" or "my" is produced.

[1] *māyākhyā parameśvarī śaktir anirvacanīyasvabhāvā triguṇātmikā*. Madhusūdana.

[2] *jaḍaprapañcopādānabhūta*. Nīlakaṇṭha.

5. *apare 'yam itas tv anyāṁ*
prakṛtiṁ viddhi me parām
jīvabhūtāṁ mahābāho
yaye 'daṁ dhāryate jagat

(5) This is My lower nature. Know My other and higher nature which is the soul, by which this world is upheld, O Mighty-armed (Arjuna).

The Supreme is Īśvara, the personal Lord o: the universe who contains conscious souls (ksetrajña) and unconscious nature (kṣetra). The two are regarded as His higher (parā) and lower (aparā) aspects. He is the life and form of every being.[1] The Universal Being of God includes the totality of the unconscious in His lower nature and the totality of the conscious in His higher. The embodiment of the soul in body, life, sense, mind and understanding gives us the ego, which uses the material setting for its activity. Each individual has two sides, the soul and the image, kṣetrajña and kṣetra. These are the two natures of Īśvara who is superior to them both.[2] The Old Testament teaches creation out of nothing. Plato and Aristotle assume a primitive matter to which God gives form. God is an artificer or architect rather than a creator, for primitive substance is thought of as eternal and uncreated and only form is due to the will of God. For Christian thinkers, God creates not from any pre-existent matter but out of nothing. Both matter and form are derived from God. A similar view is set forth in this verse. The jīva is only a partial manifestation of the Supreme.[3] The integral undivided reality of the Supreme appears divided into the multiplicity of souls.[4] The unity is the truth and multiplicity is an expression of it and so is a lower truth but not an illusion.

[1] *viśuddhāṁ prakṛtiṁ mamātmabhūtāṁ viddhi me parāṁ prakṛṣṭāṁ jīvabhūtaṁ kṣetrajñalakṣaṇaṁ, prāṇadhāraṇanimittabhūtam.* Ś.

[2] Cp. the *Bhāgavata.*

Salutations unto Thee the Self, the sovereign of all, the witness, the great spirit, the source of souls as well as of the ever productive nature.

kṣetrajñāya namas tubhyaṁ sarvādhyakṣāya sākṣiṇe
puruṣāy ātmamūlāya mūlaprakṛtaye namaḥ.

VIII, 3, 13.

[3] XV, 7. [4] XIII, 16.

6. *etadyonīni bhūtāni*
sarvāṇī 'ty upadhāraya
ahaṁ kṛtsnasya jagataḥ
prabhavaḥ pralayas tathā

(6) Know that all beings have their birth in this. I am the origin of all this world and its dissolution as well.

The world with all its becomings is from the Supreme[1] and at the time of dissolution is withdrawn into Him. Cp. *Taittīrīya Up.*, III. God includes the universe within Himself, projects it from and resumes it within Himself, that is, His own nature.

7. *mattaḥ parataraṁ nā 'nyat*
kiṁcid asti dhanaṁjaya
mayi sarvam idaṁ protaṁ
sūtre maṇigaṇā iva

(7) There is nothing whatever that is higher than I, O Winner of wealth (Arjuna). All that is here is strung on me as rows of gems on a string.

There is no other higher principle than Īśvara who effects everything and is everything. The existences of the world are held together by the Supreme Spirit even as the gems are by the string.

8. *raso 'ham apsu kaunteya*
prabhā 'smi śaśisūryayoḥ
praṇavaḥ sarvavedeṣu
śabdaḥ khe pauruṣaṁ nṛṣu

(8) I am the taste in the waters, O Son of Kuntī (Arjuna), I am the light in the moon and the sun. I am the syllable Aum in all the Vedas; I am the sound in ether and manhood in men.

9. *puṇyo gandhaḥ pṛthivyāṁ ca*
tejaś cā 'smi vibhāvasau
jīvanaṁ sarvabhūteṣu
tapaś cā 'smi tapasviṣu

[1] Cp. XIV, 3, *mama yonir mahad brahmā*. See also *Muṇḍaka Up.* I, 1, 6 and III, 1, 3. *akṣaraṁ bhūtayonim . . . puruṣaṁ bhūtayonim* *Brahma Sūtra: yonis' ca gīyate*. I, 4, 7, 27.

(9) I am the pure fragrance in earth and brightness in fire. I am the life in all existences and the austerity in ascetics.

Cp. "Thou art Reality, the Divine Spirit, not material, not lifeless. Thou art the life of the universe, the life of all creatures."[1]

10. *bījaṁ māṁ sarvabhūtānāṁ*
viddhi pārtha sanātanam
buddhir buddhimatām asmi
tejas tejasvinām aham

(10) Know Me, O Pārtha (Arjuna), to be the eternal seed of all existences. I am the intelligence of the intelligent; I am the splendour of the splendid.

11. *balaṁ balavatāṁ cā 'haṁ*
kāmarāgavivarjitam
dharmāviruddho bhūteṣu
kāmo 'smi bharatarṣabha

(11) I am the strength of the strong, devoid of desire and passion. In beings am I the desire which is not contrary to law, O Lord of the Bharatas (Arjuna).

kāmarāga: desire and passion. Ś. distinguishes kāma as desire for what is absent[2] and rāga as affection for what one has obtained.[3] Desire as such is not evil. Selfish desire requires to be rooted out. The desire for union with the Divine is not wrong. *Chāndogya Up*. refers to desires as essentially real (satya), though overlaid by what is unreal (anṛta), VIII, 3. Our desires and activities, if they are expressive of the spirit in us and derive from the true spiritual personality, become a pure overflowing of the Divine will.

12. *ye cai 'va sāttvikā bhāvā*
rājasās tāmasāś ca ye
matta eve 'ti tān viddhi
na tv ahaṁ teṣu te mayi

[1] *tvaṁ satyaṁ devadevātmaṁ na jaḍo na mṛtopi vā,*
jagatāṁ jīvitaṁ ca tvaṁ prāṇināṁ jīvitaṁ tathā

[2] *kamaḥ, tṛṣṇā asannikṛṣṭesu viṣayeṣu*

[3] *rāgaḥ, rañjanā prāpteṣu viṣayeṣu.*

(12) And whatever states of being there may be, be they harmonious (sāttvika), passionate (rājasa), slothful (tāmasa) —know thou that they are all from Me alone. I am not in them, they are in Me.

The author rejects the Sāṁkhya doctrine of the independence of prakṛti. He asserts that everything constituted by the three guṇas is in no sense a self-dependent essence independent of God, but springs from Him alone. While He contains and comprehends all, they do not contain and comprehend Him. This is the distinction between God and His creatures. They are all informed by the Divine but their changes do not touch the integrity of the Divine. He is not subject to any one else, while all things are subject to Him.

The Modes of Nature Confuse Men

13. *tribhir guṇamayair bhāvair*
ebhiḥ sarvam idaṁ jagat
mohitaṁ nā 'bhijānāti
mām ebhyaḥ param avyayam

(13) Deluded by these threefold modes of nature (guṇas) this whole world does not recognize Me who am above them and imperishable.

Ś. says that the Supreme expresses His regret that the world does not know Him, the Supreme Lord who is, by nature, eternal, pure, enlightened and free, the self of all beings, devoid of attributes; by knowing whom the seed of the evil of saṁśara is burnt up.[1]

We see the changing forms and not the Eternal Being of which the forms are the manifestations. We see the shifting forms as Plato's dwellers in the cave see the shadows on the wall. But we must see the Light from which the shadows emanate.

14. *daivī hy eṣā guṇamayī*
mama māyā duratyayā
mām eva ye prapadyante
māyām etāṁ taranti te

[1] *evambhūtam api parameśvaraṁ nityaśuddhabuddhamuktasvabhāvaṁ sarvabhūtātmānaṁ, nirguṇaṁ saṁsāradoṣabījapradāhakāraṇaṁ, māṁ, nābhijānāti jagad ity anukrośaṁ darśayati bhagavān.*

(14) This divine māyā of Mine, consisting of the modes is hard to overcome. But those who take refuge in Me alone cross beyond it.

daivī: divine. Supernatural[1] or belonging to the supreme Lord.[2]

māyām etām taranti:[3] cross beyond the māyā. They cross beyond the world of māyā which is the source of delusion.

R. makes out that māyā is that which is capable of producing marvellous effects.

The State of Evildoers

15. *na māṁ duṣkṛtino mūḍhāḥ*
prapadyante narādhamāḥ
māyayā 'pahṛtajñānā
āsuraṁ bhāvam āśritāḥ

(15) The Evil doers who are foolish, low in the human scale, whose minds are carried away by illusion and who partake of the nature of demons do not seek refuge in Me.

The evil doers cannot attain to the Supreme, for their mind and will are not instruments of the Spirit but of the ego. They do not seek to master their crude impulses but are a prey to the rajas and tamas in them. If we control them by the sattva in us, our action becomes ordered and enlightened and ceases to be the result of passion and ignorance. To get beyond the three guṇas, we have to attain first the rule of sattva. We have to become ethical, before we can become spiritual. At the spiritual level, we cross the dualities and act in the light and strength of the Spirit in us. We do not act then to gain any personal interest or avoid personal suffering but only as the instrument of the Divine.

Different Kinds of Devotion

16. *caturvidhā bhajante māṁ*
janāḥ sukṛtino 'rjuna
ārto jijñāsur arthārthī
jñānī ca bharatarṣabha

[1] *alaukikī atyadbhuteti.* Śrīdhara.

[2] *devasya jīvarūpeṇa līlayā krīḍato mamasaṁbandhinīyaṁ daivī* Nīlakaṇṭha.

[3] *māyāṁ sarvabhūtamohinīṁ taranti, saṁsārabandhanād mucyante.* Ś.

(16) The virtuous ones who worship Me are of four kinds, the man in distress, the seeker for knowledge, the seeker for wealth and the man of wisdom, O Lord of the Bharatas (Arjuna).

sukṛtinaḥ: virtuous ones. Those who are disposed towards the higher life on account of their past virtuous conduct.[1]

The afflicted, those in distress, who have suffered losses are one class. Those who are desirous of wealth, dhanakāma (Ś.), who wish to improve their material position are another. The third group are devout and upright and wish to know the truth. They are on the right way. The fourth are the jñānis, they who know. R. interprets jñāna or wisdom as devotion to one alone, *ekabhakti*.

M.B. speaks of four classes of devotees of whom three are *phalakāmā* or desirous of rewards while the best are single-minded worshippers.[2] Others ask for favours, but the sage asks nothing and refuses nothing. He yields himself completely to the Divine, accepting whatever is given to him. His attitude is one of self-oblivious non-utilitarian worship of God for His own sake.

17. *teṣāṁ jñānī nityayukta*
ekabhaktir viśiṣyate
priyo hi jñānino 'tyartham
ahaṁ sa ca mama priyaḥ

(17) Of these the wise one, who is ever in constant union with the Divine, whose devotion is single-minded, is the best. For I am supremely dear to him and he is dear to Me.

So long as we are seekers, we are still in the world of duality but when we have attained wisdom, there is no duality. The sage unites himself with the One Self in all.

18. *udārāḥ sarva evai 'te*
jñānī tv ātmai 'va me matam
āsthitaḥ sa hi yuktātmā
mām evā 'nuttamāṁ gatim

[1] *pūrvajanmasu ye kṛtapuṇyā janāḥ.* Śrīdhara.

[2] *caturvidhā mama janā bhaktā evaṁ hi me śrutam*
teṣām ekāntinaḥ śreṣṭhā ye caivanānyadevatāḥ.
Śāntiparva, 341, 33.

(18) Noble indeed are all these but the sage, I hold, is verily Myself. For being perfectly harmonized, he resorts to Me alone as the highest goal.

udārāḥ sarva evai'te: noble indeed are all these. We pray to avoid emotional suffering (ārtaḥ), gain practical advantages (arthārthī), obtain intellectual satisfaction (jijñāsuḥ) or gain wisdom (jñāni). All these are noble. Even if we pray for material things, turn prayer into a formal routine or use it as a mascot, we recognize the reality of the religious sense. Prayer is the effort of man to reach God. It assumes that there is an answering Presence in the world. If we ask, it shall be given to us. Through the exercise of prayer, we kindle a light in our consciousness which shows up our silly pride, our selfish greed, our fears and hopes. It is a means for the building up of an integral personality, a harmony of body, mind and spirit. Slowly we feel that it is degrading to pray for luck in life or success in examinations. We pray that we may know the Divine and be more and more like Him. Prayer is a way of life. Slowly it becomes the practice of the presence of God. It is jñāna, integral wisdom, divine life. The jñāni who knows God as He is, loves God for what He is. He lives in the Divine. God is dear to him as he is dear to God. While the first three types attempt to use God according to their ideas, the knowers belong to God to be used according to His will. Therefore they are the best of them all. It is possible that, when we are in deep distress, we may pray with such single-heartedness and intensity, to be relieved of our agony. If such a prayer be answered, it may be thwarting the purpose of God which we are unable to see in our blindness. The jñāni, however, has the purity of heart and singleness of will to see the plan of God and ask for its realization. "Thy will, not mine, be done."

19. *bahūnāṁ janmanām ante*
jñānavān māṁ prapadyate
vāsudevaḥ sarvam iti
sa mahātmā sudurlabhaḥ

(19) At the end of many lives, the man of wisdom resorts to Me, knowing that Vāsudeva (the Supreme) is all that is. Such a great soul is very difficult to find.

bahūnāṁ janmanām ante: at the end of many lives. The realization of the truth is a work of ages. One cannot expect to obtain the reward until one has sounded well the depths of experience in its varied complexity, and all this takes time. God lets the plant grow at its own pace. It takes nine months to make a natural baby and it will take a much longer time to make a spiritual one. The total transformation of nature is a long process.

vāsudevaḥ sarvam: Vāsudeva is all. Vāsudeva is the lord of the life which dwells in all.[1] God is all in virtue of His two natures.

R. means by this phrase that "Vāsudeva is my all." It refers to God's imperishable majesty felt by the devotee who is humble and trustful. God is all while we are nothing. Like everything else, man cannot exist without God also existing at the same time. We trustfully resign ourselves to His hands confessing that He is all. It is a consciousness of humility towards God who is everything and who truly is.

"Vāsudeva is the cause of all." Madhva.

Other forms of entreaty and prayer are not without their value. They have their reward.

Toleration

20. *kāmais tais-tair hṛtajñānāḥ*
prapadyante 'nyadevatāḥ
taṁ-taṁ niyamam āsthāya
prakṛtyā niyatāḥ svayā

(20) But those whose minds are distorted by desires resort to other gods, observing various rites, constrained by their own natures.

21. *yo-yo yāṁ-yāṁ tanuṁ bhaktaḥ*
śraddhayā 'rcitum icchati
tasya-tasyā 'calāṁ śraddhāṁ
tām eva vidadhāmy aham

(21) Whatever form any devotee with faith wishes to worship, I make that faith of his steady.

The Supreme Lord confirms the faith of each and grants the rewards each seeks. Exactly as far as the soul has risen in its

[1] *vasati sarvasmin iti vāsuḥ, tasya devaḥ.*

struggle does God stoop to meet it. Even seers who were so profoundly contemplative as Gautama the Buddha and Ś. did not repudiate the popular belief in gods. They were conscious of the inexpressibility of the Supreme Godhead as well as the infinite number of possible manifestations. Every surface derives its soil from the depths even as every shadow reflects the nature of the substance. Besides, all worship elevates. No matter what we revere, so long as our reverence is serious, it helps progress.

22. *sa tayā śraddhayā yuktas*
tasyā 'rādhanam īhate
labhate ca tataḥ kāmān
mayai 'va vihitān hi tān

(22) Endowed with that faith, he seeks the propitiation of such a one and from him he obtains his desires, the benefits being decreed by Me alone.

All forms are forms of the One Supreme; their worship is the worship of the Supreme; the giver of all rewards is the Supreme.[1] Śrīdhara.

23. *antavat tu phalaṁ teṣāṁ*
tad bhavaty alpamedhasām
devān devayajo yānti
madbhaktā yānti mām api

(23) But temporary is the fruit gained by these men of small minds. The worshippers of the gods go to the gods but My devotees come to Me.

As the Transcendent Divine cannot be known easily we resort to aspects of the Supreme and offer our worship. We realize the results we seek, for the Supreme is patient with our imperfect vision. He accepts our prayers and answers them at the level at which we approach Him. No devotion is worthless. Gradually even the illiterate devotee will seek his highest good in the Divine and grow into it. Those who rise to the worship of the Transcendent Godhead which embraces and transcends all aspects realize and attain to the highest state, integral in being, perfect in know-

[1] *sarvā api devatā mamaiva mūrtayaḥ, tad ārādhanam api vastuto mamārādhanam eva, tat tat phaladātāpi cā'hameva.*

ledge, absolute in love and complete in will. All other goods are partial and limited and have a meaning only at lower levels of development.

The Power of Ignorance

24. *avyaktaṁ vyaktim āpannaṁ*
manyante mām abuddhayaḥ
paraṁ bhāvam ajānanto
mamā 'vyayam anuttamam

(24) Men of no understanding think of Me, the unmanifest, as having manifestation, not knowing My higher nature, changeless and supreme.

The forms we impose on the Formless are due to our limitations. We turn away from the contemplation of Ultimate Reality to concentrate upon imaginative reconstructions. All gods except the One Unmanifest Eternal are forms imposed on Him. God is not one among many. He is the One behind the ever changing many, who stands beyond all forms, the immutable centre of endless mobility.

25. *nā 'haṁ prakāśaḥ sarvasya*
yogamāyāsamāvṛtaḥ
mūḍho 'yaṁ nā 'bhijānāti
loko mām ajam avyayam

(25) Veiled by My creative power (yogamāyā) I am not revealed to all. This ewildered world knows Me not, the unborn, the unchanging.

yoga: Ś. means by it union of the three guṇas: for Madhusūdana it is saṁkalpa or will.

The Supreme is not only in the world but beyond it. We mistake Him for this or that limited form.

Cp. *Bhāgavata:* "O Lord, All pervading Supreme Self, Lord of Yoga, who is there in the three worlds, who can penetrate Thy mystery, know where, when, in what manner and in how many forms Thou engagest Thyself in sport?"[1] Only Pure Being

[1] *ko vetti bhūman bhagavan parātman yogeśvarotīr bhavatas trilokyām kva vā kathaṁ vā kati vā kadeti vistārayan krīḍasi yogamāyām.*

is unmanifest, everything else belongs to the world of manifestation.

26. *vedā 'haṁ samatītāni*
vartamānān cā 'rjuna
bhaviṣyāṇi ca bhūtāni
māṁ tu veda na kaścana

(26) I know the beings that are past, that are present, O Arjuna, and that are to come but Me no one knows.

27. *icchādveṣasamutthena*
dvandvamohena bhārata
sarvabhūtāni saṁmohaṁ
sarge yānti paraṁtapa

(27) All beings are born to delusion O Bhārata (Arjuna), overcome by the dualities which arise from wish and hate, O Conqueror of the foe (Arjuna).

The Object of Knowledge

28. *yeṣāṁ tv antagataṁ pāpaṁ*
janānāṁ puṇyakarmaṇām
te dvamdvamohanirmuktā
bhajante māṁ dṛḍhavratāḥ

(28) But those men of virtuous deeds in whom sin has come to an end (who have died to sin), freed from the delusion of dualities, worship Me steadfast in their vows.

Sin is not the violation of a law or a convention but the central source of all finiteness, ignorance, the assertion of the independence of the ego which seeks its own private gain at the expense of others. When this sin is renounced, when this ignorance is overcome, our life is spent in the service of the One in all. In the process, devotion deepens and knowledge of God increases until it reaches the vision of the One Self everywhere. That is the life eternal, release from birth and death. Tukārām says:

"The self within me now is dead
And thou enthroned in its stead
Yea, this I, Tuka, testify,
No longer now is 'me' or 'my'."[1]

[1] Macnicol: *Psalms of the Maratha Saints* (1919), p. 79.

29. *jarāmaraṇamokṣāya*
māṁ āśritya yatanti ye
te brahma tad viduḥ kṛtsnam
adhyātmaṁ karma cā 'khilam

(29) Those who take refuge in Me and strive for deliverance from old age and death, they know the Brahman (or Absolute) entire (they know) the Self and all about action

adhyātmam is the reality underlying the individual self.[1]

30. *sādhibhūtādhidaivaṁ māṁ*
sādhiyajñaṁ ca ye viduḥ
prayāṇakāle 'pi ca māṁ
te vidur yuktacetasah

(30) Those who know Me as the One that governs the material and the divine aspects, and all sacrifices, they, with their minds harmonized, have knowledge of Me even at the time of their departure (from here).

We are not asked to remember at the time of departure certain speculative doctrines, but to know Him in all aspects, trust Him and worship Him.

Certain new terms are used and Arjuna in the next chapter asks for their explanations. The Supreme is to be known not only in Itself but also in Its manifestations in nature, in objective and subjective phenomena, in the principle of works and sacrifice. The teacher explains them all briefly in the next chapter.

iti . . . jñānavijñānayogo nāma saptamo 'dhyāyaḥ

This is the seventh chapter entitled The Yoga of Wisdom and Knowledge.

[1] ***pratyagātmaviṣayaṁ vastu.*** **Ś.**

CHAPTER VIII

The Course of Cosmic Evolution

Arjuna Questions

arjuna uvāca

1. *kiṁ tad brahma kim adhyātmaṁ*
kiṁ karma puruṣottama
adhibhūtaṁ ca kiṁ proktam
adhidaivaṁ kim ucyate

Arjuna said:

(1) What is Brahman (or the Absolute)? What is the Self and what is action, O the Best of persons? What is said to be the domain of the elements? What is called the domain of the gods?

What is present in the self (adhyātmam)? What is present in the gods (adhidaivam)? What is present in the sacrifice (adhiyajñam)? What is present in all beings (adhibhūtam)? The answer to these questions is that the Supreme Spirit pervades all created beings, all sacrifices, all deities and all work. These are only the varied expressions of the Supreme.[1]

2. *adhiyajñaḥ kathaṁ ko 'tra*
dehe 'smin madhusūdana
prayāṇakāle ca kathaṁ
jñeyo 'si niyatātmabhiḥ

(2) What is the domain (part) of sacrifice in this body and how, O Madhusūdana (Kṛṣṇa). How again art Thou to be known at the time of departure by the self-controlled?

How art Thou revealed at the hour of death to the spiritual-minded?

[1] *mamaiva rūpāntarāṇi.* Abhinavagupta.

Kṛṣṇa Answers

śrībhagavān uvāca

3. *akṣaraṁ brahma paramaṁ*
svabhāvo 'dhyātmam ucyate
bhūtabhāvodbhavakaro
visargaḥ karmasaṁjñitaḥ

The Blessed Lord said:

(3) Brahman (or the Absolute) is the indestructible, the Supreme (higher than all else), essential nature is called the Self. Karma is the name given to the creative force that brings beings into existence.

svabhāva: Brahman assumes the form of jīva, Chap. XV, 7.[1]

adhyātma: the lord of the body, the enjoyer.[2] It is the phase of the Divine which constitutes the individual self.

Brahman is the immutable self-existence on which all that lives, moves and has its being rests. Self is the spirit in man and nature. Karma is the creative impulse out of which life's forms issue. The whole cosmic evolution is called karma. The Supreme undertakes it and there is no reason why the individual jīva should not take part in it. The Immutable which is above all dualities of subject and object, becomes, from the cosmic end, the eternal subject, adhyātma, facing the eternal object which is mutable in nature, prakṛti, the receptacle of all forms, while karma is the creative force, the principle of movement. All these are not independent but are the manifestations of the One Supreme. The subject-object interaction which is the central pattern of the cosmos is the expression of Brahman, the Absolute Spirit which is above the distinctions of subject and object.

Māṇḍūkya Up. affirms that while the Absolute is indescribable, qualityless,[3] the living God is the ruler of the world, the in-

[1] *svasya eva brahmaṇa eva aṁśatayā jīvarūpeṇa. bhāvānāṁ svabhāvaḥ.* Śrīdhara.

[2] *sa eva ātmānaṁ deham adhikṛtya bhoktṛtvena vartamāno'dhyātma-śabdena ucyate.* Śrīdhara.

[3] *adṛṣṭam, avyavahāryam, agrāhyam, alakṣaṇam, acintyam, avyapadeśyam, ekātmapratyayasāram, prapañcopaśamam, śāntam, śivam, advaitam.* 7

dwelling soul.[1] The distinction between Godhead and God, the Absolute and the Personal God, Brahman and Īśvara, is clearly enunciated in this Upaniṣad. The personal God is the cosmic Lord, while Brahman is the supra-cosmic reality.

4. *adhibhūtaṁ kṣaro bhāvaḥ*
puruṣaś cā 'dhidaivatam
adhiyajño 'ham evā 'tra
dehe dehabhṛtāṁ vara

(4) The basis of all created things is the mutable nature: the basis of the divine elements is the cosmic spirit. And the basis of all sacrifices, here in the body is Myself, O Best of embodied beings (Arjuna).

Here again the author wishes us to possess an integral knowledge of the Divine in all aspects. There is the Immutable Divine, Brahman; there is the Personal God Īśvara, the object of all devotion; there is the Cosmic Self, Hiraṇyagarbha the presiding deity of the cosmos, and the jīva the individual soul which partakes of the higher nature of the Divine and prakṛti the mutable nature. See VII, 4 ff.

The Soul goes to that on which it is set at the Moment of Dissolution

5. *antakāle ca mām eva*
smaran muktvā kalevaram
yaḥ prayāti sa madbhāvaṁ
yāti nā 'sty atra saṁśayaḥ

(5) And whoever, at the time of death, gives up his body and departs, thinking of Me alone, he comes to My status (of being); of that there is no doubt.

This verse takes up the point raised in VII, 30. The importance of the state of mind at the moment of death is emphasized in the Upaniṣads. *Chāndogya*, III, 14, 1; *Praśna*, III, 10. We will think of God in the last moments only if we are devoted to Him previously also.

[1] *eṣa sarveśvara eṣa sarvajña, eṣo'ntaryāmī eṣa yoniḥ sarvasya prabhavāpyayau hi bhūtānām*. 6.

6. *yaṁ-yaṁ vā 'pi smaran bhāvaṁ*
tyajaty ante kalevaram
taṁ-tam evai 'ti kaunteya
sadā tadbhāvabhāvitaḥ

(6) Thinking of whatever state (of being) he at the end gives up his body, to that being does he attain, O Son of Kuntī (Arjuna), being ever absorbed in the thought thereof.

sadā tad bhāva bhāvitaḥ: ever absorbed in the thought thereof. It is not the casual fancy of the last moment but the persistent endeavour of the whole life that determines the future.

tadbhāvabhāvitaḥ: literally, made to become (*bhāvita*) in the condition (*bhāva*) of that.

The soul goes to that on which its mind is set during the last moments. What we think we become. Our past thoughts determine our present birth and our present ones will determine the future.

7. *tasmāt sarveṣu kāleṣu*
mām anusmara yudhya ca
mayy arpitamanobuddhir
mām evai 'ṣyasy asaṁśayaḥ

(7) Therefore at all times remember Me and fight When thy mind and understanding are set on Me, to Me alone shalt thou come without doubt

sarveṣu kāleṣu: at all times. Only then shall we be able to remember God in the critical last moments. Śrīdhara.

mām anusmara yudhya: remember Me and fight. It is not fight on the material plane that is intended here for it cannot be done at all times. It is the fight with the powers of darkness that we have to carry on perpetually.

We must engage in the work of the world retaining our consciousness of Eternity, the brooding presence of the Unchanging God. "Just as a dancing girl fixes her attention on the waterpot she bears on her head even when she is dancing to various tunes, so also a truly pious man does not give up (his attention) to the blissful feet of the Supreme Lord even when he attends to his many concerns."[1] All actions of our lives are to be surrendered to God who encloses, penetrates and gives meaning to our lives. The mere remembrance of God purifies all work. Cp. "I bow to the Infallible. By thinking of Him or calling on His name, every defect in austerities, sacrifice and ritual is removed."[2]

8. *abhyāsayogayuktena*
cetasā nā 'nyagāminā
paramaṁ puruṣaṁ divyaṁ
yāti pārthā 'nucintayan

(8) He who meditates on the Supreme Person with his thought attuned by constant practice and not wandering after anything else, he, O Pārtha (Arjuna), reaches the Person, Supreme and Divine.

It is not death-bed repentance that will save us but constant practice and unwavering dedication to the Supreme.

9. *kaviṁ purāṇam anuśāsitāram*
aṇor aṇīyāṁsam anusmared yaḥ
sarvasya dhātāram acintyarūpam
ādityavarṇaṁ tamasaḥ parastāt

(9) He who meditates on the Seer, the ancient, the ruler, subtler than the subtle, the supporter of all, whose form is beyond conception, who is suncoloured beyond the darkness

See *Śvetāśvatara Up.*, III, 18.

kavi: seer. It is taken to mean omniscient.[3]

Here is a description not of the relationless, immutable Absolute but of Īśvara, the Personal God, Seer, Creator and Ruler of the cosmos. He is the light opposed to darkness.[4]

[1] *punkhānupunkhaviṣayān upasevamāno*
dhīro na muñcati mukundapadāravindam
saṁgitavādyakalitā navaśaṁgatāpi
maulistha kuṁbha parirakṣana dhīr naṭīva.

[2] *yasya smṛtyā ca nāmoktyā tapoyajñakriyādiṣu nyūnaṁ saṁpūrṇatāṁ yāti sadyo vande tam acyutam.*

[3] *kaviṁ krāntadarśinaṁ sarvajñam.* Ś.

[4] *prakāśarūpatvena tamovirodhinam.* Madhūsudana.

10. *prayāṇakāle manasā 'calena*
bhaktyā yukto yogabalena cai 'va
bhruvor madhye prāṇam āveśya samyak
sa taṁ paraṁ puruṣam upaiti divyam

(10) He who does so, at the time of his departure, with a steady mind, devotion and strength of yoga and setting well his life force in the centre of the eyebrows, he attains to this Supreme Divine Person.

Apparently this practice is possible only for those who choose the moment of death by the power of yoga.[1]

11. *yad akṣaraṁ vedavido vadanti*
viśanti yad yatayo vītarāgāḥ
yad icchanto brahmacaryaṁ caranti
tat te padaṁ saṁgraheṇa pravakṣye

(11) I shall briefly describe to thee that state which the knowers of the Veda call the Imperishable, which ascetics freed from passion enter and desiring which they lead a life of self-control.

See *Kaṭha Up.*, II, 15. "The word which all the Vedas rehearse, and which all austerities proclaim, desiring which men live the life of religious studentship—that word to thee I briefly declare." Theists look upon it as the highest heaven "the highest place of Viṣṇu." *viṣṇoḥ paramam padam.*

12. *sarvadvārāṇi saṁyamya*
mano hṛdi nirudhya ca
mūrdhny ādhāyā 'tmanaḥ prāṇam
āsthito yogadhāraṇām

(12) All the gates of the body restrained, the mind confined within the heart, one's life force fixed in the head, established in concentration by yoga

The body is called the ninegated city: V, 13. The mind which is confined within the heart means the mind whose functions are checked. The yoga śāstra tells us that the soul which passes from the heart through suṣumṇanāḍi to the brahmarandhra in the head and thence goes out, becomes one with the Supreme.

[1] *yogenānte tanu tyajām.* Kālidāsa: *Raghuvaṁśa. I*, 8.

13. *aum ity ekākṣaraṁ brahma*
vyāharan mām anusmaran
yaḥ prayāti tyajan dehaṁ
sa yāti paramāṁ gatim

(13) He who utters the single syllable Aum (which is) Brahman, remembering Me as he departs, giving up his body, he goes to the highest goal.

Aum stands for the inexpressible Absolute.

mām anuṣmaran: remembering Me. The highest state can be obtained through the worship of God, according to the *Yoga Sūtra.*[1]

14. *ananyacetāḥ satataṁ*
yo māṁ smarati nityaśaḥ
tasyā 'haṁ sulabhaḥ pārtha
nityayuktasya yoginaḥ

(14) He who constantly meditates on Me, thinking of none else, by him who is a yogin ever disciplined (or united with the Supreme), I am easily reached.

15. *mām upetya punarjanma*
duḥkhālayam aśāśvatam
nā 'pnuvanti mahātmānaḥ
saṁsiddhiṁ paramāṁ gatāḥ

(15) Having come to Me, these great souls do not get back to rebirth, the place of sorrow, impermanent, for they have reached the highest perfection.

See note on IX, 33.

16. *ā brahmabhuvanāl lokāḥ*
punarāvartino 'rjuna
mām upetya tu kaunteya
punarjanma na vidyate

(16) From the realm of Brahmā downwards, all worlds are subject to return to rebirth, but on reaching Me, O Son of Kuntī (Arjuna), there is no return to birth again.

All the worlds are subject to change.[2]

[1] *samādhisiddhir īśvarapraṇidhānāt.*
[2] *punarāvartinaḥ kālaparicchinnatvāt.* Ś.

17. *sahasrayugaparyantam*
ahar yad brahmaṇo viduḥ
rātriṁ yugasahasrāntāṁ
te 'horātravido janāḥ

(17) Those who know that the day of Brahmā is of the duration of a thousand ages and that the night (of Brahmā) is a thousand ages long, they are the knowers of day and night.

Day is the period of cosmic manifestation and night of non-manifestation. These are of equal length of time and alternate.

18. *avyaktād vyaktayaḥ sarvāḥ*
prabhavanty aharāgame
rātryāgame pralīyante
tatrai 'vā 'vyaktasaṁjñake

(18) At the coming of day, all manifested things come forth from the unmanifested and at the coming of night they merge in that same, called the unmanifested.

Here the unmanifested is prakṛti.

19. *bhūtagrāmaḥ sa evā 'yaṁ*
bhūtvā-bhūtvā pralīyate
rātryāgame 'vaśaḥ pārtha
prabhavaty aharāgame

(19) This very same multitude of existences arising again and again merges helplessly at the coming of night, O Pārtha (Arjuna), and streams forth into being at the coming of day.

This periodic emergence and dissolution of all existences does not affect the Lord of all existences.

20. *paras tasmāt tu bhāvo 'nyo*
'vyakto 'vyaktāt sanātanaḥ
yaḥ sa sarveṣu bhūteṣu
naśyatsu na vinaśyati

(20) But beyond this unmanifested, there is yet another Unmanifested Eternal Being who does not perish even when all existences perish.

It is the Supracosmic Unmanifested which is changeless and eternal, in the midst of all changes. Two types of unmanifested are sometimes distinguished, an unmanifested (avyakta), into which all unredeemed beings enter, and the supercosmic avyakta, called also *śuddhatattva* which is imperceptible to the ordinary mind into which the redeemed souls enter. The perpetual rhythm of day and night is on all cosmic beings which cannot last for ever. Beyond the cosmic process is the Supreme Unmanifested Brahman, the highest goal. Those who attain It pass beyond day and night.

21. *avyakto 'kṣara ity uktas*
tam āhuḥ paramāṁ gatim
yaṁ prāpya na nivartante
tad dhāma paramaṁ mama

(21) This Unmanifested is called the Imperishable. Him they speak of as the Supreme Status. Those who attain to Him return not. That is My supreme abode.

We escape from the cycle of birth and death or cosmic manifestation (prabhava) and non-manifestation (pralaya). Even to reach the status of the Indefinable Absolute whose status goes beyond the cosmic manifestation, we have to offer our whole personality to the Supreme. Even the supracosmic condition of the Eternally Unmanifest can be won through bhakti or devotion. By union with Him of our whole conscious being, we reach the perfect consummation. The supreme abode of the personal God, Īśvara, is Parabrahma, the Absolute: see also VIII, 2.

22. *puruṣaḥ sa paraḥ pārtha*
bhaktyā labhyas tv ananyayā
yasyā 'ntaḥsthāni bhūtāni
yena sarvam idaṁ tatam

(22) This is the Supreme Person, O Pārtha (Arjuna), in whom all existences abide and by whom all this is pervaded (who) can, however, be gained by unswerving devotion.

The Two Ways

23. *yatra kāle tv anāvṛttim*
āvṛttiṁ cai 'va yoginaḥ
prayātā yānti taṁ kālaṁ
vakṣyāmi bharatarṣabha

(23) Now I shall declare to thee, O Best of Bharatas (Arjuna), the time in which yogins departing, never return and also that wherein departing they return.

24. *agnir jyotir ahaḥ śuklaḥ*
ṣaṇmāsā uttarāyaṇam
tatra prayātā gacchanti
brahma brahmavido janāḥ

(24) Fire, light, day, the bright (half of the month), the six months of the northern path (of the Sun), then going forth the men who know the Absolute go to the Absolute.

25. *dhūmo rātris tathā kṛṣṇaḥ*
ṣaṇmāsā dakṣiṇāyanam
tatra cāndramasaṁ jyotir
yogī prāpya nivartate

(25) Smoke, night, so also the dark (half of the month), the six months of the southern part (of the Sun), then going forth, the yogi obtains the lunar light and returns.

Our dead ancestors (pitṛis) are said to live in the world of the moon and remain there till the time of their return to earth.

26. *śuklakṛṣṇe gatī hy ete*
jagataḥ śāśvate mate
ekayā yāty anāvṛttim
anyayā 'vartate punaḥ

(26) Light and darkness, these paths are thought to be the world's ev rlasting (paths). By the one he goes not to return, by the other he returns again.

Life is a conflict between light and darkness. The former makes for release and the latter for rebirth. The author here uses an old eschatological belief to illustrate a great spiritual truth, that those who are lost in the night of ignorance go by the path of ancestors and are subject to rebirth and those who live in the day of illumination and tread the path of knowledge obtain release from rebirth.

27. *nai 'te sṛtī pārtha jānan*
yogī muhyati kaścana
tasmāt sarveṣu kāleṣu
yogayukto bhavā 'rjuna

(27) The yogin who knows these paths, O Pārtha (Arjuna), is never deluded. Therefore, at all times, O Arjuna, be thou firm in yoga.

Whatever work you undertake, do not lose the thought of the Eternal.

28. *vedeṣu yajñeṣu tapaḥsu cai 'va*
dāneṣu yat puṇyaphalaṁ pradiṣṭam
atyeti tat sarvam idaṁ viditvā
yogī paraṁ sthānam upaiti cā 'dyam

(28) The yogin having known all this, goes beyond the fruits of meritorious deeds assigned to the study of the Vedas, sacrifices, austerities and gifts and attains to the supreme and primal status.

The states which result from the study of the Vedas, sacrifices, austerities and gifts are all lower stages to be passed over by the Yogi who soars beyond them to the final goal.

ity . . . akṣarabrahmayogo nāmā 'ṣṭamo 'dhyāyaḥ

This is the eighth chapter entitled The Yoga of the Imperishable Absolute.

CHAPTER IX

The Lord is more than His Creation

The Sovereign Mystery

śrībhagavān uvāca

1. *idaṁ tu te guhyatamaṁ*
pravakṣyāmy anasūyave
jñānaṁ vijñānasahitaṁ
yaj jñātvā mokṣyase 'śubhāt

The Blessed Lord said:

(1) To Thee, who dost not cavil, I shall declare this profound secret of wisdom combined with knowledge, by knowing which thou shalt be released from evil.

vijñānasahitam, anubhavayuktam. Ś. We take jñāna, however, as meaning wisdom and vijñāna as detailed knowledge. If the former is metaphysical truth, the latter is scientific knowledge. We have at our disposal these different and complementary means of obtaining truth, an intuitive as well as an intellectual expansion of the human mind. We must acquire wisdom and knowledge, penetration of reality and a profound grasp of the nature of things. The philosophers prove that God exists but their knowedge of God is indirect; the seers proclaim that they have felt the reality of God in the depths of their soul and their knowledge is direct.[1] See III, 41; VI, 8.

2. *rājavidyā rājaguhyaṁ*
pavitram idam uttamam
pratyakṣāvagamaṁ dharmyaṁ
susukhaṁ kartum avyayam

(2) This is sovereign knowledge, sovereign secret, supreme sanctity, known by direct experience, in accord with the law, very easy to practise and imperishable.

râjavidyâ, râjagnhyam; literally king-knowledge, king-secret, the greatest wisdom, the greatest secrət.

[1] *asti brahmeti ced veda parokṣaṁ jñānam eva tat*
aham (or *asmi*) *brahmeti ced veda aparokṣaṁ tad ucyate.*

pratyakṣāvagamam. It is not a matter for argument but is verified by direct experience. It is knowledge by acquaintance and not by description, hearsay or report. The truth is there shining by its own light, waiting to be seen by us, if the obstructing veils are removed. The Supreme is to be seen by one as one's own self, through one's developed and purified intuition.[1] Cp. *pratibodhaviditam.*

Kena Up., II, 12.

3. *aśraddadhānāḥ puruṣā*
dharmasyā 'sya paraṁtapa
aprāpya māṁ nivartante
mṛtyusaṁsāravartmani

(3) Men who have no faith in this way, not attaining to Me, O Oppressor of the foe (Arjuna), return to the path of mortal living (saṁsāra).

The sovereign knowledge is the identity of Kṛṣṇa, the Incarnate Lord, with Brahman the source of all. Final illumination will dawn on us if we worship the Incarnate with this knowledge. The direct contemplation of the Absolute is more difficult. Because Arjuna is a man of faith, he is taught this secret. The faithless who do not accept it, do not gain release but return to birth again. The faith demanded is the faith in the reality of saving wisdom and man's capacity to attain it. The first step to grow into the freedom of the Divine is faith in the Godhead in us, which supports our being and action. When we surrender ourselves to that inner Divine, the practice of yoga becomes easy.

4. *mayā tatam idaṁ sarvaṁ*
jagad avyaktamūrtinā
matsthāni sarvabhūtāni
na cā 'haṁ teṣv avasthitaḥ

The Incarnate Lord as the Supreme Reality

(4) By Me all this universe is pervaded through My unmanifested form. All beings abide in Me but I do not abide in them.

[1] *na śāstrair nāpi guruṇā dṛśyate parameśvaraḥ*
dṛśyate svātmanaivātmā svayā sattvasthayā dhiyā.
Yogavāśiṣṭha, VI, 118, 4.

See VII, 12.

This whole universe owes its being to the Transcendent Godhead and yet the forms of this universe do not contain or express Him adequately. His absolute reality is far above the appearance of things in space and time.

5. *na ca matsthāni bhūtāni*
paśya me yogam aiśvaram
bhūtabhṛn na ca bhūtastho
mamā 'tmā bhūtabhāvanaḥ

(5) And (yet) the beings do not dwell in Me; behold My divine mystery. My spirit which is the source of all beings sustains the beings but does not abide in them.

yogam aiśvaram: divine mystery. The explanation of the rise of the limited phenomenal universe out of the Absolute Godhead is traced to the power of the Divine. The Supreme is the source of all phenomena but is not touched by them. That is the yoga of divine power. Though He creates existences, God transcends them to such a degree that we cannot even say that He dwells in them. Even the idea of immanence of God is, strictly speaking, untenable. All existences are due to His double nature but as His higher proper nature is ātman which is unconnected with the work of prakṛti, it is also true that beings do not dwell in Him nor He in them. They are one and yet separate.

"The jīva or the embodied self, bearing the body and maintaining it, remains clinging to it by ahaṁkāra or self-sense. Unlike the jīva, I, though bearing and maintaining all beings, do not remain in them, since I am free from ahaṁkāra or self-sense." Śrīdhara.

The *Gītā* does not deny the world, which exists through God and has God behind, above and before it. It exists through Him who, without the world, would yet be in Himself no less what He is. Unlike God, the world does not possess its specific existence in itself. It has therefore only limited and not absolute being. The teacher inclines not to pantheism which asserts that everything is God but to panentheism that denotes that everything subsists in God. The cosmic process is not a complete manifestation of the Absolute. No finite process can ever finally and fully express the Absolute, though this world is a living manifestation of God.

6. *yathā 'kāśasthito nityaṁ*
vāyuḥ sarvatrago mahān
atha sarvāṇi bhūtāni
matsthānī 'ty upadhāraya

(6) As the mighty air moving everywhere ever, abides in the etheric space (ākāśa), know thou that in the same manner all existences abide in Me.

Space holds them all but is touched by none.

The teacher gives here an analogy. The space is the true universal, all-pervading infinite background on which aerial phenomena take place, but its nature is stable and immutable. So also the Infinite Self is one, not many. Though it is immutable being, it is the support of all that moves. It is not contained in any of the moving entities which are all ultimately dependent on the Self. And yet the Self supports the many. Air exists in space but it does not consist of space and has nothing essentially in common with it. It is only in such a sense that we can say things exist in God.

God's utter transcendence, which is later developed by Madhva, comes out here. Even in R.'s account, the universe is the manifestation of the Divine; but in this verse it is said, that, while God causes things to exist, He does not exist in them. They are there on account of His wondrous power. God so completely transcends the universe that He is separated from all worldly being and is opposed to it as the "wholly other." This is the expression of a profound religious intuition.

7. *sarvabhūtāni kaunteya*
prakṛtiṁ yānti māmikām
kalpakṣaye punas tāni
kalpādau visṛjāmy aham

(7) All beings, O Son of Kuntī (Arjuna), pass into nature which is My own at the end of the cycle; and at the beginning of the (next) cycle, I send them forth.

8. *prakṛtiṁ svāṁ avaṣṭabhya*
visṛjāmi punaḥ-punaḥ
bhūtagrāmam imaṁ kṛtsnam
avaśaṁ prakṛter vaśāt

(8) Taking hold of nature which is My own, I send forth again and again all this multitude of beings which are helpless, being under the control of nature (prakṛti).

The unmanifested nature when lit up by the Unmanifested Self produces the objective universe with its different planes. The order and nature of development are determined by the seeds contained in nature. Only the Divine Self must take hold of it.

The ego is subject to the law of karma and is therefore helplessly obliged to take embodiment in the cosmic life. In IV, 6, it is said that the Divine assumes birth through His own māyā, *ātmamāyayā*. Human souls are not lords of their action. While they are subject to nature, the Supreme controls nature and is not helplessly driven by prakṛti through ignorance. In both cases, the means of creation is māyā. In the divine embodiment, it is yogamāyā, ātmamāyā, prakṛti which is filled with the light and joy of the Supreme and acts under His control. In human embodiment, it is avidyā māyā. The human soul is entangled in ignorance and is helplessly bound in its work, through its subjection to prakṛti.

9. *na ca māṁ tāni karmāṇi*
nibadhnanti dhanaṁjaya
udāsīnavad āsīnam
asaktaṁ teṣu karmasu

(9) Nor do these works bind Me, O winner of wealth (Arjuna), for I am seated as if indifferent, unattached in those actions.

Though the Supreme controls creation and dissolution, as their spirit and guide, He is not involved in them for He is above the procession of cosmic events. As it is the work of the nature which belongs to God, He is to be regarded as immanent in it, and yet in His supracosmic side, He exceeds the cosmic series of things and events. God is thus unweariedly active in the play of the universe and yet above the universe and free from its laws. The Self is not bound by the cosmic wheel which it projects. Countless individuals are born, grow, strive and suffer, die and come to birth again but the Self is for ever free. They reap the fruits of their actions and are bound by their past acts but He is ever free. This evolution proceeds at the cosmic dawn and is withdrawn at the cosmic night.

10. *mayā 'dhyakṣeṇa prakṛtiḥ*
sūyate sacarācaram
hetunā 'nena kaunteya
jagad viparivartate

(10) Under My guidance, nature (prakṛti) gives birth to all things, moving and unmoving and by this means, O Son of Kuntī (Arjuna), the world revolves.

Kṛṣṇa is here represented as the Supreme Self who pervades the universe, who supports all beings and yet is transcendent and unaffected. Ānandagiri advises that we should not raise the question of the purpose of creation. "We cannot say that it is meant for the enjoyment of the Supreme; for the Supreme really enjoys nothing. It is a pure consciousness, a mere witness. And there is no other enjoyer for there is no other conscious entity . . . nor is creation intended to secure mokṣa for it is opposed to mokṣa. Thus neither the question nor an answer to it is possible and there is no occasion for it, as creation is due to the māyā of the Supreme." Cp. *Ṛg. Veda:* "Who could perceive (it) directly, and who could declare whence born and why this variegated creation?"[1]

Devotion to the Supreme brings its great reward: lesser devotions bring lesser rewards.

11. *avajānanti māṁ mūḍhā*
mānuṣīṁ tanum āśritam
paraṁ bhāvam ajānanto
mama bhūtamaheśvaram

(11) The deluded despise Me clad in human body, not knowing My higher nature as Lord of all existences.

[1] *ko addhā veda ka iha pravocat kuta ājātā, kuta iyaṁ visṛiṣṭiḥ.* X, 129, 6; *Taittirīya Brāhmaṇa*, II, 8, 9.

We see only the outward human body and not the Divine in it. We see the outer appearance, not the inner reality. To recognize God in His earthly disguise means effort. Unless we turn our entire existence towards the Eternal, transcending the limits of phenomenal nature and recover the greater consciousness by which we can live in the Divine, we will be a prey to finite fascinations.

Image worship is to be used as a means to the Divine; otherwise it is faulty. In the *Bhāgavata* the Lord is represented as saying "I am present in all beings as their soul but ignoring My presence, the mortal makes a display of image worship."[1]

12. *moghāśā moghakarmāṇo*
moghajñānā vicetasaḥ
rākṣasīm āsurīṁ cai 'va
prakṛtiṁ mohinīṁ śritāḥ

(12) Partaking of the deceptive nature of fiends and demons, their aspirations are vain, their actions vain and their knowledge vain and they are devoid of judgment.

rākṣasīm: fiendish; those who are dominated by tamas and who indulge in acts of cruelty.

āsurīm: demoniac; those dominated by rajas and qualities of ambition, greed and the like. Śrīdhara.

They cling to the world of transient forms and are victims of the deceitful nature (mohinī prakṛti) and disregard the underlying Reality.

13. *mahātmānas tu māṁ pārtha*
daivīṁ prakṛtim āśritāḥ
bhajanty ananyamanaso
jñātvā bhūtādim avyayam

(13) The great-souled, O Pārtha (Arjuna), who abide in the divine nature, knowing (me as) the imperishable source of all beings, worship Me with an undistracted mind.

Deceitful nature, *mohinī prakṛti* is contrasted with Divine nature, *daivī prakṛti.* If we are of the demoniac nature, we live

[1] *ahaṁ sarveṣu bhūteṣu bhūtātmā avasthitaḥ*
tam avajñaya māṁ martyaḥ kurute arcāviḍambanam.
III, 29, 21.

in our separate ego consciousness, and make that the centre of our activities, and get lost in the fruitless cycle of saṁsāra and miss our true destiny. On the other hand, if we are of a divine nature, we open out to our true self-awareness, our whole nature is turned towards the Divine and our whole life becomes a continuous adoration of the Supreme. The endeavour to possess the Divine in knowledge and realize It in life succeeds and we act in a dedicated spirit.

14. *satataṁ kīrtayanto māṁ*
yatantaś ca dṛḍhavratāḥ
namasyantaś ca māṁ bhaktyā
nityayuktā upāsate

(14) Always glorifying Me, strenuous and steadfast in vows, bowing down to Me with devotion, they worship Me, ever disciplined.

jñātvā (13) *bhaktyā . . . . nityayuktaḥ*. These words indicate how the highest perfection is a combination of knowledge, devotion and work.

15. *jñānayajñena cā 'py anye*
yajanto mām upāsate
ekatvena pṛthaktvena
bahudhā viśvatomukham

(15) Others again sacrifice with the sacrifice of wisdom and worship Me as the one, as the distinct and as the manifold, facing in all directions.

Ś. thinks that three classes of worshippers are mentioned here.[1] R. and Madhva hold that only one class is mentioned. Tilak thinks that Advaita, Dvaita and Viśiṣṭādvaita are meant.

Men worship the Supreme facing us in all ways, as one with all existences and at the same time as separate from them.

[1] Nīlakaṇṭha says: *ekatvena aham eva bhagavān vāsudeva ity abheden aupaniṣadāḥ, pṛthaktvena ayam īśvaro mama svāmīti buddhyā prākṛtāh, anye punar bahudhā bahuprakāraṁ viśvatomukham, sarvair dvārair yat kiñcid dṛṣṭaṁ tad bhagavat svarūpam eva, yacchrutaṁ tat tan nāmaiva . . . yad uktaṁ bhuktaṁ vā, tattad arpitam evety evaṁ viśvatomukhaṁ yathā syāt tathā mām upāsate.*

16. *ahaṁ kratur ahaṁ yajñaḥ*
svadhā 'ham aham auṣadham
mantro 'ham aham evā 'jyam
aham agnir ahaṁ hutam

(16) I am the ritual action, I am the sacrifice, I am the ancestral oblation, I am the (medicinal) herb, I am the (sacred) hymn, I am also the melted butter, I am the fire and I am the offering.

Auṣadha or herb stands for the food of all creatures.[1] The Vedic sacrifice is interpreted as an offering of our whole nature, an entire selfgiving to the Universal Self. What we receive from Him, we give back to Him. The gift and the surrender are both His.

17. *pitā 'ham asya jagato*
mātā dhātā pitāmahaḥ
vedyaṁ pavitram auṁkāra
ṛk sāma yajur eva ca

(17) I am the father of this world, the mother, the supporter and the grandsire. I am the object of knowledge, the purifier. I am the syllable Aum and I am the ṛk, the sāma and the yajus as well.

18. *gatir bhartā prabhuḥ sākṣī*
nivāsaḥ śaraṇaṁ suhṛt
prabhavaḥ pralayaḥ sthānaṁ
nidhānaṁ bījam avyayam

(18) (I am) the goal, the upholder, the lord, the witness, the abode, the refuge and the friend. (I am) the origin and the dissolution, the ground, the resting place and the imperishable seed.

Cp. "I take refuge in the Buddha. He is my refuge."[2]

19. *tapāmy aham ahaṁ varṣaṁ*
nigṛhṇāmy utsṛjāmi ca
amṛtaṁ cai 'va mṛtyuś ca
sad asac cā 'ham arjuna

[1] *auṣadhaṁ sarvaprāṇibhir yad adyate tad auṣadhaśabdavācyam.* Ś.
[2] *buddhaṁ śaraṇaṁ gacchāmi eṣa me śaraṇam.*

(19) I give heat; I withhold and send forth the rain. I am immortality and also death, I am being as well as non-being, O Arjuna.

Cp. *Ṛg. Veda: yasyachāyā amṛtaṁ yasya mṛtyuh*:

Sat is the absolute reality and asat is the cosmic existence and the Supreme is both. He is being when manifested and non-being when the world is unmanifested.[1]

R. explains sat as present existence and asat as past and future existence.

The main idea is that the Supreme Lord grants our prayers in whatever form we worship Him.[2]

20. *traividyā māṁ somapāḥ pūtapāpā*
yajñair iṣṭvā svargatiṁ prārthayante
te puṇyam āsādya surendralokam
aśnanti divyān divi devabhogān

(20) The knowers of the three Vedas who drink the soma juice and are cleansed of sin, worshipping Me with sacrifices, pray for the way to heaven. They reach the holy world of Indra (the lord of heaven) and enjoy in heaven the pleasures of the gods.

21. *te taṁ bhuktvā svargalokaṁ viśālaṁ*
kṣīṇe puṇye martyalokaṁ viśanti
evaṁ trayīdharmam anuprapannā
gatāgat ṁ kāma āmā labhan e

(21) Having enjoyed the spacious world of heaven, they enter (return to) the world of mortals, when their merit is exhausted; thus conforming to the doctrine enjoined in the three Vedas and desirous of enjoyments, they obtain the changeable (what is subject to birth and death).

The teacher here refers to the Vedic theory that those who perform the prescribed ritual gain heavenly enjoyments after death and points out how it cannot be regarded as the highest goal. Such men are bound by the law of karma as they are still

[1] *kāryakāraṇe vā sad asatī*. Ś.

[2] *atas teṣām viśvatomukham mamabhajanaṁ kurvatām, sarva rūpeṇāham anugrahaṁ karomītibhāvaḥ*. Nilakaṇṭha.

lured by desire, *kāma-kāmā*, and they will return to this cosmic procession since they act from an ego-centre and since their ignorance is not destroyed. If we seek rewards in heaven, we will gain them but we return to mortal existence so long as we do not gain the true aim of life. Human life is an opportunity to develop out of the imperfect material, soul's divine nature. We operate from the ego-centred consciousness, whether we seek the pleasures of this world or of a future paradise.

22. *ananyāś cintayanto māṁ*
ye janāḥ paryupāsate
teṣāṁ nityābhiyuktānāṁ
yogakṣemaṁ vahāmy aham

(22) But those who worship Me, meditating on Me alone, to them who ever persevere, I bring attainment of what they have not and security in what they have.[1]

The teacher urges that the Vedic path is a snare to be avoided by the aspirants after the highest.

God takes up all the burdens and the cares of His devotees.[2]

To become conscious of divine love, all other love must be abandoned.[3] If we cast ourselves entirely on the mercy of God, He bears all our cares and sorrows. We can depend on His saving care and energizing grace.

23. *ye 'py anyadevatābhaktā*
yajante śraddhayā 'nvitāḥ
te 'pi mām eva kaunteya
yajanty avidhipūrvakam

(23) Even those who are devotees of other gods, worship them with faith, they also sacrifice to Me alone, O Son of Kuntī (Arjuna), though not according to the true law.

[1] *yogo'prāptasya prāpaṇam, kṣemas tad rakṣaṇam.* See II, 45.

[2] *bhagavān eva teṣāṁ yogakṣemaṁ vahati.*

[3] Rābi'a was once asked: "Do you love God Almighty?" "Yes." "Do you hate the Devil?" "My love of God," she replied, "leaves me no leisure to hate the Devil. I saw the prophet in a dream, He said, 'O Rābi'a, do you love me?' I said, 'O Apostle of God, who does not love thee?, but love of God hath so absorbed me that neither love nor hate of any other thing remains in my heart.' "
R. A. Nicholson: *A Literary History of the Arabs* (1930), 234.

The author of the *Gītā* welcomes light from every quarter of the heaven. It has a right to shine because it is light.

24. *ahaṁ hi sarvayajñānāṁ*
bhoktā ca prabhur eva ca
na tu mām abhijānanti
tattvenā 'taś cyavanti te

(24) For I am the enjoyer and lord of all sacrifices. But these men do not know Me in My true nature and so they fall.

25. *yānti devavratā devān*
pitṝn yānti pitṛvratāḥ
bhūtāni yānti bhūtejyā
yānti madyājino 'pi mām

(25) Worshippers of the gods go to the gods, worshippers of the manes go to the manes, sacrificers of the spirits go to the spirits and those who sacrifice to Me come to Me.

The shining gods, the spirits of the dead and the spirits in the psychic world all happen to be worshipped by men in different stages of development but they are all limited forms of the Supreme and cannot give the aspiring soul the peace that is beyond all understanding. The result of worship is assimilation to the form worshipped and these limited forms give limited results. No devotion fails of its highest reward. The lesser ones bring lesser rewards while devotion to the Supreme brings the supreme reward. All sincere religious devotion is a seeking after the Supreme Godhead.

Devotion and Its Effects

26. *pattraṁ puṣpaṁ phalaṁ toyaṁ*
yo me bhaktyā prayacchati
tad ahaṁ bhaktyupahṛtam
aśnāmi prayatātmanaḥ

(26) Whosoever offers to Me with devotion a leaf, a flower, a fruit, or water, that offering of love, of the pure of heart I accept.

However poor the offering, if it is made with love and earnestness, it is acceptable to the Lord. The way to the Highest is not by way of subtle metaphysics or complicated ritual. It is by sheer self-giving, which is symbolized by the offer of a leaf, a flower, a fruit or water. What is necessary is a devoted heart.

27. *yat karoṣi yad aśnāsi*
yaj juhoṣi dadāsi yat
yat tapasyasi kaunteya
tat kuruṣva madarpaṇaṁ

(27) Whatever thou doest, whatever thou eatest, whatever thou offerest, whatever thou givest away, whatever austerities thou dost practise—do that, O Son of Kuntī (Arjuna), as an offering to Me.

Self-giving results in the consecration of all acts to God. The tide of the common tasks of daily life must flow through the worship of God. Love of God is not an escape from the harshness of life but a dedication for service. Karmamārga or the way of works which starts with the duty of performance of prescribed rites concludes with the position that all tasks are sanctified when done with disinterestedness and dedication.

"My self is Thy self, my understanding is Pārvatī (Śiva's wife); my life functions are my comrades, the body is my home, my worship is the varied enjoyment of the sense objects, my sleep is the condition of concentration. My steps are movements round the temple and all utterances are prayers. Whatever act is done by me, every one of them, O Lord, is a worship of Thee."[1] If you do whatever you have to do in a spirit of dedication, it is God's worship; nothing separate need be done.[2]

[1] *ātmā tvaṁ, girijā matiḥ, sahacarāḥ prāṇāḥ śarīraṁ gṛham*
pūjā me viṣayopabhogaracanā, nidrā samādhi sthitiḥ
saṁcāraḥ pādayoḥ pradakṣiṇavidhiḥ stotraṇi sarvāgiro
yadyat karma karomi tat tad akhilaṁ śambhō tavārādhanaṁ.

[2] Madhusūdana says:

avaśyam bhāvināṁ karmaṇām mayi paramagurau samarpaṇaṁ eva madbhajanam; na tu tadarthaṁ pṛthak vyāpāraḥ kaścit kartavya ity abhiprāyaḥ.

28. *śubhāśubhaphalair evaṁ*
mokṣyase karmabandhanaiḥ
saṁnyāsayogayuktātmā
vimukto mām upaiṣyasi

(28) Thus shalt thou be freed from the good and evil results which are the bonds of action. With thy mind firmly set on the way of renunciation, thou shalt become free and attain to Me.

By such giving and consecration, the whole life of the soul is given to the service of the Supreme and the ego is freed from its barriers and its acts no more bind the soul.

29. *samo 'haṁ sarvabhūteṣu*
na me dveṣyo 'sti na priyaḥ
ye bhajanti tu māṁ bhaktyā
mayi te teṣu cā 'py aham

(29) I am the same in (alike to) all beings. None is hateful nor dear to Me. But those who worship Me with devotion they are in Me and I also in them.

God has no friends or foes. He is impartial. He does not damn any nor elect any by His capricious will. The only way to win His love is by faith and devotion and each must tread the path by himself.

30. *api cet sudurācāro*
bhajate mām ananyabhāk
sādhur eva sa mantavyaḥ
samyag vyavasito hi saḥ

(30) Even if a man of the most vile conduct worships me with undistracted devotion, he must be reckoned as righteous for he has rightly resolved.

"By abandoning evil ways in his external life and by the power of his internal right resolution." Ś. Cp. also "If he repents after he commits the sin, he is freed from sin; if he resolves that he will never commit the sin again, he will be purified."[1] The evil

[1] *kṛtvā pāpaṁ hi saṁtapya tasmāt pāpāt pramucyate*
naivaṁ kuryāṁ punar iti nivṛtyā pūyate tu saḥ.

of the past deeds cannot be washed away except by his turning to God with undivided heart. Cp. *Baudhāyana Dharma Sūtra:* "Let one feel daily repentant in mind, reflecting over misdeeds committed and practising austerity and vigilance. By this will he be freed from sin."[1] Karma never binds completely. The sinner in the lowest depths of degradation has the light in him which he cannot put out, though he may try to stifle it and turn away from it utterly. God holds us, fallen though we be, by the roots of our being and is ready to send His rays of light into our dark and rebellious hearts. The very consciousness of our imperfection and sin betrays the pressure of the Divine on our hearts. Cp. Tukārām: "Fallen of fallen, thrice fallen am I; but do Thou raise me by Thy power. I have neither purity of heart nor a faith firmly set at Thy feet. I am born of sin. How often shall I repeat it? Says Tuka." Again: "I am void of understanding, needy and worse than needy. I cannot steady my mind; I cannot stay my wayward senses. I have exhausted effort; peace and rest are far from me. I have offered Thee perfect faith; I have laid my life at Thy feet. Do now as Thou wilt, I can only look to Thee. O God, I trust in Thee, I cling firmly to Thy feet. Tuka says, It is for Thee to deal with my efforts."[2] The publican, in the parable, prays from the depth of his heart, "God, be merciful to me, a sinner."

This verse does not mean that there is an easy escape from the consequences of our deeds. We cannot prevent the cause from producing its effect. Any arbitrary interference with the order of the world is not permitted. When the sinner turns to God with undistracted devotion, a new cause is introduced. His redemption is conditional on his repentance. Repentance, as we have noticed, is a genuine change of heart and includes contrition or sorrow for the past sin and a decision to prevent a repetition of it in the future. When once the resolution is adopted, the transformation of the lower into the higher is steadily effected. If we believe in human effort, the growth may be hard. Error, imperfection and self-will are difficult to overcome, but when the soul gives up its ego and opens itself to the Divine, the Divine takes up the burden and lifts the soul into the spiritual plane.

[1] *śoceta manasā nityaṁ duṣkṛtāny anucintayan*
tapasvī cāpramādī ca tataḥ pāpāt pramucyate.

[2] Fraser and Marathes: *Tukārām*: I, p. 92.

Tulsidās says: "A piece of charcoal loses its blackness only when fire penetrates it."[1] There are no unforgivable sins.

31. *kṣipraṁ bhavati dharmātmā*
śaśvacchāntiṁ nigacchati
kaunteya pratijānīhi
na me bhaktaḥ praṇaśyati

(31) Swiftly does he become a soul of righteousness and obtain lasting peace. O Son of Kuntī (Arjuna), know thou for certain that My devotee perishes never.[2]

Once we place ourselves in the hands of the Divine, we cannot fall into utter darkness.

Cp. Rāma's statement: "To him who seeks My protection even once and requests help of Me saying 'I am yours' I shall give him fearlessness from all beings. This is My resolve."[3]

32. *māṁ hi pārtha vyapāśritya*
ye 'pi syuḥ pāpayonayaḥ
striyo vaiśyās tathā śūdrās
te 'pi yānti parāṁ gatim

(32) For those who take refuge in Me, O Pārtha (Arjuna), though they are lowly born, women, Vaiśyas, as well as Śūdras, they also attain to the highest goal.

The message of the *Gītā* is open to all without distinction of race, sex or caste. This verse is not to be regarded as supporting the social customs debarring women and Śūdras from Vedic study. It refers to the view prevalent at the time of the composition of the *Gītā*. The *Gītā* does not sanction these social rules.[4] The

[1] Cp. *Garuḍa purāṇa.*
bhaktiraṣṭavidhā hy eṣā yasmin mlecchopi vartate
sa viprendro muniḥ śrīmān sa yatiḥ sa ca paṇḍitaḥ.

[2] *pratijānīhi pratijñāṁ kuru mad bhakto na praṇaśyati.*

[3] *sakṛdeva prapannāya tavāsmīti ca yācate*
abhayaṁ sarvabhūtebhyo dadāmy etad vrataṁ mama.
Cp. the saying: *na vāsudevabhaktānām aśubhaṁ vidyate kvacit.*

[4] In the early times, there was the tendency to look upon the non-Hindus as barbarians, though this attitude of superiority was not confined to the Hindus. The ancient Greeks looked upon

Gītā gets beyond racial distinctions in its emphasis on spiritual values. Its gospel of love is open to all men and women, persons of all castes as well as those outside caste.[1]

33. *kiṁ punar brāhmaṇāḥ puṇyā*
bhaktā rājarṣayas tathā
anityam asukhaṁ lokam
imaṁ prāpya bhajasva mām

(33) How much more then, holy Brahmins and devoted royal saints; Having entered this impermanent sorrowful world, do thou worship Me.

In other words, even those who, on account of their past births, suffer from many disabilities, and are given to worldly pursuits can overcome their weakness and attain the highest. The path is easier for those Brahmins and royal sages who are spiritually disposed.

anityam asukhaṁ lokam: impermanent sorrowful world. To the Orphics life in this world is pain and weariness. We are bound to a wheel which turns through endless cycles of births and deaths. Only by purification and renunciation can we escape from the wheel and attain to the joy of union with God. John Burnet refers to the striking similarity between the Orphic beliefs and those prevalent in India at about the same time. *Early Greek*

foreigners as barbarians. The Roman general, Quntilian Varus said of the inhabitants of *Germania*: "It is true, they are men, but except the voice and limbs of the body they have nothing of human beings in them." The French philosopher, Montesquieu, (1689–1755), said of the Negroes: "One cannot well imagine that God who is so wise should have put a soul, moreover an immortal soul, into an entirely black body. It is impossible to think that these people are human beings."

[1] It is a matter of deep humiliation and shame to every sensible Hindu to think that sometimes attempts are made to justify untouchability. The Buddha welcomed antyajas into his sangha. In the *Rāmāyaṇa*, one who will now be regarded as an untouchable took Rāmā across the Ganges in his boat. The great teachers of bhakti, Śaiva and Vaiṣṇava, have striven for equality and proclaimed that believers in God, whatever their origin, are the best of the twiceborn. *caṇḍālopi dvijaśreṣṭhaḥ hari bhaktiparāyaṇāt.* Among the followers of Caitanya were Hindus and Moslems, robbers and prostitutes.

Philosophy (1930), p. 82. The teaching of the Buddha has for its starting point these features of the universe, its impermanence and pain.[1] There is a Persian saying attributed to Jesus: "The world is a bridge, pass over it but do not build upon it." Not merely the world but every phase of the cosmic process, every aspect of human history, every stage of man's life—the freshness of infancy, the crudeness of boyhood, the idealism of youth, the hot passions of adolescence and the ambitions of manhood are all bridges, meant for transit and not permanent habitation. Modern science demonstrates how miserably conditioned human life is. Jean-Paul Sartre's theory of existentialism assumes that human existence is subject to certain permanent conditions. Each of us is born, is implicated in a reality which is not dependent on him, acts on other people and is exposed to action on their part. He cannot escape from death. These conditions taken together make of human existence a tragic reality. Each of us, in this desperate condition, has to work out his salvation by the effort of his will. For the existentialist, man is left to his own resources. He has no faith in the saving grace of God. The teacher of the *Gītā* shows us a way out of the transitoriness of things, the curse of age and death, *jarāmaraṇamokṣāya*.[2] He asks us to take refuge in the Divine.

34. *manmanā bhava madbhakto*
madyājī māṁ namaskuru
mām evai 'ṣyasi yuktvai 'vam
ātmānaṁ matparāyaṇaḥ

(34) On Me fix thy mind; to Me be devoted; worship Me; revere Me; thus having disciplined thyself, with Me as thy goal, to Me shalt thou come.

It is not the personal Kṛṣṇa to whom we have to give ourselves up utterly but the Unborn, Beginningless, Eternal who speaks through Kṛṣṇa. The way to rise out of our ego-centred consciousness to the divine plane is through the focusing of all our energies, intellectual, emotional and volitional on God. Then our whole being is transformed and lifted up into the unity and universality

[1] Cp. XIII, 8.

[2] VII, 29.

of spirit. Knowledge, love and power get fused in a supreme unification. Joy and peace are the result of self-oblivion, of utter abandonment, of absolute acceptance.

iti . . . rājavidyārājaguhyayogo nāma navamo 'dhyāyaḥ

This is the ninth chapter entitled The Yoga of Sovereign Knowledge and Sovereign Mystery

CHAPTER X

God is the Source of all; to know Him is to know all

The Immanence and Transcendence of God

śrībhagavān uvāca

1. *bhūya eva mahābāho*
śṛṇu me paramaṁ vacaḥ
yat te 'haṁ prīyamāṇāya
vakṣyāmi hitakāmyayā

The Blessed Lord said:

(1) Again, O Mighty-armed (Arjuna), hearken to My supreme word. From a desire to do thee good, I will declare it to thee, now that thou art taking delight (in My words).

Prīyamāṇāya may also be rendered "who art beloved."

2. *na me viduḥ suragaṇāḥ*
prabhavaṁ na maharṣayaḥ
aham ādir hi devānāṁ
maharṣīṇāṁ ca sarvaśaḥ

(2) Neither the hosts of gods nor the great sages know any origin of Me for I am the source of the gods and the great sages in every way.

sarvaśaḥ: in every way; *sarvaprakāraiḥ.* Ś.

The Supreme is the unborn eternal and He is also the lord of the world. Though He has no birth, all existences derive from Him. The teacher announces that He is in truth the Eternal God Himself, more ancient than all else and that all manifested glory is from Him.

3. *yo māṁ ajam anādiṁ ca*
vetti lokamaheśvaram
asaṁmūḍhaḥ sa martyeṣu
sarvapāpaiḥ pramucyate

(3) He who knows Me, the unborn, without beginning,

also the mighty lord of the worlds, he, among mortals is undeluded and freed from all sins

When we learn to look at things as derived from the One Transcendent Reality, we are delivered from all groping and bewilderment.

4. *buddhir jñānam asaṁmohaḥ*
kṣamā satyaṁ damaḥ śamaḥ
sukhaṁ duḥkhaṁ bhavo 'bhāvo
bhayaṁ cā 'bhayam eva ca

(4) Understanding, knowledge, freedom from bewilderment, patience, truth, self-control and calmness; pleasure and pain, existence and non-existence, fear and fearlessness.

dama: self-control is quietude of the external senses.
śama: calmness. It is calmness of inner spirit.

5. *ahiṁsā samatā tuṣṭis*
tapo dānaṁ yaśo 'yaśaḥ
bhavanti bhāvā bhūtānāṁ
matta eva pṛthagvidhāḥ

(5) Non-violence, equal-mindedness, contentment, austerity, charity, fame and ill-fame (are) the different states of beings proceed from Me alone.

ahiṁsā: non-violence; in old texts it means non-hurting, especially non-killing.

All these separate states of being issue in accordance with the past karma of beings.[1] The Divine is indirectly responsible even for the pain and suffering of the world. He is the lord of the world and guides it, though He is unaffected by its oppositions.

6. *maharṣayaḥ sapta pūrve*
catvāro manavas tathā
madbhāvā mānasā jātā
yeṣāṁ loka imāḥ prajāḥ

(6) The seven great sages of old, and the four Manus also are of My nature and born of My mind and from them are all these creatures in the world

[1] *svakarmāṇurūpeṇa.* Ś.

These are the powers in charge of the many processes of the world. Manu according to tradition is the first man at the beginning of each new race of beings.

7. *etāṁ vibhūtiṁ yogaṁ ca*
mama yo vetti tattvataḥ
so 'vikampena yogena
yujyate nā 'tra saṁśayaḥ

(7) He who knows in truth this glory (magnifestation) and power (steady action) of Mine is united (with Me) by unfaltering yoga; of this there is no doubt.

vibhūti: glory.[1] The knower will be aware of his unity with the Divine and participate in the work of the world which is a manifestation of the Divine. The knowledge of the determinate Brahman is the way to the knowledge of the indeterminate Brahman.[2]

Knowledge and Devotion

8. *ahaṁ sarvasya prabhavo*
mattaḥ sarvaṁ pravartate
iti matvā bhajante māṁ
budhā bhāvasamanvitāḥ

(8) I am the origin of all; from Me all (the whole creation) proceeds. Knowing this, the wise worship Me, endowed with conviction.

bhāva: the right state of mind. R.

The teacher speaks now as the Lord, as Īśvara. God is the material and efficient cause of the world. The aspirant is not deluded by the passing forms but knowing that the Supreme is the source of all the forms, he worships the Supreme.

[1] *vibhūti vistāram* for Ś., *aiśvaryam* for R. right feeling, zeal, faith. Commenting on Ś., Ānandagiri says "*vividhā bhūtir bhavanaṁ vaibhavaṁ sarvātma-katvam.*" It is the glory of manifestation.

[2] *sopādhikajñānaṁ nirupādhikajñāne dvāram.* Ānandagiri.

9. *maccittā madgataprāṇā*
bodhayantaḥ parasparam
kathayantaś ca māṁ nityaṁ
tuṣyanti ca ramanti ca

(9) Their thoughts (are fixed) in Me, their lives (are wholly) given up to Me, enlightening each other and ever conversing of Me, they are contented and rejoicing in Me.

10. *teṣāṁ satatayuktānāṁ*
bhajatāṁ prītipūrvakam
dadāmi buddhiyogaṁ taṁ
yena mām upayānti te

(10) To these who are constantly devoted and worship Me with love, I grant the concentration of understanding by which they come unto Me.

buddhiyoga: the devotion of mind by which the disciple gains the wisdom which sees the One in all the forms which change and pass.

11. *teṣām evā 'nukampārtham*
aham ajñānajaṁ tamaḥ
nāśayāmy ātmabhāvastho
jñānadīpena bhāsvatā

(11) Out of compassion for those same ones, remaining within My own true state, I destroy the darkness born of ignorance by the shining lamp of wisdom.

God affects the world for man's welfare, Himself remaining apart from it. *Ātmabhāva* is also interpreted as the inner sense of beings. Here the teacher makes out how bhakti or devotion leads to the destruction of ignorance and the rise of illumination. When ignorance is destroyed, God stands revealed in the human spirit. When love and wisdom arise, the eternal is fulfilled in the individual. Bhakti is also a means to jñāna. Through it we obtain Divine grace and the power of understanding, buddhiyoga. Intellectual knowledge is rendered luminous and certain by the direct intuition of buddhi.

The Lord is the Seed and Perfection of All that Is

arjuna uvāca

12 *paraṁ brahma paraṁ dhāma*
pavitraṁ paramaṁ bhavān
puruṣaṁ śāśvataṁ divyam
ādidevam ajaṁ vibhum

Arjuna said:

(12) Thou art the Supreme Brahman, the Supreme Abode and the Supreme Purifier, the Eternal, Divine Person, the First of the gods, the Unborn, the All-pervading.

13. *āhus tvām ṛṣayaḥ sarve*
devarṣir nāradas tathā
asito devalo vyāsaḥ
svayaṁ cai 'va bravīṣi me

(13) All the sages say this of Thee, as well as the divine seer Nārada, so also Asita, Devala, Vyāsa and Thou thyself declarest it to me

Arjuna accepts the truth of what has been declared and proclaims his conviction that Kṛṣṇa who is speaking to him is the Supreme Godhead, the Absolute, the Ever-free to which we can rise by self-surrender. He gives utterance from his own experience to the truth revealed by the seers who have seen it and become one with it. The secret wisdom is revealed by God, the seers are witnesses to it and Arjuna himself verifies it from his own experience. Abstract truths uttered by the sages become now luminous intuitions, glowing experiences of one's whole being.

14 *sarvam etad ṛtaṁ manye*
yan māṁ vadasi keśava
na hi te bhagavan vyaktiṁ
vidur devā na dānavāḥ

(14) I hold as true, all this that thou sayest to me, O Keśava (Kṛṣṇa); neither the gods nor the demons, O Lord, know Thy manifestation.

15. *svayam evā 'tmanā 'tmānaṁ*
vettha tvaṁ puruṣottama
bhūtabhāvana bhūteśa
devadeva jagatpate

(15) Verily Thou Thyself knowest Thyself by Thyself, O Supreme Person; the Source of beings, the Lord of creatures; the God of gods, the Lord of the world!

16. *vaktum arhasy aśeṣeṇa*
divyā hy ātmavibhūtayaḥ
yābhir vibhūtibhir lokān
imāṁs tvaṁ vyāpya tiṣṭhasi

(16) Thou shoulds tell me of Thy divine manifestations, without exception, whereby, pervading these worlds, Thou dost abide (in them and beyond).

vibhūtayaḥ: manifestations, the divine glories by which the Supreme pervades all the worlds. They are the formative forces or spiritual powers which give to each object its essential nature. They are akin to Plato's Divine Ideas, the perfect types and patterns of all things here below. Only the word "idea" is likely to suggest a pale abstraction, a bloodless category. Vibhūti is a living formative principle.

17. *kathaṁ vidyām ahaṁ yogiṁs*
tvāṁ sadā paricintayan
keṣu-keṣu ca bhāveṣu
cintyo 'si bhagavan mayā

(17) How may I know Thee, O Yogin, by constant meditation? In what various aspects art Thou, O Blessed Lord, to be thought of by me?

Kṛṣṇa is yogin by virtue of his work as creator. Arjuna wishes to know the aspects of nature where the Lord's presence is more clearly manifest and asks Kṛṣṇa to tell him in what various aspects he should think of Him to help his meditation.

18. *vistareṇā 'tmano yogaṁ*
vibhūtiṁ ca janārdana
bhūyaḥ kathaya tṛptir hi
śṛṇvato nā 'sti me 'mṛtam

(18) Relate to me again in detail, O Janārdana (Kṛṣṇa), of Thy power and manifestation; for I am not satiated with hearing Thy nectar-like speech.

amṛtam: nectar-like. His words are life-giving.

The *Gītā* does not set up an opposition between Brahman and the world, between the Ineffable Reality and its inadequate expression. It gives a comprehensive spiritual view. It, no doubt, mentions the Indefinable (anirdeśyam), the Unmanifest Immutable (avyaktam akṣaram), the Unthinkable (aciñtyarūpam), the Absolute beyond all empirical determination. But worship of the Absolute is difficult for embodied beings.[1] It is easier to approach the Supreme through Its relations with the world and this method is more natural. The Supreme is the Personal Lord who controls the many-sided action of nature and dwells in the heart of every creature. Parabrahman is Parameśvara, the God in man and in the universe. But His nature is veiled by the series of becomings. Man has to discover his spiritual unity with God and so with all His creatures.

śrībhagavān uvāca

19. *hanta te kathayiṣyāmi*
divyā hy ātmavibhūtayaḥ
prādhānyataḥ kuruśreṣṭha
nā 'sty anto vistarasya me

The Blessed Lord said:

(19) Yes, I will declare to thee of My divine forms but only of those which are prominent, O best of the Kurus (Arjuna), for there is no end to my extent (the details).

20. *aham ātmā guḍākeśa*
sarvabhūtāśayasthitaḥ
aham ādiś ca madhyaṁ ca
bhūtānām anta eva ca

(20) I, O Guḍākeśa (Arjuna), am the self seated in the hearts of all creatures. I am the beginning, the middle and the very end of beings.

The world is a living whole, a vast interconnectedness, a cosmic harmony inspired and sustained by the One Supreme.

[1] XII, 5.

21. *ādityānām ahaṁ viṣṇur*
jyotiṣāṁ ravir aṁśumān
marīcir marutām asmi
nakṣatrāṇām ahaṁ śaśī

(21) Of the Ādityas I am Viṣṇu; of the lights (I am) the radiant Sun; I am Marīci of the Maruts; of the stars I am the moon.

Ādityas are Vedic gods. While the Supreme is in all things, He is more prominent in some than in others. There is an ascending order in the world. God is more revealed in life than in matter, in consciousness than in life and in saints and sages most of all. Within the same order, He is most revealed in the pre-eminent individuals. Some of these mythological beings were perhaps living realities to the Hindus of the period of the *Gītā*.

22. *vedānāṁ sāmavedo 'smi*
devānām asmi vāsavaḥ
indriyāṇāṁ manaś cā 'smi
bhūtānām asmi cetanā

(22) Of the Vedas I am the Sāmaveda; of the gods I am Indra; of the senses I am mind and of beings I am consciousness.

Sāmaveda is mentioned as the chief of the Vedas on account of its musical beauty.[1]

23. *rudrāṇāṁ śaṁkaraś cā 'smi*
vitteśo yakṣarakṣasām
vasūnāṁ pāvakaś cā 'smi
meruḥ śikhariṇām aham

(23) Of the Rudras I am Śaṁkara (Śiva); of the Yakṣas and the Rākṣasas (I am) Kubera; of the Vasus I am Agni (Fire) and of mountain-peaks I am Meru.

24. *purodhasāṁ ca mukhyaṁ māṁ*
viddhi pārtha bṛhaspatim
senānīnām ahaṁ skandaḥ
sarasām asmi sāgaraḥ

[1] *sāmavedo gānena ramaṇīyatvāt.* Nīlakaṇṭha.

(24) Of the household priests, O Pārtha (Arjuna), know Me to be the chief—Bṛhaspati; of the (war) generals I am Skanda; of the lakes I am the ocean.

25. *maharṣīṇāṁ bhṛgur ahaṁ*
girām asmy ekam akṣaram
yajñānāṁ japayajño 'smi
sthāvarāṇāṁ himālayaḥ

(25) Of the great sages I am Bhṛgu; of utterances, I am the single syllable Aum; of offerings I am the offering of silent meditation and of unmovable things (I am) the Himālaya.

26. *aśvatthaḥ sarvavṛkṣāṇāṁ*
devarṣīṇāṁ ca nāradaḥ
gandharvāṇāṁ citrarathaḥ
siddhānāṁ kapilo muniḥ

(26) Of all trees (I am) the Aśvattha and of divine seers (I am) Nārada; among the gandharvas (I am) Chitraratha and of the perfected ones (I am) Kapila the sage.

Kapila is the teacher of the Sāṁkhya philosophy.

27. *uccaiḥśravasam aśvānāṁ*
viddhi mām amṛtodbhavam
airāvataṁ gajendrāṇāṁ
narāṇāṁ ca narādhipam

(27) Of horses, know me to be Ucchaiśravas, born of nectar; of lordly elephants (I am) Airāvata and of men (I am) the monarch.

28. *āyudhānām ahaṁ vajraṁ*
dhenūnām asmi kāmadhuk
prajanaś cā 'smi kandarpaḥ
sarpāṇām asmi vāsukiḥ

(28) Of weapons I am the thunderbolt; of the cows I am the cow of plenty; of the progenitors I am the God of love; of the serpents I am Vāsuki.

29. *anantaś cā 'smi nāgānāṁ*
varuṇo yādasām aham
pitṝṇām aryamā cā 'smi
yamaḥ saṁyamatām aham

(29) Of the nāgas I am Ananta; of the dwellers in water I am Varuṇa; of the (departed) ancestors I am Aryama; of those who maintain law and order, I am Yama.

30. *prahlādaś cā 'smi daityānāṁ*
kālaḥ kalayatām aham
mṛgāṇāṁ ca mṛgendro 'haṁ
vainateyaś ca pakṣiṇām

(30) Of the Titans I am Prahlāda; of calculators I am Time: of beasts I am the King of beasts (lion) and of birds (I am) the son of Vinatā (Garuḍa).

31. *pavanaḥ pavatām asmi*
rāmaḥ śastrabhṛtām aham
jhaṣāṇāṁ makaraś cā 'smi
srotasām asmi jāh ıavī

(31) Of purifiers I am the wind; of warriors I am Rāma; of fishes I am the alligator and of rivers I am the Ganges.

32. *sargāṇām ādir antaś ca*
madhyaṁ cai 'vā 'ham arjuna
adhyātmavidyā vidyānāṁ
vādaḥ pravadatām aham

(32) Of creations I am the beginning, the end and also the middle, O Arjuna; of the sciences (I am) the science of the self; of those who debate I am the dialectic.

adhyātmavidyā vidyānām: of the sciences I am the science of the self. The science of the self is the way to beatitude. It is not an intellectual exercise or a social adventure. It is the way to saving wisdom and so is pursued with deep religious conviction. Philosophy as the science of the self helps us to overcome the ignorance which hides from us the vision of reality. It is the universal science according to Plato. Without it, the departmental sciences become misleading. Plato observes: "The possession of the sciences as a whole, if it does not include the best, will in some few cases aid but more often harm the owner." *Alcibiades*, II, 144 D.

33. *akṣarāṇaṁ akāro 'smi*
dvandvaḥ sāmāsikasya ca
aham evā 'kṣayaḥ kālo
dhātā 'haṁ viśvatomukhaḥ

(33) Of letters I am (the letter) A and of compounds (I am) the dual; I also am imperishable time and I the creator whose face is turned on all sides.

kāla: time. Cp. *kālasvarūpī bhagavān kṛṣṇaḥ. Viṣṇu purāṇa*, v. 38.

34. *mṛtyuḥ sarvaharaś cā 'ham*
udbhavaś ca bhaviṣyatām
kīrtiḥ śrīr vāk ca nārīṇāṁ
smṛtir medhā dhṛtiḥ kṣamā

(34) I am death, the all-devouring and (am) the origin of things that are yet to be; and of feminine beings, (I am) fame, prosperity, speech, memory, intelligence, firmness and patience.

35. *bṛhatsāma tathā sāmnāṁ*
gāyatrī chandasām aham
māsānāṁ mārgaśīrṣo 'ham
ṛtūnāṁ kusumākaraḥ

(35) Likewise, of hymns (I am) Brihatsāman, of metres (I am) gāyatrī; of months (I am) mārgaśīrṣa and of seasons (I am) the flower-bearer (spring).

36. *dyūtaṁ chalayatām asmi*
tejas tejasvinām aham
jayo 'smi vyavasāyo 'smi
sattvaṁ sattvavatām aham

(36) Of the deceitful I am the gambling; of the splendid I am the splendour; I am victory; I am effort and I am the goodness of the good.

37 *vṛṣṇīnāṁ vāsudevo 'smi*
pāṇḍavānāṁ dhanaṁjayaḥ
munīnām apy ahaṁ vyāsaḥ
kavīnām uśanā kaviḥ

(37) Of the Vṛṣṇis I am Vāsudeva; of the Pāṇḍavas (I am) the Winner of wealth (Arjuna); of the sages I am Vyāsa also and of the poets (I am) the poet Uśanā.

38. *daṇḍo damayatām asmi*
nītir asmi jigīṣatām
maunaṁ cai 'vā 'smi guhyānāṁ
jñānaṁ jñānavatām aham

(38) Of those who chastise I am the rod (of chastisement); of those that seek victory I am the wise policy; of things secret I am the silence and of the knowers of wisdom I am the wisdom.

39. *yac cā 'pi sarvabhūtānāṁ*
bījaṁ tad aham arjuna
na tad asti vinā yat syān
mayā bhūtaṁ carācaram

(39) And further, whatsoever is the seed of all existences that am I, O Arjuna; nor is there anything, moving or unmoving that can exist without Me.[1]

40. *nā 'nto 'sti mama divyānāṁ*
vibhūtīnāṁ paraṁtapa
eṣa tū 'ddeśataḥ prokto
vibhūter vistaro mayā

(40) There is no end to My divine manifestations, O Conqueror of the foe (Arjuna). What has been declared by Me is only illustrative of My infinite glory.

41. *yad-yad vibhūtimat sattvaṁ*
śrīmad ūrjitam eva vā
tat-tad evā 'vagaccha tvaṁ
mama tejoṁśasaṁbhavam

[1] Cp. Draupadī's address:
martyatā caiva bhūtānām amaratvaṁ divaukasām
tvayi sarvaṁ mahābāho lokakāryaṁ pratiṣṭhitam.

(41) Whatsoever being there is, endowed with glory and grace and vigour, know that to have sprung from a fragment of My splendour.

While all things are supported by God, things of beauty and splendour reveal Him more than others. Every deed of heroism, every life of sacrifice, every work of genius, is a revelation of the Divine. The epic moments of a man's life are inexplicably beyond the finite mind of man.

42. *athavā bahunai 'tena*
kiṁ jñātena tavā 'rjuna
viṣṭabhyā 'ham idaṁ kṛtsnam
ekāṁśena sthito jagat

(42) But what need is there, O Arjuna, for such detailed knowledge by you? I support this entire universe pervading it with a single fraction of Myself.

ekāṁśena: by a single fraction. Not that the Divine unity is broken up into fragments. This cosmos is but a partial revelation of the Infinite, is illumined by one ray of His shining light.[1] The transcendent light of the Supreme dwells beyond all this cosmos, beyond time and space.

iti . . . vibhūtiyogo nāma daśamo 'dhyāyaḥ

This is the tenth chapter entitled The Yoga of Manifestation.

[1] Cp. *Ṛg. Veda. pādo asya viśvā bhūtāni tripād asya' mṛtam divi.* X, 90, 3. The *Puruṣa Sūkta* makes out that all this is only a description of His greatness, the Puruṣa himself is much greater than this. See also *Chāndogya Up.*, III, 12, 6 and *Maitrāyaṇī Up.*, VI, 4. Commenting on N.7, Abhinavagupta who reads *tad ātmāṁśam* for *tad ātmānam* writes: *śrī bhagavān kila pūrṇa ṣāḍguṇyatvāt śarīra samparkamātrarahitopi sthitikāritvāt kāruṇikatayā ātmāṁśaṁ sṛjati; ātmā pūrṇaṣāḍguṇyaḥ aṁśaḥ upakārakatvena apradhānabhūto yatra tat ātmāṁśam śarīram gṛhnāti ity arthaḥ.*

CHAPTER XI

The Lord's Transfiguration

Arjuna wishes to see the Universal Form of God

arjuna uvāca

1 *madanugrahāya paramaṁ*
guhyam adhyātmasaṁjñitam
yat tvayo 'ktaṁ vacas tena
moho 'yaṁ vigato mama

Arjuna said:

(1) The supreme mystery, the discourse concerning the Self which thou hast given out of grace for me—by this my bewilderment is gone from me.

The illusion that things of the world exist in themselves and maintain themselves, that they live and move apart from God has disappeared.

2. *bhavāpyayau hi bhūtānāṁ*
śrutau vistaraśo mayā
tvattaḥ kamalapattrākṣa
māhātmyam api cā 'vyayam

(2) The birth and passing away of things have been heard by me in detail from Thee, O Lotus-eyed (Kṛṣṇa), as also Thy imperishable majesty

3. *evam etad yathā 'ttha tvam*
ātmānaṁ parameśvara
draṣṭum icchāmi te rūpam
aiśvaraṁ puruṣottama

(3) As Thou hast declared Thyself to be, O Supreme Lord, even so it is. (But) I desire to see Thy divine form, O Supreme Person.

It is one thing to know that the Eternal Spirit dwells in all things and another to have the vision of it. Arjuna wishes to see the Universal Form, the visible embodiment of the Unseen Divine how He is the "birth and passing away of all beings." X, 8 The abstract metaphysical truth should be given visible reality.

4 *manyase yadi tac chakyaṁ*
mayā draṣṭum iti prabho
yogeśvara tato me tvaṁ
darśayā 'tmānam avyayam

(4) If Thou, O Lord, thinkest that by me, It can be seen then reveal to me, Thy Imperishable Self, O Lord of yoga (Kṛṣṇa).

The Revelation of the Lord

śrībhagavān uvāca

5 *paśya me pārtha rūpāṇi*
śataśo 'tha sahasraśaḥ
nānāvidhāni divyāni
nānāvarṇākṛtīni ca

The Blessed Lord said:

(5) Behold, O Pārtha (Arjuna), My forms, a hundred-fold, a thousand-fold, various in kind, divine, of various colours and shapes.

The stupendous self-revelation of Divine power is manifested to Arjuna who understands the true meaning of the cosmic process and destiny. In *M.B.*, VI, 131, it is said that Kṛṣṇa appeared in His world-form to Duryodhana, who attempted to make Him a prisoner when He approached Duryodhana for a final attempt at reconciliation.

The vision is not a myth or a legend but spiritual experience In the history of religious experience, we have a number of such visions. The transfiguration of Jesus,[1] the vision of Saul on the

[1] *Mark* ix, 2–8. Saint Hildegard (1098–1180) reports a vision in which she saw a "fair human form" who declared his identity in words reminiscent of the *Gītā* description. "I am that supreme and fiery force that sends forth all the sparks of life. Death hath no part in me, yet do I allot it, wherefore I am girt about with wisdom as with wings. I am that living and fiery essence of the divine substance that glows in the beauty of the fields. I shine in the water,

Damascus Road, Constantine's vision of the Cross bearing the motto "In this sign, conquer," Joan of Arc's visions are experiences akin to the vision of Arjuna.

6. *paśyā 'dityān vasūn rudrān*
aśvinau marutas tathā
bahūny adṛṣṭapūrvāṇi
paśyā 'ścaryāṇi bhārata

(6) Behold, the Ādityas, the Vasus, the Rudras, the two Aśvins and also the Maruts. Behold, O Bhārata (Arjuna), many wonders never seen before.

7 *ihai 'kasthaṁ jagat kṛtsnaṁ*
paśyā 'dya sacarācaram
mama dehe guḍākeśa
yac cā 'nyad draṣṭum icchasi

(7) Here today, behold the whole universe, moving and unmoving and whatever else thou desirest to see, O Guḍākeśa (Arjuna), all unified in My body.

It is the vision of all in the One. When we develop our full capacity of apprehension, we see that all (past, present and future) is present.

8. *na tu māṁ śakyase draṣṭum*
anenai 'va svacakṣuṣā
divyaṁ dadāmi te cakṣuḥ
paśya me yogam aiśvaram

(8) But thou canst not behold Me with this (human) eye of yours; I will bestow on thee the supernatural eye. Behold My divine power.

I burn in the sun and the moon and the stars. Mine is that mysterious force of the invisible wind. I sustain the breath of all living. I breathe in the verdure and in the flowers, and when the waters flow like living things, it is I. I formed those columns that support the whole earth. . . . All these live because I am in them and am of their life. I am wisdom. Mine is the blast of the thundered word by which all things were made. I permeate all things that they may not die. I am life." Quoted in *Studies in the History and Method of Science*, edited by Charles Singer (1917), p. 33.

No fleshly eye can see that sovereign form. Human eye is not made for such excess of light. *Divya cakṣus* is the angelic eye while *māṁsa cakṣus* is the eye of the flesh.[1]

Human eyes can see only the outward forms; the inner soul is perceived by the eye of spirit. There is a type of knowledge that we can acquire by our own efforts, knowledge based on the deliverances of the senses and intellectual activity. Another kind of knowledge is possible when we are under the influence of grace, a direct knowledge of spiritual realities. The god-vision is a gift of god. The whole account is a poetic device to indicate the unity of the cosmic manifold in the Divine nature.

The vision is not a mental construction but the disclosure of a truth from beyond the finite mind. The spontaneity and directness of the experience are brought out here.

Saṁjaya Describes the Form

saṁjaya uvāca

9 *evam uktvā tato rājan*
mahāyogeśvaro hariḥ
darśayām āsa pārthāya
paramaṁ rūpam aiśvaram

Saṁjaya said:

(9) Having thus spoken, O King, Hari, the great lord of yoga, then revealed to Pārtha (Arjuna), His Supreme and Divine Form.

[1] The Upaniṣad says:

Hearing they hear not; knowing they know not; seeing they see not; only with the eye of enlightenment do they see.

śṛṇvanto pi na śṛṇvanti jānanto pi na jānate
paśyanto pi na paśyanti, paśyanti jñānacakṣuṣaḥ.

Mokṣadharma has the following verse:

māyā hy eṣā mayā sṛṣṭā yan māṁ paśyasi nārada
sarvabhūtaguṇair yuktaṁ na tu māṁ draṣṭum arhasi.

Commenting on it, Madhusūdana says: *sarvabhūtaguṇair yuktaṁ kāraṇopādhiṁ māṁ carmacakṣuṣā draṣṭuṁ nārhasi.*"

Cp. the Prophet's words: "Lord, open his eyes that he may see." See also the *Vision of Ezekiel, Exodus* xxxiii, 18; *Revelation* iv; and *Saddharmapuṇḍarīka*, I. "Arise, shine; for thy light is come, and the glory of the Lord is risen upon thee. Thou shalt see and be radiant and thy heart shall thrill and be enlarged" (*Isaiah* lx, 1–5).

This is Kṛṣṇa's transfiguration where Arjuna sees all the creatures in heaven and earth in the Divine Form.

10. *anekavaktranayanam*
anekādbhutadarśanam
anekadivyābharaṇaṁ
divyānekodyatāyudham

(10) Of many mouths and eyes, of many visions of marvel, of many divine ornaments, of many divine uplifted weapons.

The poet seems to feel here the dearth of words, the roughness of speech in trying to describe an experience which is essentially ineffable.

anekavaktranayanam: many mouths and eyes. He is all-devouring and all-seeing.

These are descriptions of the Universal Being. In the *Puruṣa Sūkta* also, a similar account is found. *sahasraśīrṣā puruṣaḥ sahasrākṣaḥ sahasrapāt* (*Ṛg. Vedā*, IX, 4, 90). Cp. *Muṇḍaka Up.*, II, 1, 4.

11. *divyamālyāmbaradharaṁ*
divyagandhānulepanam
sarvāścaryamayaṁ devam
anantaṁ viśvatomukham

(11) Wearing divine garlands and raiments, with divine perfumes and ointments, made up of all wonders, resplendent, boundless, with face turned everywhere.

12. *divi sūryasahasrasya*
bhaved yugapad utthitā
yadi bhāḥ sadṛśī sā syād
bhāsas tasya mahātmanaḥ

(12) If the light of a thousand suns were to blaze forth all at once in the sky, that might resemble the splendour of that exalted Being.

13. *tatrai 'kasthaṁ jagat kṛtsnaṁ*
pravibhaktam anekadhā
apaśyad devadevasya
śarīre pāṇḍavas tadā

(13) There the Pāṇḍava (Arjuna) beheld the whole universe, with its manifold divisions gathered together in one, in the body of the God of gods.

Arjuna had the vision of the One in the many and the many in the One. All things remain the same and yet all are changed. There is astonishment at the disappearance of the familiar landmarks of the everyday world. Everything is interfused, each with each and mirrors the whole. The vision is a revelation of the potential divinity of all earthly life.

Arjuna Addresses the Lord

14. *tataḥ sa vismayāviṣṭo*
hṛṣṭaromā dhanaṁjayaḥ
praṇamya śirasā devaṁ
kṛtāñjalir abhāṣata

(14) Then he, the Winner of wealth (Arjuna), struck with amazement, his hair standing on end, bowed down his head to the Lord, with hands folded (in salutation), said:

In an agony of awe, his hair uplift, his head on high, his hands clasped in supplication, Arjuna adores.

arjuna uvāca

15. *paśyāmi devāṁs tava deva dehe*
sarvāṁs tathā bhūtaviśeṣasaṁghān
brahmāṇam īśaṁ kamalāsanastham
ṛṣīṁś ca sarvān uragāṁś ca divyān

Arjuna said:

(15) In Thy body, O God, I see all the gods and the varied hosts of beings as well, Brahmā, the lord seated on the lotus throne and all the sages and heavenly nāgas.

The vision of God widens our horizon and takes us beyond the earthly tumults and sorrows which so easily obsess us. God's creation is not limited to this small planet, which is only an insignificant part of the cosmos. Arjuna sees the great and various company of spirits filling the universe.

16. *anekabāhūdaravaktranetraṁ*
paśyāmi tvāṁ sarvato 'nantarūpam
nā 'ntaṁ na madhyaṁ na punas tavā 'diṁ
paśyāmi viśveśvara viśvarūpa

(16) I behold Thee, infinite in form on all sides, with numberless arms, bellies, faces and eyes, but I see not Thy end or Thy middle or Thy beginning, O Lord of the universe, O Form Universal.

vaktra: faces or mouths.

17. *kirīṭinaṁ gadinaṁ cakriṇaṁ ca*
tejorāśiṁ sarvato dīptimantam
paśyāmi tvāṁ durnirīkṣyaṁ samantād
dīptānalārkadyutim aprameyam

(17) I behold Thee with Thy crown, mace and discus, glowing everywhere as a mass of light, hard to discern, (dazzling) on all sides with the radiance of the flaming fire and sun, incomparable.

18. *tvam akṣaraṁ paramaṁ veditavyaṁ*
tvam asya viśvasya paraṁ nidhānam
tvam avyayaḥ śāśvatadharmagoptā
sanātanas tvaṁ puruṣo mato me

(18) Thou art the Imperishable, the Supreme to be realized. Thou art the ultimate resting-place of the universe; Thou art the undying guardian of the eternal law. Thou art the Primal Person, I think.

akṣaram: imperishable. Arjuna states that the Supreme is both Brahman, and Īśvara, Absolute and God.[1]

śāsvatadharmagoptā: the undying guardian of the eternal law. Abhinavagupta reads *sāttvatadharmagoptā*, the guardian of the sāttvata dharma.

19. *anādimadhyāntam anantavīryam*
anantabāhuṁ śaśisūryanetram
paśyāmi tvāṁ dīptahutāśavaktraṁ
svatejasā viśvam idaṁ tapantam

[1] *etena saguṇarūpasya nirguṇajñāpakatvam uktam.* Nīlakaṇṭha.

(19) I behold Thee as one without beginning, middle or end, of infinite power, of numberless arms, with the moon and the sun as Thine eyes, with Thy face as a flaming fire, whose radiance burns up this universe.

20. *dyāvāpṛthivyor idam antaraṁ hı*
vyāptaṁ tvayai 'kena diśaś ca sarvāḥ
dṛṣṭvā 'dbhutaṁ rūpam ugraṁ tave 'daṁ
lokatrayaṁ pravyathitaṁ mahātman

(20) This space between heaven and earth is pervaded by Thee alone, also all the quarters (directions of the sky). O Exalted One, when this wondrous, terrible form of Thine is seen, the three worlds tremble.

21. *amī hi tvāṁ surasaṁghā viśanti*
kecid bhītāḥ prāñjalayo gṛṇanti
svastī 'ty uktvā maharṣisiddhasaṁghāḥ
stuvanti tvāṁ stutibhiḥ puṣkalābhiḥ

(21) Yonder hosts of gods enter Thee and some, in fear, extol Thee, with folded hands, And bands of great seers and perfected ones cry "hail" and adore Thee with hymns of abounding praise.

The spiritual hosts adore His glory and are lost in ecstatic worship.

22. *rudrādityā vasavo ye ca sādhyā*
viśve 'śvinau marutaś co 'ṣmapāś ca
gandharvayakṣāsurasiddhasaṁghā
vīkṣante tvāṁ vismitāś cai 'va sarve

(22) The Rudras, the Ādityas, the Vasus, the Sādhyas; the Viśvas, the two Aśvins, the maruts and the manes and the hosts of Gandharvas, Yakṣas, Asuras and Siddhas, all gaze at Thee and are quite amazed.

23. *rūpaṁ mahat te bahuvaktranetraṁ*
mahābāho bahubāhūrupādam
bahūdaraṁ bahudaṁṣṭrākarālaṁ
dṛṣṭvā lokāḥ pravyathitās tathā 'ham

(23) Seeing Thy great form, of many mouths and eyes, O Mighty-armed, of many arms, thighs and feet, of many bellies, terrible with many tusks, the worlds tremble and so do I.

This is a poetic exaggeration to bring out the universality and the omnipresence of the Supreme.

24 *nabhaḥspṛśaṁ dīptam anekavarṇaṁ*
vyāttānanaṁ dīptaviśālanetram
dṛṣṭvā hi tvāṁ pravyathitāntarātmā
dhṛtiṁ na vindāmi śamaṁ ca viṣṇo

(24) When I see Thee touching the sky, blazing with many hues, with the mouth opened wide, and large glowing eyes, my inmost soul trembles in fear and I find neither steadiness nor peace, O Viṣṇu!

25. *daṁṣṭrākarālāni ca te mukhāni*
dṛṣṭvai 'va kālānalasaṁnibhāni
diśo na jāne na labhe ca śarma
prasīda deveśa jagannivāsa

(25) When I see Thy mouths terrible with their tusks, like Time's devouring flames, I lose sense of the directions and find no peace. Be gracious, O Lord of gods, Refuge of the worlds!

kālānala: literally the doomsday fire.
Arjuna loses his bearings. The tremendous experience has in it elements of astonishment, terror and rapture.

26. *amī ca tvāṁ dhṛtarāṣṭrasya putrāḥ*
sarve sahai 'vā 'vanipālasaṁghaiḥ
bhīṣmo droṇaḥ sūtaputras tathā 'sau
sahā 'smadīyair api yodhamukhyaiḥ

(26) All yonder sons of Dhṛtarāṣṭra together with the hosts of kings and also Bhīṣma, Droṇa and Karṇa along with the chief warriors on our side too,—

27 *vaktrāṇi te tvaramāṇā viśanti*
daṁṣṭrākarālāni bhayānakāni
kecid vilagnā daśanāntareṣu
saṁdṛśyant cūrṇitair uttamāṅgaiḥ

(27) Are rushing into Thy fearful mouths set with terrible tusks. Some caught between the teeth are seen with their heads crushed to powder.

28. *yathā nadīnāṁ bahavo 'mbuvegāḥ*
samudram evā 'bhimukhā dravanti
tathā tavā 'mī naralokavīrā
viśanti vaktrāṇy abhivijvalanti

(28) As the many rushing torrents of rivers race towards the ocean, so do these heroes of the world of men rush into Thy flaming mouths.

29. *yathā pradīptaṁ jvalanaṁ pataṅgā*
viśanti nāśāya samṛddhavegāḥ
tathai 'va nāśāya viśanti lokās
tavā 'pi vaktrāṇi samṛddhavegāḥ

(29) As moths rush swiftly into a blazing fire to perish there, so do these men rush into Thy mouths with great speed to their own destruction.

These beings blinded by their own ignorance are rushing to their destruction and the Divine Controller permits it, as they are carrying out the effects of their own deeds. When we will a deed, we will its consequences also. The free activities subject us to their results. As this law of cause and consequence is an expression of the Divine mind, the Divine may be said to execute the law. The writer points out through the conception of world-form how the whole cosmos with its vastness, beauty and terror, gods, blessed souls, animals, plants are all there in the plenitude of God's life. God cannot move outside Himself, having all within Himself. We, human beings, who think discursively, are occupied, now with one object and now with another. We think consecutively but the Divine mind knows all as one. There is no past to it nor future.

30. *lelihyase grasamānaḥ samantāl*
lokān samagrān vadanair jvaladbhiḥ
tejobhir āpūrya jagat samagraṁ
bhāsas tavo 'grāḥ pratapanti viṣṇo

(30) Devouring all the worlds on every side with Thy flaming mouths, thou lickest them up. Thy fiery rays fill this whole universe and scorch it with their fierce radiance, O Viṣṇu!

31. *ākhyāhi me ko bhavān ugrarūpo*
namo 'stu te devavara prasīda
vijñātum icchāmi bhavantam ādyaṁ
na hi prajānāmi tava pravṛttim

(31) Tell me who Thou art with form so terrible. Salutation to Thee, O Thou Great Godhead, have mercy. I wish to know Thee (who art) the Primal One, for I know not Thy working.

The disciple seeks for deeper knowledge.

God as the Judge

śrībhagavān uvāca

32 *kālo 'smi lokakṣayakṛt pravṛddho*
lokān samāhartum iha pravṛttaḥ
ṛte 'pi tvāṁ na bhaviṣyanti sarve
ye 'vasthitāḥ pratyanīkeṣu yodhāḥ

The Blessed Lord said:

(32) Time am I, world-destroying, grown mature, engaged here in subduing the world. Even without thee (thy action), all the warriors standing arrayed in the opposing armies shall cease to be.

Kāla or time is the prime mover of the universe. If God is thought of as time, then He is perpetually creating and destroying. Time is the streaming flux which moves unceasingly.

The Supreme Being takes up the responsibility for both creation and destruction. The *Gītā* does not countenance the familiar doctrine that, while God is responsible for all that is good, Satan is responsible for all that is evil. If God is responsible for mortal existence, then He is responsible for all that it includes, life and creation, anguish and death.

God has control over time because He is outside of it and we also shall obtain power over time if we rise above it. As the force behind this, He sees farther than we, knows how all events are controlled and so tells Arjuna that causes have been at work for years and are moving towards their natural effects which we cannot prevent by anything we can do now. The destruction of his enemies is decided irrevocably by acts committed long ago. There is an impersonal fate, what the Christians call Providence, a general cosmic necessity, *moira*, which is an expression of a side of God's nature and so can be regarded as the will of His sovereign personality, which pursues its own unrecognizable aims. Against it, all protestations of self-determination are of no avail.

33. *tasmāt tvam uttiṣṭha yaśo labhasva*
jitvā śatrūn bhuṅkṣva rājyaṁ samṛddham
mayai 'vai 'te nihatāḥ pūrvam eva
nimittamātraṁ bhava savyasācin

(33) Therefore arise thou and gain glory. Conquering thy foes, enjoy a prosperous kingdom. By Me alone are they slain already. Be thou merely the occasion, O Savyasācin (Arjuna).

The God of destiny decides and ordains all things and Arjuna is to be the instrument, the flute under the fingers of the Omnipotent One who fulfils His own purpose and is working out a mighty evolution. Arjuna is self-deceived if he believes that he should act according to his own imperfect judgment. No individual soul can encroach on the prerogative of God. In refusing to take up arms, Arjuna is guilty of presumption. See XVIII, 58.

nimittamātram: merely the occasion. The writer seems to uphold the doctrine of Divine predestination and indicate the utter helplessness and insignificance of the individual and the futility of his will and effort. The decision is made already and Arjuna can do nothing to change it. He is a powerless tool in God's hands, and yet there is the other note that God is not arbitrary and capricious but just and loving. How are the two to be reconciled?

The numinous idea of the predestinating and solely acting God which induces in us the feeling of the utter dependence on God, the "wholly other" standing over against us in absolute antithesis, is here expressed. The intense intuition of the power of God comes out here and in Job and in Paul: "Shall the thing formed say to Him that formed it, why hast thou made me thus?"

We need not look upon the whole cosmic process as nothing more than the unfolding of a predetermined plan, the unveiling of a ready-made scenario. The writer here is not so much denying the unforeseeableness of human acts as affirming the meaning of eternity in which all the moments of the whole of time, past, present and future, are present to the Divine Spirit. The radical novelty of each moment of evolution in time is not inconsistent with Divine Eternity.

The ideas of God are worked out through human instrumentality. If we are wise, we so act that we are instruments in His hands. We allow Him to absorb our soul and leave no trace of the ego. We must receive His command and do His will with the cry "In thy will is our peace"; "Father, into Thy hands I commend my Spirit."[1] Arjuna should feel, "Nothing exists save Thy will. Thou alone art the doer and I am only the instrument." The dread horror of the war repels him. Judged by human standards, it is quite incomprehensible but when the curtain is lifted, so as to reveal the purpose of the Almighty, he acquiesces in it. What he himself desired, what he might hope to gain in this world or the next do not count any more. Behind this world of space-time, interpenetrating it, is the creative purpose of God. We must understand that supreme design and be content to serve it. Every act is a symbol of something far beyond itself.

34. *droṇaṁ ca bhīṣmaṁ ca jayadrathaṁ ca*
karṇaṁ tathā 'nyān api yodhavīrān
mayā hatāṁs tvaṁ jahi mā vyathiṣṭhā
yudhyasva jetāsi raṇe sapatnān

(34) Slay Droṇa, Bhīṣma, Jayadratha, Karṇa and other great warriors as well, who are already doomed by Me. Be not afraid. Fight, thou shalt conquer the enemies in battle.

[1] *Luke* xxiii, 46.

mayā hatām: doomed by me. God knows the direction of their lives and their appointed goal. There is nothing however small or insignificant that has not been ordained or permitted by God, even to the fall of a sparrow.

Arjuna is asked to assume the office of Providence. He will be externally master of nature and inwardly superior to all possible accidents.

saṁjaya uvāca

35. *etac chrutvā vacanaṁ keśavasya*
kṛtāñjalir vepamānaḥ kirīṭī
namaskṛtvā bhūya evā 'ha kṛṣṇaṁ
sagadgadaṁ bhītabhītaḥ praṇamya

Saṁjaya said:

(35) Having heard this utterance of Keśava (Kṛṣṇa), Kirīṭin (Arjuna), with folded hands and trembling, saluted again and prostrating himself with great fear, spoke in a faltering voice to Kṛṣṇa.

Rudolf Otto gives this whole scene as an example of the place of the numinous, the *mysterium tremendum* in religion. It presents to us the transcendent aspect of God.

Arjuna's Hymn of Praise

arjuna uvāca

36. *sthāne hṛṣīkeśa tava prakīrtyā*
jagat prahṛṣyaty anurajyate ca
rakṣāṁsi bhītāni diśo dravanti
sarve namasyanti ca siddhasaṁghāḥ

Arjuna said:

(36) O Hriṣikeśa (Kṛṣṇa), rightly does the world rejoice and delight in glorifying Thee. The Rākṣasas are fleeing in terror in all directions and all the hosts of perfected ones are bowing down before Thee (in adoration).

In an ecstasy of adoration and anguish, Arjuna praises the Supreme. He sees not only the destructive power of Time but also the spiritual presence and law governing the cosmos. While the former produces terror, the latter gives rise to a sense of rapturous ecstasy and he pours forth his soul in utter adoration.

37 *kasmāc ca te na nameran mahātman*
garīyase brahmaṇo 'py ādikartre
ananta deveśa jagannivāsa
tvam akṣaraṁ sad asat tatparaṁ yat

(37) And why should they not do Thee homage, O Exalted One, who art greater than Brahmā, the original creator? O Infinite Being, Lord of the gods, Refuge of the universe, Thou art the Imperishable, the being and the non-being and what is beyond that.

ādikartṛ: Thou art the first creator, or Thou art the creator even of Brahmā.

jagannivāsa: the Refuge of the universe. The God in whom dwells the universe.

38. *tvam ādidevaḥ puruṣaḥ purāṇas*
tvam asya viśvasya paraṁ nidhānam
vettā 'si vedyaṁ ca paraṁ ca dhāma
tvayā tataṁ viśvam anantarūpa

(38) Thou art the First of gods, the Primal Person, the Supreme Resting Place of the world. Thou art the knower and that which is to be known and the supreme goal. And by Thee is this universe pervaded, O Thou of infinite form!

39. *vāyur yamo 'gnir varuṇaḥ śaśāṅkaḥ*
prajāpatis tvaṁ prapitāmahaś ca
namo namas te 'stu sahasrakṛtvaḥ
punaś ca bhūyo 'pi namo namas te

(39) Thou art Vāyu (the wind), Yama (the destroyer), Agni (the fire), Varuṇa (the sea-god) and Śaśānka (the moon), and Prajāpati, the grandsire (of all). Hail, hail to Thee, a thousand times. Hail, hail to Thee again and yet again.

According to some, "Prajāpati and the grandsire of all."

40 *namaḥ purastād atha pṛṣṭhatas te*
namo 'stu te sarvata eva sarva
anantavīryāmitavikramas tvaṁ
sarvaṁ samāpnoṣi tato 'si sarvaḥ

(40) Hail to Thee in front, (hail) to Thee behind and hail to Thee on every side, O All; boundless in power and immeasurable in might, Thou dost penetrate all and therefore Thou art All.

The Supreme dwells everywhere, within, without, above, below and around and there is no place where He is not. See *Muṇḍaka Up.*, II. 2. 11; *Chāndogya Up.*, VII. 25
The truth that we are all the creatures of the One Supreme and that He is in each and every one of us is frequently repeated.

41 *sakhe 'ti matvā prasabhaṁ yad uktaṁ*
he kṛṣṇa he yādava he sakhe 'ti
ajānatā mahimānaṁ tave 'daṁ
mayā pramādāt praṇayena vā 'pi

(41) For whatsoever I have spoken in rashness to Thee, thinking that Thou art my companion and unaware of this (fact of) Thy greatness, "O Kṛṣṇa, O Yādava, O Comrade"; out of my negligence or may be through fondness,

tavedam. Another reading is *tavemam*.

42 *yac cā 'vahāsārtham asatkṛto 'si*
vihāraśayyāsanabhojaneṣu
eko 'thavā 'py acyuta tatsamakṣaṁ
tat kṣāmaye tvām aham aprameyam

(42) And for whatsoever disrespect was shown to Thee in jest, while at play or on the bed or seated or at meals, either alone or in the presence of others, I pray, O Unshaken One, forgiveness from Thee, the Immeasurable.

The vision of God produces a deep sense of unworthiness and sin. When Isaiah saw the Lord sitting upon a throne, high and lifted up, he said, "Woe is me! For I am undone; because I am a man of unclean lips, . . . for mine eyes have seen the King, the Lord of Hosts." (vi, 1, 5.)

43 *pitā 'si lokasya carācarasya*
tvam asya pūjyaś ca gurur garīyān
na tvatsamo 'sty abhyadhikaḥ kuto 'nyo
lokatraye 'py apratimaprabhāva

(43) Thou art the father of the world of the moving and the unmoving. Thou art the object of its worship and its venerable teacher. None is equal to Thee, how then could there be one greater than Thee in the three worlds, O Thou of incomparable greatness?

44 *tasmāt praṇamya praṇidhāya kāyaṁ*
prasādaye tvām aham īśam īḍyam
pite 'va putrasya sakhe 'va sakhyuḥ
priyaḥ priyāyā 'rhasi deva soḍhum

(44) Therefore bowing down and prostrating my body before Thee, Adorable Lord, I seek Thy grace. Thou, O God, shouldst bear with me as a father to his son, as a friend to his friend, as a lover to his beloved.

The Supreme is not to be regarded as a transcendent mystery but also as close to us, as close as a father is to the son, as a friend to the friend or as a lover to the beloved. These human relations find in God their fullest realization and later Vaiṣṇava literature utilizes these ideas more fully.

God as Father is a familiar conception to the Hindu. *Rg. Veda* says: "Be of easy approach to us, even as a father to his son. Do thou, O Self-effulgent Lord, abide with us and bring blessings to us."[1] Again, *Yajur Veda* says: "O Lord, thou art our father; do thou instruct us like a father."[2] The Old Testament uses the image of the father. "Like as a father pitieth his children, so the Lord pitieth them that fear him."[3] The idea of God as father becomes the central conception in the teaching of Jesus.

45 *adṛṣṭapūrvaṁ hṛṣito 'smi dṛṣṭvā*
bhayena ca pravyathitaṁ mano me
tad eva me darśaya deva rūpaṁ
prasīda deveśa jagannivāsa

[1] I, 1. 9.
[2] XXXVII, 20.
[3] *Psalm* ciii, 13. See also lxviii, 5.

(45) I have seen what was never seen before and I rejoice but my heart is shaken with fear. Show me that other (previous) form of Thine, O God and be gracious, O Lord of the gods and Refuge of the Universe!

There is not only the form of the Transcendent and Universal Being which is so terrifying in some of its aspects but also the form of Personal God, a mediating symbol of Godhead which is so reassuring to the terrified mortal. Arjuna, who is unable to stand the blinding blaze of light that devastates Kṛṣṇa's whole being, wishes to see the more pleasing form. The Light which for ever shines beyond the worlds is also the Light within, the teacher and friend in his own heart.

46. *kirīṭinaṁ gadinaṁ cakrahastam*
icchāmi tvāṁ draṣṭum ahaṁ tathai 'va
tenai 'va rūpeṇa caturbhujena
sahasrabāho bhava viśvamūrte

(46) I wish to see Thee even as before with Thy crown, mace, and disc in Thy hand. Assume Thy four-armed shape, O Thou of a thousand arms and of universal form.

Arjuna is asking Kṛṣṇa to assume the shape of Viṣṇu of whom He is said to be an incarnation.

The Lord's Grace and Assurance

śrībhagavān uvāca

47 *mayā prasannena tavā 'rjune 'daṁ*
rūpaṁ paraṁ darśitam ātmayogāt
tejomayaṁ viśvam anantam ādyaṁ
yan me tvadanyena na dṛṣṭapūrvam

The Blessed Lord said:

(47) By My grace, through My divine power; O Arjuna, was shown to thee this supreme form, luminous, universal, infinite and primal which none but thee has seen before.

This vision is not the final goal of man's search; in that case the *Gītā* would have ended here. The fleeting vision must become a permanent experience of the seeker. Trance or samādhi is neither the end nor an essential element of religious life. The blinding flashes, the ecstatic flights must be transmuted into permanent faith. Arjuna cannot any more forget the thrilling scene he saw but he has to work it into his life. The vision only opens; it does not enhance. Even as we test and confirm what we see by the eye, by the evidence of other senses, the knowledge acquired by the vision requires to be completed by the other elements of life.

48 *na vedayajñādhyayanair na dānair*
na ca kriyābhir na tapobhir ugraiḥ
evaṁrūpaḥ śakya ahaṁ nṛloke
draṣṭuṁ tvadanyena kurupravīra

(48) Neither by the Vedas, (nor by) sacrifices nor by study nor by gifts nor by ceremonial rites nor by severe austerities can I with this form be seen in the world of men by any one else but thee, O hero of the Kurus (Arjuna).

49. *mā te vyathā mā ca vimūḍhabhāvo*
dṛṣṭvā rūpaṁ ghoram īdṛṅ mame 'dam
vyapetabhīḥ prītamanāḥ punas tvaṁ
tad eva me rūpam idaṁ prapaśya

(49) May you not be afraid, may you not be bewildered seeing this terrific form of Mine. Free from fear and glad at heart, behold again this other (former) form of Mine.

saṁjaya uvāca

50 *ity arjunaṁ vāsudevas tatho 'ktvā*
svakaṁ rūpaṁ darśayām āsa bhūyaḥ
āśvāsayām āsa ca bhītam enaṁ
bhūtvā punaḥ saumyavapur mahātmā

Saṁjaya said:

(50) Having thus spoken to Arjuna, Vāsudeva (Kṛṣṇa) revealed to him again His own form. The Exalted One, having assumed again the form of grace, comforted the terrified Arjuna.

arjuna uvāca

51. *dṛṣṭve 'daṁ mānuṣaṁ rūpaṁ*
tava saumyaṁ janārdana
idānīm asmi saṁvṛttaḥ
sacetāḥ prakṛtiṁ gataḥ

Arjuna said:

(51) Beholding again this Thy gracious human form, O Janārdana (Kṛṣṇa), I have now become collected in mind and am restored to my normal nature.

śrībhagavān uvāca

52. *sudurdarśam idaṁ rūpaṁ*
dṛṣṭavān asi yan mama
devā apy asya rūpasya
nityaṁ darśanakāṅkṣiṇaḥ

The Blessed Lord said:

(52) This form of Mine which is indeed very hard to see, thou hast seen. Even the gods are ever eager to see this form.

53. *nā 'haṁ vedair na tapasā*
na dānena na ce 'jyayā
śakya evaṁvidho draṣṭuṁ
dṛṣṭavān asi māṁ yathā

(53) In the form in which thou hast seen Me now, I cannot be seen either by the Vedas or by austerities or by gifts or by sacrifices.

This verse is a repetition of XI, 48.

54. *bhaktyā tv ananyayā śakya*
aham evaṁvidho 'rjuna
jñātuṁ draṣṭuṁ ca tattvena
praveṣṭuṁ ca paraṁtapa

(54) But by unswerving devotion to Me, O Arjuna, I can be thus known, truly seen and entered into, O Oppressor of the foe (Arjuna).

Ṡ. defines an ideal devotee as one who, realizes by all the senses only one object, God.[1] He adores God with all his spirit and heart.[2]

Sākṣātkara or the direct perception of the divine form is possible for the true devotees.

55. *matkarmakṛn matparamo*
madbhaktaḥ saṅgavarjitaḥ
nirvairaḥ sarvabhūteṣu
yaḥ sa mām eti pāṇḍava

(55) He who does work for Me, he who looks upon Me as his goal, he who worships Me, free from attachment, who is free from enmity to all creatures, he goes to Me, O Pāṇḍava (Arjuna).

This is the essence of bhakti. See XII, 13. This verse is the substance of the whole teaching of the *Gītā*.[3] We must carry out our duties, directing the spirit to God and with detachment from all interest in the things of the world and free from enmity towards any living being.

Whatever be our vocation and character, whether we are creative thinkers or contemplative poets or humble men and women with no special gifts, if we possess the one great gift of the love of God, we become God's tools, the channels of His love and purpose. When this vast world of living spirits becomes attuned to God and exists only to do His will, the purpose of man is achieved.

The *Gītā* does not end after the tremendous experience of the celestial vision. The great secret of the Transcendental Ātman, the source of all that is and yet itself unmoved for ever is seen. The Supreme is the background for the never-ending procession of finite things. Arjuna has seen this truth but he has to live in it by transmuting his whole nature into the willing acceptance of the Divine. A fleeting vision, however vivid and permanent its effects

[1] *sarvair api karaṇaiḥ vāsudevād anyan nopalabhyate yayā sā ananyā bhaktiḥ.*

[2] *madbhaktaḥ mām eva sarvaprakāraiḥ, sarvātmanā, sarvotsāhena bhajate.* Ṡ.

[3] *gītāśāstrasya sārabhūto'rthaḥ.*

may be, is not complete attainment. The search for abiding reality, the quest of final truth cannot end, in emotional satisfaction or fitful experience.

iti . . . viśvarūpadarśanayogo nāmai 'kādaśo 'dhyāyaḥ

This is the eleventh chapter entitled The Vision of the Cosmic Form.

CHAPTER XII

Worship of the Personal Lord is better than meditation of the Absolute

Devotion and Contemplation

arjuna uvāca

1. *evaṁ satatayuktā ye*
bhaktās tvāṁ paryupāsate
ye cā 'py akṣaram avyaktaṁ
teṣāṁ ke yogavittamāḥ

Arjuna said:

(1) Those devotees who, thus ever earnest, worship Thee and those again (who worship) the Imperishable and the Unmanifested, which of these have the greater knowledge of yoga?

There are those who seek oneness with the Absolute, one and impersonal and unrelated to the universe, and others who seek unity with the Personal God manifested in the world of men and nature. Which of these have the greater yoga knowledge? Are we to turn our back on all manifestations and strain after the Unchanging Unmanifest or are we to be devoted to the Manifested Form and work in Its service? Is it Absolute or the Personal God, Brahman or Īśvara that we should worship?

śrībhagavān uvāca

2. *mayy āveśya mano ye māṁ*
nityayuktā upāsate
śraddhayā parayo 'petās
te me yuktatamā matāḥ

The Blessed Lord said:

(2) Those who fixing their minds on Me worship Me, ever earnest and possessed of supreme faith—them do I consider most perfect in yoga.

The teacher answers decisively that those, who worship God in His manifested form, have greater yoga knowledge.

Upāsana is worship.[1]

3. *ye tv akṣaram anirdeśyam*
avyaktaṁ paryupāsate
sarvatragam acintyaṁ ca
kūṭastham acalaṁ dhruvam

(3) But those who worship the Imperishable, the Undefinable, the Unmanifested, the Omnipresent, the Unthinkable, the Unchanging and the Immobile, the Constant.

4. *saṁniyamye 'ndriyagrāmaṁ*
sarvatra samabuddhayaḥ
te prāpnuvanti mām eva
sarvabhūtahite ratāḥ

(4) By restraining all the senses, being even-minded in all conditions, rejoicing in the welfare of all creatures, they come to Me indeed (just like the others).

saṁniyamya: restraining. We are asked to restrain the senses and not to reject them.

sarvabhūtahite ratāḥ: rejoicing in the welfare of all creatures. Even those who realize their oneness with the Universal Self, so long as they wear a body, work for the welfare of the world. See V, 25, where the liberated are said to rejoice in the welfare of all creatures.

Here service of humanity is declared to be an essential part of the discipline. M.B. has the following prayer: "O who would tell me of the sacred way by which I might enter into all the suffering hearts and take all their suffering on myself for now and for ever."

Cp. also Tukārām:

'That man is true
Who taketh to his bosom the afflicted:

[1] Upāsana is continuous meditation. Ś. says: *upāsanaṁ nāma yathā śāstram upāsyasya arthasya viṣayīkaraṇena sāmīpya upagamya tailadhāravat samānapratyayapravāheṇa dīrghakālaṁ yad āsanam, tad upāsanam ācakṣate.*

In such a man
Dwelleth, augustly present,
God Himself;
The heart of such a man is filled abrim
With pity, gentleness and love;
He taketh the forsaken for his own."[1]

5. *kleśo 'dhikataras teṣām*
avyaktāsaktacetasām
avyaktā hi gatir duḥkhaṁ
dehavadbhir avāpyate

(5) The difficulty of those whose thoughts are set on the Unmanifested is greater, for the goal of the Unmanifested is hard to reach by the embodied beings.

Search for the Transcendent Godhead is more difficult than worship of the Living Supreme God, the soul of all things and persons. In the *Avadhūtagītā*, Dattātreya asks: "How can I bow to Him who is formless, undifferentiated, blissful and indestructible, who has through Himself and by Himself and in Himself filled up everything?"[2] The Immutable does not offer an easy hold to the mind and the path is more arduous. We reach the same goal more easily and naturally by the path of devotion to the Personal God, by turning godward all our energies, knowledge, will and feeling. Cp. "With minds rapt in meditation, if mystics see the unqualified actionless light, let them see. As for myself, my only yearning is that there may appear before my gladdened eyes that bluish someone who keeps romping on the shores of the yamunā."[3]

[1] M. K. Gāndhi: *Songs from Prison* (1934), p. 129.

[2] *yenedaṁ pūritaṁ sarvam ātmanaivātmanātmani*
nirākāraṁ kathaṁ vande abhinnaṁ śivam avyayam

Cf. St. John of Damascus. "By the visible aspect our thoughts must be drawn up in a spiritual flight and rise to the invisible majesty of God."

[3] *dhyānāvasthita tad gatena manasā tan nirguṇaṁ niṣkriyam*
jyotiḥ kiñcana yogino yadi punaḥ paśyanti paśyantu te
asmākaṁ tu tad eva locanacamatkārāya bhūyāc ciram
kālindīpulineṣu yat kim api tan nīlaṁ tamo dhāvati.

Different Approaches

6. *ye tu sarvāṇi karmāṇi*
mayi saṁnyasya matparāḥ
ananyenai 'va yogena
māṁ dhyāyanta upāsate

(6) But those, who, laying all their actions on Me, intent on Me, worship, meditating on Me, with unswerving devotion,

7. *teṣām ahaṁ samuddhartā*
mṛtyusaṁsārasāgarāt
bhavāmi nacirāt pārtha
mayy āveśitacetasām

(7) These whose thoughts are set on Me, I straightway deliver from the ocean of death-bound existence, O Pārtha (Arjuna).

God is the deliverer, the saviour. When we set our hearts and minds on Him, He lifts us from the sea of death and secures for us a place in the eternal. For one whose nature is not steeped in vairāgya or renunciation, the path of devotion is more suitable. The *Bhāgavata* says: "The path of devotion is most suitable for him who is neither very tired of nor very attached to the world."[1] It is a matter of temperament whether we adopt the pravṛtti dharma, the path of works, or nivṛttidharma, the path of renunciation.

8 *mayy eva mana ādhatsva*
mayi buddhiṁ niveśaya
nivasiṣyasi mayy eva
ata ūrdhvaṁ na saṁśayaḥ

(8) On Me alone fix thy mind, let thy understanding dwell in Me. In Me alone shalt thou live thereafter. Of this there is no doubt.

[1] *na nirviṇṇo nātisakto bhaktiyogo'sya siddhidaḥ.* XI, 20, 7.

9. *atha cittaṁ samādhātuṁ*
na śaknoṣi mayı sthiram
abhyāsayogena tato
mām icchā 'ptuṁ dhanaṁjaya

(9) If, however, thou art not able to fix thy thought steadily on Me, then seek to reach Me by the practice of concentration, O Winner of wealth (Arjuna).

If this spiritual condition does not arise spontaneously, we must take up the practice of concentration, so that we may gradually fit ourselves for the steadfast directing of the spirit to God. By this practice, the Divine takes gradual possession of our nature.

10. *abhyāse 'py asamartho 'sı*
matkarmaparamo bhava
madartham api karmāṇi
kurvan siddhim avāpsyasi

(10) If thou art unable even to seek by practice, then be as one whose supreme aim is My service; even performing actions for My sake, thou shalt attain perfection.

If concentration is found difficult on account of the outward tendencies of the mind or our circumstances, then do all actions for the sake of the Lord. Thus the individual becomes aware of the eternal reality.

matkarma is sometimes taken to mean service of the Lord, *pūjā* or worship, offering flowers and fruits, burning incense, building temples, reading scriptures, etc.[1]

11. *athai 'tad apy aśakto 'si*
kartuṁ madyogam āśritaḥ
sarvakarmaphalatyāgaṁ
'ataḥ kuru yatātmavān

(11) If thou art not able to do even this, then taking refuge in My disciplined activity, renounce the fruit of all action, with the self subdued.

madyogam āśritaḥ: taking refuge in my wondrous power.—Śrīdhara.

[1] Abhinavagupta regards *matkarmāṇi* as equivalent to *bhagavat karmāṇi* as *pūjā, japa, svādhyāya, homa,* etc.

If you cannot dedicate all your works to the Divine, then do the work without desire of the fruit. Adopt the yoga of desireless action, *niṣkāmakarma*. We can renounce all personal striving, resign ourselves completely and solely to God's saving power, submit to self-discipline and work, abandoning all thought of reward. One must become like a child in the hands of the Divine.

12. *śreyo hi jñānam abhyāsāj*
jñānād dhyānaṁ viśiṣyate
dhyānāt karmaphalatyāgas
tyāgāc chāntir anantaram

(12) Better indeed is knowledge than the practice (of concentration); better than knowledge is meditation; better than meditation is the renunciation of the fruit of action; on renunciation (follows) immediately peace.

Śrīdhara interprets jñāna as *āveśa* or directing the spirit towards God and dhyāna as being full of God, *bhagavadmayatvam*, and this is completed in the spirit's full possession of God Himself. Cp. *Sūrya Gītā:* "Devotion is better than knowledge and desireless action is better than devotion. He who realizes this principle of Vedānta is to be regarded as the best man."[1] Devotion, meditation and concentration are more difficult than renunciation of the fruits of action, *karmaphalatyāga*. This latter destroys the sources of unrest and brings about an inner calm and peace, which are the very foundations of spiritual life. The bhakti emphasis leads to the subordination of knowledge and meditation to the devout mind and consecration of all works to God.

The True Devotee

13. *adveṣṭā sarvabhūtānāṁ*
maitraḥ karuṇa eva ca
nirmamo nirahaṁkāraḥ
samaduḥkhasukhaḥ kṣamī

(13) He who has no ill will to any being, who is friendly and compassionate, free from egoism, and self-sense, even-minded in pain and pleasure and patient.

[1] *jñānād upāstir utkṛṣṭā karmotkṛṣṭam upāsanāt*
ity yo veda vedāntaiḥ sa eva puruṣottamaḥ. 114, 77.

14. *saṁtuṣṭaḥ satataṁ yogī*
yatātmā dṛḍhaniścayaḥ
mayy arpitamanobuddhir
yo madbhaktaḥ sa me priyaḥ

(14) The Yogi who is ever content, self-controlled, unshakable in determination, with mind and understanding given up to Me—he, My devotee, is dear to Me.

In these verses the *Gītā* mentions the qualities of a true devotee, freedom of spirit, friendliness to all, patience and tranquillity.

15. *yasmān no 'dvijate loko*
lokān no 'dvijate ca yaḥ
harṣāmarṣabhayodvegair
mukto yaḥ sa ca me priyaḥ

(15) He from whom the world does not shrink and who does not shrink from the world and who is free from joy and anger, fear and agitation, he too is dear to Me.

He is not a source of grief to any; no one can make him feel grief.

16. *anapekṣaḥ śucir dakṣa*
udāsīno gatavyathaḥ
sarvārambhaparityāgī
yo madbhaktaḥ sa me priyaḥ

(16) He who has no expectation, is pure, skilful in action, unconcerned, and untroubled, who has given up all initiative (in action), he, My devotee, is dear to Me.

He renounces the fruits of all his actions. His acts are skilled, *dakṣa*, pure and passionless. He does not lose himself in reverie or dream but knows his way in the world.

17. *yo na hṛṣyati na dveṣṭi*
na śocati na kāṅkṣati
śubhāśubhaparityāgī
bhaktimān yaḥ sa me priyaḥ

(17) He who neither rejoices nor hates, neither grieves nor desires, and who has renounced good and evil, he who is thus devoted is dear to Me.

18. *samaḥ śatrau ca mitre ca*
tathā mānāpamānayoḥ
śītoṣṇasukhaduḥkheṣu
amaḥ saṅgavivarjitaḥ

(18) He who (behaves) alike to foe and friend, also to good and evil repute and who is alike in cold and heat, pleasure and pain and who is free from attachment.

samaḥ śatrau ca mitre ca. Cp. Jesus. "He maketh his sun to rise on the evil and the good, and sendeth rain on the just and the unjust."[1]

19. *tulyanindāstutir maunī*
saṁtuṣṭo yena kenacit
aniketaḥ sthiramatir
bhaktimān me priyo naraḥ

(19) He who holds equal blame and praise, who is silent (restrained in speech), content with anything (that comes), who has no fixed abode and is firm in mind, that man who is devoted is dear to Me.

aniketaḥ: no fixed abode, homeless. Though he fulfils all social duties, he is not tied to any family or home. As these souls exist, not for this family or that social group but live for mankind as a whole, they do not have a settled home. They are free to move wherever their inspiration takes them. They are not chained to one place or confined to one community. They are not tied to the past or obliged to defend an unchangeable authority. The welfare of humanity as a whole is their constant concern. These saṁnyāsins may appear in any social group. Cp. M.B.: "He who is clothed with anything, who is fed on any food, who lies down anywhere, him the gods call a Brāhmin."[2]

[1] *Matthew* v, 45.

[2] *yenakenacid ācchanno, yenakenacid āśitah,*
yatra kvacana śāyī syāt taṁ devāḥ brāhmaṇaṁ viduḥ.
Śāntiparva 245, 12.

See also *Viṣṇu Purāṇa*. III. 7. 20.
na calati nijavarṇadharmatoyaḥ samamatiḥ ātmasuhṛid vipakṣa pakṣe na harati na ca hanti kiñciduccaiḥ sitamanasam tam avehi viṣṇubhaktam.

20. *ye tu dharmyāmṛtam idaṁ*
yathoktaṁ paryupāsate
śraddhadhānā matparamā
bhaktās te 'tīva me priyāḥ

(20) But those who with faith, holding Me as their supreme aim, follow this immortal wisdom, those devotees are exceedingly dear to Me.

śraddhadhāna: (those) with faith. Before the experience arises the soul must have faith, which carries with it consent of mind and life. For those who have experience, it is a matter of sight: for others, it is faith, a call or a compulsion.

When we see the One Self in all things, equal-mindedness, freedom from selfish desires, surrender of our whole nature to the Indwelling Spirit and love for all arise. When these qualities are manifested, our devotion is perfect and we are God's own men. Our life then is guided not by the forces of attraction and repulsion, friendship and enmity, pleasure and pain, but by the single urge to give oneself to God and therefore to the service of the world which is one with God.[1]

iti . . . bhaktiyogo nāma dvādaśo 'dhyāyaḥ

This is the twelfth chapter entitled The Yoga of Devotion.

[1] In the words of Tulsidās:
"Grant me, O Master, by thy grace
To follow all the good and pure,
To be content with simple things;
To use my fellows not as means but ends
To serve them stalwartly, in thought, word, deed;
Never to utter word of hatred or of shame:
To cast away all selfishness and pride:
To speak no ill of others:
To have a mind at peace,
Set free from care, and led astray from thee
Neither by happiness nor woe;
Set thou my feet upon this path,
And keep me steadfast in it,
Thus only shall I please thee, serve thee right."
M. K. Gāndhi: *Songs from Prison* (1934), p. 52.

CHAPTER XIII

The Body called the Field, the Soul called the Knower of the Field and Discrimination between them

The Field and the Knower of the Field

arjuna uvāca

prakṛtiṁ puruṣaṁ caiva
ksetraṁ ksetrajñam eva ca
etad veditum icchāmi
jñānaṁ jñeyaṁ ca keśava

Arjuna said:

Prakṛti and puruṣa, the field and the knower of the field, knowledge and the object of knowledge, these I should like to know, O Keśava (Kṛṣṇa).

This verse is not found in some editions. Ś. does not comment on it. If it is included, the total number of verses in the *Bhagavadgītā* will be 701 and not 700, which is the number traditionally accepted. So we do not include it in the numbering of verses.

śrībhagavān uvāca

1. *idaṁ śarīraṁ kaunteya*
kṣetram ity abhidhīyate
etad yo vetti taṁ prāhuḥ
kṣetrajña iti tadvidaḥ

The Blessed Lord said:

(1) This body, O Son of Kuntī (Arjuna), is called the field and him who knows this, those who know thereof call the knower of the field.

Prakṛti is unconscious activity and puruṣa is inactive consciousness. The body is called the field in which events happen; all growth, decline and death take place in it. The conscious principle, inactive and detached, which lies behind all active states as witness, is the knower of the field. This is the familiar distinction between consciousness and the objects which that consciousness observes. Kṣetrajña is the light of awareness, the knower of all objects.[1] The witness is not the individual embodied mind but the cosmic consciousness for which the whole cosmos is the object. It is calm and eternal and does not need the use of the senses and the mind for its witnessing.

Kṣetrajña is the supreme lord, not an object in the world. He is in all fields, differentiated by the limiting conditions, from Brahmā, the creator, to a tuft of grass though he is himself devoid of all limitations and incapable of definition by categories.[2] The immutable consciousness is spoken of as cognizer only figuratively (*upacārāt*).

When we try to know the nature of the human soul, we may get to know it from above or from below, from the divine principle or the elemental nature. Man is a twofold, contradictory being, free and enslaved. He is godlike, and has in him the signs of his fall, that is, descent into nature. As a fallen being, man is determined by the forces of prakṛti. He appears to be actuated solely by elemental forces, sensual impulses, fear and anxiety. But man desires to get the better of his fallen nature. The man studied by objective sciences as biology, psychology and sociology is a natural being, is the product of the processes which take place in the world. But man, as a subject, has another origin. He is not a child of the world. He is not nature. He does not belong to the objective hierarchy of nature, as a subordinate part of it. Puruṣa or kṣetrajña cannot be recognized as an object among other objects or as a substance. He can only be recognized as subject, in which is hidden the secret of existence, a complete universe in an individual form. He is not therefore a part of the world or of any other whole. As an empirical being he may be like a Leibnitian monad closed, shut up without doors or windows. As a subject he enters into infinity and infinity enters into him. Ksetrajña is the universal in an individually unrepeatable form. The human being is a union of the universal-infinite and the universal-particular. In his subjective aspects, he is not a part of

[1] See also *Śvetāśvatara Up.*, VI, 16; and *Maitrāyaṇī Up.*, II, 5.

[2] *kṣetrajñaṁ māṁ parameśvaram asaṁsāriṇaṁ viddhi sarvakṣetreṣuyaḥ. kṣetrajṇaḥ brahmādistambaparyantāneka kṣetropādhipravibhaktaṁ tam nirastasarvopādhibhedaṁ sadasadādiśabdapratyayagocaraṁ viddhi.* Ś.

a whole but is the potential whole. To actualize it, to accomplish the universality is the ideal of man. The subject fills itself with universal content—achieves unity in wholeness at the end of its journey. Man's peculiarity is not the possession of the common pattern of two eyes and two hands, but the possession of the inward principle which impels the creative acquisition of a qualitative content of life. He has a unique quality, which is non-common. The ideal personality is unique and unrepeatable. Each person at the end of the road becomes a distinct, unrepeatable, unreplaceable being with a unique form.

2. *kṣetrajñaṁ cā 'pi māṁ viddhi*
sarvakṣetreṣu bhārata
kṣetrakṣetrajñayor jñānaṁ
yat taj jñānaṁ mataṁ mama

(2) Know Me as the Knower of the field in all fields, O Bhārata (Arjuna). The knowledge of the field and its knower, do I regard as true knowledge.

Ś. holds that the Supreme Lord seems to be saṁsārin, by reason of the cosmic manifestation, even as the individual self appears to be bound by its identification with the body.[1] The Fall, according to the Christian doctrine, is the forgetting of the image of God within man, which is freedom, and lapsing into the external, which is necessity. Man, essentially, is not a part of nature but is spirit that interrupts the continuity of nature.

3. *tat kṣetraṁ yac ca yādṛk ca*
yadvikāri yataś ca yat
sa ca yo yatprabhāvaś ca
tat samāsena me śṛṇu

(3) Hear briefly from Me what the Field is, of what nature, what its modifications are, whence it is, what he (the knower of the field) is, and what his powers are.

[1] *tatraivaṁ sati kṣetrajñasyeśvarasyaiva sato'vidyākṛtopādhibhedataḥ saṁsāritvam iva bhavati yathā dehādyātmatvam ātmanaḥ.*

The Constituents of the Field

4\. *ṛṣibhir bahudhā gītaṁ*
chandobhir vividhaiḥ pṛthak
brahmasūtrapadaiś cai 'va
hetumadbhir viniścitaiḥ

(4) This has been sung by sages in many ways and distinctly, in various hymns and also in well-reasoned and conclusive expressions of the aphorisms of the Absolute (brahmasūtra).

The *Gītā* suggests that it is expounding the truths already contained in the Vedas, the Upaniṣads and the *Brahma Sūtra* or the aphorisms of Brahman, later systematized by Bādarāyaṇa. The Vedic hymns are called cchandas or rhythmical utterances.

5 *mahābhūtāny ahaṁkāro*
buddhir avyaktam eva ca
indriyāṇi daśai 'kaṁ ca
pañca ce ndriyagocarāḥ

(5) The great (five gross) elements, self-sense, understanding as also the unmanifested, the ten senses and mind and the five objects of the senses.

These are the constituents of the field of Kṣetra, the contents of experience, the twenty-four principles of the Sāṁkhya system. The distinction of mental and material belongs to the object side. They are distinctions within the "field" itself.

The body, the forms of sense with which we identify the subject belong to the object side. The ego is an artificial construction obtained by abstraction from conscious experience. The witnessing consciousness is the same whether it lights up the blue sky or a red flower. Though the fields which are lit up may be different, the light which illumines them is the same.

6\. *icchā dveṣaḥ sukhaṁ duḥkhaṁ*
saṁghātaś cetanā dhṛtiḥ
etat kṣetraṁ samāsena
savikāram udāhṛtam

(6) Desire and hatred, pleasure and pain, the aggregate (the organism), intelligence and steadfastness described, this in brief is the field along with its modifications.

Even the mental traits are said to qualify the field because they are objects of knowledge.

The knower is a subject and the turning of it into an object or a thing means ignorance, avidyā. Objectivization is the ejection of the subject into the world of the objects Nothing in the object world is an authentic reality. We can realize the subject in us only by overcoming the enslaving power of the object world, by refusing to be dissolved in it. This means resistance, suffering. Acquiescence in the surrounding world and its conventions diminishes suffering; refusal increases it. Suffering is the process through which we fight for our true nature.

Knowledge

7 *amānitvam adambhitvam*
ahiṁsā kṣāntir ārjavam
ācāryopāsanaṁ śaucaṁ
sthairyam ātmavinigrahaḥ

(7) Humility (absence of pride), integrity (absence of deceit), non-violence, patience, uprightness, service of the teacher, purity (of body and mind), steadfastness and self-control.

8. *indriyārtheṣu vairāgyam*
anahaṁkāra eva ca
anmamṛtyujarāvyādhi-
duḥkhadoṣānudarśanam

(8) Indifference to the objects of sense, self-effacement and the perception of the evil of birth, death, old age, sickness and pain.

9. *asaktir anabhiṣvaṅgaḥ*
putradāragṛhādiṣu
nityaṁ ca samacittatvam
iṣṭāniṣṭopapattiṣu

(9) Non-attachment, absence of clinging to son, wife, home and the like and a constant equal-mindedness to all desirable and undesirable happenings.

10. *mayi cā 'nanyayogena*
bhaktir avyabhicāriṇī
viviktadeśasevitvam
aratir janasaṁsadi

(10) Unswerving devotion to Me with wholehearted discipline, resort to solitary places, dislike for a crowd of people.

11. *adhyātmajñānanityatvaṁ*
tattvajñānārthadarśanam
etaj jñānam iti proktam
ajñānaṁ yad ato 'nyathā

(11) Constancy in the knowledge of the Spirit, insight into the end of the knowledge of Truth—this is declared to be (true) knowledge and all that is different from it is non-knowledge.

It is clear from this list of qualities that jñāna or knowledge includes the practice of the moral virtues. Mere theoretical learning will not do.[1] By the development of moral qualities the light of the ever changeless Self witnessing all but attached to none is discriminated from the passing forms and is no more confused with them.

12. *jñeyaṁ yat tat pravakṣyāmi*
yaj jñātvā 'mṛtam aśnute
anādimat paraṁ brahma
na sat tan nā 'sad ucyate

(12) I will describe that which is to be known and by knowing which life eternal is gained. It is the Supreme Brahman who is beginningless and who is said to be neither existent nor non-existent.

anādimat param: beginningless supreme. Ś.
anādi matparam: beginningless, ruled by Me. R.

It is eternal, lifted above all empirical oppositions of existence and non-existence, beginning and end, and if we realize It, birth and death happen to be mere outward events which do not touch the eternity of the self.

[1] *nāyam ātmā pravacanena labhyo, na medhayā, na bahunā śrutena. Kaṭha Up.*, II, 22; *Muṇḍaka Up.*, III, 2–3.

The Knower of the Field

13. *sarvataḥpāṇipādaṁ tat*
sarvatokṣiśiromukham
sarvataḥśrutimal loke
sarvam āvṛtya tiṣṭhati

(13) With his hands and feet everywhere, with eyes, heads and faces on all sides, with ears on all sides, He dwells in the world, enveloping all.

As the one subject of all objects of experience, He is said to envelop all and have hands and feet, ears and eyes everywhere. Without the seeing Light, there is no experience at all. As the Supreme has the two aspects, the one of transcendence and detachment and the other of immanence in each particular union with the not-self, It is described in a series of paradoxes. He is without and within, unmoving and moving, far away and near, undivided and yet divided. M.B. says that when the self is associated with the modes of nature, it is called kṣetrajña; when it is released from these it is called the paramātman or the Supreme Self.[1]

14. *sarvendriyaguṇābhāsaṁ*
sarvendriyavivarjitam
asaktaṁ sarvabhṛc cai 'va
nirguṇaṁ guṇabhoktṛ ca

(14) He appears to have the qualities of all the senses and yet is without (any of) the senses, unattached and yet supporting all, free from the guṇas (dispositions of prakṛti) and yet enjoying them.

This verse makes out that the Supreme is the mutable and the immutable, the all and the one. He sees all but not with the physical eye, He hears all but not with the physical ear, He knows all but not with the limited mind. Cp. *Śvetāśvatara Up.*, III, 19, "He sees without the eye, He hears without the ear." The immensity of the Supreme is brought out by the attribution of qualities (adhyāropa) and denial (apavāda).

[1] *ātmā kṣetrajña ity uktaḥ saṁyuktaḥ prakṛtair guṇair*
tair eva tu vinirmuktaḥ paramātmety udāhṛtaḥ.
Śāntiparva, 187, 24.

15 *bahir antaś ca bhūtānām*
acaraṁ caram eva ca
sūkṣmatvāt tad avijñeyaṁ
dūrasthaṁ cā 'ntike ca tat

(15) He is without and within all beings. He is unmoving as also moving. He is too subtle to be known. He is far away and yet is He near.

16 *avibhaktaṁ ca bhūteṣu*
vibhaktam iva ca sthitam
bhūtabhartṛ ca taj jñeyaṁ
grasiṣṇu prabhaviṣṇu ca

(16) He is undivided (indivisible) and yet He seems to be divided among beings. He is to be known as supporting creatures, destroying them and creating them afresh.

Cp. Dionysius: "Undivided in things divided." All things derive from Him, are supported by Him and taken back into Him.

17. *jyotiṣām api taj jyotis*
tamasaḥ param ucyate
jñānaṁ jñeyaṁ jñānagamyaṁ
hṛdi sarvasya dhiṣṭhitam

(17) He is the Light of lights, said to be beyond darkness. Knowledge, the object of knowledge and the goal of knowledge—He is seated in the hearts of all.

The Light dwells in the heart of every being. Many of these passages are quotations from the Upaniṣads. See *Śvetāśvatara Up.*, III, 8 and 16; *Īśa Up.*, 5; *Muṇḍaka Up.*, XIII, 1, 7; *Bṛhad-āraṇyaka Up.*, IV, 4, 16.

The Fruit of Knowledge

18. *iti kṣetraṁ tathā jñānaṁ*
jñeyaṁ co 'ktaṁ samāsataḥ
madbhakta etad vijñāya
madbhāvāyo 'papadyate

(18) Thus the field, also knowledge and the object of knowledge have been briefly described. My devotee who understands thus becomes worthy of My state.

When the devotee sees the Eternal Indwelling Divine, he puts on the divine nature with the characteristics of freedom, love and equality. "He attains unto my state."

Nature and Spirit

19. *prakṛtiṁ puruṣaṁ cai 'va*
viddhy anādī ubhāv api
vikārāṁś ca guṇāṁś cai 'va
viddhi prakṛtisaṁbhavān

(19) Know thou that prakṛti (nature) and puruṣa (soul) are both beginningless; and know also that the forms and modes are born of prakṛti (nature).

As the Supreme is eternal, so are His prakṛtis.[1]

Through the possession of the two prakṛtis, nature and soul, Īśvara causes the origin, preservation and dissolution of the universe. The puruṣa described in this section is not the multiple puruṣa of the Sāṁkhya but the ksetrajña who is one in all fields. The *Gītā* does not look upon prakṛti and puruṣa as two independent elements as the Sāṁkhya does but looks upon them as the inferior and the superior forms of one and the same Supreme.

20. *kārya karaṇa kartṛtve*
hetuḥ prakṛtir ucyate
puruṣaḥ sukhaduḥkhānāṁ
bhoktṛtve hetur ucyate

(20) Nature is said to be the cause of effect, instrument and agent (ness) and the soul is said to be the cause, in regard to the experience of pleasure and pain.

For *kāryakaraṇakartṛtve,* there is another reading "*kāryakāraṇakartṛtve.*" See Franklin Edgerton: *Bhagavadgīta,* Vol. I, p. 187 note.

[1] *nityeśvaratvād īśvarasya, tat prakṛtyor api yuktaṁ nityatvena bhavitum. Ś.*

The body and the senses are produced by prakṛti and the experience of pleasure and pain is by the puruṣa subject to certain limitations. The blissful nature of the self is stained by joy and sorrow on account of its identification with the objects of nature.

21. *puruṣaḥ prakṛtistho hi*
bhuṅkte prakṛtijān guṇān
kāraṇaṁ guṇasaṅgo 'sya
sadasadyonijanmasu

(21) The soul in nature enjoys the modes born of nature. Attachment to the modes is the cause of its births in good and evil wombs

22. *upadraṣṭā 'numantā ca*
bhartā bhoktā maheśvaraḥ
paramātme 'ti cā 'py ukto
dehe 'smin puruṣaḥ paraḥ

(22) The Supreme Spirit in the body is said to be the Witness, the Permitter, the Supporter, the Experiencer, the Great Lord and the Supreme Self.

Here the Supreme Self is different from the psychophysical individual who becomes the immortal self by transcending the separatist consciousness, due to entanglement in the activities of prakṛti. In the *Gītā*, no distinction is made between the knower of the field and the Supreme Lord.[1]

23. *ya evaṁ vetti puruṣaṁ*
prakṛtiṁ ca guṇaiḥ saha
sarvathā vartamāno 'pi
na sa bhūyo 'bhijāyate

(23) He who thus knows soul (puruṣa) and nature (prakṛti) together with the modes, though he acts in every way, he is not born again.

sarvathā vartamano 'pi: though he acts in every way, whatever state of life he may be in. R.

[1] *kṣetrajñeśvarayoḥ bhedānabhyupagamād gītāśāstre.* Ś.

Different Roads to Salvation

24. *dhyānenā 'tmani paśyanti*
kecid ātmānam ātmanā
anye sāṁkhyena yogena
karmayogena cā 'pare

(24) By meditation some perceive the Self in the self by the self; others by the path of knowledge and still others by the path of works.

Sāṁkhya here stands for jñāna.

25. *anye tv evam ajānantaḥ*
śrutvā 'nyebhya upāsate
te 'pi cā 'titaranty eva
mṛtyuṁ śrutiparāyaṇāḥ

(25) Yet others, ignorant of this (these paths of yoga) hearing from others worship; and they too cross beyond death by their devotion to what they have heard.

Even those who rely on the authority of teachers[1] and worship according to their advice, have their hearts opened out to the grace of the Lord and thus reach life-eternal.

26. *yāvat saṁjāyate kiṁcit*
sattvaṁ sthāvarajaṅgamam
kṣetrakṣetrajñasaṁyogāt
tad viddhi bharatarṣabha

(26) Whatever being is born, moving or unmoving, know thou, O Best of the Bharatas (Arjuna), that it is (sprung) through the union of the field and the knower of the field.

All life is a commerce between self and not-self. According to Ś., the union of the two is of the nature of adhyāsa, which consists in confounding the one with the other. When the confusion is cleared, bondage terminates.

[1] *śrutiparāyaṇāh, kevalaparopadeśapramāṇāḥ svayaṁ vivekarahitāḥ*. Ś.

27. *samaṁ sarveṣu bhūteṣu*
tiṣṭhantaṁ parameśvaram
vinaśyatsv avinaśyantaṁ
yaḥ paśyati sa paśyati

(27) He who sees the Supreme Lord abiding equally in all beings, never perishing when they perish, he, verily, sees.

He who sees the Universal Spirit in all things, sees and becomes himself universal.

"*Never perishing when they perish.*" If all things are in a continual state of evolutionary development, then there is no unchanging God. Bergson, for example, makes God wholly immanent in the world, changing as it changes. An evolving God who is conceived as a part of the process of development of the world will cease to exist, when the universe ceases to move. The second law of Thermodynamics suggests a condition of eventless stagnation and perfect rest. An evolving or emergent God cannot be either the creator or the saviour of the world. He is not an adequate object for the religious emotions. In this verse, the *Gītā* assures us that God lives and endures even when the universe ceases to exist.

28. *samaṁ paśyan hi sarvatra*
samavasthitam īśvaram
na hinasty ātmanā 'tmānaṁ
tato yāti parāṁ gatim

(28) For, as he sees the Lord present, equally everywhere, he does not injure his true Self by the self and then he attains to the supreme goal.

29. *prakṛtyai 'va ca karmāṇi*
kriyamāṇāni sarvaśaḥ
yaḥ paśyati tathā 'tmānam
akartāraṁ sa paśyati

(29) He who sees that all actions are done only by nature (prakṛti) and likewise that the self is not the doer, he verily sees.

The true self is not the doer but only the witness. It is the spectator, not the actor. Ś. says that there is no evidence to show that there is any variety in him who is non-agent, unconditioned and free from all specialities, as there is no variety in the sky.[1] Actions affect the mind and understanding and not the self.

30. *yadā bhūtapṛthagbhāvam*
ekastham anupaśyati
tata eva ca vistāraṁ
brahma saṁpadyate tadā

(30) When he sees that the manifold state of beings is centred in the One and from just that it spreads out, then he attains Brahman.

When the variety of nature and its development are traced to the Eternal One, we assume eternity. "He realizes the all-pervading nature of the Self, inasmuch as the cause of all limitation is absorbed into the unity of the Self." Ānandagiri.

31. *anāditvān nirguṇatvāt*
paramātmā 'yam avyayaḥ
śarīrastho 'pi kaunteya
na karoti na lipyate

(31) Because this Supreme Self imperishable is without beginning, without qualities, so, O Son of Kuntī (Arjuna), though It dwells in the body, It neither acts nor is tainted.

32. *yathā sarvagataṁ saukṣmyād*
ākāśaṁ no 'palipyate
sarvatrā 'vasthito dehe
tathā 'tmā no 'palipyate

(32) As the all-pervading ether is not tainted, by reason of its subtlety, even so the Self that is present in every body does not suffer any taint.

33. *yathā prakāśayaty ekaḥ*
kṛtsnaṁ lokam imaṁ raviḥ
kṣetraṁ kṣetrī tathā kṛtsnaṁ
prakāśayati bhārata

[1] *kṣetrajñam akartāraṁ sarvopādhivivarjitam. nirguṇasyākartur nirviśeṣasy ākāśasyeva bhede pramāṇānupapattiḥ.*

(33) As the one sun illumines this whole world, so does the Lord of the field illumine this entire field, O Bhārata (Arjuna).

The knower of the field illumines the whole field, the entire world of becoming.

34. *kṣetrakṣetrajñayor evam*
antaraṁ jñānacakṣuṣā
bhūtaprakṛtimokṣaṁ ca
ye vidur yānti te param

(34) Those who perceive thus by their eye of wisdom the distinction between the field and the knower of the field, and the deliverance of beings from nature (prakṛti), they attain to the Supreme.

bhūtaprakṛti: the material nature of beings.

iti . . . kṣetrakṣetrajñavibhāgayogo nāma trayodaśo 'dhyāyaḥ

This is the thirteenth chapter entitled The Yoga of the Distinction between the Field and the Knower of the Field.

CHAPTER XIV

The Mystical Father of All Beings

The Highest Knowledge

śrībhagavān uvāca

1. *paraṁ bhūyaḥ pravakṣyāmi*
jñānānāṁ jñānam uttamam
yaj jñātvā munayaḥ sarve
parāṁ siddhim ito gatāḥ

The Blessed Lord said:

(1) I shall again declare that supreme wisdom, of all wisdom the best, by knowing which all sages have passed from this world to the highest perfection.

2. *idaṁ jñānam upāśritya*
mama sādharmyam āgatāḥ
sarge 'pi no 'pajāyante
pralaye na vyathanti ca

(2) Having resorted to this wisdom and become of like nature to Me, they are not born at the time of creation; nor are they disturbed at the time of dissolution.

Life eternal is not dissolution into the indefinable Absolute but attainment of a universality and freedom of spirit, which is lifted above the empirical movement. Its status is unaffected by the cyclic processes of creation and dissolution, being superior to all manifestations. The saved soul grows into the likeness of the Divine and assumes an unchangeable being, eternally conscious of the Supreme Lord who assumes varied cosmic forms. It is not *svarūpatā* or identity but only *samānadharmatā* or similarity of quality. He becomes one in nature with what he seeks, attains *sādṛśyamukti*. He realizes the divine in his outer consciousness and life. Cp. "Be ye therefore perfect, even as your Father which is in heaven is perfect." *Matthew* v, 48. Ś.'s view is different from this. He holds that *sādharmya* means identity of nature and not equality of attributes.[1]

3. *mama yonir mahad brahma*
tasmin garbhaṁ dadhāmy aham
saṁbhavaḥ sarvabhūtānāṁ
tato bhavati bhārata

(3) Great brahma (prakṛti) is My womb: in that I cast the seed and from it is the birth of all beings, O Bhārata (Arjuna).

If we were merely products of nature, we could not attain life eternal. This verse affirms that all existence is a manifestation of the Divine. He is the cosmic seed. With reference to this world, He becomes Hiraṇyagarbha, the cosmic soul. Ś. says: "I unite the kṣetra with the kṣetrajña, giving birth to Hiraṇyagarbha, hence to all beings." The Lord is the Father who deposits in the womb which is not-self, the seed which is essential life, thus causing the birth of every individual. The world is the play of the Infinite on the finite. See note on II, 12. The author here adopts the theory of creation as the development of form from non-being, chaos or night. The forms of all things which arise out of the abysmal void are derived from God. They are the seeds He casts into non-being.

4. *sarvayoniṣu kaunteya*
mūrtayaḥ saṁbhavanti yāḥ
tāsāṁ brahma mahad yonir
aham bījapradaḥ pitā

(4) Whatever forms are produced in any wombs whatsoever, O Son of Kuntī (Arjuna), great brahma is their womb and I am the Father who casts the seed.

Prakṛti is the mother and God is the father of all living forms. As prakṛti is also of the nature of God, God is the father and

[1] *mama parameśvarasya sādharmyaṁ mat svarūpatāṁ na tu samānadharmatāṁ sādharmyam kṣetrajneśvarayor bhedān abhyupagamāt gītāśāstre. Ś. mama īśvarasya sādharmyaṁ sarvātmatvaṁ, sarvaniyantṛtvaṁ, ityādidharmasāmyaṁ sādharmyam.* Nīlakaṇṭha.
mamasādharmyaṁ madrūpatvam. Śrīdhara.

mother of the universe. He is the seed and the womb of the universe. This conception is utilized in certain forms of worship which are developed out of what some modern puritans deride as obscene phallicism. The Spirit of God fertilizes our lives and makes them what God wants them to be.

The Supreme is the Seminal Reason of the world. All beings result from the impregnation of matter through *logoi spermatikoi* or animating souls. Through them God carries out His work in the world. These seeds of the Logos are the ideal forms which mould the gross world of matter into beings. The ideas, the patterns of things to be, are all in God. Every possibility of manifestation has its root in a corresponding possibility in the unmanifest, wherein it subsists as in its eternal cause, of which the manifestation is an explicit affirmation. God has an eternal vision of creation in all its details. Whereas in Socrates and Plato, ideas and matter are conceived as a dualism, where the relation between the subtle world of ideas and the gross world of matter is difficult to understand, in the *Gītā* the two are said to belong to the Divine. God Himself incarnates the seminal ideas in the forms of the gross world. These seminal ideas which have a divine origin, which belong to the causal Logos are the explanation of our love for God. While God is in one sense transcendent to human nature, there is also in the soul a direct expression of the Divine. The cosmic process continues until the causal origin, *alpha*. and the final consummation, *omega*, coincide.

Goodness, Passion and Dullness

5. *sattvaṁ rajas tama iti*
guṇāḥ prakṛtisaṁbhavāḥ
nibadhnanti mahābāho
dehe dehinam avyayam

(5) The three modes (guṇas) goodness (sattva), passion (rajas), and dullness (tamas) born of nature (prakṛti) bind down in the body, O Mighty-armed (Arjuna), the imperishable dweller in the body.

What leads to the appearance of the immortal soul in the cycle of birth and death is the power of the guṇas or modes. They are "the primary constituents of nature and are the bases of all substances. They cannot therefore be said to be qualities inhering in these substances." Ānandagiri. They are called guṇas, because their emergence is ever dependent on the puruṣa of the Sāṁkhya or the Kṣetrajña of the *Gītā*. The guṇas are the three tendencies of prakṛti or the three strands making up the twisted rope of nature. Sattva reflects the light of consciousness and is irradiated by it, and so has the quality of radiance (prakāśa). Rajas has an outward movement (pravṛtti) and tamas is characterized by inertia (apravṛtti) and heedless indifference (pramāda).[1] It is difficult to have adequate English equivalents for the three words, sattva, rajas and tamas. Sattva is perfect purity and luminosity while rajas is impurity which leads to activity and tamas is darkness and inertia. As the main application of the guṇas in the *Gītā* is ethical, we use goodness for sattva, passion for rajas and dullness for tamas.

The cosmic trinity reflects the dominance of one of the three modes, sattva in Viṣṇu, the preserver, rajas in Brahmā, the creator and tamas in Śiva, the destroyer. Sattva contributes to the stability of the universe, rajas to its creative movement and tamas represents the tendency of things to decay and die. They are responsible for the maintenance, origin and dissolution of the world. The application of the guṇas to the three aspects of the Personal Lord shows that the latter belongs to the objective or the manifested world. God is struggling in humanity to redeem it and the godlike souls co-operate with Him in this work of redemption.[2]

When the soul identifies itself with the modes of nature, it forgets its own eternity and uses mind, life and body for egoistic satisfaction. To rise above bondage, we must rise above the modes of nature, become *triguṇātītā*; then we put on the free and incorruptible nature of spirit. Sattva is sublimated into the light of consciousness, jyoti, rajas into austerity, tapas and tamas into tranquillity or rest, śānti.

[1] 11 and 22, 12 and 22, 13.

[2] Cp. *Isaiah* who speaks of the Messiah in these words: "He hath borne our griefs and carried our sorrows. He was wounded for our transgressions. The chastisement of our peace was upon Him and with His stripes we are healed" (liii, 45).

6. *tatra sattvaṁ nirmalatvāt*
prakāśakam anāmayam
sukhasaṅgena badhnāti
jñānasaṅgena cā 'nagha

(6) Of these, goodness (sattva) being pure, causes illumination and health. It binds, O blameless one, by attachment to happiness and by attachment to knowledge.

Knowledge here means lower intellectual knowledge.

Sattva does not rid us of the ego-sense. It also causes desire though for noble objects. The self which is free from all attachment is here attached to happiness and knowledge. Unless we cease to think and will with the ego-sense, we are not liberated. Jñāna or knowledge relates to buddhi which is a product of prakṛti and is to be distinguished from the pure consciousness which is the essence of ātman.

7. *rajo rāgātmakaṁ viddhı*
tṛṣṇāsaṅgasamudbhavam
tan nibadhnāti kaunteya
karmasaṅgena dehinam

(7) Passion (rajas), know thou, is of the nature of attraction, springing from craving and attachment. It binds fast, O Son of Kuntī (Arjuna), the embodied one by attachment to action

Though the self is not the agent, rajas makes him act with the idea "I am the doer." Ānandagiri.

8. *tamas tv ajñānajaṁ viddhı*
mohanaṁ sarvadehinām
pramādālasyanidrābhis
tan nibadhnāti bhārata

(8) But dullness (tamas), know thou, is born of ignorance and deludes all embodied beings. It binds, O Bhārata (Arjuna), by (developing the qualities of) negligence, indolence and sleep.

9. *sattvaṁ sukhe sañjayati*
rajaḥ karmaṇi bhārata
jñānam āvṛtya tu tamaḥ
pramāde sañjayaty uta

(9) Goodness attaches one to happiness, passion to action, O Bhārata (Arjuna), but dullness, veiling wisdom, attaches to negligence.

10. *rajas tamaś cā 'bhibhūya*
sattvaṁ bhavati bhārata
rajaḥ sattvaṁ tamaś cai 'va
tamaḥ sattvaṁ rajas tathā

(10) Goodness prevails, overpowering passion and dullness, O Bhārata (Arjuna). Passion prevails, (overpowering) goodness and dullness and even so dullness prevails (overpowering) goodness and passion.

The three modes are present in all human beings, though in different degrees. No one is free from them and in each soul one or the other predominates. Men are said to be sāttvika, rājasa or tāmasa according to the mode which prevails. When the theory of the "humours" of the body dominated physiology, men were divided into the sanguine, the bilious, the lymphatic and the nervous, according to the predominance of one or the other of the four humours. In the Hindu classification, the psychic characteristics are taken into account. The sāttvika nature aims at light and knowledge: the rājasa nature is restless, full of desires for things outward. While the activities of a sāttvika temperament are free, calm and selfless, the rājasa nature wishes to be always active and cannot sit still and its activities are tainted by selfish desires. The tāmasa nature is dull and inert, its mind is dark and confused and its whole life is one continuous submission to environment.

11 *sarvadvāreṣu dehe 'smin*
prakāśa upajāyate
jñānaṁ yadā tadā vidyād
vivṛddhaṁ sattvam ity uta

(11) When the light of knowledge streams forth in all the gates of the body, then it may be known that goodness has increased.

sarvadvāreṣu dehesmin: all the gates of the body. The light of knowledge can have a full physical manifestation. The truth of consciousness is not opposed to expression in matter. The Divine can be realized on the physical plane. To divinize the human consciousness, to bring the light into the physical, to transfigure our whole life is the aim of yoga.

When our minds are illumined and senses quickened, then sattva predominates.

12. *lobhaḥ pravṛttir ārambhaḥ*
karmaṇām aśamaḥ spṛhā
rajasy etāni jāyante
vivṛddhe bharatarṣabha

(12) Greed, activity, the undertaking of actions, unrest and craving—these spring up, O Best of the Bharatas (Arjuna), when rajas increases.

The passionate seeking of life and its pleasures arises from the dominance of rajas.

13. *aprakāśo 'pravṛttiś ca*
pramādo moha eva ca
tamasy etāni jāyante
vivṛddhe kurunandana

(13) Unillumination, inactivity, negligence and mere delusion—these arise, O Joy of the Kurus (Arjuna), when dullness increases.

While prakāśa or illumination is the effect of sattva, aprakāśa or non-illumination is the result of tamas. Error, misunderstanding, negligence and inaction are the characteristic marks of a tāmasa temperament.

14. *yadā sattve pravṛddhe tu*
pralayaṁ yāti dehabhṛt
tado 'ttamavidāṁ lokān
amalān pratipadyate

(15) When the embodied soul meets with dissolution, when goodness prevails, then it attains to the pure worlds of those who know the Highest.

They do not obtain release but birth in *brahmaloka*. *Nistraiguṇya* or the transcendence of the three guṇas is the condition of release.

15 *rajasi pralayaṁ gatvā*
karmasaṅgiṣu jāyate
tathā pralīnas tamasi
mūḍhayoniṣu jāyate

(15) Meeting with dissolution when passion prevails, it is born among those attached to action; and if it is dissolved when dullness prevails, it is born in the wombs of the deluded.

16. *karmaṇaḥ sukṛtasyā 'huḥ*
sāttvikaṁ nirmalaṁ phalam
rajasas tu phalaṁ duḥkham
ajñānaṁ tamasaḥ phalam

(16) The fruit of good action is said to be of the nature of "goodness" and pure; while the fruit of passion is pain, the fruit of dullness is ignorance.

17. *sattvāt saṁjāyate jñānaṁ*
rajaso lobha eva ca
pramādamohau tamaso
bhavato 'jñānam eva ca

(17) From goodness arises knowledge and from passion greed, negligence and error arise from dullness, as also ignorance.

The psychological effects of the three modes are here set forth.

18. *ūrdhvaṁ gacchanti sattvasthā*
madhye tiṣṭhanti rājasāḥ
jaghanyaguṇavṛttisthā
adho gacchanti tāmasāḥ

(18) Those who are established in goodness rise upwards; the passionate remain in the middle (regions); the dull steeped in the lower occurrences of the modes sink downwards.

The soul evolves through these three stages; it rises from dull inertia and subjection to ignorance, through the struggle for material enjoyments to the pursuit of knowledge and happiness. But so long as we are attached, even though it may be to very noble objects, we are limited and there is always a sense of insecurity since rajas and tamas may overcome the sattva in us. The highest ideal is to transcend the ethical level and rise to the spiritual. The good man (sāttvika) should become a saint (triguṇāttīa). Until we reach this stage, we are only in the making; our evolution is incomplete.

19. *nā 'nyaṁ guṇebhyaḥ kartāraṁ*
yadā draṣṭā 'nupaśyati
guṇebhyaś ca paraṁ vetti
madbhāvaṁ so 'dhigacchati

(19) When the seer perceives no agent other than the modes, and knows also that which is beyond the modes, he attains to My being.

"Then his identity with Brahman becomes manifest." Ānandagiri.

20. *guṇān etān atītya trīn*
dehī dehasamudbhavān
janmamṛtyujarāduḥkhair
vimukto 'mṛtam aśnute

(20) When the embodied soul rises above these three modes that spring from the body, it is freed from birth, death, old age and pain and attains life eternal.

dehasamudbhavān: this implies that the modes are caused by the body. "Which are the seed out of which the body is evolved." Ś.[1] Even sāttvika goodness is imperfect since this goodness has for its condition the struggle with its opposite. The moment the struggle ceases and the goodness becomes

[1] *dehotpattibījabhūtān.*

absolute, it ceases to be goodness and goes beyond all ethical compulsion. By developing the nature of sattva, we rise beyond it and obtain transcendent wisdom.[1]

The Character of Him Who is Beyond the Three Modes

arjuna uvāca

21. *kair liṅgais trīn guṇān etān*
atīto bhavati prabho
kimācāraḥ kathaṁ cai 'tāṁs
trīn guṇān ativartate

Arjuna said

(21) By what marks is he, O Lord, who has risen above the three modes characterized? What is his way of life? How does he get beyond the three modes?

What are the marks of the jīvanmukta, of him who achieves perfection in the present life? The characteristics are more or less the same as those of the sthitaprajña (II, 55 ff.) of the bhaktimān, devotee (XII, 13 ff.). From this it is evident that the marks of perfection are the same, however it may be reached.

śrībhagavān uvāca

22. *prakāśaṁ ca pravṛttiṁ ca*
moham eva ca pāṇḍava
na dveṣṭi saṁpravṛttāni
na nivṛttāni kāṅkṣati

The Blessed Lord said:

(22) He, O Pāṇḍava (Arjuna), who does not abhor illumination, activity and delusion when they arise nor longs for them when they cease.

[1] Just as we pull out a thorn by a thorn, so renouncing worldly things we must renounce renunciation. *kaṇṭakaṁ kaṇṭakeneva yena tyajasi taṁ tyaja.* By means of sattva we overcome rajas and tamas and then get beyond sattva itself.

23. *udāsīnavad āsīno*
guṇair yo na vicālyate
guṇā vartanta ity eva
yo 'vatiṣṭhati ne 'ṅgate

(23) He who is seated like one unconcerned, unperturbed by the modes, who stands apart, without wavering, knowing that it is only the modes that act.

He sees the mutations of nature but is not entangled in them. The modes or guṇaś are lifted up into pure illumination, divine activity and perfect calṁ.

24. *samaduḥkhasukhaḥ svasthaḥ*
samaloṣṭāśmakāñcanaḥ
tulyapriyāpriyo dhīras
tulyanindātmasaṁstutiḥ

(24) He who regards pain and pleasure alike, who dwells in his own self, who looks upon a clod, a stone, a piece of gold as of equal worth, who remains the same amidst the pleasant and the unpleasant things, who is firm of mind, who regards both blame and praise as one.

25. *mānāpamānayos tulyas*
tulyo mitrāripakṣayoḥ
sarvārambhaparityāgī
guṇātītaḥ sa ucyate

(25) He who is the same in honour and dishonour and the same to friends and foes, and who has given up all initiative of action, he is said to have risen above the modes.

26. *māṁ ca yo 'vyabhicāreṇa*
bhaktiyogena sevate
sa guṇān samatītyai 'tān
brahmabhūyāya kalpate

(26) He who serves Me with unfailing devotion of love, rises above the three modes, he too is fit for becoming Brahman.

He is fit for liberation.

27. *brahmaṇo hi pratiṣṭhā 'ham*
amṛtasyā 'vyayasya ca
śāśvatasya ca dharmasya
sukhasyai 'kāntikasya ca

(27) For I am the abode of Brahman, the Immortal and the Imperishable, of eternal law and of absolute bliss.

Here the personal Lord is said to be the foundation of the Absolute Brahman. Ś. makes out that the Supreme Lord is Brahman in the sense that He is the manifestation of Brahman. Brahman shows His grace to His devotees through Īśvaraśakti and He is that power in manifestation and therefore Brahman Himself. Ś. gives an alternative explanation. Brahman is the personal Lord and the verse means "I, the unconditioned and the unutterable, am the abode of the conditioned Brahman who is immortal and indestructible." Nīlakaṇṭha takes Brahma to mean Veda. R. interprets it as the emancipated soul and Madhva as māyā. Madhusūdana takes it for the personal Lord. Kṛṣṇa identifies Himself with the absolute, unconditioned Brahman.

iti . . . guṇatrayavibhāgayogo nāma caturdaśo 'dhyāyaḥ

This is the fourteenth chapter entitled The Yoga of the Differentiation of the Three Modes.

CHAPTER XV

The Tree of Life

The Cosmic Tree

śrībhagavān uvāca

1 *ūrdhvamūlam adhaḥśākham*
aśvatthaṁ prāhur avyayam
chandāṁsi yasya parṇāni
yas taṁ veda sa vedavit

The Blessed Lord said:

(1) They speak of the imperishable aśvattham (peepal tree) as having its root above and branches below. Its leaves are the Vedas and he who knows this is the knower of the Vedas

Cp. *Kaṭha Up.* "With root above and branches below, this world tree is eternal."[1] It is *saṁsāravṛkṣa*, the cosmic tree. M.B. compares the cosmic process to a tree which can be cut off by the mighty sword of knowledge, *jñānena paramāsinā*.[2] As the tree originates in God, it is said to have its roots "above"; as it extends into the world, its branches are said to go "downwards." The world is a living organism united with the Supreme.

According to ancient belief, the Vedic sacrificial cult is said to sustain the world and so the hymns are said to be the leaves which keep the tree with its trunk and branches alive.

[1] V, 1. See also *Ṛg. Veda*, I, 24, 7.
I am the originator of the world tree. *Taittirīya Up.*, I, 10.
The Petelia Orphic tablet suggests that our body comes from the earth and our soul from heaven. "I am a child of Earth and of Starry Heaven; but my race is of Heaven alone." Cp. Plato: "As regards the most lordly part of our soul, we must conceive of it in this wise; we declare that God has given to each of us, as his demon, that kind of soul which is housed in the top of our body and which raises us—seeing that we are not an earthly but a heavenly plant—up from earth towards our kindred in heaven." *Timaeus*, 90–A.

[2] *Aśvamedhaparva* 47, 12–15.

2. *adhaś co 'rdhvaṁ prasṛtās tasya śākhā*
guṇapravṛddhā viṣayapravālāḥ
adhaś ca mūlāny anusaṁtatāni
karmānubandhīni manuṣyaloke

(2) Its branches extend below and above, nourished by the modes, with sense objects for its twigs and below, in the world of men stretch forth the roots resulting in actions.

Ś. makes out that the downward spreading roots are the secondary ones, vāsanas, which the souls carry as results of past deeds.

3. *na rūpam asye 'ha tatho 'palabhyate*
nā 'nto na cā 'dir na ca saṁpratiṣṭhā
aśvattham enaṁ suvirūḍhamūlam
asaṅgaśastreṇa dṛḍhena chittvā

(3) Its real form is not thus perceived here, nor its end nor beginning nor its foundation. Having cut off this firm-rooted Asvattham (peepal tree) with the strong sword of non-attachment.

4. *tataḥ padaṁ tat parimārgitavyaṁ*
yasmin gatā na nivartanti bhūyaḥ
tam eva cā 'dyaṁ puruṣaṁ prapadye
yataḥ pravṛttiḥ prasṛtā purāṇī

(4) Then, that path must be sought from which those who have reached it never return, saying "I seek refuge only in that Primal Person from whom has come forth this ancient current of the world" (this cosmic process).

The disciple, detaching himself from the objective, takes refuge in the primal consciousness from which cosmic energies issue.

5. *nirmānamohā jitasaṅgadoṣā*
adhyātmanityā vinivṛttakāmāḥ
dvandvair vimuktāḥ sukhaduḥkhasaṁjñair
gacchanty amūḍhāḥ padam avyayaṁ tat

(5) Those, who are freed from pride and delusion, who have conquered the evil of attachment, who, all desires stilled,

are ever devoted to the Supreme Spirit, who are liberated from the dualities known as pleasure and pain and are undeluded, go to that eternal state.

Manifested Life is Only a Part

6. *na tad bhāsayate sūryo*
na śaśāṅko na pāvakaḥ
yad gatvā na nivartante
tad dhāma paramaṁ mama.

(6) The sun does not illumine that, nor the moon nor the fire. That is My supreme abode from which those who reach it never return.

Cp. *Kaṭha Up.*, V, 15; *Muṇḍaka Up.*, II, 2–10.

This verse refers to the Immutable Brahman which can be reached by ascetic practices.

The Lord as the Life of the Universe

7. *mamai 'vā 'ṁśo jīvaloke*
jīvabhūtaḥ sanātanaḥ
manaḥṣaṣṭhānī 'ndriyāṇi
prakṛtisthāni karṣati

(7) A fragment (or fraction) of My own self, having become a living soul, eternal, in the world of life, draws to itself the senses of which the mind is the sixth, that rest in nature.

mamaivāṁśaḥ: a fragment (or fraction) of myself. This does not mean that the Supreme is capable of division or partition into fragments. The individual is a movement of the Supreme, a focus of the one great Life. The self is the nucleus which can enlarge itself and embrace the whole world, with heart and mind, in an intimate communion. The actual manifestations may be partial but the reality of the individual soul is the Divine which the human manifestation does not fully bring out. God's image in man is the bridge between heaven and earth. Each individual has eternal significance in the cosmos. When he rises above his limitations, he is not dissolved in the Superpersonal Absolute but lives in the Supreme[1] and enters into a co-partnership with God in the cosmic activity.

Ś. makes out that the self is a part of the Supreme in the same way as the space in an earthen jar or a house is a part of the universal space. For R., the soul is an actual fragment (aṁśa) of God. It becomes a substantial individual soul in the world and suffers bondage by entering the service of the sense objects.

jīvabhūtaḥ: having become a living soul. Śaṁkarānanda says, "The eternal portion, having assumed the condition of the knower of the field, for the purpose of manifesting name and form, becomes the cognizer."[2] The Supreme becomes the jīva in some mode (*prakārāntareṇa*). It is not in essence the jīva but assumes that form. It is jīvabhūta and not jivātmika.

The jīvātman is one centre of the multiple Divine and expresses one aspect of the Divine consciousness. The jīva belongs to the world of manifestation and is dependent on the One; the Ātman is the one supporting the manifestation. The jiva's fulfilment consists in the expression of his characteristic nature. If he adopts the right attitude to the Divine, his nature becomes purified of the influences which diminish and distort it and the truth of his personality comes out with distinctiveness. While the individuals are in essence one with the Divine, in the world of manifestation, each is a partial manifestation of the Divine. Each of us is a ray of the Divine consciousness into which our being, if we will only allow it, can be transfigured.

prakṛtisthāni: in their natural places. Ś. Abiding in bodies made of prakṛti. R.

8. *śarīraṁ yad avāpnoti*
yac cā 'py utkrāmatī 'śvaraḥ
gṛhītvai 'tāni saṁyāti
vāyur gandhān ivā 'śayāt

(8) When the lord takes up a body and when he leaves it, he takes these (the senses and mind) and goes even as the wind carries perfumes from their places.

The subtle body accompanies the soul in its wanderings through cosmic existence.

[1] *nivasiṣyası mayyeva*, XII, 8.
[2] *nāmarūpavyākaraṇāya kṣetrajñatāṁ gataḥ pramātā bhūtvā tiṣṭhati.*

9. *śrotraṁ cakṣuḥ sparśanaṁ ca*
rasanaṁ ghrāṇam eva ca
adhiṣṭhāya manaś cā 'yaṁ
viṣayān upasevate

(9) He enjoys the objects of the senses, using the ear, the eye, the touch sense, the taste sense and the nose as also the mind.

10. *utkrāmantaṁ sthitaṁ vā 'pi*
bhuñjānaṁ vā guṇānvitam
vimūḍhā nā 'nupaśyanti
paśyanti jñānacakṣuṣaḥ

(10) When He departs or stays or experiences, in contact with the modes, the deluded do not see (the indwelling soul) but they who have the eye of wisdom (or whose eye is wisdom) see.

11. *yatanto yoginaś cai 'naṁ*
paśyanty ātmany avasthitam
yatanto 'py akṛtātmāno
nai 'naṁ paśyanty acetasaḥ

(11) The sages also striving perceive Him as established in the self, but the unintelligent, whose souls are undisciplined, though striving, do not find Him.

12. *yad ādityagataṁ tejo*
jagad bhāsayate 'khilam
yac candramasi yac cā 'gnau
tat tejo viddhi māmakam

(12) That splendour of the sun that illumines this whole world, that which is in the moon, that which is in the fire, that splendour, know as Mine.

13. *gām āviśya ca bhūtāni*
dhārayāmy aham ojasā
puṣṇāmi cau 'ṣadhīḥ sarvāḥ
somo bhūtvā rasātmakaḥ

(13) And entering the earth, I support all beings by My vital energy; and becoming the sapful soma (moon), I nourish all herbs (or plants).

14. *ahaṁ vaiśvānaro bhūtvā*
prāṇināṁ deham āśritaḥ
prāṇāpānasamāyuktaḥ
pacāmy annaṁ caturvidham

(14) Becoming the fire of life in the bodies of living creatures and mingling with the upward and downward breaths, I digest the four kinds of food.

pacāmy: literally cook.

15. *sarvasya cā 'haṁ hṛdi saṁniviṣṭo*
mattaḥ smṛtir jñānam apohanaṁ ca
vedaiś ca sarvair aham eva vedyo
vedāntakṛd vedavid eva cā 'ham

(15) And I am lodged in the hearts of all; from Me are memory and knowledge as well as their loss. I am indeed He who is to be known by all the Vedas. I indeed (am) the author of the Vedānta and I too the knower of the Vedas.[1]

apohanam: loss, destruction, rejection.

The Supreme Person

16. *dvāv imau puruṣau loke*
kṣaraś cā 'kṣara eva ca
kṣaraḥ sarvāṇi bhūtāni
kūṭastho 'kṣara ucyate

(16) There are two persons in this world, the perishable and the imperishable, the perishable is all these existences and the unchanging is the imperishable.

17. *uttamaḥ puruṣas tv anyaḥ*
paramātme 'ty udāhṛtaḥ
yo lokatrayam āviśya
bibharty avyaya īśvaraḥ

[1] Cp. Bhīṣma, who in the M.B. says of Kṛṣna, *vedavedāṅgavijñānaṁ balaṁ cāpy adhikaṁ tathā.*

(17) But other than these, the Highest Spirit called the Supreme Self who, as the Undying Lord, enters the three worlds and sustains them.

The soul in the ever changing cosmos is kṣara; akṣara is the eternal spirit, unchanged and immobile, the immutable in the mutable.[1] When the soul turns to this immutable, the cosmic movement falls away from it and it reaches its unchanging eternal existence. These two are not irreconcilable opposites, for Brahman is both one and many, the eternal unborn as also the cosmic streaming forth.

For the *Gītā*, this moving world is a creation of the Lord. The Divine accepts the world and acts in it; *varta eva ca karmaṇi*. From the cosmic end, the Supreme is Īśvara, the Highest Person, Puruṣottama, the Lord of the universe who dwells in the heart of every creature.[2]

paramātmā: the Supreme Self. God in the soul. *Gītā* refers here, not to the unknown abyss of the Godhead but to the Spirit, indwelling and moving creation.

The *Gītā* exalts the conception of the Personal God who combines in Himself the timeless existence (akṣara) and the temporal beginning (kṣara).

Ś. interprets the mutable as the changing universe, the immutable as the māyāśakti or the power of the Lord and the Supreme is said to be eternal, pure and intelligent and free from the limitations of the mutable and the immutable.

R. takes akṣara to be the emancipated soul. The universe consists of two essences distinguished as the self and the inanimate (jaḍa), the immutable and the mutable. Above them is the Supreme transcending the universe and yet at the same time permeating it. The two puruṣas may be interpreted as referring to the two natures, the one higher, His own essential nature, adhyātma, and the other lower, prakṛti. Cp. *Śvetāśvatara Up.*, I, 10.

18. *yasmāt kṣaram atīto 'ham*
akṣarād api co 'ttamaḥ
ato 'smi loke vede ca
prathitaḥ puruṣottamaḥ

[1] Cp. *Amarakośa: ekarūpatayā tu yaḥ kālavyāpī sa kūṭasthaḥ.*

[2] *avyayaḥ, sarvajñatvena īśvaradharmeṇa, alpajñatvena jīvadharmeṇa vā, na vyeti vardhate kṣīyate vety arthaḥ.* Nīlakaṇṭha.

(18) As I surpass the perishable and am higher even than the imperishable, I am celebrated as the Supreme Person in the world and in the Veda.

Cp. *Muṇḍaka Up.*, II, 1, 1–2. *akṣarāt parataḥ paraḥ puruṣaḥ.*

19. *yo mām evam asaṁmūḍho*
jānāti puruṣottamam
sa sarvavid bhajati māṁ
sarvabhāvena bhārata

(19) He who, undeluded, thus knows Me, the Highest Person, is the knower of all and worships Me with all his being (with his whole spirit), O Bhārata (Arjuna).

Knowledge leads to devotion.

20. *iti guhyatamaṁ śāstram*
idam uktaṁ mayā 'nagha
etad buddhvā buddhimān syāt
kṛtakṛtyaś ca bhārata

(20) Thus has this most secret doctrine been taught by Me, O blameless one. By knowing this, a man will become wise and will have fulfilled all his duties, O Bhārata (Arjuna).

iti . . . puruṣottamayogo nāma pañcadaśo 'dhyāyaḥ

This is the fifteenth chapter entitled The Yoga of the Supreme Person.

CHAPTER XVI

The Nature of the Godlike and the Demoniac Mind

Those of Divine Nature

śrībhagavān uvāca

1. *abhayaṁ sattvasaṁśuddhir*
jñānayogavyavasthitiḥ
dānaṁ damaś ca yajñaś ca
svādhyāyas tapa ārjavam

The Blessed Lord said:

(1) Fearlessness, purity of mind, wise apportionment of knowledge and concentration, charity, self-control and sacrifice, study of the scriptures, austerity and uprightness.

In Indian religious symbolism, the distinction between the devas, the shining ones and the asuras, the titans, the children of darkness is an ancient one. In the *Ṛg. Veda* we have the struggle between the gods and their dark opponents. The *Rāmāyaṇa* represents a similar conflict between the representatives of high culture and those of unbridled egoism. *M.B.* tells us of the struggle between the Pāṇḍavas, who are devotees of dharma, of law and justice, and the Kauravas who are lovers of power. Historically, mankind remains remarkably true to type, and we have today as in the period of the *M.B.* some men who are divinely good, some who are diabolically fallen and some who are damnably indifferent. These are the possible developments of men who are more or less like ourselves. The devas and the asuras are both born of Prajāpati. *Chāndogya Up.*, I, 2, 1.

2. *ahiṁsā satyam akrodhas*
tyāgaḥ śāntir apaiśunaṁ
dayā bhūteṣv aloluptvaṁ
mārdavaṁ hrīr acāpalam

(2) Non-violence, truth, freedom from anger, renunciation, tranquillity, aversion to fault finding, compassion to living beings, freedom from covetousness, gentleness, modesty and steadiness (absence of fickleness).

3. *tejaḥ kṣamā dhṛtiḥ śaucam*
adroho nā 'timānitā
bhavanti saṁpadaṁ daivīm
abhijātasya bhārata

(3) Vigour, forgiveness, fortitude, purity, freedom from malice and excessive pride—these, O Pāṇḍava (Arjuna), are the endowments of him who is born with the divine nature.

The human race is not divided into the kingdom of Ormuzd and the kingdom of Ahriman. In each man are these two kingdoms of light and of darkness.

The teacher has set forth the distinctive qualities of those who are seeking for the divine perfection. Now he states the qualities of those who aim at power, glory and easy life. The distinction is neither exclusive nor comprehensive. Many beings partake of the natures of both. *M.B.* says: "Nothing is wholly good or wholly evil."[1]

The Demoniac

4. *dambho darpo 'timānaś ca*
krodhaḥ pāruṣyam eva ca
ajñānaṁ cā 'bhijātasya
pārtha saṁpadam āsurīm

(4) Ostentation, arrogance, excessive pride, anger, as also harshness and ignorance, these, O Pārtha (Arjuna), are the endowments of him who is born with the demoniac nature.

Their Respective Results

5. *daivī saṁpad vimokṣāya*
nibandhāyā 'surī matā
mā śucaḥ saṁpadaṁ daivīm
abhijāto 'si pāṇḍava

(5) The divine endowments are said to make for deliverance and the demoniac for bondage. Grieve not, O Pāṇḍava (Arjuna), thou art born with the divine endowments (for a divine destiny).

[1] *nātyantaṁ guṇavat kiñcin nātyantaṁ doṣavat tathā.*

The traditional virtues of a devout Hindu are brought together as indicating a "godly" state of life. The asuras are clever and energetic but suffer from an exaggerated egoism and have no moral scruples or spiritual aims.

The Nature of the Demoniac

6. *dvau bhūtasargau loke 'smin*
daiva āsura eva ca
daivo vistaraśaḥ prokta
āsuraṁ pārtha me śṛṇu

(6) There are two types of beings created in the world—the divine and the demoniac. The divine have been described at length. Hear from me, O Pārtha (Arjuna), about the demoniac.

See *Bṛhadāraṇyaka Up.*, I, 3, 1.

7. *pravṛttiṁ ca nivṛttiṁ ca*
janā na vidur āsurāḥ
na śaucaṁ nā 'pi cā 'cāro
na satyaṁ teṣu vidyate

(7) The demoniac do not know about the way of action or the way of renunciation. Neither purity, nor good conduct, nor truth is found in them

8. *asatyam apratiṣṭhaṁ te*
jagad āhur anīśvaraṁ
aparasparasaṁbhūtaṁ
kim anyat kāmahaitukam

(8) They say that the world is unreal, without a basis, without a Lord, not brought about in regular causal sequence, caused by desire, in short

apratiṣṭham: without a basis, without a moral basis. This is the view of the materialists.

aparasparasaṁbhūtam: not brought about in regular sequence. It is interpreted in other ways also. The world presided over by

Īśvara conforms to a settled order, where things proceed from others according to law and the materialists deny the order in the world and hold that things arise any how. They believe that there is no regular succession and that the world is there only for the sake of enjoyment.

"This is the view of the Lokāyatikas that sexual passion is the sole cause of all living creatures." Ś

9. *etāṁ dṛṣṭim avaṣṭabhya*
naṣṭātmāno 'lpabuddhayaḥ
prabhavanty ugrakarmāṇaḥ
kṣayāya jagato 'hitāḥ

(9) Holding fast to this view, these lost souls of feeble understanding, of cruel deeds, rise up as the enemies of the world for its destruction.

10. *kāmam āśritya duṣpūraṁ*
dambhamānamadānvitāḥ
mohād gṛhītvā 'sadgrāhān
pravartante 'śucivratāḥ

(10) Giving themselves up to insatiable desire, full of hypocrisy, excessive pride and arrogance, holding wrong views through delusion, they act with impure resolves

Cp. *Bṛhaspati Sūtra*, which declares that kāma is the supreme end of man.[1]

11. *cintām aparimeyāṁ ca*
pralayāntām upāśritāḥ
kāmopabhogaparamā
etāvad iti niścitāḥ

(11) Obsessed with innumerable cares which would end only with (their) death, looking upon the gratification of desires as their highest aim, assured that this is all.

This is the materialist doctrine which asks us to eat, drink and be merry, for death is certain and there is nothing beyond.[2]

[1] *kāma evaikaḥ puruṣārthaḥ.*

[2] Cp. *yāvad jīvet sukhaṁ jīvet, ṛṇaṁ kṛtvā ghṛtaṁ pibet*
bhaśmībhūtasya dehasya punar āgamanaṁ kutaḥ.

12. *āśāpāśaśatair baddhāḥ*
kāmakrodhaparāyaṇāḥ
īhante kāmabhogārtham
anyāyenā 'rthasaṁcayān

(12) Bound by hundreds of ties of desire, given over to lust and anger, they strive to amass hoards of wealth, by unjust means, for the gratification of their desires.

13. *idam adya mayā labdham*
imaṁ prāpsye manoratham
idam astī 'dam api me
bhaviṣyati punar dhanam

(13) "This today has been gained by me: this desire I shall attain, this is mine and this wealth also shall be mine (in future).

14. *asau mayā hataḥ śatrur*
haniṣye cā 'parān api
īśvaro 'ham ahaṁ bhogī
siddho 'haṁ balavān sukhī

(14) "This foe is slain by me and others also I shall slay. I am the lord, I am the enjoyer, I am successful, mighty and happy.

This is the greatest sin of all, the sin of Lucifer, the claim to be oneself the god-head.

The temptation to achieve power and exercise sovereignty has been widespread. The disposition to dominate others has made man a slave. The divine souls reject the temptation as Jesus did in the wilderness. But the demoniac souls accept these ends and exalt pride, self-conceit, cupidity, hatred, brutality as virtues.

15. *āḍhyo 'bhijanavān asmi*
ko 'nyo 'sti sadṛśo mayā
yakṣye dāsyāmi modiṣya
ity ajñānavimohitāḥ

(15) "I am rich and well-born. Who is there like unto me? I shall sacrifice, I shall give, I shall rejoice," thus they (say), deluded by ignorance.

16. *anekacittavibhrāntā*
mohajālasamāvṛtāḥ
prasaktāḥ kāmabhogeṣu
patanti narake 'śucau

(16) Bewildered by many thoughts, entangled in the meshes of delusion and addicted to the gratification of desires, they fall into a foul hell.

17. *ātmasaṁbhāvitāḥ stabdhā*
dhanamānamadānvitāḥ
yajante nāmayajñais te
dambhenā 'vidhipūrvakam

(17) Self-conceited, obstinate, filled with the pride and arrogance of wealth, they perform sacrifices which are so only in name with ostentation and without regard to rules.

18. *ahaṁkāraṁ balaṁ darpaṁ*
kāmaṁ krodhaṁ ca saṁśritāḥ
mām ātmaparadeheṣu
pradviṣanto 'bhyasūyakāḥ

(18) Given over to self-conceit, force and pride and also to lust and anger, these malicious people despise Me dwelling in the bodies of themselves and others.

"God dwells as witness of their evil life." Ś.

19. *tān ahaṁ dviṣataḥ krūrān*
saṁsāreṣu narādhamān
kṣipāmy ajasram aśubhān
āsurīṣv eva yoniṣu

(19) These cruel haters, worst of men, I hurl constantly these evil-doers only into the wombs of demons in (this cycle of) births and deaths.

20. *āsurīṁ yonim āpannā*
mūḍhā janmani-janmani
mām aprāpyai 'va kaunteya
tato yānty adhamāṁ gatim

(20) Fallen into the wombs of demons, these deluded beings from birth to birth, do not attain to Me, O Son of Kuntī (Arjuna), but go down to the lowest state.

We are advised to shake off this demoniac nature. This does not mean predestination, for it is said that it is always open to us to turn godward and achieve perfection. It is not impossible at any stage. The Indwelling Spirit is in each soul and that means the hope of immortality is always there. Even the greatest sinner, if he turns to God, can achieve freedom. See IV, 36.

The Triple Gate of Hell

21. *trividhaṁ narakasye 'daṁ*
dvāraṁ nāśanam ātmanaḥ
kāmaḥ krodhas tathā lobhas
tasmād etat trayaṁ tyajet

(21) The gateway of this hell leading to the ruin of the soul is threefold, lust, anger and greed. Therefore these three, one should abandon.

22. *etair vimuktaḥ kaunteya*
tamodvārais tribhir naraḥ
ācaraty ātmanaḥ śreyas
tato yāti parāṁ gatiṁ

(22) The man who is released from these, the three gates to darkness, O son of Kuntī (Arjuna), does what is good for his soul and then reaches the highest state.

Scripture the Canon for Duty

23. *yaḥ śāstravidhim utsṛjya*
vartate kāmakārataḥ
na sa siddhim avāpnoti
na sukhaṁ na parāṁ gatim

(23) But he who discards the scriptural law and acts as his desires prompt him, he does not attain either perfection or happiness or the highest goal.

24. *tasmāc chāstraṁ pramāṇaṁ te*
kāryākāryavyavasthitau
jñātvā śāstravidhānoktaṁ
karma kartum ihā 'rhasi

(24) Therefore let the scripture be thy authority for determining what should be done and what should not be done. Knowing what is declared by the rules of the scripture, thou shouldst do thy work in this world.

śāstra: scripture.[1]

The drive of desire must be displaced by the knowledge of right action, but when the supreme end of the freedom of spirit is attained, the individual acts not from instinct, not from law but from a deep insight into the spirit of all life. We generally act according to our personal desire, then regulate the course of our conduct by reference to prescribed social codes and ultimately attain a deeper intention of life's meaning and act according to its guidance. The prompting of desire (XVIII, 59), the guidance of law (XVI, 24) and the spontaneity of spirit (XVIII, 64; XI, 33) are the three stages.

iti . . . daivāsurasaṁpadvibhāgayogo nāma ṣoḍaśo 'dhyāyaḥ

This is the sixteenth chapter entitled The Yoga of the Distinction between the Divine and the Demoniac Endowments.

[1] Cp. *śāsti yaḥ sādhanopāyaṁ puruṣārthasya nirmalam,*
tathā eva bādhanāpāyaṁ tat śāstram iti kathyate.

CHAPTER XVII

The Three Modes Applied to Religious Phenomena

Three Kinds of Faith

arjuna uvāca

1. *ye śāstravidhim utsṛjya*
yajante śraddhayā 'nvitāḥ
teṣāṁ niṣṭhā tu kā kṛṣṇa
sattvam āho rajas tamaḥ

Arjuna said:

(1) Those who, neglecting the ordinances of scriptures, offer sacrifices filled with faith—what is their position, O Kṛṣṇa? Is it one of goodness or of passion or of dullness?

These do not wilfully defy the rules of scripture but are ignorant of them.

Ś. argues that the nature of one's faith does not depend upon conformity to scriptural injunctions but on his character and the worship he adopts.

R. adopts a less liberal view and thinks that those who violate the śāstras out of ignorance or wilful neglect, whether with faith, or without faith, are to be condemned.

śrībhagavān uvāca

2. *trividhā bhavati śraddhā*
dehināṁ sā svabhāvajā
sāttvikī rājasī cai 'va
tāmasī ce 'ti tāṁ śṛṇu

The Blessed Lord said:

(2) The faith of the embodied is of three kinds, born of their nature, good, passionate and dull. Hear now about it.

3. *sattvānurūpā sarvasya*
śraddhā bhavati bhārata
śraddhāmayo 'yaṁ puruṣo
yo yacchraddhaḥ sa eva saḥ

(3) The faith of every individual, O Bhārata (Arjuna), is in accordance with his nature. Man is of the nature of his faith: what his faith is, that, verily, he is.

The author here takes up for consideration a number of questions which probably aroused interest at the time, about faith, diet, sacrifice, asceticism, almsgiving, renunciation and relinquishment.

sattva: svabhāva, nature.

śraddhā or faith, is not acceptance of a belief. It is striving after self-realization by concentrating the powers of the mind on a given ideal.

Faith is the pressure of the Spirit on humanity, the force that urges humanity towards what is better, not only in the order of knowledge but in the whole order of spiritual life. Faith, as the inward sense of truth, points to the object over which fuller light is shed later.

After all, the ultimate and incontrovertible evidence of any religious faith is the evidence of the believer's heart.

A popular verse makes out that the aims which religion offers prove effective according to one's faith in them.[1] *Bhāgavata* says that the fruit of worship follows the faith of the doer.[2] We are what we are on account of our past and we can create our future. Cp. Plato: "Such as are the trend of our desires and the nature of our souls, just such each of us becomes."[3] Cp. Goethe: "Earnestness alone makes life eternity."

4. *yajante sāttvikā devān*
yakṣarakṣāṁsi rājasāḥ
pretān bhūtagaṇāṁś cā 'nye
yajante tāmasā janāḥ

(4) Good men worship the gods, the passionate worship the demigods and the demons and the others (who are) the dull, worship the spirits and ghosts.

Men of darkness are they who make a cult of the departed and of spirits.

1 *mantre, tīrthe, dvije, deve, daivajñe, bheṣaje, gurau*
yādṛśī bhāvanā yasya siddhir bhavati tādṛśī.

2 *śraddhānūrupaṁ phalahetukatvāt.* VIII, 17.

3 *Laws,* 904–C.

5. *aśāstravihitaṁ ghoraṁ*
tapyante ye tapo janāḥ
dambhāhaṁkārasaṁyuktāḥ
kāmarāgabalānvitāḥ

(5) Those men, vain and conceited and impelled by the force of lust and passion, who perform violent austerities, which are not ordained by the scriptures,

6. *karśayantaḥ śarīrasthaṁ*
bhūtagrāmam acetasaḥ
māṁ cai 'vā 'ntaḥśarīrasthaṁ
tān viddhy āsuraniścayān

(6) Being foolish oppress the group of elements in their body and Me also dwelling in the body. Know these to be demoniac in their resolves

The methods of self-torture undertaken by some for purposes of display such as wearing hair-shirts, or piercing the body with sharp spikes, are here condemned. Bodily weakness sometimes produces hallucinations which are mistaken for spiritual visions. Self-discipline is not to be confused with bodily torture. Cp. with this, Gautama the Buddha's admonition: "The habitual practice of asceticism or self-mortification, which is painful, unworthy, and unprofitable, ought not to be followed."[1] The true discipline of the body by the practice of cleanliness, etc., is given in verse 14.

Three Kinds of Food

7. *āhāras tv api sarvasya*
trividho bhavati priyaḥ
yajñas tapas tathā dānaṁ
teṣāṁ bhedam imaṁ śṛṇu

(7) Even the food which is dear to all is of three kinds. So are the sacrifices, austerities and gifts. Hear thou the distinction of these.

[1] *Dhammacakkappavattana Sutta.*

8. *āyuḥsattvabalārogya-*
sukhaprītivivardhanāḥ
rasyāḥ snigdhāḥ sthirā hṛdyā
āhārāḥ sāttvikapriyāḥ

(8) The foods which promote life, vitality, strength, health, joy and cheerfulness, which are sweet, soft, nourishing and agreeable are dear to the "good."

9. *kaṭvamlalavaṇātyuṣṇa-*
tīkṣṇarūkṣavidāhinaḥ
āhārā rājasasye 'ṣṭā
duḥkhaśokāmayapradāḥ

(9) The foods that are bitter, sour, saltish, very hot, pungent, harsh and burning, producing pain, grief and disease are liked by the "passionate."

10. *yātayāmaṁ gatarasaṁ*
pūti paryuṣitaṁ ca yat
ucchiṣṭam api cā 'medhyaṁ
bhojanaṁ tāmasapriyam

(10) That which is spoiled, tasteless, putrid, stale, refuse and unclean is the food dear to the "dull."

As the body is built up of the food taken, the quality of food is important.[1]

Three Kinds of Sacrifice

11. *aphalākāṅkṣibhir yajño*
vidhidṛṣṭo ta ijyate
yaṣṭavyam eve 'ti manaḥ
samādhāya sa sāttvikaḥ

[1] *Chāndogya Up.*, VII, 26, 2, *āhāra śuddhau sattvasuddhiḥ* where sattva means *antaḥkaraṇa*.

The kind of diet we take has its influence on our power of self-control.

Cp. *viśvāmitra-parāśara-prabhṛtayaḥ vātāmbuparṇāśanāḥ*
tepi strīmukhapankajaṁ sulalitaṁ dṛṣṭvaiva mohaṁ gatāh
śālyānnaṁ dadhidugdhagoghṛtayutaṁ ye bhuñjate mānavāḥ
teṣām indriyanigraho yadi bhavet, vindhyas taret sāgaram.

(11) That sacrifice which is offered, according to the scriptural law, by those who expect no reward and believe firmly that it is their duty to offer the sacrifice, is "good."

The yajña of the *Gītā* is not the same as the ceremonial sacrifice of the Veda. It is sacrificial action in general by which man dedicates his wealth and deeds to the service of the One Life in all. People with such a sacrificial spirit will accept even death gladly, though unjustly meted out to them, so that the world may grow through their sacrifice. Sāvitrī tells Yama that good people maintain the world through their suffering and sacrifice. *santo bhūmiṁ tapasā dhārayanti.*

aphalākāṅkṣibhiḥ: those who expect no reward. They do the right but are indifferent to the consequences. A Socrates or a Gāndhi is concerned only whether he is doing right or wrong, acting the part of a good man or of a bad, and not whether he has a chance of living or dying.

12. *abhisaṁdhāya tu phalaṁ*
dambhārtham api cai 'va yat
ijyate bharataśreṣṭha
taṁ yajñaṁ viddhi rājasam

(12) But that which is offered in expectation of reward or for the sake of display, know, O best of the Bharatas (Arjuna), that sacrifice to be "passionate."

13. *vidhihīnam asṛṣṭānnaṁ*
mantrahīnam adakṣiṇam
śraddhāvirahitaṁ yajñaṁ
tāmasaṁ paricakṣate

(13) The sacrifice which is not in conformity with the law, in which no food is distributed, no hymns are chanted and no fees are paid, which is empty of faith, they declare to be "dull."

The distribution of food and the payment of fee are symbolic of help to others without which all work is self-regarding.

Three Kinds of Penance

14. *devadvijaguruprājña-*
pūjanaṁ śaucam ārjavam
brahmacaryam ahiṁsā ca
śārīraṁ tapa ucyate

(14) The worship of the gods, of the twice-born, of teachers and of the wise, purity, uprightness, continence and non-violence, this is said to be the penance of the body.

15. *anudvegakaraṁ vākyaṁ*
satyaṁ priyahitaṁ ca yat
svādhyāyābhyasanaṁ cai 'va
vāṅmayaṁ tapa ucyate

(15) The utterance (of words) which gives no offence, which is truthful, pleasant and beneficial and the regular recitation of the Veda—this is said to be the penance of speech.

Cp. "Of what is disagreeable and beneficial the speaker and the hearer are hard to find."[1]

16. *manaḥprasādaḥ saumyatvaṁ*
maunam ātmavinigrahaḥ
bhāvasaṁśuddhir ity etat
tapo mānasam ucyate

(16) Serenity of mind, gentleness, silence, self-control, the purity of mind—this is called the penance of mind.

17 *śraddhayā parayā taptaṁ*
tapas tat trividhaṁ naraiḥ
aphalākāṅkṣibhir yuktaiḥ
sāttvikaṁ paricakṣate

[1] *apriyasya ca pathyasya vaktāśrotā hi durlabhaḥ. M.B. Śāntiparva* 63, 17.

If you your lips would keep from slips
Five things observe with care;
Of what you speak, to whom you speak,
And how, and when, and where.
"*Uncensored Recollections.*"
(See *Thirlby Hall*, by W. E. Norris, Vol. I, p. 35.)

(17) This threefold penance practised with utmost faith by men of balanced mind without the expectation of reward, they call "good."

18. *satkāramānapūjārthaṁ*
tapo dambhena cai 'va yat
kriyate tad iha proktaṁ
rājasaṁ calam adhruvam

(18) That penance which is performed in order to gain respect, honour and reverence and for the sake of show is said to be "passionate"; it is unstable and not lasting.

19. *mūḍhagrāheṇā 'tmano yat*
pīḍayā kriyate tapaḥ
parasyo 'tsādanārthaṁ vā
tat tāmasam udāhṛtam

(19) That penance which is performed with a foolish obstinacy by means of self-torture or for causing injury to others is said to be "dull."

Now the three kinds of gifts follow.

Three Kinds of Gifts

20. *dātavyam iti yad dānaṁ*
dīyate 'nupakāriṇe
deśe kāle ca pātre ca
tad dānaṁ sāttvikaṁ smṛtam

(20) That gift, which is made to one from whom no return is expected, with the feeling that it is one's duty to give and which is given in proper place and time and to a worthy person, that gift is held to be "good."

It will lead to complete self-giving, *ātmasamarpaṇa*.

Gifts to the poor not only help the poor but help the givers. He who gives receives.

21. *yat tu pratyupakārārthaṁ*
phalam uddiśya vā punaḥ
dīyate ca parikliṣṭaṁ
tad dānaṁ rājasaṁ smṛtam

(21) But that gift which is made with the hope of a return or with the expectation of future gain or when it hurts to give, is held to be "passionate."

22. *adeśakāle yad dānam*
apātrebhyaś ca dīyate
asatkṛtam avajñātaṁ
tat tāmasam udāhṛtam

(22) And that gift which is made at a wrong place or time or to an unworthy person, without proper ceremony or with contempt, that is declared to be "dull."

The Mystical Utterance: Aum Tat Sat

23. *auṁ tat sad iti nirdeśo*
brahmaṇas trividhaḥ smṛtaḥ
brāhmaṇās tena vedāś ca
yajñāś ca vihitāḥ purā

(23) "Aum Tat Sat"—this is considered to be the threefold symbol of Brahman. By this were ordained of old the Brāhmins, the Vedas and the sacrifices

See III, 10.

"Aum" expresses the absolute supremacy, "tat" the universality and "sat" the reality of Brahman. The *Taittirīya Up.* says "*sacca tyaccābhavat.*"[1] It became sat (which is existent) and tat (that which is beyond). It is the cosmic universe as well as that which is beyond it. It stands for the three states of consciousness, waking (jāgrat), dream (svapna) and sleep (suṣupti) leading up to the transcendental state (turīya). See *Māṇḍūkya Up.* See also B.G., VII, 8 and VIII, 13.

24. *tasmād aum ity udāhṛtya*
yajñadānatapaḥkriyāḥ
pravartante vidhānoktāḥ
satataṁ brahmavādinām

(24) Therefore with the utterance of "aum" the acts of sacrifice, gift and penance enjoined in the scriptures are always undertaken by the expounders of Brahman.

[1] II, 6.

25. *tad ity anabhisaṁdhāya*
phalaṁ yajñatapaḥkriyāḥ
dānakriyāś ca vividhāḥ
kriyante mokṣakāṅkṣibhiḥ

(25) And with the utterance of the word "tat" the acts of sacrifice and penance and the various acts of giving are performed by the seekers of salvation, without aiming at the reward.

26. *sadbhāve sādhubhāve ca*
sad ity etat prayujyate
praśaste karmaṇi tathā
sacchabdaḥ pārtha yujyate

(26) The word "sat" is employed in the sense of reality and goodness; and so also, O Pārtha (Arjuna), the word "sat" is used for praiseworthy action.

27. *yajñe tapasi dāne ca*
sthitiḥ sad iti co 'cyate
karma cai 'va tadarthīyaṁ
sad ity evā 'bhidhīyate

(27) Steadfastness in sacrifice, penance, gift is also called "sat" and so also any action for such purposes is called "sat."

28. *aśraddhayā hutaṁ dattaṁ*
tapas taptaṁ kṛtaṁ ca yat
asad ity ucyate pārtha
na ca tat pretya no iha

(28) Whatever offering or gift is made, whatever penance is performed, whatever rite is observed, without faith, it is called "asat," O Pārtha (Arjuna); it is of no account hereafter or here.

iti . . . śraddhātrayavibhāgayogo nāma saptadaśo 'dhyāyaḥ

This is the seventeenth chapter entitled The Yoga of the Threefold Division of Faith

CHAPTER XVIII

Conclusion

Renunciation is to be practised not towards Work but to the Fruits of Work

arjuna uvāca

1. *saṁnyāsasya mahābāho*
tattvam icchāmi veditum
tyāgasya ca hṛṣīkeśa
pṛthak keśiniṣūdana

Arjuna said:

(1) I desire, O Mighty-armed (Kṛṣṇa), to know the true nature of renunciation and of relinquishment, O Hṛṣīkeśa (Kṛṣṇa), severally, O Keśiniṣūdana (Kṛṣṇa).

The *Gītā* insists not on renunciation of action but on action with renunciation of desire. This is true saṁnyāsa. In this verse, saṁnyāsa is used for the renunciation of all works and tyāga for the renunciation of the fruits of all works. Not by karma, not by progeny or wealth but by tyāga or relinquishment is release obtained.[1]

The *Gītā* urges that the liberated soul can remain in service even after liberation and is opposed to the view which holds that, as all action springs from ignorance, when wisdom arises, action ceases. The teacher of the *Gītā* considers the view, that he who acts is in bondage and he who is free cannot act, to be incorrect.

śrībhagavān uvāca

2. *kāmyānāṁ karmaṇāṁ nyāsaṁ*
saṁnyāsaṁ kavayo viduḥ
sarvakarmaphalatyāgaṁ
prāhus tyāgaṁ vicakṣaṇāḥ

The Blessed Lord said:

(2) The wise understand by "renunciation" the giving up

[1] *na karmaṇā na prajayā dhanena tyāgen aike amṛtatvam ānaśuḥ.*

of works prompted by desire: the abandonment of the fruits of all works, the learned declare, is relinquishment.

Inertia or non-action is not the ideal. Action without any selfish desire or expectation of gain, performed in the spirit that "I am not the doer, I am surrendering myself to the Universal Self" is the ideal set before us. The *Gītā* does not teach the complete renunciation of works but the conversion of all works into *niṣkāma karma* or desireless action.

Ś., however, contends that tyāga as taught here is applicable only to karmayogins, while for jñānins complete abandonment of works is imperative. He holds that knowledge is incompatible with work.

3. *tyājyaṁ doṣavad ity eke*
karma prāhur manīṣiṇaḥ
yajñadānatapaḥkarma
na tyājyam iti cā 'pare

(3) 'Action should be given up as an evil,' say some learned men: others declare that 'acts of sacrifice, gift and penance are not to be given up.'

4. *niścayaṁ śṛṇu me tatra*
tyāge bharatasattama
tyāgo hi puruṣavyāghra
trividhaḥ saṁprakīrtitaḥ

(4) Hear now from Me, O Best of the Bharatas (Arjuna), the truth about relinquishment: relinquishment, O Best of men (Arjuna), has been explained as threefold.

R. divides relinquishment into (1) relinquishment of fruit, (2) relinquishment of the idea that the self is the agent and so of attachment also, and (3) relinquishment of all idea of agency with the realization that the Lord is the author of all action.

5. *yajñadānatapaḥkarma*
na tyājyaṁ kāryam eva tat
yajño dānaṁ tapaś cai 'va
pāvanāni manīṣiṇām

(5) Acts of sacrifice, gift and penance are not to be relinquished but should be performed. For sacrifice, gift and penance are purifiers of the wise.

Against the view that all action should be abandoned, since it leads to bondage, the *Gītā* asserts that sacrifice, gift and penance[1] should not be abandoned.

6. *etāny api tu karmāṇi*
saṅgaṁ tyaktvā phalāni ca
kartavyānī 'ti me pārtha
niścitaṁ matam uttamam

(6) But even these works ought to be performed, giving up attachment and desire for fruits. This, O Pārtha (Arjuna), is my decided and final view.

The teacher is decidedly for the practice of Karmayoga. Actions are not to be set aside: only they have to be done without selfish attachment or expectation of rewards. Salvation is not a matter of outward action or inaction. It is the possession of the impersonal outlook and inner renunciation of ego.

Ś.'s observation that this does not refer to the devotees of wisdom who renounce all works (*jñānaniṣṭhāḥ sarvakarma-saṁnyāsinaḥ*) is not borne out by the text. Cp. *Bṛhadāraṇyaka Up*, IV, 4, 22. "It is the Brahman whom the Brahmins wish to know by the study of the Vedas, and also by means of sacrifice, gift, and austerities performed without attachment."

7. *niyatasya tu saṁnyāsaḥ*
karmaṇo no 'papadyate
mohāt tasya parityāgas
tāmasaḥ parikīrtitaḥ

(7) Verily the renunciation of any duty that ought to be done is not right. The abandonment of it through ignorance is declared to be of the nature of "dullness."

8. *duḥkham ity eva yat karma*
kāyakleśabhayāt tyajet
sa kṛtvā rājasaṁ tyāgaṁ
nai 'va tyāgaphalaṁ labhet

[1] Cp. *trayo dharmaskandhā yajña tapo dānam iti.*

(8) He who gives up a duty because it is painful or from fear of physical suffering, performs only the relinquishment of the "passionate" kind and does not gain the reward of relinquishment.

9. *kāryam ity eva yat karma*
niyataṁ kriyate 'rjuna
saṅgaṁ tyaktvā phalaṁ cai 'va
sa tyāgaḥ sāttviko mataḥ

(9) But he who performs a prescribed duty as a thing that ought to be done, renouncing all attachment and also the fruit—his relinquishment is regarded as one of "goodness."

What ought to be done is what is in harmony with the cosmic purpose.

10. *na dveṣṭy akuśalaṁ karma*
kuśale nā 'nuṣajjate
tyāgī sattvasamāviṣṭo
medhāvī chinnasaṁśayaḥ

(10) The wise man, who renounces, whose doubts are dispelled, whose nature is of goodness, has no aversion to disagreeable action and no attachment to agreeable action.

11. *na hi dehabhṛtā śakyaṁ*
tyaktuṁ karmāṇy aśeṣataḥ
yas tu karmaphalatyāgī
sa tyāgī 'ty abhidhīyate

(11) It is indeed impossible for any embodied being to abstain from work altogether. But he who gives up the fruit of action, he is said to be the relinquisher.

12. *aniṣṭam iṣṭaṁ miśraṁ ca*
trividhaṁ karmaṇaḥ phalam
bhavaty atyāgināṁ pretya
na tu saṁnyāsināṁ kvacit

(12) Pleasant, unpleasant and mixed—threefold is the fruit of action accruing after death to those who have not relin-

quished: there is none whatever for those who have renounced.

Ś. considers atyāgins to be karmayogins and saṁnyāsins to be those who have renounced all work except that which is essential for the maintenance of the body.

Work is a Function of Nature

13. *pañcai 'tāni mahābāho*
kāraṇāni nibodha me
sāṁkhye kṛtānte proktāni
siddhaye sarvakarmaṇām

(13) O Mighty-armed (Arjuna), learn of Me, these five factors, for the accomplishment of all actions, as stated in the Sāṁkhya doctrine.

Sāṁkhya here means the Vedānta. Ś.
kṛtānte is interpreted as the end of the kṛta age, that is, as taught in the original Sāṁkhya.

14. *adhiṣṭhānaṁ tathā kartā*
karaṇaṁ ca pṛthagvidham
vividhāś ca pṛthakceṣṭā
daivaṁ cai 'vā 'tra pañcamam

(14) The seat of action and likewise the agent, the instruments of various sorts, the many kinds of efforts and providence being the fifth.

adhiṣṭhāna or the seat refers to the physical body.
kartā: agent. He is, according to Ś., the phenomenal ego, *upādhilakṣaṇo avidyākalpito bhoktā*, the psychophysical self which mistakes the organism for the true self; for R. it is the individual self, the jīvātman; for Madhva, it is the supreme Lord Viṣṇu.

The kartā or the agent is one of the five causes of action. According to the Sāṁkhya doctrine, puruṣa or the self is a mere witness. Though, strictly speaking, the self is akartṛ or non-doer, still its witnessing starts the activities of prakṛti and so the self is included among the determining causes

cheṣṭā: efforts: functions of the vital energies within the body.

daivam: providence: represents the non-human factor that interferes and disposes of human effort. It is the wise, all-seeing will that is at work in the world. In all human actions, there is an unaccountable element which is called luck, destiny, fate or the force accumulated by the acts of one's past lives. It is called here daiva.[1] The task of man is to drop a pebble into the pond of time and we may not see the ripple touch the distant shore. We may plant the seed but may not see the harvest which lies in hands higher than our own. Daiva or the superpersonal fate is the general cosmic necessity, the resultant of all that has happened in the past, which rules unnoticed. It works in the individual for its own incalculable purposes.

Belief in daiva should not be an excuse for quiescence. Man is a term of transition. He is conscious of his aim, to rise from his animal ancestry to the divine ideal. The pressure of nature, heredity and environment can be overcome by the will of man.

15. *śarīravāṅmanobhir yat*
karma prārabhate naraḥ
nyāyyaṁ vā viparītaṁ vā
pañcai 'te tasya hetavaḥ

(15) Whatever action a man undertakes by his body, speech or mind, whether it is right or wrong, these five are its factors.

16. *tatrai 'vaṁ sati kartāram*
ātmānaṁ kevalaṁ tu yaḥ
paśyaty akṛtabuddhitvān
na sa paśyati durmatiḥ

(16) Such being the case, the man of perverse mind who, on account of his untrained understanding, looks upon himself as the sole agent, he does not see (truly).

The agent is one factor among five and so he misapprehends the facts when he looks upon the agent as the sole cause.

Ś. reads "looks on the pure self as the doer." If he attributes agency to the pure self, he misapprehends the facts. The ego is generally taken to be the doer but it is only one of the main

[1] Cp. *pūrvajanmakṛtaṁkarma tad daivam iti kathyate. Hitopadeśa.*

determinants of human action, which are all the products of nature. When the ego is recognized as such, we are freed from its binding influence and we live in the greater knowledge of the Universal Self, and in that self-vision all acts are the products of prakṛti.

17. *yasya nā 'haṁkṛto bhāvo*
buddhir yasya na lipyate
hatvā 'pi sa imāṁl lokān
na hanti na nibadhyate

(17) He who is free from self-sense, whose understanding is not sullied, though he slay these people, he slays not nor is he bound (by his actions).

The freed man does his work as the instrument of the Universal Spirit and for the maintenance of the cosmic order. He performs even terrific deeds without any selfish aim or desire but because it is the ordained duty. What matters is not the work but the spirit in which it is done. "Though he slays from the worldly standpoint, he does not slay in truth." Ś.[1]

This passage does not mean that we can commit crimes with impunity. He who lives in the large spiritual consciousness will not feel any need to do any wrong. Evil activities spring from ignorance and separatist consciousness and from consciousness of unity with the Supreme Self, only good can result.

Knowledge and Action

18. *jñānaṁ jñeyaṁ parijñātā*
trividhā karmacodanā
karaṇaṁ karma karte 'ti
trividhaḥ karmasaṁgrahaḥ

(18) Knowledge, the object of knowledge and the knowing subject, are the threefold incitement to action: the instrument, the action and the agent are the threefold composite of action.

See XIII, 20.

[1] *laukikīṁ dṛṣṭim āśritya hatvāpi . . . pāramārthikīṁ dṛṣṭim āśritya na hanti.*

Karmacodanā refers to the mental planning and karma-saṁgraha to the actual execution of the action and each has three aspects.

19. *jñānaṁ karma ca kartā ca*
tridhai 'va guṇabhedataḥ
procyate guṇasaṁkhyāne
yathāvac chṛṇu tāny api

(19) Knowledge, action and the agent are said, in the science of modes, to be of three kinds only, according to difference in the modes. Hear thou duly of these also.

The Sāṁkhya system is referred to and it is authoritative in some matters though not in regard to the highest truth.

Three Kinds of Knowledge

20. *sarvabhūteṣu yenai 'kaṁ*
bhāvam avyayam īkṣate
avibhaktaṁ vibhakteṣu
taj jñānaṁ viddhi sāttvikam

(20) The knowledge by which the one Imperishable Being is seen in all existences, undivided in the divided, know that that knowledge is of "goodness."

21. *pṛthaktvena tu yaj jñānaṁ*
nānābhāvān pṛthagvidhān
vetti sarveṣu bhūteṣu
taj jñānaṁ viddhi rājasam

(21) The knowledge which sees multiplicity of beings in the different creatures, by reason of their separateness, know that that knowledge is of the nature of "passion."

22. *yat tu kṛtsnavad ekasmin*
kārye saktam ahetukam
atattvārthavad alpaṁ ca
tat tāmasam udāhṛtam

(22) But that which clings to one single effect as if it were the whole, without concern for the cause, without grasping the real, and narrow is declared to be of the nature of "dullness."

Three Kinds of Work

23. *niyataṁ saṅgarahitam*
arāgadveṣataḥ kṛtam
aphalaprepsunā karma
yat tat sāttvikam ucyate

(23) An action which is obligatory, which is performed without attachment, without love or hate by one undesirous of fruit, that is said to be of "goodness."

24. *yat tu kāmepsunā karma*
sāhaṁkāreṇa vā punaḥ
kriyate bahulāyāsaṁ
tad rājasam udāhṛtam

(24) But that action which is done in great strain by one who seeks to gratify his desires or is impelled by self-sense, is said to be of the nature of "passion."

bahulāyāsam: with great strain.

The consciousness of suffering, the sense that we are doing something disagreeable, that we are passing through grim suffering and toil takes away from the value of the act. To feel consciously that we are doing something great, that we are sacrificing something vital is a failure of the sacrifice itself. But when the work is undertaken for the cause, it is a labour of love and sacrifice itself is not felt as a sacrifice. Doing unpleasant things from a sense of duty, feeling the unpleasantness all the time is of the nature of "passion," but doing it gladly in utter unself-consciousness, with a smile on the lips, as Socrates drank hemlock, is of the nature of "goodness." It is the difference between an act of love and an act of law, an act of grace and an act of obligation.

25. *anubandhaṁ kṣayaṁ hiṁsām*
anapekṣya ca pauruṣam
mohād ārabhyate karma
yat tat tāmasam ucyate

(25) The action which is undertaken through ignorance, without regard to consequences or to loss and injury and without regard to one's human capacity, that is said to be of "dullness."

The effects of actions on others must always be considered; only selfish aims are to be renounced.

Three Kinds of Doer

26. *muktasaṅgo 'nahaṁvādī*
dhṛtyutsāhasamanvitaḥ
siddhyasiddhyor nirvikāraḥ
kartā sāttvika ucyate

(26) The doer who is free from attachment, who has no speech of egotism, full of resolution and zeal and who is unmoved by success or failure—he is said to be of the nature of "goodness"

27. *rāgī karmaphalaprèpsur*
lubdho hiṁsātmako 'śuciḥ
harṣaśokānvitaḥ kartā
rājasaḥ parikīrtitaḥ

(27) The doer who is swayed by passion, who eagerly seeks the fruit of his works, who is greedy, of harmful nature, impure, who is moved by joy and sorrow—he is said to be of "passionate" nature.

28. *ayuktaḥ prākṛtaḥ stabdhaḥ*
śaṭho naikṛtiko 'lasaḥ
viṣādī dīrghasūtrī ca
kartā tāmasa ucyate

(28) The doer who is unbalanced, vulgar, obstinate, deceitful, malicious, indolent, despondent and procrastinating, he is said to be of the nature of "dullness."

prākṛtaḥ: "quite uncultured in intellect and like a child." Ś.

Three Kinds of Understanding

29. *buddher bhedaṁ dhṛteś cai 'va*
guṇatas trividhaṁ śṛṇu
procyamānam aśeṣeṇa
pṛthaktvena dhanaṁjaya

(29) Hear now the threefold distinction of understanding as also of steadiness, O winner of wealth (Arjuna), according to the modes, to be set forth fully and separately.

30. *pravṛttiṁ ca nivṛttiṁ ca*
kāryākārye bhayābhaye
bandhaṁ mokṣaṁ ca yā vetti
buddhiḥ sā pārtha sāttvikī

(30) The understanding which knows action and non-action, what ought to be done and what ought not to be done, what is to be feared and what is not to be feared, what binds and what frees the soul (that understanding), O Pārtha (Arjuna), is of the nature of "goodness."

31. *yayā dharmam adharmaṁ ca*
kāryaṁ cā 'kāryam eva ca
ayathāvat prajānāti
buddhiḥ sā pārtha rājasī

(31) That by which one knows in a mistaken way the right and the wrong, what ought to be done and what ought not to be done—that understanding, O Pārtha (Arjuna), is of the nature of "passion."

32. *adharmaṁ dharmam iti yā*
manyate tamasā 'vṛtā
sarvārthān viparītāṁś ca
buddhiḥ sā pārtha tāmasī

(32) That which, enveloped in darkness, conceives as right what is wrong and sees all things in a perverted way (contrary to the truth), that understanding, O Pārtha (Arjuna), is of the nature of "dullness."

Three Kinds of Steadiness

33. *dhṛtyā yayā dhārayate*
manaḥprāṇendriyakriyāḥ
yogenā 'vyabhicāriṇyā
dhṛtiḥ sā pārtha sāttvikī

(33) The unwavering steadiness by which, through concentration, one controls the activities of the mind, the life breaths and the senses, that, O Pārtha (Arjuna), is of the nature of "goodness."

dhṛtiḥ: steadiness of attention which makes us aware of much that our ordinary vision is not able to observe. Its power is proportional to our detachment from regrets over the past and anxieties for the future.

34. *yayā tu dharmakāmārthān*
dhṛtyā dhārayate 'rjuna
prasaṅgena phalākāṅkṣī
dhṛtiḥ sā pārtha rājasī

(34) The steadiness by which one holds fast to duty, pleasure and wealth desiring the fruit in consequence thereof—that, O Pārtha (Arjuna), is of the nature of "passion."

35. *yayā svapnaṁ bhayaṁ śokaṁ*
viṣādaṁ madam eva ca
na vimuñcati durmedhā
dhṛtiḥ sā pārtha tāmasī

(35) That steadiness by which a fool does not give up sleep, fear, grief, depression and arrogance, that, O Pārtha (Arjuna), is of the nature of dullness.

Three Kinds of Happiness

36. *sukhaṁ tv idānīṁ trividhaṁ*
śṛṇu me bharatarṣabha
abhyāsād ramate yatra
duhkhāntaṁ ca nigacchati

(36) And now hear from Me, O Best of the Bharatas (Arjuna), the three kinds of happiness. That in which a man comes to rejoice by long practice and in which he reaches the end of his sorrow.

37. *yat tad agre viṣaṁ iva*
pariṇāme 'mṛtopamam
tat sukhaṁ sāttvikaṁ proktam
ātmabuddhiprasādajam

(37) That happiness which is like poison at first and like nectar at the end, which springs from a clear understanding of the Self is said to be of the nature of "goodness."

38. *viṣayendriyasaṁyogād*
yat tad agre 'mṛtopamam
pariṇāme viṣam iva
tat sukhaṁ rājasaṁ smṛtam

(38) That happiness which arises from the contact of the senses and their objects and which is like nectar at first but like poison at the end—such happiness is recorded to be "passionate."

39. *yad agre cā 'nubandhe ca*
sukhaṁ mohanam ātmanaḥ
nidrālasyapramādotthaṁ
tat tāmasam udāhṛtam

(39) That happiness which deludes the soul both at the beginning and at the end and which arises from sleep, sloth and negligence—that is declared to be of the nature of "dullness."

Happiness is the universal aim of life. Only it is of different kinds according to the modes which dominate our nature. If the tamas predominates in us, we are satisfied with violence and inertia, blindness and error. If rajas prevails, wealth and power, pride and glory give us happiness. True happiness of human beings lies not in the possession of outward things but in the fulfilment of the higher mind and spirit, in the development of what is most inward in us. It may mean pain and restraint but it will lead us to joy and freedom. We can pass from the happiness of knowledge and virtue to the eternal calm and joy, ānanda of the spirit, when we become one with the Highest Self and one with all beings.

Various Duties determined by One's Nature (Svabhāva) and Station (Svadharma)

40. *na tad asti pṛthivyāṁ vā*
divi deveṣu vā punaḥ
sattvaṁ prakṛtijair muktaṁ
yad ebhiḥ syāt tribhir guṇaiḥ

(40) There is no creature either on earth or again among the gods in heaven, which is free from the three modes born of nature.

41. *brāhmaṇakṣatriyaviśāṁ*
śūdrāṇāṁ ca paraṁtapa
karmāṇi pravibhaktāni
svabhāvaprabhavair guṇaiḥ

(41) Of Brāhmins, of Kṣatriyas, and Vaiśyas as also of Śūdras, O Conqueror of the foe (Arjuna), the activities are distinguished, in accordance with the qualities born of their nature.

The fourfold order is not peculiar to Hindu society. It is of universal application. The classification depends on types of human nature. Each of the four classes has certain well-defined characteristics though they are not to be regarded as exclusive. These are not determined always by heredity.

The *Gītā* cannot be used to support the existing social order with its rigidity and confusion. It takes up the theory of the four orders and enlarges its scope and meaning. Man's outward life must express his inward being; the surface must reflect the profundity. Each individual has his inborn nature, svabhāva, and to make it effective in his life is his duty, svadharma. Each individual is a focus of the Supreme, a fragment of the Divine. His destiny is to bring out in his life this divine possibility. The one Spirit of the universe has produced the multiplicity of souls in the world, but the idea of the Divine is our essential nature, the truth of our being, our svabhāva, and not the apparatus of the guṇas, which is only the medium for expression. If each individual does what is appropriate to him, if he follows the law of his being, his svadharma, then God would express Himself in the free volitions of human beings. All that is essential for the world will be done without a conflict. But men rarely do what they ought to do. When they undertake to determine events believing that they know the plan of the whole, they work mischief on earth. So long as our work is done in accordance with our nature, we are righteous, and if we dedicate it to God, our work becomes a means of spiritual perfection. When the divine in the individual is completely manifested, he attains the eternal imperishable status, *śāsvataṁ padam avyayam.*[1] The problem that human life sets to us is to discover our true self and live according to its truth; otherwise we would sin against our nature. The emphasis on svabhāva indicates that human beings are to be treated as individuals and not as types. Arjuna is told that he who fights gallantly as a warrior becomes mature for the peace of wisdom.

There are four broad types of nature and answering to them are four kinds of social living. The four classes are not determined by birth or colour but by psychological characteristics which fit us for definite functions in society.

42. *śamo damas tapaḥ śaucaṁ*
kṣāntir ārjavam eva ca
jñānaṁ vijñānam āstikyaṁ
brahmakarma svabhāvajam

(42) Serenity, self-control, austerity, purity, forbearance and uprightness, wisdom, knowledge and faith in religion, these are the duties of the Brāhmin, born of his nature.

Those who belong to the order of Brahminhood are expected to possess mental and moral qualities. Cp. *Dhammapada*, 393: "Not by matted hair, nor by lineage, nor by birth is one a Brāhmin. He is a Brāhmin in whom there are truth and righteousness." Power corrupts and blinds insight. Uncontrolled power is fatal to mental poise. So the Brāhmins eschew direct power

[1] XVIII, 56.

and exercise a general control through persuasion and love and save the wielders of power from going astray.

43. *śauryaṁ tejo dhṛtir dākṣyaṁ*
yuddhe cā 'py apalāyanam
dānam īśvarabhāvaś ca
kṣātraṁ karma svabhāvajam

(43) Heroism, vigour, steadiness, resourcefulness, not fleeing even in a battle, generosity and leadership, these are the duties of a Kṣatriya born of his nature.

Though the Kṣatriyas cannot claim to be spiritual leaders, they have the qualities which enable them to adapt spiritual truths to the requirements of action.

44. *kṛṣigaurakṣyavāṇijyaṁ*
vaiśyakarma svabhāvajam
paricaryātmakaṁ karma
śūdrasyā 'pi svabhāvajam

(44) Agriculture, tending cattle and trade are the duties of a Vaiśya born of his nature; work of the character of service is the duty of a Śūdra born of his nature.

It is not a question of *identical* opportunities for all men to rise to the highest station in social life, for men differ in their powers, but a question of giving *equal* opportunities for all so that they may bring their respective gifts to fruition. Each one should have the opportunity of achieving his human fullness, the fruits of wisdom and virtue, according to his effort and condition. It makes little difference whether we dig the earth or do business or govern a state or meditate in a cell. The varṇa rules recognize that different men contribute to the general good in different ways, by supplying directly urgent wants of which all are conscious and by being in their lives and work witnesses to truth and beauty. Society is a functional organization and all functions which are essential for the health of society are to be regarded as socially equal. Individuals of varying capacities are bound together in a living organic social system. Democracy is not an attempt at uniformity which is impossible but at an integrated variety. All men are not equal in their capacities but all men are equally necessary for society, and their contributions from their different stations are of equal value.[1]

45. *sve-sve karmaṇy abhirataḥ*
saṁsiddhiṁ labhate naraḥ
svakarmanirataḥ siddhiṁ
yathā vindati tac chṛṇu

(45) Devoted each to his own duty man attains perfection. How one, devoted to one's own duty, attains perfection, that do thou hear.

svesve karmaṇy abhirataḥ: devoted each to his own duty. Each of us should be loyal at our level to our feelings and impulses; it is dangerous to attempt work beyond the level of our nature, our svabhāva. Within the power of our nature, we must live up fully to our duty.

46. *yataḥ pravṛttir bhūtānāṁ*
yena sarvam idaṁ tatam
svakarmaṇā tam abhyarcya
siddhiṁ vindati mānavaḥ

[1] Mr. Gerald Heard in his book on *Man the Master* (1942) emphasizes the need for a "quadritype organization of society." He writes: "It would seem then, that there have always been present in human community four types or strata of consciousness. We have already spoken of the first level. These are the eyes or antennae, the emergent seers and sensitives. . . . Below the eyes are the hands; behind the forebrain are the motor centres. The two mental classes below the seers, the upper and lower middle classes, the politician and the technician—it is to them that is mainly due our present crisis. The one by its great advances in administration, in social instruments, has made it possible for the monster states to exist—and so for their unresolved internal stresses to become more acute. The other, by its even greater technical advances in plant, in power machinery, in material instruments has made our societies hypertrophies—organisms of unbalanced internal structure and mutually deadly. Besides the two middle classes already made unstable and disruptive by their becoming individualized, there remained the basic, unspecialized, unquestioning class or mass—the coherers. This class is not only capable of faith: it will not hold together, it will not live without it" (pp. 133–7). Mr. Heard reminds us that "the Aryan–Sanskrit sociological thought, which first defined and named this fourfold structure of society, is as much ours as India's" (p. 145).

(46) He from whom all beings arise and by whom all this is pervaded—by worshipping Him through the performance of his own duty does man attain perfection.

Work is worship of the Supreme, man's homage to God.

The *Gītā* holds that quality and capacity are the basis of functional divisions. Accepting the theory of rebirth, it holds that a man's inborn nature is determined by his own past lives. All forms of perfection do not lie in the same direction. Each one aims at something beyond himself, at self-transcendence, whether he strives after personal perfection, or lives for art or works for one's fellows. See also XVIII, 48 and 60.

47. *śreyān svadharmo viguṇaḥ*
paradharmāt svanuṣṭhitāt
svabhāvaniyataṁ karma
kurvan nā 'pnoti kilbiṣam

(47) Better is one's own law though imperfectly carried out than the law of another carried out perfectly. One does not incur sin when one does the duty ordained by one's own nature.

See III, 35. It is no use employing our minds in tasks which are alien to our nature. In each of us lies a principle of becoming, an idea of divine self-expression. It is our real nature, svabhāva, finding partial expression in our various activities. By following its guidance in our thought, aspiration and endeavour, we progressively realize the intention of the Spirit for us. What we call democracy is a way of life which requires us to respect the rights of every human being to be a person, a unique entity. We should never despise any man, for he can do something which others cannot.

48. *sahajaṁ karma kaunteya*
sadoṣam api na tyajet
sarvārambhā hi doṣeṇa
dhūmenā 'gnir ivā 'vṛtāḥ

(48) One should not give up the work suited to one's nature, O Son of Kuntī (Arjuna), though it may be defective, for all enterprises are clouded by defects as fire by smoke.

Karma Yoga and Absolute Perfection

49. *asaktabuddhiḥ sarvatra*
jitātmā vigataspṛhaḥ
naiṣkarmyasiddhiṁ paramāṁ
saṁnyāsenā 'dhigacchati

(49) He whose understanding is unattached everywhere, who has subdued his self and from whom desire has fled—he comes through renunciation to the supreme state transcending all work.

The *Gītā* repeats that restraint and freedom from desire are essential to spiritual perfection. Attachment to objects, a sense of ego, are the characteristics of our lower nature. If we are to rise to a knowledge of our true self, self-possessed and self-luminous, we must conquer our lower nature with its ignorance and inertia, its love of worldly possessions, etc.

naiṣkarmya: the state transcending all work. It is not a complete withdrawal from all work. Such a quietism is not possible so long as we live in the body. The *Gītā* insists on inner renunciation. As the ego and nature are akin, the liberated soul becoming Brahman, the Pure Self described as silent, calm, inactive, acts in the world of prakṛti, knowing what the latter is.

The highest state is here described, not positively as entering into the Lord but negatively as freedom from kāma.

Perfection and Brahman

50. *siddhiṁ prāpto yathā brahma*
tathā 'pnoti nibodha me
samāsenai 'va kaunteya
niṣṭhā jñānasya yā parā

(50) Hear from me, in brief, O Son of Kuntī (Arjuna), how, having attained perfection, he attains to the Brahman, that supreme consummation of wisdom.

Ś. writes: "Though thus quite self-evident, easily knowable, quite near and forming the very self, Brahman appears—to the unenlightened, to those whose understanding is carried away by the differentiated phenomena of names and forms created by ignorance, as unknown, difficult to know, very remote, as though he were a separate thing."[1] As there is no need of evidence for knowing one's own body, even so there is no need of evidence for knowing the self which is nearer than the body. When we turn away from the outward and train our understanding, it is immediately comprehended. See IX, 2.

51. *buddhyā viśuddhayā yukto*
dhṛtyā 'tmānaṁ niyamya ca
śabdādīn viṣayāṁs tyaktvā
rāgadveṣau vyudasya ca

(51) Endowed with a pure understanding, firmly restraining oneself, turning away from sound and other objects of sense and casting aside attraction and aversion.

52. *viviktasevī laghvāśī*
yatavākkāyamānasaḥ
dhyānayogaparo nityaṁ
vairāgyaṁ samupāśritaḥ

(52) Dwelling in solitude, eating but little, controlling speech, body and mind, and ever engaged in meditation and concentration and taking refuge in dispassion.

Dhyānayoga is taken as a dvandva compound meaning "meditation on the nature of the self and mental concentration thereon." Ś.

53. *ahaṁkāraṁ balaṁ darpaṁ*
kāmaṁ krodhaṁ parigraham
vimucya nirmamaḥ śānto
brahmabhūyāya kalpate

(53) And casting aside self-sense, force, arrogance, desire, anger, possession, egoless and tranquil in mind, he becomes worthy of becoming one with Brahman.

[1] *avidyākalpitanāmarūpaviśeṣākārāpahṛtabuddhīnām, atyantaprasiddhaṁ, suvijñeyam, āsannataram, ātmabhūtam apy, aprasiddhaṁ, durvijñeyam, atidūram, anyad iva ca pratibhāty avivekinām.*"

Aṭṭār quotes a saying of Ibrāhim Adham: "Three veils must be removed from before the pilgrim's heart ere the door of Happiness is opened to him. First, that, should the dominion of both worlds be offered to him as an eternal gift, he should not rejoice, since whosoever rejoiceth on account of any created thing is still covetous, and the covetous man is debarred from the knowledge of God. The second veil is this, that, should he possess the dominion of both worlds, and should it be taken from him, he should not sorrow for his impoverishment, for this is the sign of wrath and he who is in wrath is tormented. The third is that he should not be beguiled by any praise or favour, for whosoever is so beguiled is of mean spirit, and such a one is veiled (from the Truth): the pilgrim must be high-minded." Browne: *A Literary History of Persia*, Vol. I (1902), p. 425.

The Highest Devotion

54. *brahmabhūtaḥ prasannātmā*
na śocati na kāṅkṣati
samaḥ sarveṣu bhūteṣu
madbhaktiṁ labhate paraṁ

(54) Having become one with Brahman, and being tranquil in spirit, he neither grieves nor desires. Regarding all beings as alike he attains supreme devotion to Me.

This verse is another indication that, for the *Gītā*, disappearance of the individual in a featureless Absolute is not the highest state but devotion to the Supreme Lord who combines in Himself the immobile and the mobile.

55. *bhaktyā mām abhijānāti*
yāvān yaś cā 'smi tattvataḥ
tato māṁ tattvato jñātvā
viśate tadanantaram

(55) Through devotion he comes to know Me, what My measure is and who I am in truth; then, having known Me in truth, he forthwith enters into Me.

The knower, the devotee, becomes one with the Supreme Lord, the Perfect Person, in self-knowledge and self-experience, Jñāna, supreme wisdom and bhakti, supreme devotion have the same goal. To become Brahman is to love God, to know Him fully and to enter into His being.

Application of the Teaching to Arjuna's Case

56. *sarvakarmāṇy api sadā*
kurvāṇo madvyapāśrayaḥ
matprasādād avāpnoti
śāśvataṁ padam avyayam

(56) Doing continually all actions whatsoever, taking refuge in Me, he reaches by My grace the eternal, undying abode.

It is also the goal of karmamārga. In these three verses, the author indicates that wisdom, devotion and work go together. Only the work is done with the knowledge that nature or prakṛti is the power of the Divine and the individual is only an instrument of God. With his heart fixed on the Eternal and through His grace, whatever he does, he dwells eternally within the Great Abode.

57. *cetasā sarvakarmāṇi*
mayi saṁnyasya matparaḥ
buddhiyogam upāśritya
maccittaḥ satataṁ bhava

(57) Surrendering in thought all actions to Me, regarding Me as the Supreme and resorting to steadfastness in understanding, do thou fix thy thought constantly on Me.

"Be always one with Me in heart, will and consciousness." A perfect self-giving to the Universal Lord makes Him the spirit of our life.

58. *maccittaḥ sarvadurgāṇi*
matprasādāt tariṣyasi
atha cet tvam ahaṁkārān
na śroṣyasi vinaṅkṣyasi

(58) Fixing thy thought on Me, thou shalt, by My grace cross over all difficulties; but if, from self-conceit, thou wil not listen (to Me), thou shalt perish.

Man is free to choose salvation or perdition. If we fondly believe that we can resist the will of the Almighty, we will come to grief. Defiance of God is due to self-sense (ahaṁkāra) and it is powerless ultimately.

59. *yad ahaṁkāram āśritya*
na yotsya iti manyase
mithyai 'ṣa vyavasāyas te
prakṛtis tvāṁ niyokṣyati

(59) If indulging in self-conceit, thou thinkest "I will not fight," vain is this, thy resolve. Nature will compel thee.

The desire 'not to fight" will only be the expression of his surface nature: his deeper being will lead him to fight. If he casts down his arms for fear of suffering and holds back from the fight, and if the war proceeds without him, and he realizes that the consequences of his abstention would be disastrous to humanity, he will be impelled to take up arms by the remorseless pressure of the Cosmic Spirit. He should try therefore to further and co-operate with the cosmic evolution instead of denying and opposing it. If he does so, he will change from an essentially determined to a determining factor. It is Arjuna's lower nature that will cause the confusion and the fall from the greater truth of his being. Now Arjuna has seen the truth and he can act, not for selfish ends, but as a conscious instrument of the Divine. The disciple must put aside all selfish fear and obey his Inner Light which will carry him past all dangers and obstacles.

God lays down the conditions and it is for us to accept them. We should not waste our strength in fighting against the stream. Most of us are natural men, eager, impulsive and definite about our own little schemes, but we must change. The way in which we can be most useful is by submission to God's choice. St. Francis de Sales' favourite prayer sums up this spirit of total subordination: 'Yes, Father! yes, and always Yes!"

60. *svabhāvajena kaunteya*
nibaddhaḥ svena karmaṇā
kartuṁ ne 'cchasi yan mohāt
kariṣyasy avaśo 'pi tat

(60) That which, through delusion, thou wishest not to do, O son of Kuntī (Arjuna), that thou shalt do even against thy will, fettered by thy own acts born of thy nature.

You will be driven to do it by the compulsive power of your nature.

61. *īśvaraḥ sarvabhūtānāṁ*
hṛddeśe 'rjuna tiṣṭhati
bhrāmayan sarvabhūtāni
yantrārūḍhāni māyayā

(61) The Lord abides in the hearts of all beings, O Arjuna, causing them to turn round by His power as if they were mounted on a machine.

The relations of our unborn nature and its fateful compulsion are regulated by the Divine who dwells in our hearts and guides and constrains our development. The power that determines events is not, as in Hardy, a blind, unfeeling, unthinking will to which we give the name of "Fate," "Destiny," or "Chance."[1] The Spirit that rules the cosmos, the Lord who presides over the evolution of the cosmic plan, is seated also in the heart of every being and will not let him rest. "Without Thee we cannot live for a moment. As the truth Thou dost exist eternally within and without."[2]

The Supreme is the inmost self of our existence. All life is a movement of the rhythm of His life and our powers and acts are all derived from Him. If, in our ignorance, we forget this deepest truth, the truth does not alter. If we live consciously in His truth, we will resign all actions to God and escape from our ego. If we do not, even then the truth will prevail. Sooner or later we will yield to the purpose of God but in the meanwhile there is no compulsion. The Supreme desires our free co-operation when beauty and goodness are born without travail and effortlessly. When we become transparent media for the light of God, He uses us for His work.

[1] Like a knitter drowsed,
Whose fingers play in skilled unmindfulness
The will has woven with an absent heed
Since life first was, and ever will so weave.

[2] *tvāṁ vihāya na śaknomi jīvituṁ kṣaṇam eva hi*
antar bahis' ca nityaṁ tvaṁ satyarūpeṇa vartase.

62. *tam eva śaraṇaṁ gaccha*
sarvabhāvena bhārata
tatprasādāt parāṁ śāntiṁ
sthānaṁ prāpsyasi śāśvatam

(62) Flee unto Him for shelter with all thy being, O Bhārata (Arjuna). By His grace shalt thou obtain supreme peace and eternal abode.

sarvabhāvena: with all thy being. We must grow conscious of the Divine on all the planes of our being. The love of Rādhā for Kṛṣṇa is the symbol of integral love in all planes of being from the spiritual to the physical.

Arjuna is called upon to co-operate with God and do his duty. He must change the whole orientation of his being. He must put himself at the service of the Supreme. His illusion will then be dispelled, the bond of cause and consequence will be broken and he will attain shadowless light, perfect harmony and supreme blessedness.

63. *iti te jñānam ākhyātaṁ*
guhyād guhyataraṁ mayā
vimṛśyai 'tad aśeṣeṇa
yathe 'cchasi tathā kuru

(63) Thus has wisdom more secret than all secrets, been declared to thee by Me. Reflect on it fully and do as thou choosest.

vimṛśyaitad aśeṣeṇa: reflect on it fully. We must use our intelligence,[1] exercise our discrimination.

yathā icchasi tathā kuru: do as thou choosest. God is seemingly indifferent, for He leaves the decision to Arjuna's choice. His apparent indifference is due to His anxiety that each one of us should get to Him of his own free choice. He constrains no one since free spontaneity is valuable. Man is to be wooed and not coerced into co-operation. He is to be drawn, not driven, persuaded, not compelled. The Supreme does not impose His command. We are free at any moment to reject or accept the Divine call. The integral surrender should be made with the fullest con-

[1] Cp. M.B., XII, 141, 102.
tasmāt kaunteya viduṣā dharmādharmaviniścaye
buddhim āsthāya lokesmin vartitavyaṁ kṛtātmanā.

sent of the seeker. God does not do the climbing for us, though He is ever ready to help us when we stumble, comfort us when we fall. God is prepared to wait in patience till we turn to Him.

The conflict between the doctrine of human freedom and that of predestination has roused much discussion in Europe and India. Thomas Aquinas holds that freedom of the will and human effort play a chief part in man's salvation, though the will itself may need the support of God's grace. "Whence, the predestined must strive after good works and prayer; because through these means predestination is most certainly fulfilled . . . and therefore predestination can be furthered by creatures, but it cannot be impeded by them."[1] Man has the freedom to refuse the grace offered to him by God. Bonaventura thinks that it is God's intention to offer grace to man but only those who prepare themselves for its reception by their conduct, receive it. For Duns Scotus, since freedom of the will is God's command, even God has no direct influence on man's decision. Man can co-operate with God's grace but he can also refrain from it.

Spiritual leaders act on us not by physical violence, miracle-mongering or spell-binding. A true teacher does not assume a false responsibility. Even if the pupil takes a wrong turn, he would only counsel but not compel him to turn back, if such a procedure should interfere with his individual freedom of choice. Even error is a condition of growth. The teacher encourages the pupil's early steps even as the father does the tottering steps of the child. He stretches out a hand to help, when he trips but he leaves it to the disciple to choose his path and control his steps.

Kṛṣṇa is only the charioteer; he will obey Arjuna's direction. He bears no arms. If he influences Arjuna, it is through his all-conquering love which is inexhaustible. Arjuna should think for himself and discover for himself. He should not act from simple and blind beliefs acquired from habit or authority. Inarticulated assumptions adopted inevitably and emotionally have led to fanatic bigotries and caused untold human misery. It is therefore important that the mind should seek rational and experiential justification for its beliefs. Arjuna must have a sense of real integrity, that his ideas are his own and not those imposed on him by his teacher. Teaching is not Indoctrination.

[1] *Summa Theologica* E.T. by the Fathers of the English Dominican. Province. Second Edition (1929), Part I Q. 23, Art. 8.

Final Appeal

64. *sarvaguhyatamaṁ bhūyaḥ*
śṛṇu me paramaṁ vacaḥ
iṣṭo 'si me dṛḍham iti
tato vakṣyāmi te hitam

(64) Listen again to My supreme word, the most secret of all. Well beloved art thou of Me, therefore I shall tell thee what is good for thee.

65. *manmanā bhava madbhakto*
madyājī māṁ namaskuru
mām evai 'ṣyasi satyaṁ te
pratijāne priyo 'si me

(65) Fix thy mind on Me; be devoted to Me; sacrifice to Me; prostrate thyself before Me; so shalt thou come to Me. I promise thee truly, for thou art dear to Me.

The ultimate mystery, the supreme teaching with which the teacher wound up Chapter IX (34) is repeated here.

Thought, worship, sacrifice and reverence, all must be directed to the Lord. We must let ourselves go in a simple, sustained, trustful surrender of oneself to God, open ourselves out to Him in the words of the Christian hymn.

O Love, I give myself to Thee,
Thine ever, only Thine to be.

God discloses His nature, His graciousness and love and eagerness to take us back to Him. He is waiting, ready to enter and take possession of us, if only we open our hearts to Him. Our spiritual life depends as much on our going to Him, as on His coming to us. It is not only our ascent to God but His descent to man. Look at the words of the poet Tagore:

Hast thou not heard His silent steps?
He comes, comes, ever comes.

The love of God is pressing in on our souls and if we throw ourselves open to His perpetual coming, He will enter our soul, cleanse and redeem our nature and make us shine like a blazing light. God, who is ever ready to help, is waiting only for our trustful appeal to Him.

66. *sarvadharmān parityajya*
mām ekaṁ śaraṇaṁ vraja
ahaṁ tvā sarvapāpebhyo
mokṣayiṣyāmi mā śucaḥ

(66) Abandoning all duties, come to Me alone for shelter. Be not grieved, for I shall release thee from all evils.

We should willingly yield to His pressure, completely surrender to His will and take shelter in His love. If we destroy confidence in our own little self and replace it by perfect confidence in God He will save us. God asks of us total self-giving and gives us in return the power of the spirit which changes every situation.

Arjuna was perturbed by the various duties, ritualistic and ethical, that the war will result in the confusion of castes and indifference to the ancestors as well as in the violation of sacred duties of reverence for the teachers, etc. Kṛṣṇa tells him not to worry about these laws and usages but to trust Him and bow to His will. If he consecrates his life, actions, feelings and thoughts, and surrenders himself to God, He will guide him through the fight of life and he need have no fears. Surrender is the easiest way to self-transcendence. "He only is fit to contemplate the Divine light who is the slave to nothing, not even to his virtues." Ruysbroeck.

If we are to realize our destinies, we must stand naked and guileless before the Supreme. We, now and then, vainly try to cover ourselves up and hide the truth from the Lord. That way the gopīs failed to realize their destinies.

We do not even seek God as await His touch. When we turn to Him and let Him fill our whole being, our responsibility ceases. He deals with us and leads us beyond all sorrow. It is an unreserved surrender to the Supreme who takes us up and raises us to our utmost possible perfection. Though the Lord conducts the world according to fixed laws and expects us to conform to the law of right action based on our nature and station in life, if we take shelter in Him, we transcend all these. A seemingly outer help must come to man, for his soul cannot deliver itself from the trap in which it is caught by its own effort. When we wait on God without words and desire only His taking hold of us, the help comes. Cp. "He, who cares nothing for merits and demerits even though taught by Me, who, setting aside all duties, serves Me alone, is the greatest."[1]

The followers of R. look upon this verse as the carama śloka or the final verse of the whole book.

The Reward of following the Doctrine

67. *idaṁ te nā 'tapaskāya*
nā 'bhaktāya kadācana
na cā 'śuśrūṣave vācyaṁ
na ca māṁ yo 'bhyasūyati

(67) Never is this to be spoken by thee to one who is not austere in life or who has no devotion in him or who is not obedient or who speaks ill of Me.

Only those who are disciplined, loving and have a desire to serve are capable of understanding the message; others may listen to it and abuse it.

68. *ya idaṁ paramaṁ guhyaṁ*
madbhakteṣv abhidhāsyati
bhaktiṁ mayi parāṁ kṛtvā
mām evai 'ṣyaty asaṁśayaḥ

(68) He who teaches this supreme secret to My devotees, showing the highest devotion to Me, shall doubtless come to Me.

It is the duty of those who are previously initiated to initiate their uninitiated brethren.[2]

69. *na ca tasmān manuṣyeṣu*
kaścin me priyakṛttamaḥ
bhavitā na ca me tasmād
anyaḥ priyataro bhuvi

[1] *ajñāyaivaṁ guṇān doṣān mayādiṣṭān api svakān*
dharmān saṁtyajya yaḥ sarvān bhajet sa hi sattamaḥ.

[2] *asaṁskṛtās tu saṁskāryāḥ bhrātṛbhiḥ pūrvasaṁskṛtaiḥ.*
Cp. *durjanaḥ sajjano bhūyāt sajjanaḥ śāntim āpnuyāt*
śānto mucyeta bandhebhyo muktaś cānyān vimocayet.

May the wicked become virtuous, may the virtuous attain tranquillity, may the tranquil be freed from bonds, may the freed make others free.

(69) There is none among men who does dearer service to Me than he; nor shall there be another dearer to Me in the world.

The great ones who have crossed the ocean of saṁsāra and help others to cross are the dearest to God

70. *adhyeṣyate ca ya imaṁ*
dharmyaṁ saṁvādam āvayoḥ
jñānayajñena tenā 'ham
iṣṭaḥ syām iti me matiḥ

(70) And he who studies this sacred dialogue of ours, by him I would be worshipped through the sacrifice of knowledge, so I hold.

71. *śraddhāvān anasūyaś ca*
śṛṇuyād api yo naraḥ
so 'pi muktaḥ śubhāṁl lokān
prāpnuyāt puṇyakarmaṇām

(71) And the man who listens to it with faith and without scoffing, even he, being liberated, shall attain to the happy worlds of the righteous.

72. *kaccid etac chrutaṁ pārtha*
tvayai 'kāgreṇa cetasā
kaccid ajñānasaṁmohaḥ
praṇaṣṭas te dhanaṁjaya

(72) O Pārtha (Arjuna), has this been heard by thee with thy thought fixed to one point? O Winner of wealth (Arjuna), has thy distraction (of thought) caused by ignorance been dispelled?

Conclusion

arjuna uvāca

73. *naṣṭo mohaḥ smṛtir labdhā*
tvatprasādān mayā 'cyuta
sthito 'smi gatasaṁdehaḥ
kariṣye vacanaṁ tava

Arjuna said:

(73) Destroyed is my delusion and recognition has been gained by me through Thy grace, O Acyuta (Kṛṣṇa). I stand firm with my doubts dispelled. I shall act according to Thy word.

Arjuna turns to his appointed action, not with an egoistic mind but with self-knowledge.[1] His illusions are destroyed, his doubts are dispelled. The chosen instrument of God takes up the duty set to it by the Lord of the world. He will now do God's bidding. He realizes that He made us for His ends, not our own. Freedom to choose rightly depends on moral training. Through sheer goodness we rise up to a liberty of spirit, which carries us out of the grossness to which the flesh is prone. Arjuna had the onset of temptation and won his way to a liberating victory. He feels that he will fulfil the command of God as He is there to strengthen him. It is our duty to live in the spirit of the verse, "As I am ordained by Thee, O Hṛsīkeśa, seated in my heart, so I act."[2] Jesus says: "I seek not my own will but the will of Him who sent me." We must live as God would have us live in His eternal life. To will what God wills is the secret of divine life. When Jesus cried "May this cup pass from me," He was yet having His own preferences and asked for personal satisfaction. He wished to escape the bitter humiliation and death, but when He uttered "Thy will be done," "kariṣye vacanam tava," he gave up His separate existence and identified Himself with the work of the Father who sent Him.[3] This evolution means a great shedding of all pretences and evasions, a stripping of all sheaths, a ***vastrāpaharaṇa***, the self-naughting of the soul.

saṁjaya uvāca

74. *ity ahaṁ vāsudevasya*
pārthasya ca mahātmanaḥ
saṁvādam imam aśrauṣam
adbhutaṁ romaharṣaṇam

[1] *ajñānasaṁmohanāśa ātmasmṛtitābhaḥ.* Ś.

[2] *tvayā hṛṣīkeśa hṛdisthitena, yathā niyuktosmi tathā karomi*

[3] *Mark* xiv, 32–41. "As the Father gave me commandment, even so I do." *John* xiv, 31.

Saṁjaya said:

(74) Thus have I heard this wonderful dialogue between Vāsudeva (Kṛṣṇa) and the high-souled Pārtha (Arjuna) causing my hair to stand on end.

75. *vyāsaprasādāc chrutavān*
etad guhyam ahaṁ param
yogaṁ yogeśvarāt kṛṣṇāt
sākṣāt kathayataḥ svayam

(75) By the grace of Vyāsa, I heard this supreme secret, this yoga taught by Kṛṣṇa himself, the Lord of yoga, in person.

Vyāsa granted to Saṁjaya the power to see and hear from a distance all that transpired on the battlefield so that he might report the events to the blind King Dhṛtarāṣṭra.

76. *rājan saṁsmṛtya-saṁsmṛtya*
saṁvādam imam adbhutam
keśavārjunayoḥ puṇyaṁ
hṛṣyāmi ca muhur-muhuḥ

(76) O King, as I recall again and again this dialogue, wondrous and holy; of Keśava (Kṛṣṇa) and Arjuna, I thrill with joy again and again.

77. *tac ca saṁsmṛtya-saṁsmṛtya*
rūpam atyadbhutaṁ hareḥ
vismayo me mahān rājan
hṛṣyāmi ca punaḥ-punaḥ

(77) And as often as I recall that most wondrous form of Hari (Kṛṣṇa), great is my astonishment, O King, and I thrill with joy again and again.

saṁsmṛtya, saṁsmṛtya: as often as I recall. The dialogue of Kṛṣṇa and Arjuna and the fact of God are not philosophical propositions but are spiritual facts. We do not learn their meaning by simply recounting them but by dwelling upon them in a spirit of prayer and meditation.

78. *yatra yogeśvaraḥ kṛṣṇo*
yatra pārtho dhanurdharaḥ
tatra śrīr vijayo bhūtir
dhruvā nītir matir mama

(78) Wherever there is Kṛṣṇa, the lord of yoga, and Pārtha (Arjuna), the archer, I think, there will surely be fortune, victory, welfare and morality.

The teaching of the *Gītā* is yoga and the teacher is yogeśvara. When the human soul becomes enlightened and united with the Divine, fortune and victory, welfare and morality are assured. We are called upon to unite vision (yoga) and energy (dhanuḥ) and not allow the former to degenerate into madness or the latter into savagery. "The great centralities of religion," as Baron Von Hugel loved to call them, the tremendous facts of life divine are yoga, the realization of God through worship and entire submission to His will and dhanuḥ or active participation in the furtherance of the cosmic plan. Spiritual vision and social service should go together. The double purpose of human life, personal perfection and social efficiency is indicated here.[1] When Plato prophesied that there would be no good government in the world until philosophers became kings, he meant that human perfection was a sort of marriage between high thought and just action. This, according to the *Gītā*, must be, for ever, the aim of man.

iti . . . mokṣasaṁnyāsayogo nāmā 'ṣṭādaśo 'dhyāyaḥ
iti śrīmadbhagavadgītā upaniṣadaḥ samāptāḥ

This is the eighteenth chapter entitled The Yoga of Release by Renunciation.

Here the *Bhagavadgītā-Upaniṣad* ends.

[1] Cp. "That holy world I fain would know, wherein the priesthood and the kingship move together in one accord." *Vājasaneyi Saṁhitā*, XX, 5.

Selected Bibliography

K. T. Telang: *The Bhagavadgītā.* 1882.

Edwin Arnold: *The Song Celestial* 1885.

A. Mahadeva Śāstri: *The Bhagavadgītā* 1901.

L. D. Barnett: *The Bhagavadgītā.* 1905.

Annie Besant and Bhagavan Das. *Bhagavadgītā.* 1905.

Sri Aurobindo: *Essays on the Gītā.* 1928.

W. Douglas P. Hill: *The Bhagavadgītā.* 1928.

B. G. Tilak: *Gītarahasya.* E.T. 1935.

D. S. Sarma: *The Bhagavadgītā* 1937.

Franklin Edgerton: *The Bhagavadgītā.* 1944.

Swāmi Prabhavānanda and Christopher Isherwood: *The Bhagavadgītā* 1945.

Mahadev Desai: *The Gītā according to Gāndhi.* 1946.

INDEX